Human Rights & the United Nations: a great adventure

Human Rights

&
the United Nations:
a great adventure

John P. Humphrey

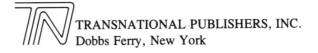

TRANSNATIONAL PUBLISHERS, INC.
Dobbs Ferry, New York

Library of Congress Cataloging in Publication Data

Humphrey, John Thomas Peters, 1905–
   Human rights and the United Nations.

   Includes index.
   1. Civil rights (International law)—History.
2. Humphrey, John Thomas Peters, 1905–   3. United
Nations. Division of Human Rights—History.   I. Title.
K3240.4.H85   1983   341.4'81   83-9307
ISBN 0-941320-14-6

Manufactured in the United States of America

''Ce sera là une grande aventure.''

Henri Laugier

Contents

Preface

Although it has none of the appointments and paraphernalia of scholarship, including foot-
notes (which I have studiously avoided), this book is as careful and objective an account of
the matters related in it as I could make it. I have not attempted a history of the human
rights program in the United Nations. My purpose has rather been to put down for the record an account based on my experience as director of the Division of Human Rights during
the first two decades of the organization's history.

Interested scholars should have no difficulty in tracing sources by consulting, under
the relevant year and organ, the United Nations Yearbook and the reports and summary
records of the various United Nations bodies concerned with human rights.

A Great Adventure Begins (1946)

It began one afternoon in June 1946. It was the end of the academic year and my wife and I were going to the Gaspé coast for the summer; I had just locked my desk at the McGill Law Faculty when the telephone rang. I picked up the receiver. The call was from New York and the man at the other end of the line was Henri Laugier, the Assistant Secretary-General of the United Nations in charge of Social Affairs. I had known him when he was a refugee in Montreal during the war; but, although we had kept in touch, this was the first time in many months that I had heard his voice.

I first met Laugier at the home of the Montreal painter, Louise Gadbois; but it was through Emile Vaillancourt that I really got to know him. Vaillancourt and I had a common passion, the future of a bilingual and bicultural Canada, and we had become close friends. He, Laugier and I occasionally lunched together in a little restaurant in the east end of the city, and I began to invite Laugier to my flat. I was soon one of his chief contacts with anglophobe Montreal, for I was one of the too rare Montrealers who at that time were fluent in both languages.

We soon discovered that we had much in common. I loved France, where I had been a student, and was committed to the cause of the Free French. I admired his meridional wit and sense of humor, his outspoken frankness, and the enthusiasm with which he pursued any cause in which he believed. He was a born partisan and a stubborn fighter and seldom took a halfway position. He had exiled himself from France because he would not live in a country which had come to terms with the Nazis; he would and did continue the fight abroad. In 1940, on the recommendation of the Rockefeller Foundation, he had been appointed—notwithstanding his open anticlericalism—to the chair of physiology (of which he was the titular professor at the Sorbonne) at the Catholic Université de Montréal, combining his academic duties with work for the Free French and commuting nearly every weekend to and from New York or Washington.

Although Montreal had a large French colony, many of these Frenchmen were either Vichyards or fence-sitters; and even in French-Canadian circles there was a good deal of sympathy for Petain. Laugier must have felt more at home with an Anglo-Saxon francophile than with some of his compatriots. In any event we became good friends. When he left Canada in 1944, after the liberation of North Africa, I wrote him that, while fully understanding his wish to return to France, I regretted that Canada was losing such a great *animateur*. I was at Percé on the Gaspé coast at the time and it was there that I next heard from him, although only indirectly. I used to walk to the Pigeon farm every morning for milk, and one morning old Mr. Pigeon greeted me with the news, heard over the radio, that I had been awarded an honorary degree by the University of Algiers. Laugier was now the rector of this institution, at that time the only Free French university, and he had included me as one of several Canadians and Americans on whom the honor had been conferred.

After the liberation of France, Laugier became the director general in charge of cultural relations at the French foreign office, and it was while he held that office that I had my next business with him. I wanted, as a gesture to France, to bring some French intellectual, preferably a jurist, to McGill to give a series of public lectures. The university gave me carte blanche but left me to make the arrangements. I cabled Laugier, and Professor René Savatier was very soon chosen to give the lectures.

Laugier now wanted me to come down to New York. There was something he wanted to talk about.

"Pouvez-vous me dire de quoi il s'agit?"

"J'aimerais savoir si vous avez l'intention de passer le reste de votre vie à McGill."

I parried the question. I was not, I said, committed to an academic career. As for going to New York, it was impossible. We had sold our car and were booked to leave that weekend by train for the Gaspé coast. The postwar strain on the railways was still so great that, if we gave up our reservations, we might have to wait up to a fortnight for others. Laugier cut short my explanations. He wanted me to be the director of the Division of Human Rights in the Department of Social Affairs at the United Nations. "Ce sera là," he added, "une grande aventure." I thought so too and was ready to accept his offer then and there. But I replied that I must have some time to think it over and to consult my wife. I talked to Jeanne, she agreed, and I wrote to Laugier putting only one condition on my acceptance: we must be allowed to continue our Percé holiday until the end of July.

On August first, Jan Stancyck, the principal director in the United Nations Department of Social Affairs, and Louis Gros, Laugier's administrative assistant, met me at Grand Central Station and drove me in a United Nations car to Hunter College in the Bronx, where the Secretariat was temporarily housed. Stancyck had been the minister of labor in the Polish government in exile and was now Laugier's second in command. Never, however, did he interfere in my work and only once did he so much as make a suggestion. This was when I was preparing the first draft of what was to become the Universal Declaration of Human Rights. A socialist of the old school, he wanted to be sure that economic and social rights would be included. He need not have worried; I had already decided to include them. Human rights without economic and social rights have little meaning for most people, particularly on empty bellies.

We drove to the Bronx by Riverside Drive. It was a bright sunny day and the Hudson sparkled with life. Behind us the dramatic New York skyline reached to the heavens. We passed under George Washington Bridge and sped on to Hunter College. Nothing could have been more unlike an international headquarters than those academic surroundings. I was led into a small office with a desk and two chairs. It was unbearably hot, there was no air conditioning, a brisk breeze blew in through the open window, and I had difficulty keeping the papers which soon began to accumulate on my desk in some order. I hadn't the faintest idea of what was expected from me or of what to do next. Some people had already been recruited for my division, although without much regard for the work that they were to do, and I met them. As both Laugier and the Secretary-General were in Europe, I was received by the Acting Secretary-General, the Russian Arkady Sobolev. I found him polite and urbane and was impressed by his excellent command of English. I liked him immediately.

One man did not welcome my arrival. Petrus Schmidt, a Dutchman who had been an underground journalist during the war and had been temporarily in charge of the division, fully expected to be its director. He poured out the story to me on my second day at Hunter College, making no attempt to hide his bitterness against Laugier. Although I understood why he might be disappointed, I was not responsible for the situation and could do nothing about it. Somewhat precipitately perhaps, I told him that I would be happy to have him remain in the division as the assistant director. But this didn't satisfy him, and he went to the Department of Security Council Affairs—Sobolev's department—where he remained until his untimely death in 1952.

I was interviewed on the same day by a *New York Times* reporter whose story got me into my first trouble. For after quoting me she went on with some general comment about people in the Secretariat, including Assistant Secretary-General Sobolev. The reporter gave the impression that the whole story had come from me, an impression that was hardly calculated to improve my prospects as a discreet international official. When the Secretary-General returned from abroad the following day, he sent me a note warning me to be more careful in the future.

Two days later, Laugier also returned to headquarters and Trygve Lie received us both, though only for the purpose of formally welcoming me to the Secretariat. As I never had much to do with Lie, I never got to know him intimately. He wasn't particularly interested in human rights, and the few times I found myself alone with him, I was hard put to find something to talk about that sounded natural. And the fact that Laugier soon quarrelled with him didn't help.

In 1948, at the first of the two sessions of the General Assembly held in Paris, Lie once called me to his office. The post of principal director in the Department of Social Affairs was vacant and he wanted to fill it by promotion, because, I gathered, certain countries were pressing candidates whom he didn't want. He asked me whether I had any administrative experience. I replied that I had none. I didn't get the job. Lie had the reputation, whether justified or not, of not liking intellectuals, a category to which I obviously belonged. But there may have been other reasons for his decision. Laugier later told me that, when the matter was discussed in Lie's board room, Abraham Feller, the legal counsel, spoke against moving me from a post where I was doing a good job in difficult circumstances. I took the explanation with a grain of salt, attributing it to Laugier's friendship. In retrospect, I was glad that I didn't get the place, for the duties of the principal director were so ill defined and his authority so limited that the post was a graveyard of reputations. Several years later, I did act in this capacity for Guillaume Georges-Picot, Laugier's successor as Assistant Secretary-General in charge of the Department of Social Affairs, and found the job uncreative and frustrating. Just as I had myself, the directors resented anyone's coming between them and the head of the department. Georges-Picot took it for granted that I would be promoted to the post; but Dag Hammarskjold, the new Secretary-General, in reorganizing the Secretariat, abolished the post, combining the grades of assistant secretary-general and principal director under the new designation of under secretary. Hammarskjold's purpose was to downgrade the political importance of the assistant secretaries general, not to abolish an office which had no essential place in the administrative scheme.

In August 1946, when I arrived at Hunter College, the most important person in the United Nations human rights program was already Eleanor Roosevelt. She had been the chairman of the so-called nuclear or preparatory Commission on Human Rights when it met in May; and it was generally expected that she would preside over the definitive commission. Within a fortnight of my arrival in New York, she invited me to spend a weekend at her Val-Kill cottage near Hyde Park. This, I imagined, would be my first real test. But I need not have worried, for nothing could have been more simple and more friendly than the way she received me. Within minutes I felt completely at ease and was talking to her as naturally as if I had known her all my life. Simplicity and the knack of giving other people confidence often go with greatness. Mrs. Roosevelt had both.

She came to the Poughkeepsie station to meet me. It was before her automobile accident and she drove the car herself. In her white summer dress, she looked younger than I was ever to see her again. At breakfast, next morning, she explained that she had been up since six and had already written her daily newspaper column, besides doing several other chores. After breakfast, we retired to the living room to continue our chat about human rights and the United Nations. We then went for a walk. She talked about herself and about F.D.R. A propos of F.D.R. she said that after one of the summit conferences he told her that, in his opinion, it would be easier for the United States to come to an understanding with the U.S.S.R. than with Britain. She also talked about her sons: she seemed especially worried about Elliot, who, with his wife Faye, was then living at Val-Kill. It was not easy, she said, to be the son of a famous man, and she seemed to regret that her sons had not had a more normal family life. She was sorry, she said, that Elliot had not been able to make a friend of some "liberal" like myself. When she said that, I knew that I had passed the test. It helped give me the confidence I needed for my new job. By lunchtime I felt that I had made a friend; Mrs. Roosevelt had the great gift of making friends quickly. She had an intuitive understanding of others and was at her best in a personal relationship, her candor, sense of humor and quick intelligence never failing her.

We had a family luncheon on the toughest roast beef I have ever eaten and that evening, with Elliot and Faye, went to dine with a Hudson River family about a half-hour's drive away. The house, the meal and the company contrasted sharply with the simplicity of Val-Kill cottage.

Although Jeanne and I went to other parties at Val-Kill, these were big affairs organized for the Commission on Human Rights. I remember a party at which Mrs. Roosevelt produced a bottle of wine that, many years earlier, had been dedicated to her uncle, Theodore Roosevelt. She brought it to the small table on the lawn where Jeanne, René Cassin, and two other guests were sitting, and explained that it had been found when they were cleaning out the cellar of the "big house" at Hyde Park. As Cassin was the French member of the commission, it seemed appropriate that he should have the famous bottle. He opened it with great ceremony, proposed a toast and we all lifted our glasses. The wine had turned to vinegar. But none of us flickered an eyelash—and Mrs. Roosevelt never knew what she had given us.

Mrs. Roosevelt was one of the greatest personalities ever to be associated with the United Nations, and her great prestige was one of the chief assets of the Human Rights Commission in the early years. I remember the crowds lined up to greet her in every town through which we passed on the rainy day during the 1948 session of the General Assembly when the French government took a party of delegates on a bus-trip from Paris to Amiens, ostensibly to see a housing project. Dr. Evatt, the Australian president of the General Assembly, was visibly annoyed by the scant attention paid to him. One day when Mrs. Roosevelt and I were lunching together in the Secretariat cafeteria at Lake Success, everyone in the large hall stood up as she entered. There was a tendency in certain parts of the Secretariat to play down the human rights program as an exotic in an international organization. But when the time came for the first session of the Human Rights Commission, we had to meet in the largest hall available, so large was the audience that wanted to see Mrs. Roosevelt. Another time—also at Lake Success—I invited Professor Vladimir Koretsky, the alternate Soviet representative on the commission (who later became a judge on the International Court of Justice) to have lunch in the delegates' lounge with Mrs. Roosevelt and me. He was so impressed with the experience and so grateful to me that on returning to my room in the Barbizon-Plaza Hotel the next day I was greeted by a parcel from him containing a bottle of vodka, some Russian cigarettes and a sausage. In the early years, Mrs. Roosevelt's prestige with the Russians was enormous, and had the state department been more imaginative, she might have become a much more important influence for the promotion of international understanding. But unfortunately she was soon exploited for short-term Cold War objectives, and in the later years her great prestige was partly dissipated.

Soon after my weekend at Val-Kill cottage, the Secretariat moved from Hunter College to the Sperry Gyroscope plant at Lake Success. Some members of the staff were upset when they learned that we were to be lodged in a factory. Dr. Brock Chisholm, the Canadian who later became the director general of the World Health Organization, addressed a mass meeting and tried, rather unconvincingly, to quell the fears of claustrophobia. But the material arrangements at Lake Success turned out to be particularly good, and many people regretted the later move to the Manhattan skyscraper. At Lake Success everything was on the same level, and in the course of a day you not only got some exercise but met your colleagues in the corridors. In the Manhattan building, traffic went up and down in lifts and the only colleagues you met were those who happened to be on the same rise. During the relatively short time we were at Lake Success, I probably made more friends in the Secretariat than in all my years at Manhattan. My own office was near the center of the building; there were no windows, and the partitions between the offices did not reach the ceiling. You could never be certain of not being overheard, but we didn't have many secrets.

Jeanne was still in Percé so, after the move to Lake Success, I found a room for myself with a hospitable Great Neck family. Sir Raphael Cilento, an Australian, who had just been appointed the director of the Social Division, also had a room there, and we soon became friends. When Jeanne joined us late in September, my kind hostess, Mrs. Bishop, also took her in while we looked for more permanent accommodations. Because of the housing shortage, my status in the organization and the fact that we had no children, we were low on the Secretariat housing list. After about a month we moved to the Lido Beach

Hotel at Long Beach on Long Island, which the United Nations had acquired from the U.S. Navy. In many ways the winter we spent at the Lido Beach Hotel was our best time at the United Nations. Never again would we meet colleagues on the same informal basis, and we made several good, lasting friends, including Emile Giraud from France, and A. H. Hekimi from Iran, whom I had just recruited. Both of them had been in the Secretariat of the League of Nations.

Also living at the hotel were Wilfred and Tressa Benson. Wilfred had been an official in the International Labor Office and was now a director in the U.N. Trusteeship Department. We too became good friends. Another was Willard Crocker, a retired Indian Army colonel who worked with Benson, and who later left the Secretariat for a career in the Australian foreign service. Crocker, who could be crusty, hated New York and never tired of explaining why. "Living in New York," he used to say, "is the lowest form of existence."

New York was indeed probably the worst possible choice for the headquarters of the United Nations. Anywhere in the United States would have been bad enough. The choice should have fallen on a small and neutral country. But of all the sites in the United States that were considered, New York was certainly the worst. The climate was indifferent, the cost of living high, and the political atmosphere not neutral for the discussion of many issues. In 1946, another reason for not having the United Nations in the United States was the difficulty encountered by most countries finding the hard American dollars to defray the expenses of the organization. I didn't share all of Crocker's prejudices about New York, but to live there was certainly not one of the reasons why I joined the Secretariat. Jeanne and I nevertheless soon adapted ourselves to living in the city and, I suppose, even became New Yorkers. Indeed, a very real disadvantage of the United States as the host country is that country's great power of assimilating foreigners. Many members of the Secretariat who come from abroad soon adopt American standards and the American way of life, becoming, for most practical intents and purposes, Americans. If this did not happen to Jeanne and me, it was partly due to the paradox that Canadians are immunized, as it were, to American life and living standards. For many Canadians New York is no novelty.

We lived, therefore, that first winter at the Lido Beach Hotel. But we were often in Manhattan, particularly when the General Assembly and the Human Rights Commission were in session. There were countless receptions and dinner parties which provided opportunities to meet members of the Secretariat and of delegations. The Lido Beach Hotel would have been an ideal place to spend the summer, but when the good weather came and we could have enjoyed the amenities of the beach, the United Nations sold the building and we were ordered out. It was still practically impossible to rent an apartment in the neighborhood of Lake Success, but we found a place in Roslyn which looked promising for the summer: the former Schwab mansion now became a residential club. We moved in just in time to enjoy the masses of azaleas and rhododendrons which remain my chief memory of the place; but we had hardly unpacked when the owner of the club went into bankruptcy and we had to move to a hotel in Manahttan. This meant commuting— something that I wanted to avoid. We finally found a room in the Colony Hotel in Great Neck and, in January 1949, after a long sojourn in Europe, an apartment in the same town. We lived there until we went to Chile in 1951. In the meantime, the United Nations had moved to its present headquarters in Manhattan and I had to commute back and forth from

Great Neck. In 1952, after another long sojourn abroad, we settled down in Manhattan, living first in hotels until we found an apartment on Sutton Place and later one on Beekman Place, both within easy walking distance of the United Nations.

For the first few months after I joined the Secretariat, I had very little idea of what was expected of me. I wasn't taking over from someone else in an established post, nor was there anyone I could turn to for instructions. I had a high-sounding title and a small staff, but there was still no program. The so-called nuclear or preparatory Commission on Human Rights had met in May; but it had been concerned mainly with the mandate and composition of the definitive commission and the creation of a sub-commission on freedom of information. It had given less attention to matters of substance and had given few instructions to the Secretariat. I knew, of course, that the Human Rights Commission was expected to draft an international bill of rights—that had been practically decided at San Francisco—but both the form the bill would take and the items it would include were matters still to be decided. New ground had to be plowed, but it was still *terra incognita*. Soon I would be working on the pragmatic basis of dealing with problems as they came up. My most important immediate task was to find something to keep my small staff busy and to recruit some new people. Since I knew that much of our work would be of a quasi-legislative character, I wanted some good lawyers, preferably with international experience. I naturally thought of the League of Nations and was surprised to discover that so few League officials had found places in the United Nations Secretariat.

Although Laugier was always available for consultation he gave me carte blanche not only in recruiting, but in planning the work of the Division and in matters of substance. Impatient of detail, his quick mind immediately grasped the essentials of a problem. He knew how to delegate authority and also how to keep up the morale of his friends and associates. As with all real leaders, his enthusiasm was contagious. Things went well—perhaps too well—for me as long as he remained in the Secretariat. Our personal relationship was so close and so warm that I could always depend on his support. His departure in 1951 did more than leave a void. Not only was he no longer there with his unfailing support, but I discovered that having been so closely identified with him also had its drawbacks, for he had many enemies, and they were usually in high places. His views on most questions were intransigent and he had a cutting and sometimes cruel wit. He would rather tell a good story than eat, which, considering that he prided himself on being a gourmet, is saying a great deal. The butts of his stories never forgot the insult. Quite innocently I inherited some of this resentment; it was, as it were, a case of guilt by association.

I particularly appreciated the freedom I had in recruiting at a time when too many people were being taken into the Secretariat because they had political support or for other irrelevant reasons. Laugier's confidence made it possible for me to build up one of the best, although smaller, divisions in the Secretariat. Intellectually, the members of the Division of Human Rights could have held their own in most groups of civil servants or academics. They were also hardworking, loyal and friendly; and they believed in the significance of what they were doing. The fact that they were of many races, nationalities and creeds added to their richness as a team; and such was their devotion to the United Nations that in professional matters they acted objectively without regard to the special interests of the countries from which they happened to come. When we disagreed, it was usually because of some personal or other reason such as would have divided officials in a national administration. This international spirit, when and where it exists, is one of the most promising features of an international organization. It was not present to the same degree in all the Secretariat services, nor did it continue always to characterize the Division of Human Rights. As the years went by, I was reluctantly obliged to qualify my first, and perhaps too romantic, assessments. From the inside looking out, the Secretariat was not only less glamorous but also less idealistic than from the outside looking in. People do not become angels simply because they are working for an international organization. In terms of human rivalry and intrigue, the United Nations Secretariat was not unlike other bureaucracies, and personal struggle for power was often compounded by international politics. I soon discovered, moreover, that many of the nationals of certain powers—and I am not referring to only one side in the Cold War—looked upon themselves, as their governments looked upon them, primarily as watchdogs for national interests. Confidential information had a way of reaching delegations with surprising speed. Some delegations were not above interfering in the affairs of the Secretariat, notwithstanding Article 100 of the Charter, by which member states undertake to respect its exclusively international character. One of the governments with the best records in these matters was the Canadian. Never once did they interfere in my work. Indeed, if I had any complaint on that score it was that, until shortly before my retirement, successive Canadian governments showed little interest in the human rights program. The Canadian delegation even abstained when the Third Committee of the General Assembly voted the Universal Declaration of Human Rights in 1948, although, embarrassed by the company in which they found themselves, they reluctantly changed their position in time for the final vote in the Assembly three days later. It was not until 1963, under the Diefenbaker administration, that Canada became for the one and only time during my twenty years at the United Nations, a member of the Human Rights Commission which, by that time, had finished its most important work, including the drafting of the Universal Declaration and of the two covenants. When engaged in United Nations business, I never thought of myself as a Canadian, although I discovered that socially, and particularly when I was on some mission abroad, to be a Canadian was an advantage. Canadians were popular at the United Nations, partly because it was recognized that they had so few political axes to grind.

At the beginning, Western Europe and the Americas were overrepresented in the Secretariat. This imbalance was probably not the fault of the Secretary-General, for the Soviet Union and other communist countries were at first not interested in sending their people to the Secretariat, and the new countries of Africa and Asia had yet to be born. After the latter became members, and after the communist countries began to insist on their fair share of the posts, a precipitate effort was made to right the balance, often with the result that people were appointed to posts for which they had no qualifications. While the new incumbent carried the title, someone else often had to do the work. What this did to morale can easily be imagined. I can remember officers recruited at high levels who never did a useful day's work, but they could be seen in the committee rooms almost any day listening to the debates. Happily there were very few such people in my own division, and then only in the last years when I had less control over recruiting. On the other hand, some officers were overworked. In a relatively small service like the Division of Human Rights, which in a given year was responsible for a whole series of meetings both at headquarters and abroad, the main burden fell on the very small group of officers capable of drafting a report or preparing a study.

Diplomats and other government officials often come to international conferences prepared to make great efforts to get through an agenda, achieve a quick result, and then go home and relax. The Secretariat official may, and in my division usually did, move on to another conference where the delegates had exactly the same sense of urgency. Both Secretariat officials and delegates often put in long days which would shock any trade union official. I have represented the Secretary-General at meetings that went on right through the night and on more than one morning have seen the sun rise over the East River. The Paris session of the General Assembly in 1948, when we were working on the Universal Declaration of Human Rights, was admittedly exceptional. But night after night, after the Third Committee had adjourned, there would be some drafting committee which my colleagues and I would have to attend; and even after that, there was usually something else that had to be done—with the result that it was often two or three o'clock in the morning before I was back in my hotel. The work is now better organized, mainly because of the strong stand taken by the interpreters, without whose help no United Nations meeting can be held.

In August 1946, I was certainly not overworked , nor was my staff. But in some other parts of the Secretariat there was great activity, for the second part of the first session of the General Assembly was to open at Flushing Meadows on 23 October. Although swept up with the other senior officials in the whirl of social activity and ceremony of which this historic event was the occasion, I had very little to do with the work of the session. Like many other officers responsible for a substantive program, I was at this session little more than an observer. The Assembly nevertheless took a number of decisions which were important in fixing the direction that the human rights program would take, one of these being especially important and the debate leading up to it highly dramatic. The issue was no less than whether the Commission on Human Rights would have a mandate, as it had been understood at the San Francisco Conference it would have, to draft the international bill of rights.

The Catalyst of the Second World War (1946)

Although certainly an early comer to the Secretariat, I was not one of the first arrivals. The Secretariat had come into formal existence in February 1946 with the appointment of Trygve Lie as Secretary-General, and had therefore been functioning for only six months on the day I reported for duty. But many of my colleagues at Hunter College had been serving the United Nations in one capacity or another since the San Francisco Conference over a year earlier. I had not been there nor had I been present at the later preparatory meetings in London, or at the first half of the first session of the General Assembly. I had also missed the first session of the Economic and Social Council and, more important from the point of view of my job, the so-called nuclear or preparatory session of the Commission on Human Rights.

The history of the international protection of human rights did not begin at San Francisco. But the decisions taken there, as reflected in the Charter, were crucial to the future development of the human rights program and, from the point of view of the theory and practice of international law, nothing short of revolutionary.

Before the Second World War, the international community was only minimally concerned with human rights. Traditional international law governed only the relations of states, individual men and women were neither subject to its rules nor protected by them, and human rights fell within the exclusive domestic jurisdiction of states. It is true that customary law protected the minimum rights of foreigners, though only indirectly. A state was duty bound to observe a certain minimum standard of justice in its treatment of the nationals of other countries whom it had admitted to its territory. But the compensation owed for any injury by failure to observe this standard belonged not to the injured individual but to his state. The injured individual had no guarantee that his state would take up his claim and, since the institution was based on self-help, only strong states were in a position to do so.

As for their own nationals, governments were with one possible exception free to treat them as they liked. What they did to their own citizens was their own business, beyond the reach of international law, and not the legitimate business of other countries or of the international community. The exception, if it really existed, was known as humanitarian intervention. If a government committed atrocities against its own people which shocked the conscience of mankind then, many international lawyers said, other countries had a right to intervene, if necessary by force. Such interventions were fairly common in the nineteenth century, usually for the protection of religious minorities. But the motives behind them were usually if not always political; and there was controversy as to whether the right really existed. One thing is certain: states were under no obligation to protect persecuted people in other countries.

A beginning was also made in the nineteenth and early twentieth centuries to protect, if only indirectly, the rights of certain other categories of people. Most important were the treaties aimed at the abolition of slavery and the slave trade. Steps were also taken for the relief of sick and wounded soldiers and prisoners of war; and several treaties protected the rights of workers in industrial employment.

To appreciate the revolutionary development in international law brought about by the Charter of the United Nations, it is enough to look at the Covenant of the League of Nations, where the term "human rights" does not even appear. President Woodrow Wilson had wanted a reference in the covenant to religious freedom, but when the Japanese quite appositely suggested that, if freedom of religion were to be included, there should also be some mention of racial equality, this so frightened some countries whose laws restricted Asiatic immigration that both suggestions were withdrawn.

Two articles of the League Covenant did, however, deal with human rights, though without using the term. One of these provided that colonies and territories, which as a consequence of the First World War had ceased to be under the sovereignty of the states which had formerly governed them, and which were inhabited by "people not yet able to stand by themselves under the strenuous conditions of the modern world," were to be put under the tutelage of advanced nations who, as mandatories on behalf of the League, would be responsible for their administration under conditions which would guarantee, *inter alia*, freedom of conscience and religion and the prohibition of abuses such as the slave trade. The mandates system was taken over by the United Nations under a different name and subject to different rules. The Charter says that one of the purposes of the Trusteeship system is "to encourage respect for human rights and fundamental freedoms for all without distinction as to race, sex, language or religion." The second article of the League Covenant dealing with human rights said that the members of the League would "endeavor to secure and maintain" fair and humane labor conditions, undertake to secure just treatment for the native inhabitants of territories under their control, and entrust the League with the supervision of agreements relating to the traffic in women and children.

The League Covenant did not even mention what would be the most important contribution of the League to the protection of human rights. At the Paris Peace Conference, the great powers had decided that certain newly created states and states the territory of which had been increased by reason of the war would be required to grant the enjoyment of certain human rights to all inhabitants of their territories and in particular to protect the rights of their linguistic, racial and religious minorities. These obligations were imposed by treaty and by the declarations that certain states were required to make on their admission to the League—the provisions relating to minorities being put under the guarantee of the League Council. The system was discriminatory in that it applied only to certain countries, which resented this exceptional incursion on their sovereignty. But it worked fairly well until it was exploited by Nazi Germany to further its expansionist policies; and from the point of view of the recognition of the rights of the individual in international law, it was a significant step forward. Amongst other things, the League developed procedures for receiving petitions on which remedial action could be taken. The United Nations did not take over the League's responsibilities for the protection of minorities, and the elaborate machinery developed to that end between the two wars has been allowed to die. Most contemporary states are more interested in assimilating their minorities than in helping them to maintain their identity.

The International Labor Organization, created like the League of Nations by the peace treaties after the First World War, now has a history of over half a century of achievement behind it. It has adopted well over a hundred conventions fixing international standards and also possesses machinery for the implementation of these standards, some of which could well be emulated by the United Nations. In its role in the promotion of the objectives discussed in this book, however, the I.L.O. has often been uncooperative—a result, perhaps, of its thwarted ambition to become, after the effective demise of the League of Nations, the principal organ of the international community responsible for the promotion of respect for all economic and social rights. Whatever the reason, its role— particularly when the international bill of rights was being drafted—was often parochial.

The Covenant of the League of Nations reflected the marginal interest of traditional international law in human rights. By 1945, however, the historical context had changed, and references to human rights run through the United Nations Charter like a golden thread. The Charter says in its very first article that one of the purposes of the organization is to promote respect for human rights and fundamental freedoms for all without distinction as to race, sex, language or religion; and by Article 56 member states pledge themselves to take joint and separate action in cooperation with the organization to promote that purpose.

The reason for this sudden concern for human rights was, of course, the traumatic experience through which the world had just passed. One of the causes of the Second World War was the cynical, studied and wholesale violation of human rights in and by Nazi Germany. This, unlike any previous war, was a war to vindicate human rights, was recognized as such by the leaders of the Grand Alliance, and was perhaps best expressed by President Roosevelt when, in January 1941, before the United States entered the war, he defined four freedoms: freedom of speech; freedom of worship; freedom from want; freedom from fear "everywhere in the world." These, he said, were "the necessary conditions of peace and no distant millenium."

Yet when in the fall of 1944 the governments of China, the United Kingdom, the United States and the Soviet Union agreed on the Dumbarton Oaks proposals, these contained only a general reference to human rights. The United Nations would, the proposals said in a chapter on arrangements for economic and social cooperation, "promote respect for human rights and fundamental freedoms," a commitment which—considering its context and the generality of the language used—hardly met the expectations of a public opinion aroused by the atrocities of the war.

The Dumbarton Oaks proposals were the work of the great powers and reflected their current absorption with military security: there was no opportunity in the circumstances in which the proposals were drafted to hear the representations of the smaller countries or of private interests. The relatively strong human rights provisions of the Charter were largely, and appropriately, the result of determined lobbying by nongovernmental organizations and individuals at the San Francisco Conference. The United States government had invited some forty-two private organizations representing various aspects of American life—the churches, trade unions, ethnic groups, peace movements, etc.—to send representatives to San Francisco, where they acted as consultants to its delegation. These people, aided by the delegations of some of the smaller countries, conducted a lobby in favor of human rights for which there is no parallel in the history of international relations, and which was largely responsible for the human rights provisions of the Charter. The United States delegation, remembering that the U.S. Senate had refused to ratify the Treaty of Versailles, wanted nothing in the Charter which might serve as a pretext for not ratifying it, and therefore resisted the pressure. But in a dramatic last-minute session, Mr. Stettinius, the secretary of state, agreed to support the minimum demands of the lobbyists. The U.S. delegation then persuaded the other great powers to accept the amendments. How this was achieved has never been explained. Perhaps, in the rush of last-minute decisions, not much thought was given to the revolutionary character of what was happening.

One very obvious lesson to be drawn from these events is that a determined group of individuals can influence even an international conference. The experiment has never been repeated on the same scale in the halls of the United Nations. Had it been repeated when procedures were being devised for the implementation of the Covenant on Civil and Political Rights, the result might have been different. A second lesson is that in matters relating to human rights, individuals and governments are usually on opposite sides of the ring. In such matters governments usually move when and only when they are forced to do so.

Some of the countries represented at San Francisco would have accepted stronger human rights provisions than the ones which were put into the Charter. Several Latin American delegations—Cuba, Mexico and Panama—even wanted it to contain an international bill of rights. But the great majority, including the great powers without whose assent no decision of this importance could be taken, were not ready for such a step. The result was that, although the Charter mentions human rights in a number of places, it does not define or even list them. But even though the proposal to include a bill of rights in the Charter was rejected, an article was inserted by which the Economic and Social Council was instructed to create a commission on human rights; and it was generally understood that this commission would draw up an international bill of rights—an understanding to which President Truman specifically referred in his closing speech to the conference. One of the first acts of the Economic and Social Council was to create this commission and to instruct it to draft the bill.

My First Session of the General Assembly (1946)

I had hardly expected to be busy at the General Assembly, which opened in the last week of October, and in fact was not. But I could hardly have been more excited, for a proposal was made challenging the arrangements that had been made for the drafting of the international bill of rights and, it seemed, undermining the very raison d'être of the Human Rights Commission. At the first part of the first session of the Assembly, which had met in London, the delegation of Panama had asked that a draft bill which it had unsuccessfully sponsored at the San Francisco Conference be adopted as an Assembly resolution. The item was now on the agenda of the second part of the session. Ricardo J. Alfaro, the Panamanian minister of foreign affairs, argued the case in both the First (political) and Third (social, humanitarian and cultural) committees. His principal opponent was Mrs. Roosevelt, who moved that the Panamanian draft be sent to the Commission on Human Rights. From the sidelines I watched the Assembly adopt an amended version of her motion. It was a good decision. For while the adoption of the United Nation's declaration of human rights was postponed for two years, the 1948 text was better than anything the Assembly would have adopted in 1946; and the long debates in the Human Rights Commission, to which much publicity was given, helped to educate both governments and world opinion. The longer process also gave the specialized agencies and nongovernmental organizations an opportunity to contribute to the final result.

There were also other human rights items on the Assembly's agenda: racial discrimination, including the treatment of Indians in South Africa, the crime of genocide, the political rights of women and freedom of information. The question of the treatment of Indians in South Africa was later expanded to cover the whole racial situation in that unhappy country, a question that was to have a profound impact on the United Nations and the work of my division; but, because it was always treated as a political matter and therefore debated not in the Third Committee but in the political organs of the Assembly, the Human Rights Division never had direct responsibility for it. When, however, in 1953 the General Assembly appointed a committee (of which Laugier, after his retirement from the Secretariat was a member) to study the racial situation in South Africa, one of my officers, Ezekiel Gordon of Israel, played an important role in the preparation of its report.

Violations of human rights in South Africa have posed one of the most difficult questions with which the United Nations has ever had to deal, and more time and energy have been devoted to it than to any other human rights issue. In one form or another the question

14

has been on the Assembly's agenda at every session except one. In 1946, it came up as an Indian complaint that Indians were being discriminated against in South Africa. The South Africans objected that the question did not concern Indian nationals, but citizens of the union; the matter was therefore essentially within its jurisdiction and, as stipulated by Article 2, paragraph 7 of the Charter, beyond the reach of any intervention by the United Nations. The Assembly ignored this challenge to its competence, whereupon South Africa asked that the question be referred to the International Court of Justice for an advisory opinion. This the Assembly also refused to do, just as it would refuse similar requests in the future. Instead, it adopted a resolution saying that Indians in South Africa should be treated in conformity with agreements between the two countries and the relevant provisions of the Charter. At a later session, the Indian complaint was merged with a similar one from Pakistan and, still later, with the much broader issue of apartheid. The United Nations has condemned South Africa for violating her obligations under the Charter and the Universal Declaration of Human Rights and has invoked mandatory sanctions against the country in a so far unsuccessful attempt to bring it to heel.

The Assembly also discussed genocide, which it defined as the denial of the right to existence to entire human groups, just as homicide is the denial of the right to life to individuals. Genocide was declared to be a crime under international law for the commission of which both principals and accomplices, whether officials or private individuals, were to be punished. This decision, like the judgments of the Nuremberg Tribunal condemning Nazi war criminals, helped to establish the principle that individuals are subjects of international law. The Assembly also requested the Economic and Social Council to undertake the necessary studies with a view to the adoption of a convention on genocide. The Division of Human Rights played a major role in the preparation of this convention, which was adopted in 1948 and has been widely ratified.

Another resolution said that it was in the interest of humanity to put an immediate end to religious and racial persecution and discrimination, and called on governments to take prompt and energetic steps to that end. The legislative history of this resolution shows that its sponsor, Egypt, intended it to be aimed against the persecution of religious minorities in certain named countries. The General Committee objected to the countries' being named and recommended that the item not be included on the agenda, whereupon a new text, from which the names of countries had been removed, was adopted without difficulty. The United Nations would soon be less squeamish.

Denmark moved a resolution calling on member states to adopt "measures necessary to fulfill the purposes and aims of the Charter by granting women the same political rights as men." It would also have had the Assembly recommend that, when dealing with applications for membership in the United Nations, the Security Council give consideration to the political rights of women in the applicant states. The resolution was easily adopted after its sponsor withdrew the part relating to membership. Finally, the Assembly called on the Economic and Social Council to convene a conference on freedom of information. "Freedom of information," the resolution said, "is a fundamental human right and is the touchstone of all the freedoms to which the United Nations is consecrated." Freedom of information has, indeed, some very special qualities, for in countries where the press is free, other human rights are likely to be respected. But the United Nations has been able to do very little to make the freedom meaningful, notwithstanding the enthusiasm with which the question was first attacked. There is probably no more frustrating story in the history of the human rights program than the story of this failure. The resolution convening the conference was moved, on behalf of the Philippines, by General Carlos Romulo—a colorful figure who had been an A.D.C. to General MacArthur during the war. He was also a professional newspaperman and the head of a chain of newspapers in the Philippines. His contagious enthusiasm infected everyone who worked with him. I did not realize, when his motion was being debated, that I would become so involved in its implementation. It was, of course, clearly a human rights question; and though the Department of Public Information thought that it should have responsibility for it and UNESCO also wanted a share, the Secretary-General decided that it should go to the Division of Human Rights. The conference was held in the spring of 1948. General Romulo was its president and I the executive secretary.

The Commission on Human
Rights (1947)

Now that the General Assembly had defeated the Panamanian motion, the Commission on Human Rights—which was to meet on 27 January—had a clear mandate to draft the international bill of rights.

The "nuclear" commission, made up of individuals, had recommended that the members of the definitive commission should also be individuals elected to act in their personal capacity. But the Soviet member of the nuclear body thought the members should represent governments; and when the matter came before the Economic and Social Council, the Russians argued that instructed representatives would be more qualified to develop practical solutions. A compromise was reached which, as it turned out, was not really one at all. The commission was to consist of one representative of each of eighteen states (like the Council itself) to be selected by the Council. But, "with a view to securing a balanced representation in the various fields covered by the Commission," the Secretary-General was to consult with the governments so selected before their representatives were finally nominated and confirmed by the Council. There were thus to be two stages: the election of the member states and the confirmation of their representatives. In practice, the consultations, when in fact they took place, were perfunctory; the Council always confirmed the nominees and no attempt was ever made to secure "a balanced representation." Sometimes we learned the names of nominees only when the Council was about to confirm them, or when the commission met; and in no case did the Secretariat ever object to a name submitted by a government. It would have been scarcely possible for us to do so, for we had neither the necessary real authority nor sufficient knowledge of the qualifications of the nominees to make a case. I remember one nominee who I had good reason to believe had been a Nazi sympathizer during the war. It was obviously impossible for me to object to his confirmation, although I did call the case to the attention of the Secretary-General. Had I raised the question in the Council, I would have been challenged to prove my suspicion, which I could not have done.

The persons sitting on the commission were therefore representatives of their governments; yet, when it suited their purposes, many of them insisted that they spoke as individual experts. Some were more independent than their colleagues and some operated without precise or any instructions from their governments; and these were not the least useful representatives. One such representative was Charles Malik of Lebanon. The Secretariat worked very closely with these delegates, who were glad to be fed ideas they could sponsor and for which they would have the credit. This was one of the ways in which we were able to make a substantive contribution. Texts and resolutions were sometimes drafted in my office or by my colleagues and later given to a delegation for which we sometimes even prepared a speech in support of the proposal. A good example—although in this case the draft was prepared with the help of the leaders of some of the nongovernmental organizations—was the resolution sponsored in the late sixties by Costa Rica calling for the appointment of a United Nations High Commissioner for Human Rights. Sometimes a delegation would itself take the initiative but would come to us asking for help in working out the details. Or the delegation might be undecided as to the correct policy to follow and would come to us for advice. ''Please let me have your personal opinion'' was a common request.

The decision that membership on the commission would be at the governmental level was probably realistic and helpful, since, in the early years in any event, its work was mainly of a quasi-legislative character. There would be no point in preparing texts which would not be accepted by governments. But now that the commission is becoming an implementing body, the character of its membership should be changed. For, as Philip Noel-Baker said at an early session of the Economic and Social Council, its members must feel ''free to raise questions which might embarrass governments, and they can hardly do this if they represent them.''

Member states can also appoint alternates (again in theoretical consultation with the Secretariat) to act in the absence of their representatives; but the alternates do not have to be confirmed by the Council. The privilege is often abused and gives an unfair advantage to large countries which often send veritable delegations to the commission. Alternates sit and vote as convenience dictates, even though the confirmed delegate may be in the chamber. Or, when a controversial question comes up, the confirmed representative may be replaced by a member of the permanent delegation.

To maintain continuity, the Council replaces a third of the members every year, the period of office being three years. But in the early years, member states having permanent seats on the Security Council were always reelected. In 1961, the membership was increased from eighteen to twenty-one, and in 1966 to thirty-two in order to permit more of the new states to become members. The membership now stands at 43, almost as large as the General Assembly in 1946. The distribution of seats is now fixed by ECOSOC resolution: the Afro-Asian countries having twenty, Latin America eight, the communist countries of Eastern Europe five, and Western Europe and ''other states'' (including Australia, Canada, Japan, New Zealand and the United States) ten. This gives the economically developing countries an easy majority, an imbalance now typical of the United Nations. Such was not the case when the Universal Declaration of Human Rights and the two covenants on human rights were being drafted.

Despite various attempts in the Economic and Social Council to limit the number of its sessions to one in every two years, the commission has met regularly at least once a year since its first session in January and February 1947. In that year it met twice and its drafting committee once. The duration of the session ranges from three weeks or a month to two months (when it was drafting the covenants). The relatively short sessions and the long intervals between them were a handicap and, paradoxically, lengthened the drafting process when the commisssion was working on the covenants. Less time would have been devoted to them had the commission remained in more or less continuous session until the work was done: for one thing there would have been less incentive to filibuster. And if the covenants had been completed earlier, some of the most highly controversial issues, such as the question of the self-determination of peoples, which became a real issue only in 1950, might have been avoided. On the other hand, some of the educational impact resulting from public participation in the work might have been lost.

The commisssion has had three sub-commissions, consisting of individual experts acting in their personal capacities. Only one, the Sub-Commission on the Prevention of Discrimination and the Protection of Minorities, has survived. The Economic and Social Council appointed a nuclear sub-commission on the status of women when it set up the nuclear Commission of Human Rights. This body met in the spring of 1946—before I came to the Secretariat. But at the second session of ECOSOC its chairman, Mrs. Bodil Begtrup of Denmark, made a statement to the effect that the women did not want to be "dependent on the pace of another commission." The sub-commission therefore recommended, she went on to say, that it be given the status of a full commission. Although there is no record that Mrs. Begtrup had any mandate to speak for her colleagues, and although the recommendation, if it indeed came from the sub-commission, should have gone through the Human Rights Commission, the Council acceded to her request and the organic link between the two bodies was severed. One consequence of the decision was that the members of the Commission on the Status of Women became states and not individuals acting in their personal capacities. Many people, including many women, thought it was a mistake and even discriminatory for the United Nations to have a separate body dealing with the rights of women. About a year after this decision was taken, a delegation representing a number of women's organizations came to me in Queen Mary Hall in London (where I had just made a speech) to protest the decision. I had a similar experience in Montreal where I went to talk to the Canadian Institute of International Affairs. At that time, the Montreal branch of the institute discriminated against women by relegating them to a separate branch to which I was also invited to speak. Not wanting to repeat what I had said the night before, I thought the women might be interested in hearing about the Commission on the Status of Women. I was not a little embarrassed when, in the discussion that followed my talk, I was criticized for having dared to talk to them on that subject: the unanimous opinion of the women present was that it had been a mistake to set up a separate commission. I thought so too, because I felt very strongly that the status of women is a human rights question and that women are entitled to the same rights as men. Many years later when, after my retirement from the Secretariat, I was a member of the Royal Commission on the Status of Women in Canada, I found myself in the unpleasant position of having to write a minority report because I did not agree that women should be given special treatment. As for the United Nations Commission on the Status of Women, I came to recognize—after it began to interest itself actively in the plight of women in the less developed parts of the world—the usefulness, from a practical point of view, of having a separate organ, even though that organ could have been a sub-commission of the Commission on Human Rights.

The Division of Human Rights was responsible in the Secretariat for the work of the Commission on the Status of Women. Some of the delegates to the commission disliked this arrangement and wanted a separate division headed by a woman: they even complained to Trygve Lie that the work of the Secretariat was badly done. But for obvious reasons of administrative efficiency—the section on the status of women was much too small to be a separate division—the *démarche* failed. Much later, however, and after my retirement from the Secretariat, the section was separated from the Division.

The Economic and Social Council had authorized the nuclear Commission on Human Rights to recommend the creation of other sub-commissions . Mrs. Roosevelt proposed a sub-commission on freedom of information and of the press. When the matter came before the Council, the Soviet Union argued that "the protection of minorities and the prevention of discrimination was as important as freedom of information." "Even in the most highly developed countries," its delegate said, "the rights of minorities are not protected." Each of the giants was obviously playing what it considered to be its trump card. In the result, the Council authorized the commission to set up three sub-commissions, one on freedom of information, another on the prevention of discrimination and the third on the protection of minorities. The commission created a Sub-Commission on Freedom of Information and of the Press. But, instead of setting up the other two sub-commissions as it had been authorized to do—one on the prevention of discrimination and the other on the protection of minorities—the commission combined their functions in the mandate of a single Sub-Commission on the Prevention of Discrimination and the Protection of Minorities. This was unfortunate, for the two functions are quite different, and giving the same body responsibility for both not only helped confuse the issues but made it easier for the United Nations to shirk the politically embarrassing job of protecting minorities.

At its first session, this sub-commission carefully distinguished, on the suggestion of the Secretariat, between the two parts of its mandate. The prevention of discrimination was, it said, "the prevention of any action which denies to individuals or groups of people equality of treatment which they may wish." The protection of minorities, on the other hand, "is the protection of non-dominant groups which, while wishing in general for equality of treatment with the majority, wish for a measure of differential treatment in order to preserve basic characteristics which they possess and which distinguish them from the majority of the population." These definitions were never approved by the Human Rights Commission, which has never shown any interest in what may be called the positive protection of minorities. An easy but false rationalization, which is still dominant in the United Nations, is that if everyone is treated alike, there is no need for special measures to protect minorities; but the argument quite misses the point, for, if linguistic, racial and religious minorities are to preserve their distinctive characteristics, they may need something more than equality.

Although the sub-commission tried in the early years of its history to act under both parts of its mandate, it was wasting its time. The national states which control the United Nations are more interested in assimilating their minorities—sometimes called nation-building—than in helping them retain their identities. Every effort which the sub-commission made to protect minorities in a positive way was frustrated by the Human Rights Commission and higher bodies. Its early concern for the protection of minorities was, indeed, a factor in an attempt made by the Economic and Social Council in 1951 to liquidate the sub-commission—since when it has concentrated almost exclusively on the prevention of discrimination. The inclusion of the protection of minorities in the mandate of the sub-commission had another unexpected result. For paradoxically, it drew a kind of red herring over the sub-commission's path which helped prevent it from making early progress with what was to prove its most important business, the prevention of discrimination.

In 1951, the Council abolished the Sub-Commission on Freedom of Information and of the Press. It wanted to abolish the other sub-commission as well; but the General Assembly, which has always been passionately interested in the elimination of racial discrimination, forced the Council to reconsider, a development that naturally improved the prestige and influence of the sub-commission. Indeed, the period of its greatest and most useful activity dates from that time. I have no doubt that, had the Sub-Commission on Freedom of Information been given the same opportunity, it would have discovered equally useful work patterns. But there was no strong party in the General Assembly interested in keeping it alive. The disappearance of this sub-commission has been an important factor in the failure of the United Nations to take adequate measures for the promotion of a freedom which, as already mentioned, the General Assembly solemnly declared at its first session to be "the touchstone of all the freedoms to which the United Nations is consecrated." I tried several times to revive interest in the sub-commission but could do nothing in the face of the strong views held by certain delegations and in the higher echelons of the Secretariat, ostensibly on grounds of the so-called proliferation of subordinate bodies of the Council. My last attempt to revive the sub-commission was at the Rome seminar on freedom of information in 1964, which recommended that the Human Rights Commission study the possibility, but nothing came of it.

The members of the sub-commission were individuals elected, with the consent of their governments and in theoretical consultation with the Secretariat, to act in their expert capacities. These consultations were, as already mentioned, mere formalities when, indeed, they ever took place. But the role of governments was important. When in 1953 Mr. Minoo Masani, one of the most brilliant persons ever to serve on it, was reelected to the Sub-Commission on the Prevention of Discrimination and the Protection of Minorities, of which he had been the chairman and was still the rapporteur for a study on discrimination in education, the Indian government (with which he had fallen into disfavor) refused to allow him to continue to serve. In the early years, however, it was still possible to get someone elected without the formal intervention of his government. I myself arranged for the election of Hernan Santa Cruz to the Sub-Commission on the Prevention of Discrimination and the Protection of Minorities at a time when the Chilean government would not take the initiative, and also of Chief Justice Abu Rannat of the Sudan (whom I had recently met in Khartoum) by finding friendly members of the Human Rights Commission willing to nominate them.

Although elected to serve in their personal capacities and, presumably in accord with the dictates of individual conscience, many of the members of the sub-commissions were in fact the instructed representatives of their governments. On the whole, however, the members were highly gifted and dedicated people animated primarily by the purposes and principles of the United Nations. This was especially true of the Sub-Commission on the Prevention of Discrimination and the Protection of Minorities, which brought together one of the best groups of people ever to meet at the United Nations. I sometimes thought the quality of representation diminished as one proceeded higher in the official hierarchy, with the lowest marks going to the Third Committee of the General Assembly. There were also very good people on the Sub-Commission on Freedom of Information, but, since the best of them were editors and journalists, who in their professional lives were preoccupied by many of the political issues that were being debated in other United Nations bodies, they found it hard to resist the temptation to use their membership in the sub-commission to fight the Cold War and to discuss issues far removed from the relatively prosaic but nevertheless important questions covered by their terms of reference. Their failure to resist this temptation was one of the reasons why the sub-commission was abolished.

The organizational and constitutional basis described above had been largely determined by the time I arrived in the Secretariat. The two commissions, but not the sub-commissions, had been created and their terms of reference defined, and a Division of Human Rights had been set up in the Secretariat. How would they function in practice? Only one thing seemed clear: the first task of the Commission on Human Rights would be to draft an international bill of rights.

First Session of the Human Rights Commission (1947)

The Commission on Human Rights held its first session from 27 January to 10 February 1947 in an atmosphere of optimistic excitement. This was the event to which we in the Human Rights Division had been looking forward. All the visitors' seats in the Council chamber were occupied when the session opened. The importance which governments attached to the commission was manifested by the quality of their representatives, many of whom were also playing or would later play important roles in the General Assembly and the Security Council. Two of them, Charles Malik and Carlos Romulo, later became presidents of the General Assembly. But the majority were not members of their permanent missions. In later years the quality of representation was not so high.

As had been expected, Mrs. Roosevelt was elected chairman, an office she held until 1951. She remained a member of the commission until 1952, when after the defeat of the Democrats in the presidential election of that year, she was replaced as the American representative by the Republican, Mrs. Oswald Lord. The vice-chairman was P.C. Chang, who also represented China in the Economic and Social Council. I was at first put off by his somewhat gruff manner and his uninhibited criticisms of the Secretariat, but I soon learned to appreciate his great human qualities and we became friends. He was a master of the art of compromise and, under cover of a quotation from Confucius, would often provide the formula which made it possible for the commission to escape from some impasse. The rapporteur, Charles Malik, came from Lebanon—a tall man with black hair and a nose like an eagle who would have made a good figure dressed as a sheik galloping across the desert. My personal relations with him were also good, though not as easy-going as they became with Chang—our philosophical assumptions were too far apart. When I was having breakfast with him one morning at the Hotel Eden in Geneva, I happened to mention the name of Hans Kelsen, the great contemporary legal scholar who was a positivist. Malik, who was by way of being a Thomist and believed in natural law, reacted with a fit of temper. Intellectually, Chang and Malik dominated the commission, but they were usually in disagreement. Both scholarly men, Chang was a pragmatist—he called himself a pluralist; Malik believed that his chosen philosophy provided the answers to most, if not all, questions, and his thinking was apt to carry him to rigid conclusions. But he was one of the most independent people ever to sit on the commission and he was dedicated to human rights.

Australia was represented by the peppery Colonel Hodgson, who also represented his country on the Security Council. He wanted a human rights convention with teeth in it. Roland Lebeau attended the first session as the alternate for Professor (later Senator) Fernand Dehousse, the Belgian delegate. A member of the Belgian permanent mission, he was one of the most brilliant of the younger men at the United Nations. He once invited my wife and me for Sunday lunch with Henri Spaak at his Long Island house. Lebeau made some derogatory remark about the United States, to which Spaak impatiently retorted that no country had ever been more generous in its relations with other countries.

René Cassin represented France. A little man with a Vandyke beard, he had a dynamic personality and a sharp and quick mind; he was one of the best public speakers I have ever heard. He could go on at great length without a note. But he was not a particularly effective debater, nor did I find him a good presiding officer when he became the chairman of the commission in 1955. He was always so preoccupied with pressing his own point of view that he sometimes forgot that he was in the chair. And forever seeking unanimity when it was obvious that none was possible, he was slow in bringing an issue to a vote. In age the doyen of the commission, he had had experience with the League of Nations, had been in London with de Gaulle during the war and was now the head of the French Conseil d'Etat. I visited him several times in his Boulevard St. Michel apartment where he had left on the door the black seal of the Gestapo the Nazis put there when they condemned him to death in absentia.

India was represented by Mrs. Hansa Mehta, a determined woman who wanted an effective international system for the implementation of human rights, a stand later rejected by the Indian government. Charles Dukes—later Lord Dukeston—represented the United Kingdom. Chile was represented by Félix Nieto del Rio, Egypt by Osmar Ebeid, Iran by Ghasseme Ghani and Uruguay by José A. Mora, none of whom attended subsequent sessions of the commission. Ricardo Alfaro, the member from Panama, who had been so active at San Francisco and in the General Assembly, did not attend this or any other session. His alternate was German Gil Guardia who again submitted the Panamanian draft bill. The representative of the Soviet Union, Alexander Bogomolov, was its ambassador to France. He did not attend the first session, the Soviet Union being represented by Valentin Tepliakov, a relatively minor official. T. Kaminsky represented Byelorussia and G.L. Stadnik—who did not come to this or any other session—the Ukraine. Yugoslavia was represented by Vladislav Ribnikar. He was one of the most interesting people on the commission, and I came to know him fairly well. He belonged to a family which had been wealthy before the war and had, indeed, owned the newspaper, *Politica*, but he had joined the partisans and was now a communist.

Such were the dramatis personae when the curtain went up on 27 January 1947. The Cold War had already begun, and the difficulties which faced the commission and all the uncertainties inherent in a new undertaking were compounded by political controversy and recrimination. But politics nevertheless played a secondary role in the early years and, by United Nations standards, the commission performed its mandate well. Specific instances of violations of human rights, real or alleged, were rarely mentioned. Paradoxically, this was the proper approach at a time when the commission was performing a quasi-legislative function. Too much name-calling would have diverted us from the work in hand, and there were other forums in the United Nations for the purpose. Mrs. Mehta nevertheless found an opportunity early in the session to mention the treatment of Indians in South Africa.

Not that human rights can be divorced from politics. In a sense nothing could be more political; and it would have been quite unreal had the great international debate on human rights not reflected the deep differences which divide nations and groups. There was much controversy but it was usually pertinent to the issues in debate. Although these issues were most sharply drawn in exchanges between the spokesmen of the traditional democracies and those of the new "popular democracies," it would be an oversimplification to think that the ideological debate was carried on only between communists and noncommunists. There were also sharp differences between the spokesmen for traditional democracy. Charles Malik—an energetic defender of liberalism and traditional values—urged the commission to recognize four principles. First, the human person is more important than any group to which he may belong. Second, his most sacred and inviolable possessions are his mind and his conscience. Third, any pressure on the part of the state, religion or race involving the automatic consent of the individual is reprehensible. And fourth, the social group to which the individual belongs may, like the human being himself, be wrong or right: the human person alone is the judge. No one was surprised when Tepliakov objected to this statement of principles, but the most vocal disagreement came from other quarters: Charles Dukes, who was a trade unionist and a member of the British Labour Party, retorted that unrestricted individual liberty was impossible in any modern community. In an organized society, groups could not be prevented from putting pressures on individuals. That was the price that had to be paid for freedom of association. And he went on to stress the coexistence and closely knit interdependence of the state and the individual. René Cassin shared his views: the human person was essentially a social being and he warned the commission against giving too little attention to social rights.

Later in the session, Mr. Ribnikar—that Yugoslav scion of a dispossessed middle class—took a more extreme view:

"We are at present in a transitional period. The commission should regard the ideals of the middle class as those of another age, and not look on certain principles as eternal. That was the mistake of the drafts presented by Panama and, more especially, in that of the American Federation of Labor. The international bill of rights should be in conformity with the aspirations of the popular masses of the world."

Cut to the quick, Toni Sender, the observer for the American Federation of Labor who interpreted her consultative function rather widely, had a sharp reply. Mr. Ribnikar, she said, "placed greater importance upon common interest than upon that of the individual and considered the ideal of individual liberty obsolete."

No decision had yet been taken regarding the form of the international bill of rights. In his closing speech to the San Francisco Conference, President Truman had referred only in general terms to "an international bill of rights acceptable to all the nations involved;" and, although Article 68 of the United Nations Charter mentioned a Commission on Human Rights, it said nothing about the bill. The mandate which the commission had received from the Economic and Social Council was also vague. Although the Panamanian draft was in the form of a declaration, there were other possibilities which I discussed in a paper I prepared for the commission. One possibility would be a resolution of the General Assembly, but this would only have the legal force of a recommendation. Another would be a multilateral convention binding in international law on all states ratifying it. If the bill were to take this form, I added prophetically, it might, "involve delays." Or, I added, the bill might be drafted as an amendment to the Charter, which would make it part of the fundamental law of the United Nations. In that case, member states could not renounce the bill and retain their membership in the organization.

The general consensus after much discussion was that the bill would be a declaration to be adopted by resolution of the General Assembly. Only at the second session was it decided that it would have three parts: a declaration, a convention and measures of implementation. Mrs. Roosevelt opened the debate by saying that she hoped the commission would discuss the first two of the Secretariat's suggestions, a declaration or a convention, which corresponded to the views of her own delegation. She did not favor the third alternative, nor did anyone else. The possibility of amending the Charter—a formidable task—was not discussed at that or at any other session. Although it was characteristic of Mrs. Roosevelt that she wanted to turn at once to the business of drafting, her colleagues felt that there should be at least a general discussion first. Mr. Tepliakov said that there should be no voting until all aspects of the proposed bill had been examined. And Mr. Dukes doubted whether a decision, even on the form of the bill, could be taken at that session. But it soon became evident that a large majority favored a declaration. P.C. Chang, who was nearly always ready with a practical solution, then suggested that the commission should not vote on the matter but should proceed on the assumption that the bill would be drafted as a resolution for adoption by the General Assembly, i.e. as a declaration. It was on this assumption that I later prepared my draft.

Colonel Hodgson and Mrs. Mehta continued to argue for a legally binding convention. The exact juridical character of the "General Act," a draft of which Mrs. Mehta submitted, was never explained. It would be adopted by the General Assembly, she said, and was to constitute "an obligation undertaken by member states." How this was to be achieved was not explained, but it was apparently not the intention of India that this general act would be ratified by states. According to the draft "the Security Council of the United Nations shall be seized of all alleged violations of human rights, investigate them and enforce redress within the framework of the United Nations." But Mrs. Mehta later said that the main responsibility for enforcing the general act would fall on the General Assembly. Colonel Hodgson and Roland Lebeau objected that the General Assembly had no power to adopt binding instruments of any kind. It could only adopt resolutions the implementation of which would be the responsibility of governments, or approve draft conventions and recommend them to governments for signature and ratification. Mrs. Mehta made no attempt to answer these objections. Had the Indian government been serious about its proposal, it could have been redrafted to take them into account; but it was never heard of after the first session of the commission. During this first session Mrs. Mehta continued to insist that her proposal be put to a vote. She herself continued to be an energetic advocate of strong measures of implementation, a position that the Indian government later abandoned. I often consulted her when I wanted a delegation to sponsor some idea relating to implementation.

The Australians wanted an international court of human rights. The idea was not as far fetched as it might have seemed in the political circumstances of 1947. Only three years later there would be a European Court of Human Rights, and a similar tribunal has now been created by the American Convention on Human Rights. The United Nations is still far from ready for such a court; but if the international community ever becomes really serious about human rights, the time will come when the European example will be followed on a universal scale. Colonel Hodgson insisted repeatedly that what was needed was "a multilateral convention binding on all states;" but he did not explain how all states could be forced to ratify it. It was he, however, who, at the last meeting of the session, moved for the insertion of a paragraph in the commission's report to the Economic and Social Council mentioning the consensus in favor of a bill to be drafted as a resolution for presentation to, and approval by, the General Assembly.

Since it was agreed that the commission could not draft the bill at its first session, a drafting committee was suggested to do the work. Although finally adopted, the suggestion met with more than one objection. Colonel Hodgson said that "no concrete results could be achieved by a drafting committee composed of government representatives expressing different points of view." Whoever did the work should act "as the servant of the commission" and he suggested the Secretariat as the most competent body. Mr. Dukes agreed, provided the Secretariat were allowed to call in experts, and Hodgson accepted the proviso. But Tepliakov objected that the task should be accomplished only "in accordance with the instructions received from the commission, after it had completed its deliberations on particular points and had determined the principles to be enunciated." He therefore moved that no decision be taken on the Australian proposal until all points concerning the bill had been discussed. The chairman ruled his motion out of order on the ground, she said, that it had already been voted on when the Russian had moved to postpone examination of the general act proposed by India. The ruling was challenged, but the commission sustained it—wrongly, I think—by a vote of six to two and a majority of abstentions. Tepliakov then moved the adjournment of the meeting, and this was also defeated. But the meeting did adjourn without taking any decision on the Australian motion.

At the next meeting, Malik had a new formula. But the issue had now become so controversial that, although the whole meeting was devoted to it, it was only on the following day that a decision was reached. Tepliakov was evidently afraid that, if the Australian proposal were adopted and a mandate given to the Secretariat, the work would be done by "outside experts." Experts might be asked to help the commission, he said, "but they should not be charged with the task of drafting the document." If there was any plot to turn the drafting over to outsiders, I knew nothing of it; and, in fact, no outside experts were consulted at any stage in the drafting. But Tepliakov was right to be on his guard. For the decision which the commission did take at its next meeting would have, had it not been modified later by the Economic and Social Council, effectively excluded the Soviet Union from participating in the first stages of the drafting process.

After some further discussion directed mainly to the role of the Secretariat, the commission decided to ask its chairman, vice-chairman and rapporteur—representing the United States, China and Lebanon respectively—to prepare, with the help of the Secretariat, a preliminary draft "in accordance with the instructions and decisions of the first session of the commission." The drafting committee would then report to the next session of the commission.

Tepliakov was obviously not satisfied. But apparently because he first wanted to consult his government it was not until later in the session that he announced that he would not support the arrangement because, he said, the function of the drafting committee had been changed from a technical to a substantive one. On the last day of the session he went further and announced that, because the powers given to the drafting committee were too wide and more countries should have been represented on it, he would not vote for the commission's report to the Economic and Social Council. The Soviet position was so obviously right that the Council soon upset the commission's arrangements.

The only other important business transacted at this session was the creation of the two sub-commissions already mentioned and the adoption of a recommendation to the Council on how to deal with communications alleging violations of human rights. The United Nations had been receiving great numbers of such communications from people and organizations in many countries. I had had a list prepared and now drew the attention of the commission to its existence. Mrs. Mehta asked that it be circulated, which it was, without, however, disclosing the names of the authors, to protect them against the possibility of reprisals. Mrs. Mehta then wanted the commission to discuss those communications coming from nongovernmental organizations in consultative status with the Economic and Social Council; communications from individuals would be made available to members on request. This procedure was at first agreed to. But General Romulo, who was also worried by the possibility that reprisals might be taken against the authors, moved that the matter be referred to a committee for study. The committee took the view that the commission had no power to take any action on any complaint and, therefore, did not look at the communications. Such was the genesis of a much-criticized doctrine that prevailed in the United Nations until 1967. The commission nevertheless recommended a procedure for dealing with the communications which became the basis for ECOSOC Resolution 75 (V) by which the Council approved the commission's view that it had no power to take any action on complaints and established a complicated procedure to be followed by the Secretariat in handling the communications, but made no provision for the relief of the petitioners. The Secretariat was to acknowledge the communications while informing the authors that the United Nations had no power to take any action on complaints; it was to send summaries (later copies) of the communications to the governments concerned (after deleting the names of the authors) and it was to prepare a confidential list for the consideration of the commission in closed meeting. It was probably the most elaborate wastepaper basket ever invented. At every session the commission went through the farce of clearing the conference room for a secret meeting which lasted only a few minutes, time enough for the commission to adopt a resolution taking note of the list, until the Soviet Union objected even to this formality. In 1959, the Secretariat was asked to classify the communications according to the countries to which they related. It happened one year that a large number of them related to Poland. When the commission met in closed meeting, the Soviet representative, Ambassador Platon Morozov, attacked the Secretariat which, he said, had not been objective. Foolishly perhaps, I jumped to its defense. Morozov then attacked me personally: "It isn't to act in that way, Mr. Humphrey," he said, "that you are paid a salary." He apologized after the meeting.

A few governments took the communications seriously enough to investigate the complaints and to write us considered replies which we circulated to the commission. Some other governments returned the "libelous" allegations to the Secretariat.

First Draft of the Universal Declaration of Human Rights (1947)

There was no reason for thinking when the commission adjourned that it had not taken a firm decision, or that the ground had not been prepared for the drafting of the international bill of rights. It was typical of Mrs. Roosevelt that she should want the drafting committee to begin work at once and she invited her two colleagues and me to meet her in her Washington Square apartment on the Sunday following the adjournment.

It soon became obvious that this committee would not draft the bill: Chang and Malik were too far apart in their philosophical approaches to be able to work together on a text. There was a good deal of talk, but we were getting nowhere. Then, after still another cup of tea, Chang suggested that I put my other duties aside for six months and study Chinese philosophy, after which I might be able to prepare a text for the committee. This was his way of saying that Western influences might be too great, and he was looking at Malik as he spoke. He had already, in the commission, urged the importance of historical perspective. There was some more discussion mainly of a philosophical character, Mrs. Roosevelt saying little and continuing to pour tea. But before the tea party was over, they had decided that I would prepare a preliminary draft. I didn't go to China nor did I study the writings of Confucius!

Before I could get down to any serious work on the draft, the Soviet Union challenged the composition of the drafting committee in the Economic and Social Council. The committee, its representative said, had been set up before any decisions had been taken on the content of the bill: its mandate was therefore much wider than had originally been intended. The committee was also too small and had no European member. He had a good case, but the Council was slow in rallying to his point of view. In the course of a long and complicated procedural debate, the president of the Council, Sir Ramaswami Mudaliar, gave an elaborate ruling on the question of whether a superior body could appoint a subcommittee of an inferior body—the kind of debate in which some diplomats excel—and the Council was itself obliged to have recourse to a drafting committee. But, as in many procedural debates, the underlying issue was strictly political, in this case, whether the Soviet Union was to have a share in the preliminary drafting of the international bill of rights, an issue which was resolved on 24 March, when Mrs. Roosevelt wrote a letter to Sir Ramaswami saying that she intended to appoint a new drafting committee of eight members of the commission: Australia, Chile, China, France, Lebanon, the United States, the United Kingdom and the Soviet Union. Strictly speaking, she had no legal right to change the decision of the commission in a matter on which it had been explicit; but her solution was realistic and politically acceptable and was approved by the Council. At the same time the Council requested the Secretariat to prepare "a documented outline" of the international bill of rights—a confirmation in effect of the mandate that I had already received from the committee of three with the difference that, whereas the committee of three had asked me to draft a declaration, the Council was now asking for an "outline," which I might have interpreted as meaning merely a list of rights. I chose not to, and prepared a draft declaration which was however always known as the Secretariat Outline. The new drafting committee was to meet in June.

The Division of Human Rights was now caught up in a routine of meetings which continued unabated for the rest of my twenty years in the Secretariat. The ECOSOC session just mentioned met from 28 February to 29 March, and before that the Commission on the Status of Women had held its first session. It opened on the same day, 10 February, the Human Rights Commission adjourned, and lasted for two weeks; and it met as a full functional commission reporting directly to ECOSOC and not, as originally intended, as a sub-commission of the Commission on Human Rights. As in the latter, its members were now states.

The League of Nations had done some useful work to improve the condition of women, and I expected that the new commission would want to go on from where the League had left off. I therefore arranged for the preparation of a questionnaire on the legal status of women based on the League's experience. This would, I hoped, elicit some useful information from governments. It proved to be a useful tool in the hands of the commission.

More perhaps than in any other United Nations body the delegates to the Commission on the Status of Women were personally committed to its objectives. Although they represented governments under whose instructions they worked, they acted as a kind of lobby for the women of the world. There was no more independent body in the United Nations. Many governments had appointed and continued to appoint as their representatives women who were militants in their own countries. My relations with them were never as close as they became with the members of the Human Rights Commission, partly because they were less inclined to seek the advice of the Secretariat. They reached many of their decisions in private, informal meetings in which we had no part. Later, after the section on the status of women in the Secretariat was better organized, the commission worked more closely with it and took its chief into their confidence. But I did make several friends in the first group to come to the commission, including Marie-Hélène LeFaucheux of France and Dorothy Kenyon of the United States. Later, I made a much closer friend of Minerva Bernadino of the Dominican Republic who, although she did not come to the first session, was one of the most influential women at the United Nations—a friendship which had its importance in the development of certain aspects of the human rights program, as will be explained later.

The commission appointed Mrs. Bodil Begtrup of Denmark, who had been the chairman of the nuclear sub-commission, as its first chairman. She was the president of the Danish Council of Women and later became an ambassador. The vice-chairman was Mrs. Jessie Street, the chairman of the Australian Women's Charter Conference and of the

United Associations of Women of New South Wales. And the rapporteur was Mrs. E. Uralova of the Byelorussian S.S.R. and a people's commissar for education.

The commission devoted most of its first session to organizational and procedural matters, including its terms of reference and the relations which it proposed to have with the specialized agencies, the Trusteeship Council, other commissions (including the Commission on Human Rights) and nongovernmental organizations. It also discussed the legal status and treatment of women, including political rights, and asked the Economic and Social Council to request governments to complete by June certain parts of the questionnaire already mentioned, indicating any change in law or practice since the adoption by the General Assembly of its resolution on political rights. There was also some ideological debate. The Soviet Union was proud of its record in the matter of the equality of men and women and, at this and other sessions, often attacked the Western countries for their "backwardness." This attitude carried over into ECOSOC and other United Nations bodies.

I cannot say that I was always at ease with the commission. Many of its members resented the fact that the section on the status of women was part of the Division of Human Rights with a man as its director, and I was sometimes made to feel that my presence was not welcome. But I made a point of attending as many of the commission's meetings as possible and, apart from some of the interpreters and summary record writers, was often the only man in the conference room. Although a few of the delegates, including Dorothy Kenyon and Mrs. E.A. Popova of the Soviet Union made a special effort to be friendly, I found the chairman somewhat formidable and unbending. One day, walking down a corridor with her I ventured to make a joke, simply to break the ice. It had some remote bearing on the status of women, I forget what. She turned to me coldly and said, "Why did you tell that story?" I never attempted to joke with her again, and thereafter I was very careful about my choice of jokes when talking to a member of the commission.

Once the Commission on the Status of Women and the fourth session of ECOSOC were out of the way, I turned my attention to preparing a draft of a declaration on human rights. The Secretariat was still housed in the Sperry plant and, while working conditions there were not bad, this was not the best place in which to do the kind of job I had to do. The director was seldom allowed any freedom from people who wanted to see him or from the telephone. If I were to draft a text of such importance, I needed to be alone and quiet for a few days with a chance to think. I talked to Laugier, who agreed that it would be a good idea for me to absent myself from my office for a week and devote my full attention to the declaration. It was therefore at the Lido Beach Hotel, where Jeanne and I were living at the time, that, with some help from Emile Giraud, I prepared the first draft of the Universal Declaration of Human Rights.

I was no Thomas Jefferson and, although a lawyer, I had had practically no experience drafting documents. But since the Secretariat had collected a score of drafts, I had some models on which to work. One of them had been prepared by Gustavo Gutierrez and had probably inspired the draft declaration of the international duties and rights of the individual which Cuba had sponsored at the San Francisco Conference. There were also texts prepared by Irving A. Isaacs, by the Rev. Wilfred Parsons, S.J., by Rollin McNitt and by a committee chaired by Viscount Sankey after a public debate conducted in Britain by the *Daily Herald*. One had been prepared by Professor Hersch Lauterpacht and another by H.G. Wells. Still others came from the American Law Institute, the American Association for the United Nations, the American Jewish Congress, the World Government Association, the *Institut de droit international* and the editors of *Free World*. The American Bar Association had sent in an enumeration of subjects. With two exceptions, all these texts came from English-speaking sources and all of them from the democratic West. The documentation which the Secretariat brought together ex post facto in support of my draft included texts extracted from the constitutions of many countries. But I did not have this before me when I prepared my draft.

The best of the texts from which I worked was the one prepared by the American Law Institute, and I borrowed freely from it. This was the text that had been unsuccessfully sponsored by Panama at the San Francisco Conference and later in the General Assembly. It had been drafted in the United States during the war by a distinguished group representing many cultures, one of whom was Alfredo Alfaro, the Panamanian foreign minister.

My draft comprised forty-eight short articles.[1] Four principles were suggested for inclusion in the preamble: there can be no peace unless human rights are respected; man—and I meant this word to include women—does not only have rights, he owes duties to the society of which he forms part; he is a citizen not only of his state but of the world; and there can be neither human freedom nor human dignity unless war and the threat of war are abolished. The only one of these principles that was included in the text of the Universal Declaration was the one which said that respect for human rights is the foundation of peace.

Although most of the articles related to civil and political rights, economic, social and cultural rights were not neglected. I did not need to be told that the former can have little meaning without the latter. It is by no means certain that economic and social rights would have been included in the final text if I had not included them in mine. There was considerable opposition in the drafting committee to their inclusion. Nor were they included in the European Convention for the Protection of Human Rights and Fundamental Freedoms of 1950.

I remember a conversation I later had with Geoffrey Wilson, Lord Dukeston's alternate on the drafting committee, when we were crossing the Atlantic together. He said that once the Secretariat had included something in its draft, it was very difficult for governments to object to its being there, an obvious reference to economic and social rights, which significantly enough were not mentioned in the draft convention which the United Kingdom presented to the drafting committee.

Two articles dealt with the prevention of discrimination and the protection of minorities. The Universal Declaration has a great deal to say about the prevention of discrimination, but it does not mention minorities. The refusal of the General Assembly to include rules designed to protect them was one of the first concrete signs that the United Nations would not continue in the role of the League of Nations as the international protector of minorities.

After cataloguing and defining the various rights and freedoms, I went on to mention three principles, the recognition of which is essential in any effective system for the inter-

1. The so-called Secretariat Outline is reproduced in the Yearbook on Human Rights for 1947 (United Nations, Lake Success, 1949), p. 484.

national protection of human rights. The first was that the right of individual petition (which I had included in Article 29 of my draft) included the right to petition the United Nations. The second was the duty of all member states to respect and protect the rights enunciated in the declaration, and the third that its provisions were to be deemed fundamental principles of international law and of the national law of each member state. "Their observance," my text went on to say, "is, therefore, a matter of international concern and it shall be within the jurisdiction of the United Nations to discuss any violation thereof." None of these principles was retained in the Universal Declaration, although some of them were put into the covenants. The Universal Declaration does not even recognize the right to petition national, let alone international authorities. In proposing these principles for inclusion in a declaration to be adopted by resolution of the General Assembly, I skated over some fundamental problems of international law and organization. Like Mrs. Mehta with her general act, I had no plan for overcoming the difficulty that the General Assembly can only make recommendations. I knew very well that it had no power to impose binding obligations; but instinct told me that the Declaration would later be recognized in some way as binding, perhaps by the force of custom; and that, I think, is what has now happened. By including the three principles in my text, I in any event raised most of the questions concerning the international implementation of human rights that needed to be discussed. The ultimate test of the United Nations human rights program would, I was sure, be whether it could create effective procedures for its implementation. To reach international agreement on the definition of human rights is one thing, and, as it turned out, this was relatively easy. But for states with disparate social systems to agree on international machinery for their implementation is quite another.

Having completed my draft, I left in April for Europe, on the first of many missions abroad, to represent the Secretary-General at meetings of the executive board of UNESCO in Paris. It was my first transatlantic flight and only my second journey by air.

It was also my first visit to Europe since the war. Landing at Dunkirk I saw some of the destruction. And in Paris, I even briefly experienced some of the minor deprivations its inhabitants had had to suffer. By contrast, the large formal dinner which Julian Huxley, the director general of UNESCO, gave for the members of the executive board was a splendid affair. In the Gare du Nord the *petits pains* had tasted like sawdust and the coffee like ink; but in the fine dining room of the recent Gestapo headquarters, now the seat of UNESCO, there was no lack of good food and wine. I was equally well taken care of across the street at the Hotel de la Perousse.

As a mere observer at the UNESCO meetings I had very little to do or say. Huxley wanted me to make a statement concerning our plans about freedom of information, and about how UNESCO could cooperate, particularly in the organization of the proposed information conference. But my ideas on the subject were still so vague that I thought it better to remain silent. It had not yet been decided, moreover, that my division would have responsibility for the conference, and I could hardly speak for the U.N. Department of Information. I spent what free time I had in Paris visiting haunts that I had known when I was a student at the *faculté de droit*.

I returned to New York by the *Mauretania*, stopping for a few days in London. Amongst other things, I wanted to see Egon Schwelb, the legal adviser of the War Crimes Commission. I had been impressed by his mastery of detail in a letter he had written to me about the work of this commission, and it had occurred to me that he might be the man I was looking for to be the assistant director of the Human Rights Division. When I learned that he was a Czech, I was even more interested. At that time—it was before the communist coup d'état—many people thought that Czechoslovakia could become a kind of bridge between East and West. Having a Czech as assistant director, I somewhat naively thought, might, failing a Russian, help give the Division a better balance.

Meeting Schwelb confirmed my good impression. But before making up my mind, I spoke to Lord Wright, the chairman of the War Crimes Commission, and to Colonel Ledingham, its secretary, both of whom enthusiastically recommended him. While we were walking through Green Park I told Schwelb that he would have the job. I have seldom seen anyone more pleased. I said nothing to him about my political motivation; and, as a matter of fact, he became a British subject before coming to the Division. And, as I soon learned, he had no special knowledge of and even less sympathy for the Soviet Union. But I never regretted my decision. He turned out to be exactly the kind of man I needed. Meticulous for detail, he was a voracious reader of official documents, which he used to take home at night; he had a phenomenal memory, was an erudite student of international law, and was familiar with both the English and continental systems of national law.

Egon Schwelb's appointment gave rise to one of the first human rights cases within the Secretariat. When it became known that a Jew with a social democratic background would be the assistant director of the Division of Human Rights, some of the Czech members of the Secretariat raised a great outcry: even the Czech delegation became involved. But with Laugier's support I stuck to my guns. It was only after the Czech deputy minister of foreign affairs, Vladimir Clementis, gave his approval that the clamor died down.

Not many months later I became involved in another case of anti-Semitism—better described as alleged anti-Semitism —in the Secretariat. Some officers in the language services had complained that they were being discriminated against on racial and religious grounds, whereupon the Secretary-General appointed a special board of inquiry to investigate the matter. The members of the board were W.B. Sutch of the New Zealand delegation, David Weintraub, an American director in the Department of Economic Affairs, and myself. This was one of the most unpleasant experiences I have ever had, and because the inquiry involved attending many meetings over a long period of time, it interfered with my normal work. We took evidence from many people in many weary sessions which sometimes lasted until late in the night. One of the curious things about the case was that one the defendants was himself a Jew. After we had collected all the evidence, my two colleagues thought that a case had been made against the defendants. But, while I agreed that the service was badly run, I did not think there was any convincing proof of discrimination; and failing such proof, the presumption of innocence applied. I thought, however, that an officer in the Secretariat has a duty not only not to discriminate, but to avoid the appearance of discrimination.

I had to resist an assumption that, as the director of the Human Rights Division, I was in some way especially qualified to deal with such matters when they arose in the Secretariat. I did not want to become a kind of Secretariat ombudsman, much less a prosecutor, partly because, if I became too involved in Secretariat controversy, my real job would suffer. I therefore refused to serve on such bodies as the disciplinary committee whenever my name was proposed either by the staff or the administration. The chairman of the staff association once told me that I was the only person on whom both the staff and the administration could agree as chairman of the disciplinary committee, but they found somebody else. I did, reluctantly, become a member of the appointments and promotion board; but I was quickly dropped from membership because, I am sure, the personnel bureau thought me a nuisance when I questioned some of their recommendations.

The Sub-Commission on Freedom of Information and of the Press held its first session a fortnight after I returned to headquarters. Its twelve members were mostly journalists. G.L. van Heuven Goedhart, the chairman, had been the editor of the Dutch underground paper *Het Parool* during the war. He later became the first United Nations High Commissioner for Refugees. The vice-chairman was Lev Sychrava from Czechoslovakia and the rapporteur, George Ferguson from Canada. Although he probably never knew it, I was responsible for Ferguson's election to the sub-commission, the Americans having asked me to suggest the name of a Canadian.

The member from France was André Géraud, better known as "Pertinax," and the member from Norway, Christen Christensen. P.C. Chang was there from China, but he was replaced at the next session by a man of the same name. From the Philippines we had Salvador Lopez, a member of the permanent mission, than whom no one did more to promote freedom of information at the United Nations. The British member, R. J. Cruikshank, never attended a meeting but was represented by his alternate, A.R.K. Mackenzie. Professor Zechariah Chafee of Harvard University, an authentic liberal, was the member for the United States. The member from the Soviet Union was the fiery and loquacious J.M. Lomakin. From Uruguay we had Roberto Fontaina. The member from Panama did not attend the session.

The sub-commission had been asked to prepare the agenda and to make other arrangements for the international conference on freedom of information which, it had now been decided, would meet in Geneva in 1948. But the members were soon in deep ideological conflict, and the often stormy debates quickly revealed the fundamental differences in approach that would characterize all future discussion of freedom of information at the United Nations. The issue was and remains whether the press should be an instrument of freedom or one of power. The communist countries often talked about the duty of the press to promote human rights, but they failed to recognize that a free press is in itself an essential factor in achieving those rights. Spokesmen for the Western tradition defined the freedom in almost absolute terms without too much regard for the responsibilities which, under contemporary conditions at least, must condition its exercise.

Lomakin said that the task of the press was to struggle for international peace and security; to develop friendly relations among nations based on respect for the principles of independence, equal rights and the self-determination of peoples; to organize the struggle for democratic principles, for the unmasking of the remnants of fascism and for the extirpation of fascism in all its forms; to promote human rights; and to organize an effective campaign against those organs of the press that were inciting the peoples to war and aggression, and for the decisive and unrelenting unmasking of warmongers. This soon to be familiar litany of good causes—provided the words meant what they appeared to say—was intoned with great vehemence. Salvador Lopez replied with a list that stressed the duty of the press to "tell the truth without prejudice and to spread knowledge without malicious intent."

The deep incompatibilities between the communist and liberal approaches to the functions of the press which this exchange manifested have never been bridged, and probably never will be. In the circumstances, the definition of freedom of information in Article 19 of the Universal Declaration of Human Rights is a considerable achievement. Later, after the adoption of the Declaration and after the developing countries joined the debate, more attention was given to the dichotomy between freedom and responsibility. Society is entitled to expect that every human right will be exercised with responsibility and due regard for the rights of others. In the case of the press and even more so with other information media, the possibility of abuse is so great that the duties corresponding to the right need to be defined with special care. Although often overstated, there was a good deal of merit in the position taken by the developing countries, which have always been critical of the monopolistic and sometimes unfair practices of the great news-gathering agencies. I always thought the tendency to define freedom of information as an absolute right weakened the Western case in the United Nations. Freedom of information has two aspects. There is the right to inform, but there is also the right of the public to be informed.

Drafting Committee and
Other Matters (1947)

The new drafting committee of eight, which she had appointed to replace the committee of three, met in June with Mrs. Roosevelt in the chair. There were some new faces, including that of Hernan Santa Cruz, who represented Chile for the first time. No one has been more continuously or for a longer period of time associated with the human rights program.

Politically left of center, he had considerable influence with delegations representing the economically developing countries, whose cases he sometimes argued with great energy —a practice which often brought him into conflict with the Western industrial powers. I remember how annoyed Mrs. Roosevelt was with him for the part he played in the drafting of the second paragraph of Article 1 of the two covenants on human rights dealing with the economic self-determination of peoples, which she thought compromised the future of the instruments. I came to know Santa Cruz well, perhaps as well as I knew any member of the Human Rights Commission, and I saw a great deal of him socially. I was several times his guest in his home in Santiago, where I met two future presidents of Chile, Eduardo Frei and Salvador Allende. A man who could be friendly with two such different personalities was likely to be politically eclectic.

Another person who first appeared at the drafting commission was Professor Vladimir Koretsky, a future judge of the International Court of Justice, whom I have already mentioned. He was then a legal adviser to the Soviet foreign office and attended the meetings of the drafting committee as the alternate for Ambassador Bogomolov. Lord Dukeston, who did not attend the session, was represented by his alternate, Geoffrey Wilson.

The drafting committee used my text, officially known as the Secretariat Outline (a misnomer if there ever was one, since it was really a draft declaration) as the basis for its work. But it also had before it a draft convention which had been presented by the United Kingdom. I regretted that the authors of this draft did not push it more energetically, for it was written with skill and imagination and might have become a solid basis for the Covenant on Civil and Political Rights. In any event, it had little if any influence on the final outcome. It included neither economic, social nor cultural rights, an omission to which attention has already been drawn. But the civil and political rights were defined with a precision appropriate to a text that was meant to become a treaty. Unlike some other delegations, it was characteristic of the British, who were good draftsmen, that they should want to know in advance exactly what obligations states were to be called on to undertake.

A feature of the British draft was that the states parties to the convention would have recognized that the rights defined in it were founded on "the general principles of law recognized by civilized nations," a term of the lawyer's art introduced in 1920 in the statute of the World Court to give the Court the right to apply rules in the settlement of disputes other than those which can be found in international treaties or custom. Since these words would have added nothing to the enforceable character of the convention as between the parties to it, the intention must have been that, on the assumption that the convention would be widely ratified, the words would add force to the argument that human rights were indeed protected by general principles of law and hence enforceable by the World Court. But the British draft would not have changed the rule of the Court's statute, which denies individuals any access to it.

When Professor Koretsky—ignoring, but I am sure not ignorant of the fact that this was a term of art—attacked the reference to "civilized nations" as an insult to certain countries, Geoffrey Wilson, who was not a lawyer, replied that the words need not be retained, a concession which would have considerably weakened the British draft. Koretsky's criticisms should have been directed not to the draft convention but to the statute of the Court itself which, because of the psychological baggage it now carries, is rightly or wrongly obnoxious to some of the newer members of the United Nations. From Koretsky's point of view, one red herring was as good as another, and the propaganda value of the issue was too great to be wasted. His legal wrangling on this and other occasions shocked my lawyer's conscience, but personally I found him a very likeable fellow. I have already mentioned his friendly gesture after I had taken him to lunch with Mrs. Roosevelt.

The British draft convention would have obliged states parties to ensure that everyone under their jurisdiction, whether citizens or not, should enjoy by their laws the exercise of the rights and freedoms defined in the instrument, and that persons whose rights were violated should have an effective remedy. This was implementation at the national level. There were also to be enforcement procedures within the United Nations, although the draft did not contemplate an individual right of petition. On receipt of a request from the Secretary-General made by authority of a resolution of the General Assembly—which under a draft resolution accompanying the draft convention would have delegated its authority in the matter to the Human Rights Commission—a state party would have been obliged to supply an explanation, certified by its highest legal authorities, of the manner in which its law gave effect to any provision of the convention. Finally, any failure of a state to fulfill its obligations under the treaty would have been:

> an injury to the community of states and a matter of concern to the United Nations as the community of states organized under the rule of law;

and:

> any one of them which is found by a resolution of the General Assembly adopted by a two-thirds majority persistently to have violated the provisions of this Bill of Rights should be deemed to have violated the principles of the United Nations and therefore liable to expulsion from the organization under Article 6 of the Charter.

I have described the British draft in some detail because it probably represented the highest point ever reached by the United Kingdom in its approach to the protection of human rights by the United Nations. I was sorry that the drafting committee did not discuss it more seriously. It is true that the assumption then was that the international bill of rights would take the form of a declaration. But once the commission had decided, as it did at its second session, that there would also be a multilateral convention (later called the covenant), the British draft would have been an excellent working basis for it. And the end result might have been better than the International Covenant on Civil and Political Rights which the General Assembly adopted in 1966. Surprisingly, because they had been insisting on a convention, the Australians sharply criticized the British draft. The proposal was commendable, said R.H. Harry in the absence of Colonel Hodgson, but it "was not sufficient to assure to the peoples of the world that the bill of rights would be more than a mere declaration of principles." Listening to this speech, I felt that the Australians had allowed themselves to be carried away by their advocacy for an international court of human rights, which was not included in the British proposal, and for which there was no support in the drafting committee.

The precision and clarity with which their proposal was drafted reflects an attitude which the British maintained throughout the work on the two covenants. Since these were to be legally binding instruments, it was necessary, the British argued, to know in advance exactly what ratifying states would be undertaking to do. The Americans on the other hand wanted short articles enunciating general principles, a method which everyone agreed was appropriate for a declaration. The quarrel between the two delegations reached a maximum of intensity when the commission was drafting the articles on freedom of information and freedom from arbitrary arrest. The Americans argued that it would not be feasible to list all foreseeable limitations to the exercise of specific rights; and to illustrate their point they produced elaborate lists of such limitations, some of which were, to say the least, far fetched. There are good arguments in favor of pithy statements—it is, for example, the method of the Code Napoleon—but the method will not work unless there is a strong tribunal empowered to interpret the law. The Americans certainly did not envisage the creation of such a tribunal; and while, as we have seen, Australia wanted one, the possibility has never been seriously considered at the United Nations. Later, at the seventh session of the commission, the International Labor Organization (one of the specialized agencies called in to advise on the drafting of the articles on economic, social and cultural rights) also argued that these rights should be defined in broad terms as general principles only; and in this they were supported by the British who continued, however, to favor precise drafting for civil and political rights. But the I.L.O. position was inspired by its determination to protect its jurisdiction against any encroachments by the United Nations.

I return to the first session of the drafting committee and a long debate lasting through six meetings during which the Secretariat draft declaration was discussed and compared with the United Kingdom draft convention. I was put on the spot at the very first meeting. Colonel Hodgson wanted to know what principles the Secretariat had used in the preparation of its draft and what was the philosophy behind it. He should have known that any answer that I could give to his question would, in that ideologically divided group, get me and my draft into hot water. I therefore replied that the draft was not based on any particular philosophy; it included rights recognized by various national constitutions and also a number of suggestions that had been made for an international bill of rights. I wasn't going to tell him that insofar as it reflected the views of its author—who had in any event to remain anonymous—the draft attempted to combine humanitarian liberalism with social democracy. Essentially my answer was true, because my draft was based on the documentation that I had had before me. But I had myself decided what to put in and what to leave out, and I had made changes and additions. A more expansive reply would have been indiscreet to the point of compromising the work of the commission. Later, Colonel Hodgson took me to task over my Article 25, which said that everything that is not prohibited by law is permitted. That, he said, was pure nonsense. It did not deserve the scorn that Hodgson poured on it; the principle is an expression of the rule of law and, as I could have told him, was enshrined in the fifth article of the French Declaration of 1789 on the Rights of Man and the Citizen.

I had some trouble with Mrs. Roosevelt over an article which said that everyone has a right to a legal personality. The principle seemed pretty clear to me: legal personality is the capacity to possess rights and to owe duties. A slave doesn't have a legal personality, and slavery still existed. There are other examples, including civil death which deprives certain categories of people, including members of certain religious communities and condemned criminals, of the legal capacity to exercise their rights. An authoritarian government could suppress the rights of minorities or of enemies of the regime. I could understand that Mrs. Roosevelt might have some difficulty about this: it was lawyers' language. But she was being advised by lawyers who, if they did not understand the vocabulary, had only to open any good book on jurisprudence. These lawyers continued to insist that they did not understand what I was talking about until I reminded them that there had been slavery in the United States up until the Civil War. The principle was retained. Article 6 of the Universal Declaration of Human Rights says that "everyone has the right to recognition everywhere as a person before the law," a more roundabout way of saying what I had said in fewer words. The principle, as far as I can remember, had not been included in any of the drafts on which I worked.

Much of the discussion still turned on the form of the bill. Mrs. Roosevelt said that, since it was to be adopted by the General Assembly, it should be a declaration. This could be followed by treaties on particular subjects which would be binding on the states which ratified them, or there might be a convention containing the substance of the declaration. In that case both instruments might be presented to the General Assembly at the same time. P.C. Chang envisaged three instruments: a declaration "drafted in simple phrases," a commentary on each of its articles, and proposals for its implementation. Later he suggested the formula for a tripartite bill—a declaration, a convention and measures of implementation—which was finally adopted.

Warning the committee that he could not express the views of the Soviet government on questions of principle and substance, Professor Koretsky said that

the committee might be embarking on a voyage which would lead it in a direction where it might cross the border which divides international from internal law—the border which divides the interrelationships of governments from the field where the sovereign rights of nations must prevail. The United Nations must first fight the remnants of fascism. Having beaten fascism it must formulate a bill of rights which would prevent the rebirth of fascist systems and of fascist ideology. Such a bill must not, however, be of such a nature as to interfere in the internal systems of various governments.

The future judge of the International Court of Justice was too intelligent not to see the inconsistency in what he was saying. Turning to my draft, he said that it wanted the committee to suggest that "the United Nations embark on an intervention in the affairs of individual countries." The United Kingdom draft, on the other hand, was an attempt "to transfer certain principles of law accepted in the United Kingdom to other countries—not only principles but also the mechanisms for their implementation. This system was not quite applicable to other countries whose historical development was different." He went on to criticize the political philosophy underlying both drafts. "The basic characterisic of the drafts that had been presented to the committee was their tendency to liberate man not from persecution but from his government, from his own people. That meant putting him in opposition to his own government and to his own people." He had, of course, hit the nail right on the head. One purpose of both drafts was to protect individuals from their governments. If the protection of human rights did not mean that, it did not mean much. Professor Koretsky wanted to fight the remnants of fascism and to prevent its rebirth, but that cannot be done without interfering in the internal affairs of governments. The struggle for human rights has always been and always will be a struggle against authority. There was perhaps something paradoxical about what the United Nations was trying to do; for the international bill of rights was being drafted by the representatives of governments. These were some of the things that I would have liked to say to Professor Koretsky had I not been the servant of the committee; for I did not think that he was very effectively answered by the members.

He then turned to the form of the bill. "Since each sovereign government must set its own standards in its relations with other nations, the only form," he said, "which would be compulsory for any government would be that of an international convention." But since it was obvious from everything he had said that the Soviet Union did not want a binding convention, he logically concluded that the committee should draft a declaration. This declaration should, he said, be simple, clear and concise. "It should not seek to separate man from his community; it should seek rather to create a man who is free in the framework of a free society." Not many people would have disagreed with his summation.

In 1947, it was an easy assumption in the West that the Soviet Union would never accept a binding convention on human rights; and Russian diplomats confirmed this by their off-the-record remarks. It was in the logic of the Cold War, however, that later, after the United States had turned against the covenants for reasons grounded in internal politics and countries like the United Kingdom were worried by the provisions put into them on the self-determination of peoples, the Soviet Union should attempt to fill the vacuum and become a champion of the covenants.

Colonel Hodgson again said that he didn't believe in a simple declaration. There should be a convention containing "practical measures for carrying out stated objectives." Even that might not be enough, because many conventions were not respected. "Provision should, therefore, be made that if a government or nation did not carry into effect the terms of the bill of rights, it should be taken to task by the aggrieved party before an international court." He had said all this before, but this time he provoked an outburst from Koretsky: "Any action creating a court which would stand higher than the separate governments as regards the interrelations between governments and their citizens would inevitably lead,'' said the future member of the World Court, ''to the destruction of governments.'' It would be an organism which would be working against governments—a new, outside, disconnected organism which would take upon itself the function of regulating the relations between governments and their citizens. This would violate the provisions of international law. This was strong language, and most of it utter nonsense.

Cassin undertook to reply, but most of what he said was beside the point. A better answer by a lawyer to another lawyer would have been to remind the future judge of the World Court that there is no limit to the right of states to bind themselves by treaty, that in the past states had undertaken by treaty to respect certain rights of their citizens, that there were examples in the past of states agreeing by treaty to refer disputes relating to human rights to the judgment of international tribunals, and that this had not resulted in the destruction of governments. There was, he could have added, the celebrated example of the minority treaties by which, after the First World War, some states had undertaken to refer any disputes arising out of the treaties to the World Court. Some governments had indeed been destroyed, but not because they had undertaken to respect the rights of their minorities or to accept the jurisdiction of the World Court.

It was Professor Koretsky who suggested that a small working group be appointed to collate the various opinions that had been expressed. The members, he added, should be the chairman, Cassin, Malik and Wilson. The working group would report back to the committee, which would be convened again for the purpose a few days before the next session of the full commission. He wanted, he explained later, to give governments an opportunity to comment on the various suggestions before the committee began drafting the bill. This suggestion was made in the course of a long speech which contained more than one political sting and in which he managed to refer to the treatment of Indians in South Africa, the failure of the ''MacArthur Constitution'' to eradicate the feudal system in Japan, and other matters. He also reached certain heights. The Declaration of Human Rights, he said, should ''imitate the style and manner of the old laws, especially their conciseness and clarity; it should have emotional appeal; conviction and provocative language;'' and he recalled ''the clear fighting spirit of the American Declaration of Independence and of the French Declaration of the Rights of Man, both of which reflected periods of freedom and of elevation. The Declaration of Human Rights should sound a bugle call and should state principles for which any man would be ready to stake his life.''

Mrs. Roosevelt chided Koretsky, reminding him that in the Economic and Social Council the Soviet Union had opposed entrusting the drafting to a small committee. She obviously interpreted his suggestion as a delaying tactic. The upshot however was the appointment of a temporary working group, consisting of Cassin, Malik and Wilson, to suggest ''a logical rearrangement'' of the articles in the Secretariat Outline and the way in which they should be redrafted in the light of the committee's discussions and divided between a manifesto and a convention. That was on a Friday at noon. The working group met immediately and asked Cassin to prepare a draft based on those articles of the Secretariat Outline that he considered appropriate for a declaration. He did this over the weekend with the help of my colleague, Emile Giraud. On Monday, the working group went over the preamble and first six articles of the new draft and sent them to the drafting committee.

Cassin's revision of my draft, written out in longhand, was displayed, at the request of the French government, at United Nations Headquarters on the tenth anniversary of the adoption of the Universal Declaration of Human Rights; and photographic reproductions of the same manuscript are reproduced in a collection of some of Cassin's articles and speeches published in 1972 under the title, *La Pensée et l'Action*. This helped create the myth that Cassin was the father of the Declaration. In an article published in 1968, the twentieth anniversary of the adoption of the Declaration and the year he received the Nobel Prize, Cassin takes credit for preparing the first draft. After referring to the documentation which had been prepared by the Secretariat, he says that "l'utilisation de ce travail . . . ne pouvait se faire directement au cours de débats oraux," a comment which fails to mention my own draft. He then says, "C'est pourquoi je fus chargé par mes collègues de rédiger, sous ma seule responsabilité, un premier avant-projet." This account, which is patently wrong, as anyone can confirm who will take the trouble to consult the official records, leaves the impression that Cassin prepared an original draft based on a more or less undigested mass of material collected by the Secretariat. The truth is that, while Cassin's role was important, it was not more important than the one played by some other members of the commission. The Universal Declaration of Human Rights has no father in the sense that Jefferson was the father of the American Declaration of Independence. Very many people—in the Commission on Human Rights, in its drafting committee, in the Commission on the Status of Women, in the two sub-commissions, in the General Assembly, in the specialized agencies, in departments of national governments and in the nongovernmental organizations—contributed to the final result. It is indeed this very anonymity which gives the Declaration some of its great prestige and authority.

Cassin's new text reproduced my own in most of its essentials and style. In many cases he merely prepared a new French version of the official United Nations translation of the original English, and when this was translated back into English the result seemed further removed from the original than it really was. This also explains why some of his suggested changes seemed awkward, at least in English. Cassin also changed the order of some of the articles, combined in one article principles that I had expressed in two, and divided some of them into two or more articles; and he left out some of the articles on the hypothesis that they could be included more appropriately in a convention. Many of his suggestions were rejected. In particular his changed order did not resist the test of time. There are almost as many possible classifications of human rights as there are people who argue about them. One of the very few new ideas in Cassin's draft was in his Article 28, which said that "the protection of human rights requires a public force" instituted "for the service of all and not for the advantage of those to whom it is entrusted. . . . Each citizen must take it as an honor to take part in military service in the states which recognize this institution." Wilson said that such an article would abridge the rights of conscientious objectors, and Mrs. Roosevelt pointed out that military service was neither a right nor a freedom. In other cases Cassin's instinct was better than mine. My draft had said that "appointments to the civil service shall be by competitive examination." Cassin quite properly added the possibility of other kinds or recruitment, but P.C. Chang tried to restore my text which, he said, reflected a Chinese tradition that went back as far as the Han dynasty. No one supported him, and Cassin's second draft omitted all reference to competitive examinations. There were several articles in the Cassin draft which stated principles that were more philosophical than legal and, to my mind at least, not appropriate for the declaration. I will discuss them presently.

When the drafting committee reconvened on 17 June, Mrs. Roosevelt, who was in a hurry to complete its work, asked the members to limit their remarks to three minutes for each article, an admonishment to which Professor Koretsky quite properly objected. The first article now read: "All men are brothers. Being endowed with reason, members of one family, they are free and possess equal dignity and rights." This was one of Cassin's additions. My own draft had carefully avoided any philosophical assertions which did not enunciate justiciable rights: if they have any place in the instrument it is in the preamble. For one thing—but this is hindsight—they weaken the case for saying that, whatever the General Assembly intended when it adopted the Declaration, it is now part of positive customary international law and therefore binding on all states. At the second session of the Human Rights Commission, Cassin's article created so much difficulty—Ambassador Bogomolov wanted to know why the Declaration should be filled with solemn affirmations lacking in sense—that Cassin and Romulo were asked to prepare a new draft of the article. It also created difficulties with the Commission on the Status of Women, which objected to its language. But the greatest harm which resulted from the introduction of unnecessary philosophical concepts was the needless controversy and useless debate they invited. The discussions the article provoked, particularly in the General Assembly, were needlessly controversial and protracted. Article 1 of the Declaration as finally adopted reads: "All human beings are born free and equal in dignity and rights. They are endowed with reason and conscience and should act towards one another in a spirit of brotherhood." Apart from the fact that at least part of this statement is of questionable truth, it is purely hortatory and adds nothing to the authority of the Universal Declaration of Human Rights.

Cassin reproduced, with minor changes mainly of style, my article on the right to own property, the writing of which had given me great difficulty because I had been searching in vain for a formula which would be applicable to rival economic and social systems. That is why it recognized only an unqualified right to own personal property. As for property in industrial, commercial and other profit-making enterprises, the right was, my article said, to be governed by the law of the country in which the enterprises were situated. The article then went on to say that "the state may regulate the acquisition and use of private property and determine those things which are susceptible of private appropriation. No one shall be deprived of his property without just compensation." My text may have been an admission of defeat; but it was probably as good as if not better than the one finally adopted by the General Assembly, which recognizes an unqualified right to own property "alone as well as in association with others." The discussions leading up to the adoption of this text were, as was to be expected, controversial; but, contrary to my expectations, there was relatively little apparent division on ideological grounds. Indeed, the General Assembly text was unanimously adopted—perhaps because it says so little. There is no article on the right of property in the Covenant on Civil and Political Rights. This was because no agreement could be reached on a formula covering the right to compensation in the event of expropriation, a difficulty that the Declaration had overcome by stating that "no one shall be arbitrarily deprived of his property."

The inclusion in my text of a series of articles on economic and social rights, which Cassin had reproduced, was quickly challenged. R.H. Harry, speaking for Australia in the absence of Colonel Hodgson, said that it would be "difficult to spell out in detail the different rights involved." In his opinion, "two or three articles in the final draft should be sufficient to cover the broad principles." Geoffrey Wilson agreed: "two or three general principles should be stated. These principles would be worked out at a later stage by the United Nations and its specialized agencies." Santa Cruz disagreed: "if the drafting committee did not introduce economic and social rights into the Declaration, it would not appear to the world to be acting realistically." Mrs. Roosevelt and Malik took a middle ground. "Some of the rights," said Malik, "would be true in a socialistic form of society; others would not. Since the Declaration had to be universal, only fundamental principles should be stated, such as the right to education, the right to participate in cultural life, the right to property, the fact that human labor is not a merchandise and so on." He then said something which showed how rigid his logic could be. Thinking probably that my article outlawing slavery and the slave trade was not sufficient, Cassin had added the principle that a person cannot "either alienate his person nor place himself in a state of servitude to another." This, said Malik, might be interpreted as "a restriction on a man's personal freedom. If he wanted to be a slave it was his right." Cassin's addition was not retained.

Before adjourning, the committee returned briefly to the idea of a convention. Article 8 of the British draft convention said that "it shall be unlawful to deprive any person of his life save in the execution of the sentence of a court following on his conviction of a crime for which this penalty is provided by law"—a principle which I had included in other language in my draft declaration. Malik wanted the words, "from the moment of conception" inserted, thus beginning in the United Nations a controversy that was to last over the years and generate much casuistical debate—not only in relation to the Universal Declaration of Human Rights, which says simply that "everyone has the right to life" and the Covenant on Civil and Political Rights, but also to the Declaration on the Rights of the Child (which was adopted in 1959), none of which take any position on the question. I would again be involved in this controversy when, after my retirement from the Secretariat, I was a member of the Royal Commission on the Status of Women in Canada. I agreed with the majority of my colleagues that the Canadian Criminal Code should be amended to permit abortion by a qualified practitioner at the request of a woman who had been pregnant for less than twelve weeks, and was myself responsible for the qualification which I thought necessary, not only from the point of view of the woman's health, but also because there is some point at which an unborn child has the right to life.

The drafting committee adjourned on 25 June. Two days later I was in Ottawa testifying before a special joint committee of the Senate and House of Commons on human rights and fundamental freedoms. I talked and answered questions for nearly two hours, tracing the United Nations human rights program since the San Francisco Conference.

Five months were to pass before the Commission on Human Rights would take up the work where the drafting committee had left off. In the meantime I had other worries. Paper work was piling up on my desk. The Division was responsible for a huge correspondence both within and outside the Secretariat. I even tried to read the numerous communications we were receiving from people complaining that their rights were being violated. But there were so many of them that I had to organize a special unit for the frustrating job. In the light of the commission's decision that it had no power to entertain complaints, there was not much that we could do about them; but the letters had to be read, acknowledged and classified, and copies sent to governments; and confidential lists had to be prepared for the commission. There were also working papers to be prepared for various bodies; and I wrote carefully drafted memoranda in French to Laugier on all important policy matters. And there were people to see and the telephone to answer. But above all, there was the constant round of Secretariat meetings. Anyone with a job to do usually began by convening a meeting to discuss it, and I was usually expected to attend. There was some method in this madness, since several minds are sometimes better than one; but it was an unconscionable waste of time. Later, as I gained more experience running the Division, I tried to discourage such meetings. Laugier, moreover, usually wanted me to be with him at meetings he had to attend; and there were long directors' meetings at which attendance was de rigueur, many of them with agendas which, while undoubtedly important, had little if anything to do with human rights.

The Economic and Social Council met three weeks after the drafting committee had adjourned. There were a number of human rights items on its agenda, including the proposed convention on genocide, trade union rights and freedom of information. It was at this session that the Council confirmed the commission's controversial decision relating to human rights communciations. I had also accepted an invitation to give a lecture to the American Academy of Political and Social Science which met at the University of Michigan in Ann Arbor. This lecture and its repercussions dogged me for the rest of my career in the Secretariat. My remark that what the United Nations was trying to do in the matter of human rights was ''revolutionary in character'' was, in context, a correct and reasonable thing to say, particularly to an audience of scholars. In the very next sentence I went on to say:

> Human rights are largely a matter of relationships between the state and individuals, and therefore a matter which has been traditionally regarded as being within the domestic jurisdiction of states. What is now being proposed is, in effect, the creation of some kind of supranational supervision of this relationship between the state and its citizens.

But quite innocently, I had played right into the hand of enemies in the United States of the United Nations human rights program. My remark about its revolutionary character was immediately picked up by the American Bar Association and used out of context in the energetic campaign it was conducting against the program. The cry was taken up by the Republican Party and, as late as the presidential elections of 1964, Barry Goldwater did me the honor of quoting me, again out of context, in his book, *Why Not Victory* ? My blunder embarrassed American supporters of the human rights covenants and I regretted having made it. But since recovering my freedom of speech on my retirement from the Secretariat, I have said the same thing countless times because it is true. There has never been a more revolutionary development in the theory and practice of international law and organization than the recognition that human rights are matters of international concern.

The General Assembly, in the work of which I was now more involved, met on 16 September; but I had to leave New York before the end of the session to attend the first session of the Sub-Commission on the Prevention of Discrimination and the Protection of Minorities and the second session of the Human Rights Commission, both in Geneva. This was my first visit to Switzerland since 1929, when my wife and I had been there for our honeymoon. In late November the city was grey and cold; and on most days the *bise* blew down over the lake. Later, after I had spent much of my time in Geneva because there were so many meetings there, I came to like the place better than New York. But when, many years later, an attempt was made to move my division to Geneva, I opposed the move because I thought that a service as politically important as the Human Rights Division should be at headquarters near the Secretary-General.

During my twenty years at the United Nations, the level of representation on the Sub-Commission on the Prevention of Discrimination was always high, and the first session was no exception. I came to know some of the members very well. I already knew Joseph Nisot, the member from Belgium and the sub-commission's first rapporteur. A member of the Minorities Section in the League of Nations Secretariat, he had taken refuge in Montreal during the war and, although we were poles apart in our political thinking, we had become friends. Later he became the head of the Belgian mission to the United Nations. Eric Extrand from Sweden was the chairman, and Hérard Roy from Haïti was vice-chairman. Minoo Masani, the Indian member, a man of great personal charm, with one of the quickest minds I have ever encountered, was, like many other Indians at the United Nations, an accomplished debater. I have already mentioned that his government refused to allow him to continue to serve on the sub-commission after his reelection in 1955.

Elizabeth Monroe, the British member, was one of the most capable women ever to come to the United Nations. I tried to recruit her as chief of the section on the status of women, but when, misled by her use of the prefix "Miss," I put the question to her one day over lunch, she replied that she didn't think that her husband, who it seems was a London surgeon, would approve. The member from the United States was Jonathan Daniels, at one time President Roosevelt's administrative assistant and now the editor of a newspaper in Raleigh, North Carolina. Samuel Spanien, a French lawyer with a fine mind, had defended Léon Blum in the prosecution trumped up against him by the Pétainist government. The Soviet expert was A.P. Borisov, the same man who had been a member of the nuclear commission on human rights. Other members attending the first session were Chang-fu from China, W.M.J. McNamara from Australia, Arturo Meneses Pallares from Ecuador and Rezazada Shafaz from Iran.

The sub-commission devoted most of this first session to the draft declaration: the important first paragraph of Article 2[1] of the Universal Declaration is largely its work, except that the General Assembly added, "color" to the list of grounds on which discrimination is proscribed. The sub-commission had thought this word unnecessary and even dangerous. In its opinion "color" was included in "race" and to mention it expressly might throw doubt on the meaning of "race" as it is used in the Charter. It also recommended an article on the protection of minorities, but, for reasons already discussed, no such article was included in the final text. The sub-commission wanted the Economic and Social Council to ask the International Court of Justice for an opinion on whether the treaties and

1. "Everyone is entitled to all the rights and freedoms set forth in this Declaration, without distinction of any kind, such as race, colour, sex, language, religion, political or other opinion, national or social origin, property, birth or other status." Paragraph two was added by the General Assembly.

declarations by which, after the First World War, certain countries had undertaken to protect their racial, religious and linguistic minorities, were still in force. Regrettably, the Council decided instead to ask the Secretary-General for his opinion. Emile Giraud, who prepared the opinion, concluded that, with certain exceptions, the treaties and declarations were no longer binding. I did not agree with this but, partly out of respect for Giraud's greater experience, I sent his study to the legal department as a basis for further discussion. The question was then discussed at a meeting in Laugier's office with Ivan Kerno, the Assistant Secretary-General in charge of the legal department, who was himself a citizen of Czechoslovakia, one of the countries bound by the treaties. Kerno, who had the final say, considered that all the treaties and declarations had lapsed and rewrote part of the opinion. The result was that, when published in April 1950, the opinion read that "between 1939 and 1947 circumstances as a whole changed to such an extent that generally speaking the system should be considered as having ceased to exist." I have always considered it ironical that an international secretariat should have thus countenanced one of the most questionable and disruptive institutions of international law, the so-called *rebus sic stantibus* clause which, according to the doctrine, is presumed to form part of every treaty. The sub-commission also asked the Secretariat to prepare a study on the main types and causes of discrimination. This study was written by Professor Recasens-Siches whom I had recently recruited. He later also prepared a study on the definition and classification of minorities. Recasens-Siches was a legal philosopher with an international reputation who had once been a member of the cabinet in the Loyalist government of Spain. He left the Secretariat a few years later to accept a post in the National University of Mexico. Another useful initiative taken at this session was the request to UNESCO to undertake a program to disseminate the scientific facts about race. UNESCO published declarations on the question in 1950 and subsequently on three other occasions.

At the expense of several night meetings, the sub-commission did a great deal of work in the short space of two weeks. The Human Rights Commission also met for only two weeks, a very short time considering the heavy agenda. But Mrs. Roosevelt drove the members very hard—she wanted to be home for Christmas—with the result that a great deal of work was done; several night meetings continued into the early hours of the morning. Although most of the delegates, and even more the Secretariat, suffered from loss of sleep, Mrs. Roosevelt remained as alert as she had been when she opened the session. There were some relaxing interludes, including an elaborate dinner party which Ambassador Bogomolov, who was representing the Soviet Union for the first time, gave at the Hotel Richmonde, and where René Cassin and I were the only guests from noncommunist countries. There was a great deal to drink—vodka, Russian brandy and just about every kind of Crimean wine—and many toasts, but I suspected that some of our hosts had water in their glasses instead of vodka. After the party, Professor Koretsky and I, both perfectly sober, gave an exhibition of international comity, swaying from side to side, arm in arm, as we came down the staircase from the hotel mezzanine. I remember another of Bogomolov's parties when Jeanne was with me. Anything served as a pretext for a toast. After one to the director of the Human Rights Division, the guests drank to the wife of the director and then to the husband of the wife of the director and so on.

The commission decided that it would prepare both a declaration and a convention (to be called a covenant) as well as provisions for implementation. On the suggestion of Fernand Dehousse, who was representing Belgium for the first time, the commission then divided into three working groups. The first worked on the declaration, where the most significant development of the session took place; for the Soviet Union, in the person of Ambassador Bogomolov, began to take an active part in the drafting, particularly of the articles on economic, social and cultural rights. The commission never had a more cooperative Soviet spokesman than Bogomolov, who was also one of its most urbane. The second group worked on the convention, and the third was to devise a system of implementation. I spent most of my time in the third group, because I already thought that the real test of the United Nations as an international organization dedicated to the promotion of respect for human rights and fundamental freedoms would be its ability to agree on effective measures of implementation. If I expected any immediate results I was to be disappointed; it was the implementation group that achieved the least in terms of lasting results. The Ukrainian member was apparently afraid that some progress might be made, for he remained with the group only long enough to say that there should be no question of implementation until agreement had been reached on the content of the international bill of rights. All the recommendations of this group were directed to the proposed covenant or to other possible human rights conventions. For it was not then thought that the Declaration would ever be binding in international law, and very few people had begun to recognize the important possibilities inherent in the Charter itself. Everybody agreed that the first responsibility for enforcement should be at the state level and that each state party would be under an obligation to incorporate the rules of the convention into its own national law, a principle which has survived in Article 2 of the International Covenant on Civil and Political Rights. The group also recommended that the Economic and Social Council appoint a standing committee for the mediation and conciliation of disputes arising out of alleged violations of the convention and, if possible, provide a remedy. Disputes not settled by the ECOSOC committee would be sent to the Human Rights Commission, which would decide whether they should be referred to an international human rights tribunal, the creation of which was recommended. The decisions of the tribunal, which were to be binding on the parties, were to be implemented by the General Assembly. Never again would such far-reaching procedures be contemplated for the implementation of the covenant. The commission paid little attention to these recommendations, none of which it discussed in any detail; but it did complete a careful draft of the Declaration and an admittedly preliminary draft of a convention, both of which were forwarded to governments for their comments.

The Geneva Conference on Freedom of Information and Mondanités in Paris (1948)

The New Year ushered in one of my busiest and best years at the United Nations, a year of meetings—so many that they sometimes overlapped. Some were at Lake Success, others in Geneva, and the General Assembly met in Paris. I attended them all, and, although I now had an assistant director on whom I could rely, I also had my division to run.

The Commission on the Status of Women met at Lake Success on 5 January. My relations with its new chairman, Hélène Lefaucheux of France, were easier than they had been with her predecessor; but I still felt that my presence was resented in the conference room. I now had a good chief of the section on the status of women in the person of Amanda Labarca, who had a national reputation as an educationalist in Chile where she had been the president of the Federation of Women. It was a great disappointment when that summer she told me that she was leaving the Secretariat.

The Economic and Social Council had asked this commission to look at the draft declaration. It recommended changes in two articles, one of them the famous article beginning with "All men are brothers," for which Cassin had been responsible. Pointing out that the word "men" was often interpreted restrictively, Jessie Street said that it should be replaced by "human beings." The Chinese member then said that another word should be found for "brothers." It was the Begum Hamid Ali who suggested the formula, "in the spirit of brothers and sisters," which wasn't far from "in a spirit of brotherhood" finally adopted by the General Assembly.

The women also recommemded a new text for the article on the right to marry. The Human Rights Commission had referred simply to the equal right of both men and women to marry. Mrs. Street wanted the article to mention divorce. In some countries, she recalled, a wife could be divorced on the slightest pretext but could not divorce her husband. The chairman suggested that the article say that men and women have equal rights to contract and to dissolve marriage. While I have no documentary evidence, I believe that the text finally adopted by the General Assembly which speaks of "equal rights as to marriage, during marriage and at its dissolution" and, like Madame Lefaucheux's suggestion, avoids any mention of divorce, was approved by the Vatican. Other items on the agenda included the political rights of women, the property rights of married women, educational opportunities and the employment and remuneration of women—items which kept reappearing on the commission's agenda as long as I was at the United Nations.

The second session of the Sub-Commission on Freedom of Information opened the day the Commission on the Status of Women adjourned. Its first session had been devoted chiefly to the organization of the international conference on freedom of information (which was to open in a few weeks) and the agenda of the conference—an agenda that had survived the criticisms of the communist countries in the General Assembly. The sub-commission had now to draft the articles on freedom of information for the Declaration and covenant on human rights. My own draft of the Declaration had devoted four articles to the question, one of which mentioned the duty "to present information and news in a fair and impartial manner." Cassin had reproduced this in his draft and added a specific reference to the responsibility of editors and printers. But in the drafting committee Mrs. Roosevelt had said that her government could not accept the reference to editors and printers, and the matter was later referred to the sub-commission. The American position was, and apparently still is, that a good press will compensate for a bad one; remove all restrictions and the public will be served. The sub-commission skated over the problem; but it nevertheless improved the drafting committee's text and prepared an article which, with minor amendments, became Article 19 of the Universal Declaration of Human Rights. The drafting committee's text had also said that "every person shall be free to express and publish his ideas." Professor Chafee, the American member who had more than once been attacked for his liberal opinions, suggested a change in the wording. In the United States, he said, people had been forced by committees of the congress to reveal their intimate opinions, for example about communism. The text was therefore changed to read: "Everyone has the right to freedom of opinion and expression." Professor Chafee was replaced as the American member of the sub-commission at its next session, but whether this had anything to do with his reference to congressional witch-hunting I do not know.

The sixth session of ECOSOC began the day before the sub-commission adjourned. It was just as well for me that the economists were monopolizing the session, because in February I had my hands full making last minute arrangements for the information conference. This was the largest conference yet to be held under the auspices of the United Nations—both member and nonmember states were to be represented—and to be its executive secretary was therefore a heavy responsibility, particularly since it was to be held away from headquarters. My difficulties were compounded by jealousies and controversy within the Secretariat. Not only did the Department of Public Information feel that it should have been given responsibility for running the conference, but there was some feeling in the higher echelons of the Secretariat that the conference should not be held under United Nations auspices. I learned about the views of one high-ranking official almost by accident. I was waiting for a U.N. car—such things existed in those days—to take me back to Lake Success after a reception given by General A.G.L. McNaughton, the permanent representative of Canada, in his Long Island residence. Byron Price, the American Assistant Secretary-General, was also waiting for a car. I hardly knew him, but I did know that together with the Secretary-General himself and Andrew Cordier, he was one of the most powerful men in the establishment. During the war he had been the director of censorship in the United States; he had also been a general manager of Associated Press and had worked with United Press. A propos of nothing, he began to complain to me about the proliferation of meetings at the United Nations on matters which, in his view, were of only peripheral interest to the organization, mentioning the information conference as an example.

The Department of Public Information was a service department responsible for making the United Nations known throughout the world. It seemed natural to them that they should also have substantive responsibility for freedom of information. The result was that, while I was ready to agree that some of its officers probably knew far more about the question than I or any member of my staff did, and while I would have welcomed any help that they could have given us—which was not forthcoming—I had to carry on a running battle with the department.

Freedom of information is not only obviously a human right, but, as the General Assembly had said at its first session, it is the touchstone of all other rights. Both the Economic and Social Council and the Human Rights Commission had recognized this when they gave responsibility for organizing the conference and drawing up its agenda to a subcommission of the Commission on Human Rights. And the Secretary-General had appointed me as the executive secretary of the conference. By the time I left headquarters for Geneva, I had every reason to believe, therefore, that my authority had been confirmed. I was surprised when, without consulting either Laugier or me, Benjamin Cohen, the Chilean Assistant Secretary-General in charge of the Department of Public Information, turned up in Geneva a day or two before the conference opened and began to take over. Amongst other things, he convened and chaired an informal meeting of heads of delegations the day before the opening to discuss the business of the conference, including the choice of officers. The delegations resented this interference. Hector McNeil, the British minister of state and head of the United Kingdom delegation, was so incensed that he sent a message to the Secretary-General—the contents of which he later disclosed to me—congratulating him on the way the conference had been planned and was being run by the Division of Human Rights. He was impressed, he told me, that such a small staff could run so big a conference with such efficiency. I had no doubt that this gesture was partly inspired by the obvious difficulties under which I was working. As for Cohen, he very soon left Geneva and left the field to us. I should add that my future relations with him were very good, and that I came to admire his devotion to the purposes of the United Nations.

It was a foregone conclusion that General Romulo would be the president of the conference. I have never had a more satisfactory relationship with a presiding officer. We had at least a half hour together regularly every morning before the committees met, a rare experience, since most chairmen arrive just in time to open a meeting and have to be briefed during the heat of the battle. He also took me into his full confidence, consulting me about the progress that was being made or the difficulties that had come up. Romulo had a cocky manner and some people refused to take him seriously, but he had real value: he had a quick mind, was full of enthusiasms and got things done; and he liked to do things in a big way. I helped him make arrangements for a reception he intended to be the most spectacular in the Palais des Nations since the Aga Khan was the president of the Assembly of the League of Nations, but it had to be cancelled when the President of the Philippines died. I was so impressed by Romulo as a presiding officer that I recommended him as a possible president of the General Assembly, an office to which he was in fact elected in 1949.

When after four weeks the conference ended on a note of optimism, it had prepared and sent to the Economic and Social Council three draft conventions: one on the gathering and international transmission of news; one on the institution of an international right of correction; and one on freedom of information. The first of these had been sponsored by the United States, the second by France, and the third by the United Kingdom—a political imbalance that should have been a warning of stormy waters ahead. It had also adopted forty-three resolutions and, its most lasting achievement, draft articles for the international bill of rights based on the work of the sub-commission. Over three decades later, only one of the conventions, the Convention on an International Right of Correction, the least important of the three, is in force, and that only between a very small number of states.

But in 1948 the conference was hailed as a great success. And so it would have been had the three conventions been opened for signature and ratification immediately after the end of the conference. I soon realized that a great mistake had been made. If the countries invited to the conference had been asked to give their delegations full powers to sign any conventions approved by it, the three conventions would undoubtedly be in force today. But because it was thought that their prestige and authority would be enhanced if the conventions were approved by the United Nations before they were opened for signature, the three drafts together with the rest of the final act were sent to the Economic and Social Council for further action. This gave the opposition the time to organize its forces as well as unlimited time in which to press its point of view. In ECOSOC and later in the General Assembly, there began a long and frustrating process of discussion and amendment. In brief, the amendments which the communist and developing countries forced on the United Nations were from the Western point of view so radical that the draft conventions became unacceptable. What was coming to the surface was the resentment felt in many countries toward the monopolistic practices of the great news-gathering agencies, and the too simple concept of freedom of information current in the West, particularly among professional journalists. And as so often happens, the opposition overreacted.

The atmosphere at the conference was highly political, the committee rooms becoming arenas for fighting the Cold War which (after the Prague coup d'état) had become more intense. Positions hardened and there was very little room left for compromise. As so often happens in the United Nations, it was a dialogue between the deaf. I was involved in one—and as far as I know the only one—attempt to reach a compromise. One afternoon Vladislav Ribnikar, the head of the Yugoslav delegation, invited me for a drink. After an appropriate introduction—for he was a civilized man—he began to explain the minimum aims of the communist countries. What they wanted most of all, he said, was a condemnation of warmongering. If they got that they would be willing to compromise on other things. Although he did not say so, I was fairly sure that he wanted me to pass this on to the leaders of the Western group. It happened that I was having dinner that night with Jean Desy, the head of the Canadian delegation. When I spoke to him about my conversation with Ribnikar, he advised me to talk to William Benton, the leader of the American delegation. But when I stopped Benton in the corridor the next day he brushed me aside impatiently, scarcely listening to my story.

The conference over, I returned to New York on the R.M.S. *Media*, leaving Jeanne in Europe where I would soon rejoin her. There were a number of people from the conference on board, including General Romulo and the whole of the Philippine delegation, which gave me a birthday party on 30 April. I was at headquarters in time for the second session of the drafting committee. It reviewed the work of the Human Rights Commission in the light of the comments that had been received from governments, from the Commission on the Status of Women and from the two sub-commissions, prepared a new draft of the covenant and of part of the declaration; but it did not discuss measures of implementation. The session ended on 21 May, three days before the opening of the third session of the Human Rights Commission, which also met at Lake Success.

In the meantime, the ECOSOC ad hoc committee on genocide had met. It worked on the draft which, on 9 December, the General Assembly adopted as the International Convention on the Prevention and Punishment of the Crime of Genocide. My division was not responsible for piloting the convention through the General Assembly, where it was discussed in the Sixth or Legal Committee, but we were responsible for the item in the earlier stages. In 1947, we had worked with three consultants on a draft which, if memory serves, was prepared by Emile Giraud. Two of these consultants were highly colorful personalities. Professor Lemkin has as much right as anyone to be called the father of the convention. Strongly motivated by the fact that members of his own family in Poland had been exterminated by the Nazis, he devoted all his considerable energies to the cause. Never in the history of the United Nations has one private individual conducted such a lobby. He could be seen everywhere in the committee rooms and, by common consent, was accorded privileges denied to other private individuals. But he was a very difficult man who looked for enemies under every bench, which was probably the reason we had difficulty getting the jurists to sit down around one table: they even refused to have their picture taken together. The second expert was Professor V.V. Pella, an expatriate Romanian criminologist whom I also remember as a bon vivant. The third jurist whom we had invited to help us was Donnedieu de Vabres of France, but he never turned up and was represented by a member of the French delegation.

The Human Rights Commission met for four weeks. After some delay caused by the late arrival of the Byelorussian and Ukrainian representatives, who had had difficulty getting United States visas—a difficulty interpreted as an act of reprisal—the commission decided to give priority to the Declaration, to which it devoted most of the session. Its final draft of this historic instrument was adopted on 18 June, the last day of the session, twelve delegations voting in favor; four—Byelorussia, the Soviet Union, the Ukraine and Yugoslavia—anticipating the position they would take in the General Assembly on 10 December, abstained from voting. Explaining the views of the Soviet Union, A.P. Pavlov said that "while it could not be said that the document contained nothing at all, since it did in a somewhat vague way repeat certain generally accepted democratic concepts of fundamental rights, it did nothing to ensure respect for human rights." Its chief faults, he went on to say, lay in the absence of any effective measure to combat fascism and nazism, its inadequate references to democracy, the limitation of certain rights, the absence of any provisions for implementation and the rejection of any specific definition of the obligations of individuals to the state—a very mixed bag of objections when one remembers the position his delegation had taken on some of these issues.

The commission had no time to review the work that its drafting committee had done on the covenant, nor did it recommend any measures for implementation; but it did ask its members to circulate their views on such measures in writing. Some of them merited more attention than they received. The Soviet Union's reaction to all of them was that they interpreted implementation as

not a system of measures for ensuring that human rights are implemented and guaranteed in every country by the state and society, but rather a system of international measures of pressure to be exercised through special organs established for this purpose (e.g., an international court, international committee or a United Nations public prosecutor, etc.) and intended to force individual states to take particular steps connected with the execution of the Convention on Human Rights.

The Soviet paper then went on to say that it was therefore clear that "such 'implementation' could become a means of interfering in the internal affairs of states." The plans if adopted would transform disputes between private individuals and their governments into international disputes "thereby substantially enlarging the area of international differences, frictions and incidents, unnecessarily burdening and aggravating international relations and undermining the foundations of peace." They would also upset the balance of power established by the Charter. The Soviet Union therefore disapproved "all the drafts and proposals on implementation presented to the commission and considered them unsatisfactory." Its position, which remains the same today, had at least the virtue of frankness. Were some other governments equally candid their positions on the international implementation of human rights would reveal themselves as not very different.

Having decided to forward its draft declaration, together with the draft covenant as prepared by its drafting committee, and also the report of the Geneva working group on implementation to the Economic and Social Council, the commission adjourned on 18 June. By United Nations standards, and considering the relatively short time it had actually met since the drafting had begun, it had done its work well. Possibly the best tribute that can be paid to it is to say that when its draft of the declaration reached the General Assembly later that year, many delegations were prepared to accept it as it stood; and that, notwithstanding the many long hours which the Third Committee of the Assembly devoted to it, the final result was remarkably like the commission's text.

I had a whole month between the adjournment of the commission and the beginning of the seventh session of ECOSOC, which was to be held in Geneva. It gave me a much needed opportunity to catch up with my desk work, but I was soon crossing the Atlantic for the third time that year. I first went to Biarritz to fetch my wife, and I remember going with her to Bayonne to see a bullfight and both of us being disgusted with the *mise à mort* we saw for the first time.

There were so many human rights items on the Council's agenda, including the draft declaration on human rights, the draft convention on genocide and the final act of the information conference, that a special human rights committee was set up to deal with them. But like the Council itself, this committee did very little of lasting value. There was a great deal of talk, most of it directed to procedure, but neither the Council nor the committee itself changed a comma in either the draft declaration or the draft genocide convention. It must have been at this time that I began to question the usefulness of the Economic and Social Council as part of the United Nations human rights structure. Its indifferent record in human rights matters was partly due to the fact that, with a few outstanding exceptions, the member countries were represented either by economists or by relatively junior civil servants, many of whom were cynical about human rights. More basic, however, was the fact that, situated as it was between the Commission on Human Rights with its relatively high level of representation, and the General Assembly, it had no well-defined role to play. It had neither the expertise required to deal with the technical problems involved nor the representative character of the General Assembly. Limited in its membership—like the commission it had only eighteen members—it did not have the political authority of the General Assembly, on which all members of the United Nations were represented; for while its member states were elected by the General Assembly and, theoretically, were supposed to act in the interest of the whole international community, in fact they consulted only their own interests.

Since the Council had no effective substantive contribution to make, it occupied its time with endless procedural debate. It was a bottleneck through which we had to pass. And because many of the people who frequented it were not distinguished by their sympathy for the human rights program, many of the commission's difficulties and those of my division in the Secretariat originated in it, either because the Council itself initiated them or because it was influenced by unsympathetic senior members of the Secretariat who could maneuver better there than in either the Commission on Human Rights or the General Assembly, where they had relatively little influence. It was the Council, for example, which abolished the Sub-Commission on Freedom of Information and of the Press and which tried to wind up the Sub-Commission on the Prevention of Discrimination and the Protection of Minorities. It even tried to limit the Human Rights Commission to biannual sessions, and this at a time when the latter's agenda was so heavy that many important matters could not be discussed. These were some of the reasons why I came to think that the commission should not be a functional commission of ECOSOC but rather a Council of Human Rights reporting directly to the General Assembly.

Some of the things that happened at the seventh session of the Economic and Social Council would be hard to believe were they not written on the record. After it had set up its special human rights committee, several delegations objected to sending the draft declaration to it. A.A. Arutinuian speaking for the Soviet Union said that, if this were done, the Declaration which "should be one of the major achievements of the Council would be relegated to the background where few people would notice its existence." As it turned out there was some truth in what he said, for the special human rights committee took so long discussing other matters that it never reached the report of the Human Rights Commission or the text of the draft declaration. But the Soviet delegation was itself partly responsible for the fiasco.

The special human rights committee spent two weeks discussing the report of the Commission on the Status of Women, the only item on its agenda that could not be said to be urgent, since nothing in it required action at the forthcoming session of the General Assembly. Some of the many interventions of A.P. Pavlov—who was now becoming the principal Russian spokesman in human rights matters—lasted for over an hour. He was a ferocious yet distinguished-looking man with a jet black goatee, pink cheeks and a mass of pure white hair. More to the point, he was also one of the most loquacious speakers I have ever listened to and the most difficult of all the Russians who worked on the Declaration. Some people said that his bourgeois background—he was the nephew of the great Pavlov— made him vulnerable to criticism back home and that this accounted for the show he never failed to provide.

Charles Malik, the president of the Council, also chaired the special human rights committee. He was obviously impressed by the historical importance of this role, but he tried so hard to please everybody that he seemed to invite debate, and the filibuster went on unabated. Laugier, exasperated by the chairman's failure to conclude debate on the Declaration, exclaimed: "Il sera le parrain d'un avortement." Finally, on 5 August, the committee decided to wind up the debate on the status of women even if it meant an all-night meeting. This proved unnecessary; the committee adjourned at six o'clock, in time for the delegates to attend a Soviet cocktail party. I could not be sure whether it was the threat of a long night-meeting or an appetite for vodka and caviar that did the trick. Madame LeFaucheux, to whom I talked at the party, seemed very pleased about the attention which had been given to the commission of which she was the chairman.

The fact that the committee had completed its work on the report of the Commission on the Status of Women did not mean that the way was now clear for the Declaration; for the next item on the agenda was the information conference, including the three draft conventions, a proper discussion of which could take weeks. The committee would then have to fix new terms of reference for the Sub-Commission on Freedom of Information and discuss the draft genocide convention before reaching the Declaration. The outlook was grim, therefore, that Sunday when the French delegation took the Council and Secretariat to Génissiat to inspect a new dam. By the end of the next week the situation was critical: there were only two weeks left, and it seemed that the special committee would not get through its agenda. One heard talk of an attempt to sabotage the Declaration or, at the very least, to prevent its reaching the General Assembly that year.

Over the objections of the Russians it was finally decided to recall to plenary not only the draft declaration but also the draft convention on genocide and two of the draft conventions on freedom of information. A.A. Arutinuian who, it will be remembered, had objected to sending the declaration to the special committee, now argued that it should be left there. "A committee on human rights," he said, "should naturally consider matters pertaining to human rights." The result of all this was that the discussion of all these matters in Council was limited to a series of brief position statements; but the draft instruments did get to the next session of the General Assembly and that was the important thing.

I continued to sit in the special committee, which now had a new chairman in the person of Leonid Kaminsky of Byelorussia. He caused a sensation and much debate when he ruled out of order an amendment sponsored by the loquacious Pavlov. And at one point Pavlov and Katz-Suchy of Poland both seriously argued that a treaty ratified by two states could not impose legal obligations. They had already argued that the sovereign right of states to refuse foreigners admission to their territories could not be interfered with by treaty. However, the pressure was now off and I could listen to this kind of nonsense with a certain degree of equanimity. On 20 August I returned to plenary for the debate on the Declaration. All was plain sailing until the Chileans brought up an issue that had been simmering in the Commission on the Status of Women and in the Council's human rights committee: the right of married couples to live together and hence the right of a wife to leave her country of origin and reside with her husband in another country. This was no academic discussion, for the Soviet government had just refused to allow the Russian wife of the son of a Chilean diplomat to leave the Soviet Union with her husband. When a motion deploring such practices was made, the Soviet and Polish delegations reacted so sharply that no more business was done that day. In the evening, Malik gave a big dinner party. I sat opposite to Pavlov, who looked tired and, I thought, unhappy.

The next day I was back in the special human rights committee, which had not yet completed its business. The Russians were accusing the British of trying to close a debate that had never been opened. Chairman Kaminsky was so upset that he left the chair. In the afternoon, the committee spent over three hours arguing about whether the morning meeting had been properly adjourned. At six thirty, it returned to and finally completed its discussion of the draft convention on freedom of information. The meeting adjourned at eight thirty.

On Monday, after a weekend which included an excursion to Gruyères, the Council returned to the Chilean motion and the communists now had an answer. Freedom of movement, they said, fell within domestic jurisdiction and, a typical non sequitur, there was discrimination in the capitalist countries. Pavlov spoke at great length. His language was always colorful, but he now excelled himself. The situation in Britain, he said, was one "qui fait de la femme une espèce d'article de chambre à coucher"—as it came in the French interpretation to which I was listening. The interpreters later told me that his language was sometimes so violent that they did not translate. Pavlov then proposed an amendment to the Chilean resolution by which the Council would deplore "all legislative measures which forbid mixed marriages between persons differing in color, race, nationality, citizenship or religion." Although obviously a red herring, no one could object to the sentiments expressed in the amendment and it was adopted. More to the point, the Council deplored "legislative or administrative provisions which deny to a woman the right to leave her country of origin and reside with her husband in any other." At its next session the General Assembly would declare (after citing Articles 13 and 16 of the Universal Declaration of Human Rights on freedom of movement and the right to marry without any limitations due to race, nationality or religion) that such measures were not in conformity with the Charter and call on the Soviet Union to withdraw them. This was the first of many times that the General Assembly would use the Declaration to interpret the Charter.

The next day there was a night meeting. René Cassin, with whom I had just had dinner, made a brilliant speech. Pavlov, who could be counted on to take the floor at every meeting, surprised me when he said that "in general" the Soviet Union approved the draft declaration; but he then went on with a list of particulars with which it was in disagreement. It did not, Pavlov said, consistently maintain the principle of full equality. Nor did it make any provisions for the eradication of fascism or the prohibition of fascist and Nazi propaganda and of racial and national hostility. The obligations which the individual owed to his family, nation and society were not expressed, and the Declaration did not sufficiently guarantee the enjoyment of economic rights. Some of this criticism was repeated by the delegate from Poland, who added that the Declaration might become an instrument for interfering in the domestic affairs of states. Another night meeting followed, this time to discuss freedom of information. But since the Council had already decided to send the conventions on to the General Assembly, the proceedings were again limited to a series of position statements.

I had now begun to keep a diary and, with occasional lapses, continued to do so until my retirement from the Secretariat in 1966. Its first entry deals with a dinner party at the flat of Stephane Hessel, Laugier's executive assistant. Two of the guests, Henri Laugier and Pierre Mendès-France, then the French representative on the Council, got into a heated argument about the international role of France. Laugier, reverting to a familiar theme, said that the time had come for the rest of the world to unite against the two great superpowers which were responsible for the Cold War and most of the current trouble in the world. "Il faudrait un troisième colosse," he said, and the spokesman for this third colossus should be France. Nonsense, objected Mendès-France: "Pour la France il y a maintenant pas d'action internationale, il y a seulement une action interne."

Because of Laugier, but also because I was a Canadian who spoke their language fluently, my relations with the French were always very close. I think they sometimes forgot that I was not French. I remember once when Laugier, Mendès-France and I were discussing the failure of the Council to adopt a resolution which the French supported, Mendès-France turned to me and said somewhat irritably: "If Humphrey had spoken up the result would have been different." I said something about the duty of the Secretariat to be neutral.

There was a gap of three weeks between the adjournment of ECOSOC and the opening of the third session of the General Assembly, which was to be in Paris. Jeanne and I spent most of this time holidaying in Brittany. But first I had to represent the United Nations at a conference of the International Law Association in Brussels, the high point of which was Professor Hersch Lauterpacht's brilliant but devastating talk on human rights. A perfectionist who wanted quick results, he didn't take sufficient account of the political difficulties we were working under in the United Nations. But his criticism of the overcautious position the Human Rights Commission had taken in the matter of the treatment of communications alleging violations of human rights was later fully vindicated.

The only person in Brussels whom I knew at all was Roland Lebeau, on leave from his post in the Belgian mission at U.N. Headquarters, who took my wife and me to pay our respects to the Mannekin Pis and afterwards for a drink in a café on the Grand' Place. That night there was a banquet at the Cercle Gaullois. I have never seen so many medals and ribbons. The Belgians like decorations, and I felt very humble in my dark, undecorated business suit. When I went to the United Nations, I was well supplied with formal attire; but while I occasionally wore a dinner jacket, I never once wore a dress suit all the time I was in the Secretariat. It was assumed that United Nations people didn't have room in their baggage for formal dress, and some delegations had ideological objections. When the second anniversary of the adoption of the Universal Declaration of Human Rights was celebrated by a symphony concert in the Metropolitan Opera House, the invitations, which went to all the delegations and to important New Yorkers, read "black tie." Laugier scolded me for this: "Les droits de l'homme en 'black tie' c'est une honte." I told him that he was talking like a demagogue. In my opinion human rights go as well with black ties as with blue collars.

The Brussels conference over, we travelled on to Concarneau in Brittany, where we were greeted by a little harbor filled with sailing boats painted a bright blue, with light blue mainsails and rusty pink jibs, used in the sardine fisheries. Although it was Sunday, many of the women, dressed in the black Breton fashion and wearing white headdresses, were washing clothes in the community basins. The men, dressed in the colors of the sardine boats, stood around talking and smoking. On arriving at the Grand Hotel de Cornouilles, I noticed a Manitoba license on a car parked outside, which was such a rarity in France that I inquired about the owner. This turned out to be Gabrielle Roy, the Canadian writer, who with her husband Dr. Marcel Carbotte, were also holidaying in Brittany. We had many talks. I introduced them to Prévert's *Paroles* some of which Gabrielle read to us, and very well. I detected in her a certain intellectualism which, for some reason, surprised me in the author of *Bonheur d'Occasion*. Later we saw her several times in Paris and once had a long argument about religion. She told us that although she believed in God and some kind of survival after death she was no longer a Catholic. She advised me to read Lecompte de Noüy's *L'Homme et sa Destinée*, which I did. When I spoke to Laugier about the book, he said that Lecompte de Noüy was a) an indifferent scientist, b) a poor philosopher and c) a Vichyard. Laugier was always forthright in his opinions.

On 12 September, we boarded a train for Paris, not without difficulty because the *wagon-lit* conductor said we had too much luggage. My explanation that I was a United Nations official on my way to the General Assembly could not have impressed him less. We were in Paris the next morning in time for breakfast at the Hotel de la Perousse, where I had stayed on my mission to UNESCO. I then walked down the Avenue Kléber to the Palais de Chaillot where the General Assembly was meeting, but the offices for the Secretariat were not yet ready, although mine—notwithstanding the presence of carpenters, electricians and painters—was more habitable than Laugier's. When he moved in, I had no place to work, so I spent most of the day listening to the speeches at the opening session. To compensate me for my sacrifice Laugier took me for a good lunch at the *Petit Clos*. Louis Dolivet, who was also there, showed me an account in the *New York Times* of a speech by Frank E. Holman, president of the American Bar Association, in which he had said that the United Nations human rights program was an attempt to establish state socialism, if not communism. Dolivet also told me that in another speech Holman had quoted me as admitting that the program was revolutionary. Holman, of course, was exploiting my Ann Arbor speech, already mentioned. The next day I had my office to myself, but the noise was deafening and it was almost impossible to work: my secretary could hardly hear me dictating.

As always in the General Assembly, it was several days before we could get the Third Committee (which dealt with social, cultural and humanitarian matters) organized. Mrs. Roosevelt, who had just arrived, asked me to meet her in her Hotel Crillon apartment with some people from the United States delegation. They were looking for some way to limit debate on the draft declaration, but none of their suggestions sounded very practical. Debate can be limited when there is a will on all sides to do so, but the United Nations is practically defenseless against a filibuster. The number and length of interventions can be limited by majority vote; but long and repetitious speeches are only one means of obstructing business. Much more subtle is the simple device of introducing numerous amendments and sub-amendments, each one of which has to be debated. In any event, our conversations in the Hotel Crillon led to no visible result. I was always embarrassed when Mrs. Roosevelt asked me to come to this kind of meeting and would try to find some excuse for not attending if I thought that it was to be in the nature of a delegation meeting. The Americans assumed that the Secretariat necessarily shared their objectives. In this particular case I did share them personally; but as an official in a politically oriented organization, I knew that there were other delegations whose objectives were quite different.

Mrs. Roosevelt spoke at the Sorbonne on the following evening. The great amphitheater was packed by an enthusiastic audience which gave her a reception the like of which I have seldom witnessed. Paul Ramadier, René Cassin and the rector of the university spoke in glowing terms. But Mrs. Roosevelt lost a great opportunity. The crowd had come to hear the chairman of the Human Rights Commission and the widow of a great president. It heard a speech obviously written by someone in the state department and chiefly devoted to attacking the Soviet Union. I didn't blame the Americans for talking back, but I disliked their using Mrs. Roosevelt in these polemics. For she had become a symbol which should have been kept above the Cold War—a symbol around which reasonable men and women everywhere might have rallied. When after the meeting I joined Laugier and some of his friends for a drink at *La Source*, we all agreed that Mrs. Roosevelt's international position had been compromised.

I worked very hard at this session of the General Assembly, often until late into the night. When in the last week of the session we were putting the Declaration into final shape, it was sometimes three or four o'clock in the morning before I got to bed. There was also, as might be expected, a very active social life. Nothing was too good for the United Nations, and Paris put on a brilliant show. In retrospect, I wonder how we did it. Jeanne and I were at most of the receptions, lunches, dinner parties, theater parties and concerts. It was a real relief when we missed the ball at the *Chambre de Commerce* because Jeanne's dress was not ready. A random glance at my diary shows that on 28 October I had lunch with Laugier and others at the *Rotisserie Perigourdine*; Jeanne and I dined with Minerva Bernadino—easily the most active member of the Commission on the Status of Women and a power in the Third Committee—and after dinner went to see Laugier in his rue de Babylonne apartment. Since I had already seen him at lunch he must have wanted to consult me on some matter of business.

A few days later, Jeanne and I had lunch with René Cassin. The other guests were Alexandre Parodi, the permanent representative of France to the United Nations, Benjamin Cohen of the United States Department of State and Sir Hartley (later Lord) Shawcross. Although the lights did not work and the apartment was cold, the conversation was as good as the food. That evening the Indians gave a reception at the Ritz. All Paris and the United Nations were there. No alcohol was served. There was something wrong, I thought, about the fact that the Indians all drank at other parties and in their homes but forced their guests to abstain at their public functions.

One of the first of the big events was a special mass at Notre Dame. We arrived late, after the sermon; but we saw the procession which ended the ceremony and were given an opportunity to kiss Cardinal Suhard's ring. Another spectacular affair was a gala performance at the Opera. The ballet was indifferent, but the ambiance—Garde républicaine and all the rest—made up for it. Julian Huxley drove us back to our hotel, and not long afterwards I went to a cocktail party in his apartment which was *pour prendre congé* because he was leaving for Istanbul and would, indeed, soon leave his post as director general of UNESCO. I did not know then that my name would be proposed for the post he was leaving. Although I did not know Huxley well, I had seen enough of him to recognize his great qualities. That summer we had had a long tête-à-tête about human rights over lunch in Geneva.

Although diplomatic cocktail parties are an easy target for envious or uninformed persons, the fact is that they are part of a diplomat's job. He can pick up a great deal of information at these parties and also convey informally a suggestion or opinion which his government is still unprepared to advance officially. Glamor and good food and drink apart, attending a diplomatic cocktail party can be a tiring business, especially if one has just come from three or four hours' work in a committee. Later, when the membership of the United Nations grew to well over a hundred countries, the cocktail round became a real problem. When the General Assembly was in session, one might have several invitations to receptions for the same evening and perhaps some other commitment as well. Partly to cope with these receptions, after the United Nations move from Lake Success to Manhattan, Jeanne and I always lived in the vicinity of Turtle Bay. Many of the receptions were held in the headquarters building where, I discovered, it was possible to put in an appearance, shake hands with the host and, unless there was someone present with whom I particularly wanted to talk, take my leave discreetly through a back door. On such evenings I was home only a few minutes late for dinner which was, of course, impossible when the party was in a private home where one had to stay until one could decently take one's leave. These parties could be very trying if one did not know the other guests, which was the position in which I found myself at Huxley's party. Huxley himself was late, and though Mrs. Huxley had received me graciously and introduced me to other guests, I soon found myself alone with nobody to turn to. Three people whom I did know arrived later: Thanassis Agnides, the chairman of the U.N. Advisory Committee on Administrative and Budgetary Questions, Ronald Walker, an Australian member of the UNESCO executive board and H.M. Phillips of the United Kingdom. I greeted them like old friends and certainly knew them much better by the time the party ended. Phillips drove me back to the Palais de Chaillot where I had not yet finished my day.

The worst of the receptions were the monster affairs given every year jointly by the Secretary-General and the president of the Assembly. At the one in Paris it was hardly possible to move among several thousand guests and the only champagne that came our way fell on Jeanne's dress. And when we were invited to taste the wines of France at the *Halles des Vins* there was such a crowd that we never got near the tables.

A feature of the session was the dinner parties which Laugier and Marie Cutolli gave at their rue de Babylonne apartment. They owned a fine collection—it has since been given to the Republic—of modern French painting. Laugier and Marie were not only collectors; they knew the painters.

I once sent my cousin, Jack Humphrey, to see the rue de Babylonne paintings. I hoped that Laugier might be able to help him, because at the time he badly needed recognition, but neither Laugier nor Marie showed any interest. Once when I showed Laugier a Humphrey in my apartment, he brushed it aside with a remark about "la peinture familiale." I suspected that, notwithstanding his reputation as a connoisseur, he was interested only in established painters. But when I once mentioned to him the name of Morrice, he had never heard of it.

Not only were we entertained, we did some entertaining ourselves. One night we took P.C. Chang to the *Bal Tabarin*. He had had to refuse our invitation to dinner because there was a meeting that evening of Chinese ambassadors from, it seemed, all over the world. Chang invented some kind of excuse to get away early and met us in Montmartre. When we got to the *Bal Tabarin*, some of the ambassadors of whom he had taken leave were already there.

The Magna Carta of the World (1948)

Most of the business of the General Assembly is done in committee, agenda items being usually first considered in one of the main standing committees on which all delegations are represented and where a first vote is taken. The item is then referred for a final vote to the Assembly sitting in plenary. The international bill of rights was sent to the Committee on Social, Cultural and Humanitarian Questions or Third Committee. In 1948, a fortnight passed before this committee convened, and the long debate on the Declaration, which consumed most of the session, did not begin until 30 September.

We were fortunate in having Charles Malik in the chair, for as rapporteur of the Human Rights Commission he was familiar with the legislative history of the document. He did a much better job presiding over the Third Committee than he had done as president of the Economic and Social Council. Presiding over a much more turbulent body—perhaps the most turbulent in the United Nations—he conducted the proceedings with a firmness that at first surprised me. There were indeed times when he approached arrogance, even losing his temper and, with a bang of his gavel, refusing the floor to delegations. But my respect for him grew as the session progressed, and he got the Declaration through the committee.

The committee devoted eighty-one long meetings to the Declaration and dealt with one hundred and sixty-eight resolutions containing amendments. But first there was a general debate in which most of the fifty-nine delegations participated, and then a long procedural discussion before we could get down to the actual final drafting of the instrument.

We got away to a bad start. It was already time to adjourn the morning meeting on September 30, when a Latin American delegate opened the general debate. He talked on into the afternoon. Malik, when he was finally able to adjourn the meeting, drew the attention of the delegates to the article in the draft declaration stating that in the exercise of one's rights one must respect the rights of others, a reminder which was much appreciated by the hungry delegates.

The general debate over, it took the committee a whole week before deciding that, at this session, it would deal only with the Declaration. Mrs. Roosevelt had explained that the Human Rights Commission intended to finish at its next session its work on the covenant and measures for implementation—the other parts of the bill—a promise which, as it turned out, was overoptimistic because the commission did not complete its work on the two covenants (as they had by that time become) until 1954.

Several delegations regretted that the covenant would not be adopted at the same time as the Declaration. New Zealand in particular was against adopting any declaration until the convention was ready, its representative warning the committee that "if the Declaration were adopted first, there was less likelihood that the covenant would be adopted at all;" and, when the question was put to a vote, that country, Haiti and Uruguay abstained. Had their advice been followed the adoption of the Declaration might have been postponed indefinitely. It should have been clear, even in 1948, that reaching agreement on a convention setting forth precise legal obligations would be infinitely more difficult than drafting the Declaration, and that it would take a long time to complete. In the meantime, it would be nothing short of a miracle if, in the rapidly changing atmosphere at the United Nations, the convention did not become a focus for political controversy; and that is what did happen. By 1950, the burning issue of the self-determination of peoples had, for example, become a principal theme in the human rights debates. The covenants ran into rough weather, and it was not until 1966 that they were completed and opened for signature, nineteen years after the first session of the Human Rights Commission; and it was ten more years before they came into force. Not only would the adoption of the Declaration have been indefinitely postponed had the New Zealanders had their way, but it would never have been adopted with its present content. For at any time after 1949 it would have been quite impossible to prevent the inclusion in it of the kind of politically controversial assertions; for example, those relating to self-determination, which have adversely affected the authority of the covenants.

Although I could not foresee the political controversies that would arise over the covenants, there were other reasons why I was happy about the decision to concentrate on the Declaration. It was important, given the expectations that had been aroused since San Francisco, that the United Nations achieve some concrete result as quickly as possible. It wasn't simply a question of choosing the easiest path. Although a lawyer and therefore naturally prejudiced in favor of a binding instrument, I had always thought that the Declaration would be the most important part of the international bill of rights. There was little likelihood that any convention covering the totality of human rights would be quickly or universally ratified; nor was there any way by which all states could be forced to ratify. The Declaration, even though it might not be technically binding, would apply to all states and would have the great authority of the United Nations behind it. It would also be a catalyst of national and international legislation. The best strategy, therefore, was for the General Assembly to adopt it as quickly as possible. The logic of my position took me even further; for I thought that it might be better if the international community were given some time to digest the Declaration before attempting to adopt a convention. In the meantime, everything possible should be done, both within and outside the United Nations, to strengthen the authority of the Declaration. I knew, of course, that it was not meant to be legally binding and that it could not be made binding simply by having the Assembly adopt it. But, even in 1948, my instinct told me that eventually it would become part of international law whatever the intentions of its authors, or the form in which it was adopted. That result could be delayed or even frustrated by the mere fact of working on a convention. For if it were ever to be successfully argued that it had become part of the customary law of nations, it would have to be shown that the great majority of states accepted it as such. The adoption of a convention would make that demonstration more difficult. For, why have a convention if the Declaration were binding? The strategy I favored would not have prevented the United Nations from sponsoring special conventions on particular rights or groups of rights, including the conventions on freedom of information and on the prevention and punishment of the crime of genocide, both of which were on the agenda of this session of the General Assembly.

Looking back after many years, I can find no reason for thinking that I was wrong in 1948. The Universal Declaration of Human Rights is now part of the customary law of nations and therefore binding on all states. I do not remember anyone in 1948 who shared my views. As a United Nations official, I could not properly campaign for them openly, and, to do so would have been self-defeating; for most delegations did not then want the Declaration to become part of the customary law. But whenever I had the opportunity to do so privately, I did explain my views to friendly delegates. This was not easy because even lawyers—and they weren't all lawyers—found it difficult to understand the processes by which customary law is made unless they also happened to be specialists in international law. I remember one night in the Palais de Chaillot saying to Mrs. Roosevelt, while having missed her dinner she drank tea and ate sandwiches, that I thought that the Declaration would be much more important than the covenant. She must have thought me slightly daft, for by that time it had been drilled into her head that only treaties could be binding on states. Much later, when she was making speeches in the United States and elsewhere urging the early completion of the covenants (as they had become) she invariably argued that they were needed because the Universal Declaration of Human Rights was not binding. It was a mistake so to play down the Declaration; a better argument on behalf of the covenants would have been that they were necessary because, unlike the Declaration, they would contain provisions for implementation. Some of her other public statements were also unfortunate. In a speech she made in Washington in November 1949, she insisted that the draft covenant could not be accepted by the communists. This was an impolitic statement for the chairman of the Human Rights Commission to make; nor has it been confirmed by events. For in 1973, the Soviet Union ratified both covenants, something which the United States has yet to do.

Some of the people who had represented their governments on the Human Rights Commission were also sitting as delegates in the Third Committee. Charles Malik and Mrs. Roosevelt have already been mentioned. Others included René Cassin, P.C. Chang, Alexei Pavlov and Hernan Santa Cruz. With their full knowledge of the commission's draft and of the difficulties that had had to be overcome preparing it, they provided the leadership which made it possible for the Third Committee to produce a text which was very similar to the one that had been prepared by the commission. Some delegations would have accepted the commission's text as it stood, but it soon became apparent that the committee would examine every article *de novo* and indeed reopen all the questions that had been discussed by the commission. There was even a well-organized attempt, under the leadership of the Cuban Guy Perez Cisneros, to replace the commission's text in most of its essentials by the text of the American Declaration on the Rights and Duties of Man which the Organization of American States had adopted at Bogotá earlier in the year. Since twenty out of the fifty-nine delegations were from Latin America, this was no small threat. At one point, the Latin Americans tried to have a committee appointed to compare the two texts. Thanks partly to Santa Cruz, himself a Latin American, they didn't succeed. But the

Bogotá menace continued to hang over us. Highly intelligent, Perez Cisneros used every procedural device to reach his end. His speeches were laced with Roman Catholic social philosophy, and it seemed at times that the chief protagonists in the conference room were the Roman Catholics and the communists, with the latter a poor second.

The political atmosphere in which the committee had to work was charged to the point of explosion by the Cold War with irrelevant recriminations coming from both sides. But in one respect the historical context was still favorable, for the debates on human rights had not yet become occasions for political duelling in the growing conflict over colonialism. The Soviet Union did attempt to introduce a reference to the "right" of peoples to self-determination, but it failed. Had the Declaration been adopted at any time after 1949 a more serious attempt would have been made and would probably have succeeded, with results easy to imagine in the light of what happened to the covenants. Most people would agree with the political principle of self-determination as expressed in the United Nations Charter—which I take to mean that it is politically and morally right that all peoples, assuming you can define what a people is, should be allowed to determine their own political destiny, if all other factors are equal—but to try to enunciate this as a legal right is quite a different matter. It was something of a miracle that the great General Assembly debate on the Declaration took place in 1948.

The committee worked hard and, by United Nations standards, efficiently. Some of the difficulties were resolved in small drafting committees which usually met at night after the adjournment of the main committee. One of these did not arise until after three o'clock in the morning. The problem this time was how to render into the other official languages the Russian word "soslovie." Cassin, Pavlov, their advisers and interpreters had been in my office earlier about the same matter. It was finally decided that the nearest equivalent in English was "birth," and this word is used in Article 2 of the Declaration. The Secretariat's interpreters and translators were very good and seldom needed this kind of help.

Some of the most controversial issues came up in connection with matters that should never have been discussed. There was substantial agreement even between the spokesmen for different ideologies on the definition of the traditional rights, such as the right to a fair trial, even though agreement on a text sometimes concealed an unexpressed disagreement over the meaning of particular words. Thus the word "democratic" in Article 29 would probably be interpreted differently in London and Moscow.[1] More controversial were the fortunately few instances where the text asserted philosophical principles. An article which Cassin had proposed in the drafting committee was one of these. The draft article now read: "All human beings are born free and equal in dignity and rights. They are endowed by nature with reason and conscience and should act towards one another in a spirit of brotherhood." An unsuccessful attempt was now made to transfer the substance of this article to the preamble, its proper place if it were to be in the Declaration at all. Feeling ran so high that the vote was taken by roll call. One reason for leaving it where it was may have been a South African attempt to limit its scope by substituting the words "fundamental

---

1. Art. 29(2): "In the exercise of his rights and freedoms, everyone shall be subject only to such limitations as are determined by law solely for the purpose of securing due recognition and respect for the rights and freedoms of others and of meeting the just requirements of morality, public order and the general welfare in a democratic society."

rights and freedoms" for "dignity and rights." While everyone might be entitled to the enjoyment of certain fundamental rights, the South Africans argued, the principle could not be extended to all rights. This so electrified the meeting that it united in protest. But the South African delegate seemed unperturbed by the reaction to his intervention; he did not change his attitude even when the chairman pointed out, on my prodding, that if the word "dignity" had been used in the United Nations Charter,[2] it was because Field Marshal Smuts had wanted it there. Although the principle of equality was clearly enough expressed in other articles, this incident may have led delegations to think that there was some value in having the controversial article in the Declaration.

But the most controversial issue to which the article gave rise was whether it should contain some reference to the deity. At the second session of the Human Rights Commission, and again at the second session of the drafting committee, Malik had unsuccessfully tried to bring a reference to the Creator into the article on the family. Now it was the Brazilian delegation which wanted Article 1 to say that human beings are created in the image of God. The article as it then stood said that human beings are endowed "by nature" with reason and conscience, and the Brazilians wanted this statement to be preceded by a reference to the deity. But Count Carton de Wiart of Belgium, fearing an endless philosophical debate, moved that the words "by nature" be deleted. P.C. Chang supported him in a speech in which he pleaded for "two-man-mindedness" and asked the delegates not to impose philosophical concepts such as natural law on countries where they are alien to the thinking of many millions of people. The words "by nature," he added, "had a ring of Rousseau and evoked memories of the theory that man was naturally good." In the result, the Belgian amendment to delete the words was adopted and the Brazilians withdrew their amendment. Later, when the preamble was being discussed, Father Beaufort of the Netherlands moved that it mention the divine origin and immortal destiny of man. In support of his amendment he used the extraordinary argument that nonbelievers could simply ignore the words. Mrs. Kalinowska of Poland quite properly pointed out that it would be extremely dangerous to admit the possibility that any part of the Declaration could be ignored. Count Carton de Wiart again came to the rescue. It would be inconceivable, he said, if the Third Committee were to try to settle such a question by a vote. And when it became clear to Father Beaufort that his amendment would not be supported by the majority, he withdrew it. The result was that the Universal Declaration of Human Rights mentions neither God nor nature.

But something as important as religion, which is so intimately related to the life of the individual and which has played such a role, for good and for bad, in the long struggle for human rights, could not be ignored by the Declaration. Much thought and discussion was given at every stage of the drafting to Article 18, which recognizes and defines the right to freedom of thought, conscience and religion. Predictably, the article gave rise to controversy. In the drafting committee, Charles Malik—a citizen of a country the population of which was almost evenly divided between Christians and Moslems—had obtained the insertion in the article of the principle that freedom of religion includes the right to change

2. "We the peoples of the United Nations determined . . . to reaffirm faith in fundamental human rights, in the dignity and worth of the human person, in the equal rights of men and women and of nations large and small. . . ." Preamble to the Charter written by Field Marshal Smuts.

one's religion or belief. When this addition was discussed in the Third Committee, another Lebanese Christian (who was, however, representing Saudi Arabia) energetically opposed its inclusion. It would, Jamil Baroody said, favor the proselytizing activities of missionaries who were often the precursors of foreign intervention; and to include the principle would also be an affront to Moslems, since the Koran forbade them to change their religion. Although Baroody was supported at this stage by the delegations of Afghanistan, Iraq, Pakistan and Syria, the right was included in the article as it was adopted. It will be remembered that Malik had not been so successful when, also in the drafting committee, he had tried to have the right to life protected from the moment of conception.

Other controversies reflected political conflict between states and groups of states, one of them in connection with Article 2. The commission's text read: "Everyone is entitled to all the rights and freedoms set forth in this Declaration, without distinction of any kind, such as race, color, sex, language, religion, political or other opinion, property or other status, or national or other origin." The article was, as already noted, amended by the addition of the Russian word "soslovie," which was rendered into English by "birth;" but this had been only a technical difficulty. The great political controversy to which the article gave rise began when Yugoslavia moved that its protection be specifically extended to the populations of Trust and Non-Self-Governing Territories. Mrs. Roosevelt objected that the amendment was unnecessary, since it was perfectly clear that the Declaration was meant to apply to everyone. The colonial powers interpreted the Yugoslav motion as an attack against them, as it indeed was. Conditions in the colonies were better, said Ernest Davies for the United Kingdom, than they were behind the Iron Curtain. The representative of the Ukraine then said that the colonial powers didn't want their colonies to enjoy human rights. The amendment was adopted. But when, later, a style committee was appointed to go over the whole Declaration, it reported back a text of Article 2 which differed substantially from the one which the Third Committee had adopted by also extending its protection to the population of countries under foreign occupation. Since the style committee had obviously gone beyond its mandate, the chairman ruled that it would be necessary to return to the text which the Third Committee had adopted. But a new paragraph was adopted in plenary which softened the bite implicit in the Yugoslav amendment in that Trust and Non-Self-Governing Territories were no longer singled out for special mention.

In Cold War terms, the most controversial issue related to forced labor. On the morning of 15 October, just as the meeting was about to adjourn, Christopher Mayhew of the United Kingdom, holding in his hand a document which he said was a copy of the Soviet Corrective Labor Code, began to read extracts from it. He then described conditions in the Russian forced labor camps. There can be no doubt whatsoever that the conditions described by Mayhew really did exist, but, since the British were not proposing any change in the article relating to forced labor, their intervention could be interpreted as a move in the Cold War. The Yugoslav had been more subtle when he raised the question of colonialism. The controversy continued over the years, in particular at the next two sessions of the Economic and Social Council which, in 1951, invited the International Labor Organization to join the United Nations in setting up an ad hoc committee on forced labor. The Division of Human Rights provided part of the secretariat for this committee and one of the five committee members was Enrique Garcia Sayan, a one-time Peruvian foreign affairs minister who had been an officer in the Division. The ad hoc committee held five sessions at which it examined witnesses and other evidence. It concluded that there were two principal systems of forced labor in the world. One was used as a means of political coercion or punishment for holding or expressing political views, the other for economic purposes. The inquiry revealed "systems of forced labor of so great a nature that they seriously threaten fundamental human rights and jeopardize the freedom and status of workers in contravention of the obligations and provisions of the Charter of the United Nations."

The articles on economic, social and cultural rights were hotly debated; nor was the controversy limited to exchanges between protagonists of the two main ideologies. Article 20, which proclaims the freedoms of assembly and of association, is still controversial. The commission's text had mentioned the freedoms without any qualification, but in the Third Committee it was amended, over the objections of the British and New Zealand delegations that this would prohibit the "closed shop," to recognize the right not to belong to an association.

Some of the articles could have been better drafted, and there were some important omissions. The failure to include an article on the protection of minorities has already been mentioned. I had included one in my own draft which, because of the importance of the principle enunciated, I quote in full:

> In states inhabited by a substantial number of persons of a race, language or religion other than those of the majority of the population, persons belonging to such ethnic, linguistic or religious minorities shall have the right to establish and maintain, out of an equitable proportion of any funds available for the purpose, their schools and cultural and religious institutions, and to use their own language before the courts and other authorities and organs of the state and in the press and in public assembly.

Cassin dropped the most important part of my text—the part referring to public funds—from his revision because, as Samuel Spanien later explained in the Sub-Commission on the Prevention of Discrimination and the Protection of Minorities, France did not allocate public funds to private educational institutions. The article gave rise to so much controversy that the Human Rights Commission finally dropped it, with the result that the draft it sent to the General Assembly did not even mention minorities. Several attempts were made in the Third Committee to reintroduce an article which would have extended a measure of protection to minorities; but the opposition, particularly from some of the Latin Americans, who insisted that there were no minorities in Latin America, was so strong that these too were doomed to failure. The Americans and the British said that any compromise between the views of the New World, where countries wanted to assimilate immigrants, and views held in Europe, where there were historical national minorities, would be impossible. This was an oversimplification not only because there are in fact indigenous and other national minorities in the Americas but because most European governments are just as keen to assimilate their minorities as are governments on the other side of the Atlantic. The British even argued that since the Declaration would protect the equal rights of everyone, including those of members of minorities, no special provision was needed—thereby quite missing the point that if their right to retain their cultural identity is to be protected, the minorities may need something more than equality. Chile then suggested that the question be referred to the Sub-Commission on the Prevention of Discrimination and the Protection of Minorities for further study, and this was done. The sub-commission did its best, but the opposition in the government-controlled Human Rights Commission was so great that nothing came of its efforts. There can be little doubt that the sub-commission's continued interest in the fate of minorities was one of the reasons why, in 1951, the Economic and Social Council tried to abolish it.

Another important omission is the failure of the Declaration to recognize any right of petition. My own draft had said that "everyone has the right, either individually or in association with others, to petition the government of his state or the United Nations for redress of grievance." Slightly improved—Cassin had added that a person also had the right to petition the government of his country of residence—the article was approved by the drafting committee. But although it also survived the second session of the commission, it was deleted at the drafting committee's second session on the initiative of the United Kingdom. This deletion was confirmed by the commission, which however forwarded the draft article to the General Assembly with a note saying that it had not had the time to study it—a prevarication that can be taken to mean that the commission was not too sure about its decision. The Third Committee discussed the question during three meetings; but notwithstanding the efforts of the French to restore the article, the question was referred back to the commission for further study in connection with the covenant. As a result neither the Declaration nor the covenants mention the fundamental right of petition, a right which exists even in some authoritarian countries. Indeed the right is more important in such countries than in democracies, where there are alternative procedures of redress. It is a historical fact that, in English law, for example, the right was first recognized at a time when other remedies had not yet been developed. There was no good reason for refusing a right to petition national governments and authorities, even if the General Assembly was not yet ready to recognize an international right to petition the United Nations.

No article in the Declaration has been more criticized than Article 14, which says that everyone has the right "to seek and to enjoy" asylum from persecution. This gives no right to asylum but only a right to enjoy it once it has been granted. It was probably too much to expect that governments would give up their discretionary power under international law to refuse to allow foreigners to enter their territories. I had recognized this in my own draft, which also sidetracked the issue saying merely that "every state shall have the right to grant asylum to political refugees," a right which was already recognized by international law. It is something of an achievement, however, that both the 1951 Convention of the Status of Refugees and the Declaration on Territorial Asylum of 1967 say that persons entitled to seek asylum are not to be rejected at the frontier, expelled to or made to return to the countries from which they have fled, if this would expose them to persecution.

I have touched on only a few of the issues that came up. Every one of the thirty articles of the Declaration was discussed in great detail and most of the meetings were full of interest and even drama. There was a constant clash, not only of ideologies but of personalities. Most of the delegates were past masters in the art of debate; some of them were politicians on the make, some were almost fanatically attached to a point of view, a few only occasionally if ever opened their mouths; but most of them were conscious of the historic role they were playing and rose to the occasion. Sitting next to the chairman, and both professionally and emotionally involved, I wished at times that I were a delegate; the silent role of an international official can sometimes be very frustrating. Whenever I had an idea that had any merit I could usually give it expression through some friendly delegate; but there were times when I felt that I must speak, if only to set the record straight. I was soon preoccupied by another worry: Would the committee get through the draft before the end of the session? At times it seemed that it could not, and as it turned out it was a very near thing. We finished just in time for the General Assembly to vote the final text in the night of 10 December—only two days before the end of the session. Had the discussions gone on any longer the adoption of the Declaration would have had to be postponed for another year, or perhaps indefinitely. The Soviet Union did try both in the committee and in the plenary Assembly to postpone its adoption but was supported only by the five other communist countries then members of the United Nations.

At one o'clock in the night of 6 December, by roll call vote, the Third Committee adopted its draft of the Declaration and sent it on to the Assembly. Although no delegation voted against, there were seven abstentions: Byelorussia, Canada, Czechoslovakia, Poland, the Ukraine, the Soviet Union and Yugoslavia. Saudi Arabia and South Africa did not vote. The South Africans had made it abundantly clear that they would not accept the Declaration: it should, they had said, include only those fundamental rights the universal existence of which was recognized everywhere in the world.

Most people had expected that the Soviet Union and the other communist countries would vote against the Declaration. Ambassador Bogomolov, who had replaced Pavlov in the final days of the committee's proceedings, had said that his government attached the greatest importance to its many objections and criticisms. And the fact that at the very time that the Declaration was being discussed in the Third Committee it was already being invoked against the Soviet Union in another part of the General Assembly, in the case of the Russian wives of foreign diplomats, was hardly calculated to endear it to that government. The fact that the communist countries merely abstained and did not cast negative votes was a positive occurrence, for it made possible the later statement that the Declaration had been adopted without dissenting vote. Also the communist countries would not be in the position of having voted against an instrument which, in the future, they would if it suited their purposes be as quick as anyone to invoke. I remember, some months later, after Yugoslavia's break with the Cominform, talking to a senior Yugoslav diplomat who insisted that his country had voted for the Declaration.

It was the Canadian abstention which shocked everyone, including me. The Canadians had given me no warning, and I was quite unprepared for what happened. Although I knew that the international promotion of human rights had no priority in Canada's foreign policy, it had never occurred to me that the government would carry its indifference to the point of abstaining in such an important vote. I could hardly have prevented the scandal even if the delegation had taken me into their confidence, but I could at least have warned them of the company in which they would probably find themselves. After the voting, a man from the Canadian Press came to interview me, sent, he said, by the delegation. He wanted me to say that I was shocked, but I lectured him on the duties of an international official. The next day, Dana Wilgress, a senior career diplomat who was on the Canadian delegation, stopped me in the corridor. He had something to tell me, he said, that would take the iron out of my soul: it had just been decided that Canada would vote for the Declaration in the plenary Assembly. I had no doubt whatsoever that this quick change in position was dictated solely by the fact that the government did not relish the company in which it found itself.

It was therefore with bad grace that Canada joined the majority when the General Assembly adopted the Universal Declaration of Human Rights on the night of 10 December. Lester Pearson, explaining my country's vote, said that many of the articles of the Declaration were vague and lacking in precision. It would have been better, he said, if a body of jurists, such as the International Law Commission, had gone over the text before it was submitted to the General Assembly. This was probably ex post facto rationalization. The Canadians had certainly never made the suggestion before; nor had they made any effort, either in the Economic and Social Council or in the Third Committee, to make the Declaration more precise. Had the course Pearson preferred been followed, the Declaration could not have been adopted in 1948, with the consequences already suggested. A possible real reason for the Canadian abstention in the Third Committee may have been the government's fear that if they voted for the Declaration they might be accused of trespassing on the jurisdiction of the provinces under the constitution. But although this was mentioned in the explanation of vote, it is difficult to believe that it could have been a compelling reason. For in 1948 everyone agreed that the Declaration would not be binding in international law and would not, therefore, impose any legal obligations on member states. As one of the greatest contemporary international lawyers, Sir Hersch Lauterpacht, put it in a book published not long afterwards, "the Canadian delegate in the Third Committee refrained from voting for the Declaration for reasons which could have had validity only if the Declaration were legally binding."

The countries which did abstain in the final vote in the night of 10 December were the six communist countries then members of the United Nations, plus Saudi Arabia and South Africa. After the vote had been taken, many delegations exercised their right to explain their votes or their reasons for abstention. For me, and probably for everyone else, their explanations were an anticlimax. In a long speech, Ambassador Andrei Vishinsky of the Soviet Union said that the Declaration suffered from serious defects and omissions: the article on slavery was too abstract; the article on freedom of information failed to solve the problem because it did nothing to prevent warmongering and fascist ideas; there could be no freedom of information unless the workers had the means to voice their opinions, and that meant having at their disposal printing presses and newspapers; the right to demonstrate in the streets should have been guaranteed; there were no guarantees that scientific research would not be used for war purposes; and there were no provisions protecting the rights of minorities. Finally, he regretted, there was no mention in the Declaration of the sovereign rights of states. The representative of the Ukraine rationalized his abstention in traditional Marxist terms: the Declaration proclaimed rights that could not be exercised under existing conditions and within the economic structure of many countries. Before the right to work, to rest and to education could be implemented, the economic system of free enterprise would have to be drastically altered. True equality, he said, was possible only under a system which guaranteed to everyone equal conditions and opportunities for the development of their potential, and that was not the kind of equality contemplated by the Declaration. Speaking for Czechoslovakia, its representative complained that the Declaration was not imbued with revolutionary spirit; it was neither bold nor modern. It was merely a proclamation, said the representative of Byelorussia: it did not guarantee the rights proclaimed. The rights included, said the Pole, did not go beyond the rights recognized by the old liberal school. There was no mention of the duties which an individual owed to his neighbors, his family, his group or his nation. Compared to the Declaration of 1789 on the Rights of Man and of the Citizen, and the Communist Manifesto, and especially the principles which inspired the October Revolution, it was a step backward. The Yugoslavs found more measured language in which to explain their abstention: the traditional categories of human rights (meaning civil and political rights) needed to be widened, and a system of social rights recognized which would include the collective rights of certain communities.

In the Third Committee, the South Africans had said that the list of rights included in the Declaration was too wide and that it should have been limited to those fundamental rights which were universally recognized. The explanation which they gave for their abstention in plenary was more interesting and, from the point of view of the future of the Declaration, most discerning. They reminded the Assembly that in the Third Committee they had alreay made the point that the Declaration, although not a treaty, would nevertheless impose certain obligations on member states, since it would probably be recognized as an authoritative definition of the fundamental rights and freedoms mentioned in the Charter which that instrument had left undefined. "If such an interpretation were accepted," they said, "those member states which voted for the Declaration would be bound in the same manner as if they had signed a convention embodying those principles." This was, as it has turned out, an understatement; for, if the principles set forth in the Declaration are now part of the customary law of nations—and there can be little doubt that they are—they are binding on all states including South Africa, whether they voted for the Declaration or not.

Saudi Arabia did not explain its abstention, but in the Third Committee Jamil Baroody had said that the provision in Article 18, which recognizes the right of everyone to change his religion or belief, was contrary to the rule of the Koran, an interpretation which was challenged in plenary by Sir Mohammed Zafrullah Khan, a Pakistani Moslem, in a speech I knew that he was going to make, because he had told me so over lunch the day before.

Although the Declaration was clearly not meant to be binding, a number of delegations felt it necessary to labor the point. Mrs. Roosevelt, predicting that it "might well become the international Magna Carta of all mankind," stressed that it was not a treaty or international agreement and did not impose legal obligations; it was rather a statement of principles of inalienable human rights, setting up a common standard of achievement for all peoples and all nations. Most of the delegates who discussed the point agreed with her, but there were a few who tried to breathe some legal life into the document. The Chinese recalled that the Charter committed member states to the observance of human rights and said that the Declaration "stated these rights explicitly." The French said that it could be considered as "an authoritative interpretation of the Charter," the very thing that the South Africans had warned that it might become. They also mentioned the possibility that the principles proclaimed by the Declaration could now be considered as "general principles of law" which the statute of the International Court of Justice says are a source of international law. And the representative of Chile said any state that violated the rights proclaimed by the Declaration would be in violation of the principles of the United Nations.

Apart from a few discordant notes, some of which were, I regret to say, sounded in Canada, the adoption of the Declaration was hailed, both inside and outside the United Nations, as a great achievement. And a great achievement it was. In less than two years, international agreement had been reached on the principles which should govern the relations of the individual with society, and this at a time when a hotly contested ideological conflict over this very relationship was dividing the world into two camps. The paradox is more apparent than real. The legislative history of the Declaration shows that, while there was deep disagreement on how they should be implemented, there was substantial agreement on the stated objectives. The adoption of the Declaration was, however, a much greater achievement than anyone could have imagined in 1948. For while its adoption by the General Assembly gave it great moral and political authority, it is its subsequent history which has given the Declaration the unique status it now possesses in international law and politics.

Among the very few dissenting voices was that of someone for whom I had the greatest respect and friendship. Sir Hersch Lauterpacht had come over from Cambridge University for the final days of the debate in the Third Committee, and Jeanne and I had dinner with him one evening after the vote in committee and before the final vote in the Assembly. Sir Hersch told me that he would soon be bringing out a long book on human rights, and I gathered that it would be highly critical of the Human Rights Commission, the Universal Declaration of Human Rights and practically everything the United Nations had done since the San Francisco Conference. He sent me some of the proofs some months later. Sir Hersch, in his impatience, went so far as to question even the moral authority of the Declaration. I thought this argument far fetched:

> The moral authority and influence of an international instrument of this nature must be in direct proportion to the degree of sacrifice of the sovereignty of states which it involves . . . The Declaration does not purport to imply any sacrifice of the sovereignty of the state on the altar of the inalienable rights of man and, through them, of the peace of the world.

He was even more peremptory regarding its possible legal significance:

> It is idle to attempt to kindle sparks of legal vitality in the Universal Declaration of Human Rights by regarding it as a recommendation of the General Assembly and by inquiry into its legal effects as such.

It is only fair to add that these lines were written only shortly after the adoption of the Declaration, before it began to have any real impact and before the subtle processes began to work which would make it part of the customary law of nations.

Sir Hersch was not only a great international lawyer—perhaps the greatest of his time—he was also a dedicated human rights partisan. He thought and said that the United Nations already possessed important powers under the Charter to promote and even enforce respect for human rights which it had failed to use; and in this history has proved him to be right. As a partisan he was also disappointed that the General Assembly had not immediately adopted a legally binding human rights convention. He was, of course, right in thinking that the Declaration could not be binding simply because it had been adopted by the General Assembly; such resolutions ordinarily only have the force of recommendations. If sparks of legality were to be kindled in it, it would be because of subsequent events and a growing consensus that, whatever the intentions of its authors, it is in fact now part of the customary law—a development which the great lawyer failed to foresee but which, had he lived longer, he would have been among the first to recognize and welcome. As for his attack on the moral authority of the Declaration, it was without any doubt a function of his dedication to the purpose the instrument was meant to serve. For he was an impatient man who wanted to move faster than political realities would permit. He could be satisfied with nothing less than an immediately binding commitment to respect human rights. But, while I could understand and sympathize with his attitude, the stand taken by the International Law Association, of which he was one of the most distinguished members, so annoyed me that I allowed my membership to lapse. Many years later, after I had retired from the Secretariat and rejoined the association to become its rapporteur on human rights, I reminded its Buenos Aires conference of an incident which occurred at a meeting of the Economic and Social Council in 1949. The Council was discussing arrangements for the celebration of the first anniversary of the adoption of the Declaration when the observer for the International Law Association asked for the floor. I was shocked to hear him say that the best way to celebrate the adoption of the Declaration would be to forget it.

I would need a very long chapter to review all the evidence that could be marshalled in support of the proposition that the Universal Declaration of Human Rights is now part of the customary law of nations. As far as I know, no one has ever attempted to bring together and analyze the countless times that the Declaration has been invoked, either within or outside the United Nations, or been used as the standard of permissible action. I will mention only two exhibits, as it were, which I have chosen partly because they show that even those states which abstained in the 1948 vote now say that the Declaration is binding. The first is Article 7 of the Declaration on the Granting of Independence to Colonial Countries and Peoples, which the General Assembly adopted in 1960. This article says that "all states shall observe faithfully and strictly the provisions of the Charter of the United Nations, the Universal Declaration of Human Rights and the present Declaration. . . ." With the exception of South Africa, all the countries that abstained in 1948 voted for that article. They could hardly now argue before an international tribunal with any sense of conviction that the Universal Declaration of Human Rights is not now binding. In 1963, the General Assembly unanimously adopted (with the exception of South Africa) another declaration, on the elimination of all forms of racial discrimination, which uses similar language.

Even more important are the numerous resolutions by which certain countries, including South Africa, have been condemned for failing to live up to their obligations under the human rights provisions of the Charter—provisions which, as already noted, neither list nor define the human rights to which they refer. Most of these resolutions also refer to the Universal Declaration of Human Rights and this in a manner which shows that, just as the South Africans predicted, the United Nations uses the Declaration to interpret the Charter.

It is out of such stuff that the customary law of nations is made. For custom is simply the consensus of states as to what the law is and it is proved out of their own mouths, as it were, by their official statements and practice. What could be more official than a vote cast at the United Nations? When a member state votes for a resolution that purports to say what the law is, that is evidence that, in the opinion of that state, such is the law. So while resolutions of the General Assembly are not ordinarily binding in themselves, they may be evidence of customary law. The question of the juridical character of the Universal Declaration of Human Rights has yet to come squarely before the International Court of Justice, and it is perhaps just as well that it has not; for an adverse opinion from a conservative court could have arrested the evolution of the law, perhaps forever. But in its advisory opinion on the legal consequences of the continued presence of South Africa in Namibia, the Court came very near to considering the point; and the separate concurring opinion of Judge Fuad Ammoun shows how the Court might go if the question were now to come before it. The principles enunciated in the Universal Declaration of Human Rights could be considered binding, said Judge Ammoun, because "they have acquired the force of custom through a general practice accepted as law."

I am satisfied in my own mind that the Declaration is now binding on all states. But whatever its juridical force may be, its great political and moral force, which it owes to the fact that it was adopted by the United Nations and its response to the deepest aspirations of mankind, cannot be denied; and this authority increases with the years. Its impact on world public opinion has been as great as if not greater than that of any contemporary international instrument, including the Charter of the United Nations. Some publicists have not hesitated to say that the adoption of the Declaration is the greatest achievement of the United Nations. In his great Encyclical *Pacem in Terris,* Pope John not only endorsed the Declaration but in large measure based the encyclical on it. In the United Nations, where the Declaration is constantly invoked, it has become the criterion for judging the conduct of states in their relations with individuals and groups. It has played a particularly important role in the deliberations of the General Assembly and in the Trusteeship Council, where it quickly became a criterion for judging the conduct of the administering powers in trust and non-self-governing territories. It has inspired or influenced so many resolutions in various organs of the United Nations and the specialized agencies that it would be difficult to count them. It has also inspired a growing body of treaties, including the important European Convention of 1950 for the Protection of Human Rights and Fundamental Freedoms.

The final judgment of history will be determined by the impact which the Declaration has and will have on the actual conduct of states and of individual men and women everywhere. There is unfortunately little reason for thinking that human rights, with the possible exception of economic, social and cultural rights and the rights of certain classes of people not to be discriminated against, are better respected now than they were before 1948. But while the gap between commitment and performance may still be wide, governments are now formally committed to respect and observe human rights. And the international community now possesses "a common standard of achievement" by reference to which the conduct of these governments can be and is judged. Some measure of the impact which the Declaration has had on the expectations of individual men and women can be found in the many thousands of communications received by the United Nations every year from people everywhere alleging that their rights have been violated and invoking the Declaration in their appeals for help. But if the adoption of the Declaration is one of the greatest achievements of the United Nations, the inability of the organization to respond effectively to these appeals is one of its greatest failures.

Back to New York (1949)

Once the Declaration had been adopted, there was nothing to keep my wife and me in Paris and, since we both needed a holiday, we decided to spend a fortnight in Italy before returning to New York. We went first to Rome where, after settling down in the Hotel Quirinale, we walked to the Piazza Venezia and then took a taxi to see the Colosseum in the moonlight. Where we got the energy I cannot imagine, for we had both reached the end of our tethers. I was tempted to stay on in Rome, for as a one-time professor of Roman Law, I was interested in the antiquities. But what we needed was rest; so after two days, we made our way by car to Naples and across the bay to Sorrento.

The Hotel Cocumela had once been a monastery. Situated in an orange grove high on a cliff, it commanded a fine view across the bay with Pompeii and Vesuvius in the distance. There was an old church on the grounds where we attended mass on Christmas Eve. The ceremony began with a procession out of the church, into the garden, through the hotel lobby and back into the church. As the priest carrying a *bambino* doll led us out of the church, we were greeted by a fusillade of firecrackers and rockets, which whizzed over our heads, burst under our feet and deafened our ears. But my best memories are of the long walks I took up beyond the hemmed-in streets of Sorrento to the heights where the orange groves, lemon trees and bougainvillea gave way to olive trees, and from where I could get a view of both sides of the peninsula.

Sorrento provided the rest that we needed. When we returned to New York, I was shocked to discover that I had gained nearly twenty pounds, which I attributed to relaxation after the strains of the General Assembly, the excellent *cucina* at the Hotel Cocumela and a sea voyage back to the United States. We had also lived well in Paris. Within five months I had lost the extra pounds; and considering the pace at which I went that spring I was just as glad that I had put them on.

We celebrated the New Year on board the S.S. *Excambion* then on the last lap of her maiden voyage. Our first stop was at Leghorn where we had time for a quick excursion to Pisa. The next day we were in Genoa, where the ship remained for four days. Some of the effigies of Mussolini and fascist slogans we had seen on a previous visit in 1936 were still on the walls. Our last port of call was Marseilles, a city of memories, which we had first visited on our honeymoon in 1929.

The *Excambion* remained in Marseilles for only a day. We were beginning to know some of the other passengers. One of our table companions, an officer of the Canadian Department of External Affairs who had been at the Paris Assembly, volunteered some information which helped explain the Canadian abstention in the voting on the Universal Declaration of Human Rights. In Canada, she said, the campaign against the Declaration had been led by the president of the Canadian Bar Association, John T. Hackett. On arriving in New York, I had some further interesting information and I put the two items together. A friend had sent me an editorial published in the *Montreal Gazette* of 17 January. It carried the revealing title "Human Rights on Pink Paper" and *inter alia* quoted, again out of context, my notorious remark about the revolutionary nature of the United Nations human rights program. It also quoted the president of the American Bar Association who had so virulently attacked the Declaration in the United States. I wondered whether the latter had ever been in Montreal. The evidence was at hand: I found a report in a publication of the American Bar Association of a trip that he had made to Montreal in August, and of his talks with John Hackett. Hackett had also attended meetings of the American association when the Declaration was discussed and, it seemed, the positions of the two organizations were the same. I concluded that constitutional difficulties were not the only reason for the Canadian abstention. When the American lawyers had discovered that they were getting nowhere in Washington, they had apparently turned their attention to their northern neighbors. My disgust with the Canadian abstention was compounded by the realization that it was not even home grown.

Another passenger on the *Excambion* was Francis Biddle, a sometime attorney-general of the United States, with whom I had several long walks on the ship's deck. Biddle, though skeptical about the future of the United Nations, praised the social and human rights programs out of which he thought something useful might come.

The voyage over, we docked on the Jersey side of the Hudson. A United Nations car drove us to Great Neck, and early the next morning I was in my office in the Sperry plant. We were beginning another busy period; in 1949 there would be sessions of the Human Rights Commission, the Commission on the Status of Women, the two sub-commissions, two sessions of ECOSOC and, in effect, two sessions of the General Assembly, since the Paris session had been adjourned to April. Working papers had to be prepared and other arrangements made for all these meetings, and recruiting and other administrative problems that I hadn't been able to handle properly abroad had to be attended to. Much of this entailed infighting with the bureaus of personnel and finance over the needs of the Division. These fights were sometimes very unpleasant, and my difficulties were compounded by Laugier's unpopularity in both places. There was a disposition in the Secretariat to treat the human rights program as something of minor importance and even exotic in an international organization. But these, had I only known it, were halcyon days. My real difficulties would begin with Laugier's retirement and would become worse with the arrival of Hammarskjold as Secretary-General. Another distraction was the special board of inquiry on anti-Semitism which was beginning to hear witnesses, usually at night.

I had to find someone to replace Amanda Labarca as chief of the section on the status of women and one or two experts in information matters to help us with new responsibilities resulting from the decisions of the Geneva information conference. I found a new chief for the section on the status of women in the person of Mrs. Lakshmi Menon, who had been on the Indian delegation to the third session of the General Assembly and had just become the Indian member of the Commission on the Status of Women. Finding anyone expert in the highly specialized field of information was harder. I tried to recruit Fernand Terrou and, later, Jacques Kayser, both Frenchmen, but neither could be tempted into the Secretariat. Kayser said that he would take the job if he did not have to live in New York, and, when he did accept a short-term appointment as a consultant, he insisted on working in Geneva. He was the most knowledgeable person in the field I have ever known. Finally, I found a good man in Hilding Eek, but after a few years he returned to academic life in Sweden. As it turned out, all my efforts to build up an efficient section on freedom of information came to very little. For the Sub-Commission on Freedom of Information and of the Press met for the last time in 1952 and, as explained in an earlier chapter, the draft conventions approved by the Geneva conference soon fell into the political morass where they still are.

Among the people I did recruit at this time were Luis Recasens-Siches and Mousheng Lin. Recasens had an international reputation as a legal philosopher; but the fact that he had been a minister in the loyalist government of Spain weighed just as much in my choice. Lin came to us on the recommendation of P.C. Chang. I was impressed by the ability of some of the younger men on the Chinese delegation and, after the fall of Peking to the communists, thought that some of them might be tempted into the Secretariat. I telephoned Chang, who invited me to come to his office high up in the Empire State Building. He practically gave me the choice of his assistants, the best of whom, he said, was Mousheng Lin. I never regretted the choice: Lin was one of the most civilized men I have ever known, a talented writer—as anyone can see who reads his *Men and Ideas*—and a loyal colleague and friend. After Schwelb's retirement, he became the deputy director of the Division.

My first business after my return to headquarters was a picayune row about the text of the Universal Declaration of Human Rights. As adopted by the General Assembly, Article 3 read: "Everyone has the right to life, liberty and security of person." The documents service inserted the word "the" before "security" and the amended text had been published by the Department of Public Information. I didn't think much of the improvement nor did I think that the Secretariat had the right to change even a comma in the General Assembly's text, which I wanted restored. I had an unpleasant exchange with the chief editor, who told me that I was being difficult and unreasonable. But I had my way and the correct text was restored in subsequent editions.

The spring session of the Economic and Social Council began on 7 February. Of the fifty-nine items on its agenda, the Council decided to give priority to the ten concerning human rights so that the Secretariat could get ahead with its heavy spring program. These ten items covered a wide range of subjects: forced labor, freedom of association, equal pay for equal work, trade union rights, three resolutions of the General Assembly (on the draft covenant, the right of petition and the fate of minorities), the Sub-Commission on Freedom of Information and of the Press, a report of the International Refugees Organization, a proposed declaration on the rights of the aged, a study that we had prepared on statelessness, and those parts of the report of the third session of the Human Rights Commission which the Council had not discussed at its last session.

Much as I wanted to do so, and notwithstanding the urging of Alva Myrdal, the new top-ranking director of the Social Department, I did not attend the session of the Commission on the Status of Women, which met in Beirut. My long absences from headquarters in

1948 had made me an easy target for criticism; so after discussing the matter with Laugier I decided to remain in New York. In retrospect, I think this was a mistake; my place was with the commission, however an unsympathetic bureaucracy might react.

The second part of the third session of the General Assembly opened on 5 April; and the next day I was listening to the debate in the General Committee on the question whether items should be included in the agenda on the observance of human rights in Bulgaria and Hungary—neither of which were yet members of the United Nations. The Bulgarians and Hungarians and their friends were arguing that the inclusion of the items in the agenda would be intervention in a matter essentially within domestic jurisdiction and hence beyond the competence of the United Nations. In the case of Hungary, the charges were based on the conduct and outcome of the trial of Cardinal Mindzenty by a People's Court. Julius Katz-Suchy of Poland made one of the best speeches. But although he was a forceful if sharp-tongued speaker, on this occasion his eloquence was ineffective, for the committee proceeded to recommend the inclusion of both cases under a single item, which the General Assembly referred, not to the Third, but to the Ad Hoc Political Committee, which meant that I would have no responsibility for it. On 30 April, the Assembly adopted a resolution expressing its deep concern and drawing the attention of the two countries to their obligations under the peace treaties.

When the General Assembly was in session, my place was in the Third Committee. Laugier wanted me to be there whenever human rights were being discussed and this notwithstanding how busy I might be with office work or how irrelevant the discussions, some of which were not much better than political name calling. One day, when I had left him alone in the conference room, he sent me a message saying that he enjoyed acting as my deputy but he would rather have me in the room. Later, I learned how to do part of my paper work in the conference room while pretending to listen to the debates, but I always had someone sitting behind me to warn me when to listen. Laugier also complained that too many papers were coming up to him in English. I explained that my people drafted them in the working language, usually English, which they understood best. Both English and French were working languages in the Secretariat: papers published in one language had to be translated into the other (and usually also into Russian) before being circulated to delegations; but this was time-consuming and expensive and under the rules could be begun only when I had Laugier's approval. Laugier's spoken English was not good; but he could read the language fairly easily. I myself worked in both languages, and when I had anything that required Laugier's signature, for example a note to the Secretary-General, I always had it prepared for him in French and used that language in my notes to him.

In Paris, the General Assembly had not had the time to study the three conventions that had been drafted by the Geneva information conference. It now began its long and still uncompleted consideration of the instruments, beginning with the Convention on the Gathering and International Transmission of News. After a long debate, several amendments to the Geneva text were adopted. The French then proposed that the convention be amalgamated with the draft Convention on the Institution of an International Right of Correction, which they had sponsored at Geneva. But although the proposal was adopted, the Indians then moved that the adoption of the amalgamated convention be postponed until the next session of the Assembly. I waited an hour for van Heuven Goedhart, the chairman of the Sub-Commission on Freedom of Information and of the Press, to join me at lunch while he lobbied against the Indian motion. In the afternoon, the Indians withdrew their motion but only on condition that the amalgamated convention not be opened for signature until the more controversial Convention on Freedom of Information had been approved. It might have been better had their first motion been adopted, for the decision to tie the fate of the amalgamated convention to the convention on freedom of information has had the result that, like the latter convention, the articles on the gathering and international transmission of news have never been adopted. In 1952, the French were able to have those parts of the amalgamated convention which dealt with the right of correction detached and made into a separate convention, which is now in force between a few states.

About this time, Jeanne and I had dinner with V.V. Pella, one of the experts who had helped prepare the genocide convention. Manley Hudson, the American judge on the International Court of Justice, was there. I had known Hudson when I was at McGill and he was teaching international law at Harvard. Towards the end of the war he had come to Montreal to drum up support for a statement on the international law of the future, and I helped him arrange a meeting of Montreal lawyers to discuss the statement. Apart from Hudson, I was the only person there who had any real knowledge of international law. It was therefore easy for him to get the meeting to endorse his project; for he refused to entertain or indeed listen to any suggestions.

To return to Pella's party, Manley, as usual at that hour of the night, had had too much to drink; and when I made some remark about the American Bar Association—I was still incensed by what I had learned about its campaign against the Universal Declaration of Human Rights—he lost his temper, bursting out with "Don't you say anything against the American Bar Association." He also reprimanded me for not having sought his assistance in the drafting of the Declaration. On another occasion he lectured me on the danger of allowing the human rights program to fall into the hands of Jews.

Not long after this, I went to Washington for meetings of the American Society of International Law, one of which was devoted to human rights. Carl Aix, who had taken me to lunch before the meeting, attacked the draft covenant. This started a controversial debate during which Professor Myers McDougal of Yale University came to our defense in a spirited speech. George Finch, the editor of the American Journal of International Law, took the other side. Some day perhaps someone will write a book about how the United Nations human rights program split the American legal profession down the middle.

Back in the Division, we were working on a paper for the Human Rights Commission. The suggestions we put into it were among the boldest the Secretariat ever made to the commission. The decision taken by the commission in 1947, and confirmed by ECOSOC—that the commission had no power to act on complaints—has already been mentioned. Fortified by the opinion of Sir Hersch Lauterpacht, I was convinced that this decision was wrong. In our paper we therefore suggested that the commission review its position which, we said, was based on a restrictive interpretation of the Charter. We pointed out that both the General Assembly and the Economic and Social Council were then acting on various allegations that human rights had been violated and concluded that such action must be based on the Charter. In the circumstances, the commission should consider asking the Council to revise its Resolution 75(V), and give the commission the right to make recommendations on matters which came to its attention while examining communications alleging violations of human rights. We also suggested that the Council ask the commission to draw up a report on cases "affecting very great numbers of people or having international repercussions." The working paper could be interpreted as criticizing both the commission and ECOSOC and another Assistant Secretary-General might have been reluctant to approve it, but Laugier did so without any difficulty. Our position was fully vindicated over two decades later, in 1970, when the Council instructed the Sub-Commission on the Prevention of Discrimination and the Protection of Minorities (of which, having retired from the Secretariat, I was that year the chairman) to examine the communications with a view to bringing the attention of the commission to situations which appeared to reveal consistent patterns of gross violation of human rights. Situations so referred to the commission were to be thoroughly studied by it with a view to making recommendations to ECOSOC, or the commission could decide with the consent of the state concerned to appoint an ad hoc committee to investigate the situation. This arrangement stemmed partly from a resolution for which I took the initiative in the sub-commission in 1967 and a report which I myself drew up in 1968.

On 6 April, the commission held a short session of one meeting for the sole purpose of electing new members of the Sub-Commission on Freedom of Information and of the Press. It was one of the most shocking performances I ever witnessed at the United Nations, for the member countries were interested only in assuring the election of their own nationals. Since there were fewer seats on the sub-commission than on the electing body, nationals of states not members of that body had no chance of being chosen. Gerrit van Heuven Goedhart, who was the out-going chairman of the sub-commission and one of its best and most distinguished members, was not reelected because the Netherlands was not a member of the commission. Two days later I lunched with him and two members of the Dutch delegation to discuss how he could be put back on the sub-commission. I suggested asking the Economic and Social Council to increase the membership. But although a similar stratagem was later used to get Mohammed Awad reelected to the Sub-Commission on the Prevention of Discrimination (after the Egyptian government had forgotten to nominate him) this was not tried in this instance; and we lost van Heuven Goedhart for freedom of information.

The commission's fifth session began on Monday, 9 May. Before the opening meeting, I drove Jeanne to the Lennox Hill Hospital where she was to have a serious operation. I was back at Lake Success in time to see Mrs. Roosevelt reelected chairman of the commission. It was a bad week both for me and for the commission. On Thursday, P.C. Chang was chairing the commission and having a very bad time of it. At one point, he gave the floor to Pavlov simply to clarify a point, notwithstanding the fact that the list of speakers was closed. Pavlov then delivered one of his long harangues. While this was going on, Mrs. Roosevelt came into the chamber and, prompted by one of her advisers, raised a point of order which Chang maintained. She then left the chamber and Pavlov said that Chang could now conduct the meeting in his own fashion, the insinuation being that he was acting in the American interest. I admired his short dignified reply.

On the Friday, Schwelb and I talked to Wilfred Jenks, the legal counsel of the I.L.O., about the possibility of creating machinery for the protection of trade union rights. Schwelb and I had been working on a suggestion that a joint United Nations–I.L.O. Commission should be established for this purpose; but Jenks dismissed the proposal out of hand with the remark that the director-general of the I.L.O. would never consider it. Notwithstanding his refusal even to discuss it, we put the suggestion in a paper for consideration by the Economic and Social Council that summer. There was another meeting on the question at the Geneva headquarters of the I.L.O. in July, when David Morse, its director-general, was also present and Laugier and I represented the United Nations. The position of the I.L.O. remained adamant, although I suspected that Morse might have been open to conviction had it not been for the strong line taken by his advisers. As Laugier and I left the room, Morse turned to me and said that I was a tough fighter. I never knew him well, but what I saw of him I liked.

When the item on trade union rights came up in the Council, our suggestion was strongly supported by the French, who moved a resolution which, had it been adopted, would have created the joint machinery. But the I.L.O. lobby was so strong that the Council asked it to set up a fact-finding and conciliation commission on freedom of association to act on behalf of both organizations. The Soviet Union, in opposing this decision, made the point that I would have made had I been a delegate. Safeguarding trade union rights is intimately related to other human rights, which are the direct concern of the United Nations. Another argument that I had stressed in my talks with the I.L.O. was that there were some members of the United Nations, including the Soviet Union, which were not members of the I.L.O.

Because the proposed conciliation commission was also to act on behalf of the United Nations, we were entitled to have our views heard on its structure and mandate. The Council asked the two secretariats to prepare procedures for making the commission available to the United Nations and to members of the United Nations which were not members of the I.L.O. When I saw the I.L.O. proposals in the fall of 1949 there were one or two things about them that I did not like, including the suggestion that the commission would entertain complaints only if the accused state agreed. Nor did I think that the right to bring complaints should be limited to the governing body of the I.L.O. and the Economic and Social Council. I wanted individuals and organizations to have the same right. I was thinking, of course, about the bad precedent that the I.L.O. proposal would be when the time came to set up machinery for the implementation of other human rights. I also thought that the conciliation commission should report not only to the I.L.O. but also to the Economic and Social Council. Jenks would listen to none of these objections, and in January 1950, the I.L.O. set up the commission on its own terms, without even giving the Economic and Social Council the right to refer cases to it. It was fourteen years before any government consented to a case being referred to the commission. The governing body of the I.L.O. must have soon realized that the machinery that it had created would have only limited usefulness. For in 1951 it created a new body, the governing body committee on freedom of association, to examine complaints with a view to advising the governing body whether it should seek the consent of states to refer the cases to the conciliation commission. The consent of governments to send cases to this committee was not to be required. The idea was brilliant and has produced results; for the issues which can be heard by the commission only if governments agree are now heard by the committee without their consent as part of the debate on whether that consent should be sought.

This was only one of our first jurisdictional conflicts with the International Labor Organization. I do not think I was being chauvinistic or trying to build up an empire. It was my clear duty to protect the interests of the United Nations—as it was Jenks' duty to protect the interests of the I.L.O. I believed, moreover, and still do, that one of the best ways to strengthen the authority of the United Nations—even in its primary function of maintaining international peace and security—is to involve the organization as deeply as possible in every kind of nonpolitical activity. The specialized agencies, including the I.L.O., were becoming more and more independent of the United Nations, at whose expense their powers were being strengthened. I knew something about Jenks' views on these questions, for I had known him fairly well during the war when the I.L.O. was housed on the McGill campus. When Percy Corbett, then my colleague at the university, once drove both of us to Washington for meetings of the American Society of International Law, Jenks talked at length about the future of the I.L.O. Amongst other things, he said that he did not think that it should become too closely linked with the United Nations because if, like the League of Nations, the new world political organization should fail, the I.L.O. might be brought down with it.

I have wandered far from the fifth session of the Human Rights Commission where Chang was still presiding; why Mrs. Roosevelt missed so many meetings at this session, I do not know. "P.C." was still in trouble and Pavlov again accused him of hiding behind Mrs. Roosevelt's skirt.

About this time Mrs. Roosevelt gave a buffet luncheon for the commission at Hyde Park. I went with a light heart because Jeanne seemed so much better. It was good to get out of the city, if only for a few hours. The commission was working on the covenant. An entry in my diary says that the British lost a hard-fought battle with the Americans. Everyone agreed that there were certain necessary limitations on the enjoyment of some of the rights listed in the covenant; and the British wanted these to be mentioned in the articles setting forth the rights. The Americans wanted one general limitations clause applicable to the whole covenant, which I thought could become an escape clause because it would have to be drafted in such general terms. A right begins to have meaning only when you know all the limitations placed on it. The Indians now moved an amendment to the article on arbitrary arrest and detention, the purpose of which was to delete the permissible limitations mentioned in the article as then drafted. The adoption of this amendment seemed to establish the principle favored by the United States that all limitations should be dealt with together in one place. But, when the Covenant on Civil and Political Rights was approved by the General Assembly in 1966, it contained no general limitations clause. Limitations there are in abundance—I sometimes think that you could drive a team of oxen through the instrument—but all of them are expressed in the articles enunciating the rights.

Mrs. Roosevelt was not always a good chairman. But she was more sinned against than sinning; and when she made a mistake, it was usually because she had been badly advised by her state department assistants. In my opinion they had no business advising her on procedural questions relating to the conduct of the meetings. As chairman, she was the servant of the commission and not the agent of her government. The British thought so too, and came to me to complain. They had, they added sarcastically, congratulated one of the state department officials on his appointment to the Secretariat, inasmuch as he was performing one of its duties. My own position was not always easy. It was sometimes hard enough to advise the chairman under any conditions, but when the state department began to interfere my position was impossible. On one occasion at this session, I was tempted to leave the chamber because I did not want the commission to think that the chairman was getting her advice from me. Pavlov was admittedly often provocative and often out of order, but she sometimes treated him unfairly. Once at this session she gave him a public spanking when calling him to order, but this time he was not altogether at fault. His attack on Belgian colonial policy may have been provocative and perhaps irrelevant; but the Belgian member had made an unsatisfactory answer to Pavlov's point that the Forced Labor Convention of 1930 distinguished between metropolitan and colonial territories.

The Australians again proposed the creation of an international court of human rights but received no support and, although the proposal remained on the agenda for several years, no more was heard of it. A majority, which did not include the communists who were opposed to any kind of international implementation, favored the creation of some kind of conciliation commission which would hear complaints that the covenant was being violated. The debate got away to a bad start. I thought Mrs. Roosevelt's contribution was one of her weakest. She did not seem to have her heart in it, possibly because she did not agree with her instructions. The United States and the United Kingdom were proposing that only states should have the right to bring complaints before the conciliation body. The Secretariat had suggested in a working paper that this right be given also to individuals and groups. I was pretty sure that if it were given only to states, it would be used only when the latter had some political reason for doing so. That was the lesson of the complaints procedure under the constitution of the International Labor Organization, where in nearly three decades states had used their right to complain only twice, and in both cases the motivation had been political. It was also the logical conclusion, since governments are unlikely to bring a friendly government before an international instance. All this and more I said to a member of the British delegation after one of the meetings. He agreed, but added that nothing could be done about it.

The commission was equally divided on the issue; and when the vote was taken, it resulted in a tie, eight to eight. This meant, under the rules of procedure, that the proposal to give a right of petition to individuals had been lost. It was for me one of the most disappointing decisions the commission ever took. The situation could hardly have been more unsatisfactory. By a tie vote in which only sixteen states of the total membership of the United Nations had participated, the commission had disposed of one of the most important questions that would ever come before it. The commission itself was not satisfied with the result, although it never changed its position. This may partly explain the unexpected and indeed incompatible decision that it now took. Obviously inspired by the Secretariat paper already mentioned, it asked the Economic and Social Council to request the Secretariat to prepare a study on, amongst other things, the receivability and preliminary consideration of petitions and also to examine the communications which were being currently received, with a view to submitting to the commission at its next session those communications which might be receivable under the conditions suggested by the study. In the light of what it had just decided in the matter of petitions under the covenant, this was a surprising decision indeed. It also implied a rejection of the position which it had taken in 1947 that it had no power to take any action on complaints. It was much more radical to contemplate action on the communications that were then being received by the United Nations than to provide for a right of individual petition under the covenant. For it implied that the United Nations already had the right under the Charter to consider them. Had the Council approved this recommendation, which it did not, it would have anticipated its decision of

1970—taken in a different political context—establishing procedures for considering communications which appear to reveal consistent patterns of gross violations. The commission's decision to ask for the study was energetically opposed by the Soviet Union, whose representative said that it virtually asked the Secretary-General to distort the Charter. It would, said Pavlov, have "the deplorable result of making it possible for fascist organizations to call upon the United Nations to consider their complaints."

When in 1966, the General Assembly approved the Covenant on Civil and Political Rights (there being by that time two covenants) it gave no right of complaint to individuals or private groups. It did vote, but only reluctantly and by a much smaller majority, an optional protocol which allows the Human Rights Committee, the conciliation body created by the covenant, to entertain communications from certain individuals. Provided a state has accepted this protocol, individuals subject to its jurisdiction can address communications to the committee complaining that this state has violated rights set forth in the covenant. The committee may then, after considering the matter in the light of "all written information" which they make available to it, forward its "views" to the individual and state party concerned. Even the right of states to complain under the covenant is on an optional basis. For, by Article 41, no communication from a state party alleging that another state party has violated its obligations under the covenant can be entertained unless the latter state has made a special declaration recognizing the competence of the committee to receive such communications; and only states which have made similar declarations can address complaints to the committee. By contrast, the International Convention on the Elimination of All Forms of Racial Discrimination, which the General Assembly approved in 1965, gives states parties a right to complain to the Racial Discrimination Committee without any special declaration being necessary, and individual petitions are on an optional basis. The fact that the covenant does not follow this precedent throws a great deal of light on human rights priorities in the United Nations.

When the Sub-Commission on the Prevention of Discrimination met on 13 June, the Secretariat came under criticism. I sympathized with the complaint that no provision had been made for simultaneous interpretation; for I had been arguing this very matter with the department of conferences and general services. On instructions I explained that the fault lay, not with the Secretariat (although I was not too sure about this), but with the budgetary limitations fixed by the Fifth Committee of the General Assembly. It was not easy to explain why the axe should fall on the sub-commission. I could not tell them that human rights had a low priority in the Secretariat. I could have said, but of course did not, that it was not very good economics to bring experts to New York at very great expense and even to pay them a living allowance, only to cut their efficiency by more than a half once they got there; for that is what consecutive interpretation meant. Because all speeches had to be interpreted into the other working language and those in Russian into both, the time consumed was doubled and sometimes trebled. We had the same trouble in the commission, which was still meeting.

In the sub-commission, A.P. Borisov of the Soviet Union held me personally responsible for its failure to meet in 1948. I replied that the decision had been taken by the Economic and Social Council, which he knew as well as I, but he wanted to pose as the protector of persecuted minorities. At another meeting he ranted on about the "sloth" of the Secretariat. Jonathan Daniels of the United States complained that some of the documents were late. This was true and I knew the reason why, but I could hardly say in public that my staff was much too small for the work that it now had to do. I pointed out that no one had asked us to prepare the late documents, which we had prepared because we thought that they would be useful; it was better for the sub-commission to have them late than not at all. My patience was wearing thin, but I consoled myself with the thought that one of the functions of an international secretariat is to be a butt of criticism. It came almost as a relief when, in the commission a few days later, Pavlov attacked the legal counsel of the Secretary-General, Abraham Feller, for an opinion he had given relating to the states which should be invited to adhere to the covenant.

I had to divide my time between the sub-commission and the commission. In the latter body, Mrs. Roosevelt again put on a poor performance which I attributed to the state department. It had been understood that, once the amendments to the articles already in the Geneva draft of the covenant had been dealt with, the commission would study the proposals for new articles, most of which related to economic and social rights and had come from the Soviet Union. The United States did not want them in the covenant, and Mrs. Roosevelt announced that the new articles would have to be considered *en bloc* and that there would be no voting. She also made certain other suggestions which made it look as if she wanted to deprive Pavlov of his place on the speakers' list. I whispered that she was making a mistake, but she was getting other advice from her state department assistants who, as usual, were sitting behind her. Pavlov immediately challenged her ruling. After a long discussion, his right to have the articles voted on was maintained by a vote of eight in favor and two against, including the chairman. After the meeting, one of Mrs. Roosevelt's advisers accused me of bias in favor of the Soviet Union. "Yes," I said, "I get my instructions straight from Moscow." In the afternoon he came to apologize. I had the satisfaction that week of knowing that my objectivity was being attacked by both sides in the Cold War—which I interpreted as meaning that I was being objective. Later, Pavlov repeated Borisov's charge that I was personally responsible for the failure of the sub-commission to meet in 1948.

That weekend my wife scolded me: I was too thin and I looked tired. True, I had lost some weight since returning to New York; but what was really wrong with me was that I was frustrated and, for the first time since coming to the United Nations, discouraged. If the United Nations was to realize the high purposes of the Charter, it would not be enough simply to proclaim certain human rights and fundamental freedoms. Some effective international procedures needed to be set up for their implementation, and it was beginning to look as though this would not be done. I was, of course, suffering from the impatience of an activist. I should have realized that, after the successes of 1948, the momentum would slow down. It would, moreover, be vastly more difficult to reach agreement on procedures for implementation than it had been to agree on standards of conduct.

The Sub-Commission on the Prevention of Discrimination continued to meet for a week after the commission adjourned, and by then I had forgotten the attacks on the Secretariat at its opening meetings, to which I had probably overreacted, perhaps because I was working under so much pressure. Actually, I had a very high opinion of this sub-commission, which was probably the best qualified and, with a few exceptions, the most strongly motivated group I ever worked with at the United Nations. Only a few of its members were professional diplomats and, in theory at least, they acted as individuals and not on the instructions of governments. Yet, because they did not have a well-thought-out program, they had accomplished very little apart from their contributions to the Universal Declaration and the covenant. Nor would they have such a program until the Secretariat provided them with one in 1952. The sub-commission had been created on the suggestion of the Soviet Union in response to American sponsorship of the Sub-Commission on Freedom of Information; but, while there was general agreement that there should be such a body, very little thought had been given to its mandate. Its initial difficulties were compounded by the commission's decision to combine the prevention of discrimination and the protection of minorities in the mandate of the same body; for much time was lost in a fruitless attempt, given the attitude of most governments, to set up standards and procedures for the positive protection of minorities. It was only after the members realized that the United Nations did not intend to protect minorities, which most governments wanted assimilated, that the sub-commission began to concentrate on what was to be its real work, the prevention of discrimination. In the meantime, its preoccupation with minorities actually prevented it from making any significant contribution. Although the General Assembly had refused to put an article on the protection of minorities in the Universal Declaration of Human Rights—a fairly good sign of the way the wind was blowing—it had nevertheless asked the sub-cmomission to continue its study of the question. In attempting to perform the mandate, the sub-commission drafted a resolution for adoption by the Assembly which would have requested member states to provide adequate facilities for the use of minority languages in judicial proceedings and state-supported schools in areas where recognized minorities constituted a considerable part of the population. The Belgian member, Joseph Nisot, opposed this because, he said, it would be a violation of Article 2, paragraph 7 of the Charter, which prohibits any intervention by the United Nations in matters which are "essentially within the domestic jurisdiction of any state." Shortly afterwards, I listened to a heated argument over lunch between Nisot and Samuel Spanien of France. Nisot said that it would be dangerous if any attempt were ever made to enforce the principles that the sub-commission was then trying to formulate, because this would only worsen an already explosive international situation; it would be better if the United Nations were to do nothing. Nisot had probably more international experience than any of us, for he had been an official in the League of Nations; but he was easily the most conservative member of the sub-commission. I knew him well but I don't remember ever having agreed with him on anything.

A European Convention and a First Anniversary (1949)

I brought Jeanne back from the hospital a few days before the sub-commission adjourned; but we had only five days together before I had to leave for Geneva to attend the summer session of the Economic and Social Council. Jeanne's doctor did not want her to go to Europe, but he did want her out of the New York heat. She therefore decided to go to Nova Scotia, where I would join her later in the summer.

I was booked on the R.M.S. *Queen Elizabeth*. As the ship steamed out of the Hudson, I watched the Manhattan skyline disappear and then, tired out, fell asleep in my deck chair. When I awoke, I found that two Canadians were sitting near me, Norman Robertson, the under secretary of state for external affairs, and Louis Rasminsky who later became the governor of the Bank of Canada. I wasn't so lucky with my table companions in the dining saloon. At lunch one day, one of them made a cutting remark about Sir Stafford Cripps. I said that this was the kind of thing people were saying about Léon Blum before the war and still saying about Roosevelt. Roosevelt's name triggered a long argument in which I was a minority of one. I was tired and probably irritable; the other people at the table must have thought me a dangerous United Nations radical.

The ship docked at Cherbourg late on a Tuesday afternoon, so it was quite late when the boat train arrived in Paris, although still early enough to go to the *Bal Tabarin* with some United Nations friends. Next morning, after a long walk, I went to the Palais Royal, the seat of the *Conseil d'Etat*, whose head, René Cassin, had invited me to lunch. Cassin was not in his office and was nowhere to be found; he had forgotten the appointment. So I walked over to a modest little restaurant where Jeanne and I had often eaten in my student days.

Bad news was waiting the next day in Geneva. A letter dictated by Jeanne—she couldn't write it herself—said that the phlebitis was worse and that she was now flat on her back in a Halifax hospital. I was on the point of flying to Nova Scotia when a reassuring cablegram arrived. Laugier's typical reaction to this news was to invite me to dinner at the Hotel du Parc in Gex, where he and Marie Cutolli always stayed during Geneva sessions of the Economic and Social Council.

On the same day, I had lunch with Hector McNeil, who was the head of the British delegation to the Council, and who had been so complimentary about my handling of the conference on freedom of information. We talked about the future of the Council: the British favored retrenchment, a stance which for them would become characteristic. I could hardly agree. I even thought the Council should remain in more or less permanent session; there was so much to be done. The next day I dined with Emile Vaillancourt, then the Canadian ambassador to Yugoslavia, who was in Geneva as the head of the Canadian delegation to an important conference which was drafting new conventions for the protection of victims of armed conflict. He said that he was on a diet, but he was as exuberant as ever and very pleased and excited about his work.

My first important business in Geneva was the meeting, already mentioned, at I.L.O. headquarters on machinery for safeguarding trade union rights. The next was the first of a series of meetings in my office on the urgent matter of refugees; the International Refugee Organization was to terminate its activities in June 1950, and something had to be created to replace it. I favored the appointment of a United Nations High Commissioner for Refugees, and my division later prepared the first draft of the statute of that office. In 1951, I was also the executive secretary of the conference which drew up the convention relating to the protection of refugees.

One of the first items discussed by the Council's Social Committee at this session was freedom of information. The General Assembly had referred back to the Council some of the resolutions adopted by the 1948 conference, one of them on war propaganda (the Russians called it warmongering) and false and distorted news. It was an old theme which had been gone over many times, and the delegations no longer had much enthusiasm for it; I had the impression that they were simply saying their pieces. The committee then turned to the report of the Sub-Commission on Freedom of Information. The report was not too good, nor was it well received. Jacques Kayser of the French delegation had warned me in advance that he was going to ask me some embarrassing questions, so I was prepared for them when they came. His purpose, I am sure, was to exonerate the Secretariat and to put the blame for the poor performance where it belonged, on the sub-commission.

At the last session of the General Assembly, the Belgians had proposed, probably on the suggestion of the Anti-Slavery Society, that a committee of experts on slavery be appointed. The matter had been referred to the Council and was discussed in plenary from 16 to 20 July. It was common knowledge that despite over a century and a half of international effort to abolish them, slavery and even the slave trade still existed in certain parts of the world. Both practices were prohibited by a League of Nations convention and by the Universal Declaration of Human Rights, but there was no international enforcement machinery. Some delegations wanted the study the Belgians were asking for to be made by the Secretariat, an idea which did not commend itself to me. What was needed was a survey which, naming countries when necessary, would throw more light on the real situation. No study prepared on the sole responsibility of the Secretariat could do this; for, as I intervened in the debate to say, we could not be put in the position where we might have to point a finger of shame at member states. We could do the work, but we needed a political umbrella such as a rapporteur or committee who could accept responsibility for the study and defend it in the Council. I was confirmed in this opinion, several days later, when P.C. Chang complained to me about something that the British had said about *mui tsai*, which they called involuntary servitude but Chang said was a kind of adoption. The Chinese would have been furious had the Secretariat even mentioned this. I was therefore relieved when the Council asked the Secretary-General to appoint an ad hoc committee to study slavery in all its aspects.

The Social Committee then turned to the report of the Commission on the Status of Women, an occasion which the Russians used, as they had at the last session, to attack the Western democracies. The report was badly received, the committee even refusing to vote on some of the recommendations, one of which asked the Council to urge the Secretary-General to set up a separate division on the status of women; but the committee refused to interfere with the business of the Secretariat. That evening I took Laugier and Marie to dinner in Annemasse across the French border. Next day I had lunch with Brock Chisholm, the Canadian director-general of the World Health Organization and his assistant, Dr. W.P. Forrest, who wanted to talk about the article in the draft covenant on cruel, inhuman and degrading treatment.

On 28 July, after dealing fairly rapidly in plenary with the report of the Sub-Commission on Freedom of Information, the Council turned to trade union rights (the debate on which has already been mentioned). The Secretariat had recommended that joint United Nations–I.L.O. machinery be set up for their enforcement. But although the French sponsored a resolution to this effect, the proposal of the American and British delegations that the I.L.O. should have exclusive responsibility was adopted. There was then a controversial debate on forced labor. Corley Smith of the United Kingdom read extracts from the R.F.S.S.R. Corrective Labor Codes. Arutinuian, usually a good speaker, made a weak but offensive reply. The United States then proposed setting up a commission of inquiry, but the Council decided that it would first ask governments if they would cooperate.

I had to intervene several times in the debate on the report of the Human Rights Commission. What I wanted most was to have the Council approve the commission's recommendation that the Secretariat prepare the study on the right of petition already mentioned; but, rationalizing its decision by the unconvincing argument that the commission had not taken a final decision in the matter, the Council decided to take no action. The real reason, of course, was that governments were not ready to recognize an international right of petition or, indeed, to take any other effective measures for the implementation of human rights law.

The last of the human rights items dealt with refugees and statelessness, particularly the problem of how to resettle or repatriate the great numbers of refugees and displaced persons who would still be homeless after the impending liquidation of the International Refugees Organization. The Council requested the Secretariat to prepare a plan for the creation of new machinery. One of the possibilities mentioned (and to my great satisfaction finally adopted) was a high commissioner's office. There was a meeting that afternoon to decide who in the Secretariat would be responsible for preparing the plan. The legal department was anxious to do the work, but it was decided that it would be the responsibility of the Division of Human Rights.

As usual in Geneva the social life was intense and became more so as the end of the session approached. One Saturday, the French gave their annual big party, which this year was at Thonon. We returned to Geneva by lake boat to the accompaniment of music and champagne. On Sunday, the third anniversary of my joining the Secretariat, I drove to Interlaken and back with Laugier and Marie. Laugier wanted me to go to Strasbourg to attend at least some of the meetings of the first session of the Consultative Assembly of the Council of Europe, at which the proposed European convention on human rights was to be discussed. We both felt that there should be some United Nations representation on such an important occasion. But when we consulted Lake Success, the bureaucrats replied that I would have to pay my own expenses and that the time would be deducted from my annual leave. I decided to go nevertheless.

A *bise* was blowing over the lake when I left Geneva on Sunday afternoon. In Strasbourg, the streets were festooned with flags, including the new flag of the Council of Europe. Monday turned out to be a holiday, something that I had not known about when I left Geneva, and the Assembly did not meet. I spent the day walking, admiring the cathedral, and reading William James' *Varieties of Religious Experience*. Thinking that I would cross over into Germany, I also went to Kehl. But the border formalities were so complicated that even though I had a diplomatic passport, I abandoned my plan and walked around Kehl instead. The place had been badly damaged in the war and very little had been done to clean it up.

The next morning I went to the university where the consultative assembly was meeting. Fernand Dehousse, on whom I had counted to introduce me to some of the delegates, had not arrived. The delegates were discussing the future of Europe. The speakers included Churchill, Macmillan, Herbert Morrison and De Valera. Churchill pleaded for the admission of Germany as a member of the Council of Europe. In another part of his speech he mentioned the Universal Declaration of Human Rights which, he said, had been adopted in Geneva, a blunder which showed that he did not know too much about it. But the association of the two ideas made sense: if Germany were to be readmitted to the European community it would have to be on conditions that guaranteed respect for human rights. Macmillan made the best speech. I was not very much impressed by Morrison's speech, but I liked him when Toni Sender (from the American Federation of Labor) later introduced me to him and to Hugh Dalton. I also met De Valera. We talked about the self-determination of peoples, about the rights of minorities and about the article on marriage in the Universal Declaration of Human Rights. Pulling a copy of the Declaration out of his pocket, De Valera pointed to where Article 16 says that men and women "are entitled to equal rights as to marriage, during marriage and at its dissolution."

"Ireland could never accept that," he said.

"But why, Mr. De Valera?"

"Because we don't believe in divorce."

I explained that the Human Rights Commission had carefully avoided using the word and that there had even been informal consultations with the Vatican, which had raised no objections. Marriage could be dissolved, I went on to say, by causes other than divorce.

"How?" he said.

"For one thing by death."

"I don't admit that," he said. "Marriages are made in heaven and they continue in heaven."

I was in Strasbourg to listen to the debate on a report recommending the adoption of a European convention on human rights. This report had been commissioned before the Council of Europe came into existence; and the Hague conference on movements for European unity, which met in May 1948 and had recommended the creation of the Council, had also recommended that only states undertaking to respect a charter on human rights should be admitted to the Council. In February 1949 at a meeting in Brussels under the same auspices, a committee, chaired by Pierre Henri Teitgen, had been set up to prepare a preliminary draft of a convention. I listened to Teitgen present his report. The convention was, he said, needed as a defense against three threats to the freedom of Europeans: *raison d'état*, fascism and the exploitation by communists of contemporary economic and social conditions. An Irish delegate then began to analyze some of the articles in the Universal Declaration of Human Rights of which he was critical. His wrath was chiefly directed to Article 21 on elections. I soon realized that this was a pretext for attacking British policy in Ulster. Henri Spaak, the president of the Assembly, called him to order, bringing the speech to a quick end.

The European Convention for the Protection of Human Rights and Fundamental Freedoms was signed in November 1950 and came into force on 3 September 1953. Its stated purpose was "to take the first steps for the collective enforcement of certain of the rights stated in the Universal Declaration." The committee of experts which prepared the convention had been asked to take into consideration the work that had been done by the United Nations which, in practice, was taken to mean the draft covenant as it existed in 1949. Like that draft, the European convention did not include economic and social rights, although in 1961 some nineteen of these rights were set forth in a European Social Charter. The chief difference between the European convention and the Covenant on Civil and Political Rights lies in their provisions for implementation. The former created a commission of human rights which can consider complaints from states parties and, on an optional basis, petitions from individuals, organizations and groups. There is also a European Court of Human Rights which can adjudicate cases referred to it by the contracting parties or by the commission, but not by individuals. If the commission fails to bring about a friendly settlement of a matter, it draws up a report to the Commission of Ministers of the Council of Europe which, unless the matter has been referred to the Court, decides whether there has been a violation of the convention, and what effect shall be given to its decision. This committee also supervises the execution of judgments of the Court.

By comparison the procedures provided for the implementation of the Covenant on Civil and Political Rights are weak. No provision is made in it for either a court or a committee of ministers. The human rights committee, which is the conciliation body corresponding to the European commission, has nothing like the powers of the latter; its right to receive complaints from states parties depends, under an optional article, upon whether its jurisdiction is accepted by the state complained against; and the right of individual petition is relegated to an optional protocol. There can be no doubt that, in terms of practical results achieved, the European experience has been more successful than the universal approach in the United Nations; and this had led many people to conclude that a regional approach to the international protection of human rights is more likely to succeed than a universal one. But it does not necessarily follow that what has been true of Europe would be true for other parts of the world. Compared to other regions, Western Europe is a relatively cohesive community which was, moreover, as M. Teitgen had pointed out in his speech, motivated by its recent experience of gross violations of human rights in one of its parts and by a strong desire to erect ideological barriers against the spread of communism as practiced in Eastern Europe or any revival of fascism.

The special conditions which obtain in Europe hardly exist in any other part of the world. It does not necessarily follow, therefore, that the regional approach which has been successul there would succeed elsewhere. Moreover, as the history of the United Nations shows, some of the most difficult human rights problems have roots which extend beyond regions and affect the whole international community. Politically difficult as it may be, the efforts of the international community must therefore continue to be directed towards the creation of effective procedures for the protection of human rights under the auspices of the United Nations. But the difficulties facing a divided United Nations were, and remain, vastly greater than those which had to be overcome in a relatively cohesive Western Europe. It is relatively easy for states with radically different social systems to agree on ultimate objectives, but they have radically differing views as to how these objectives can be translated into reality. Here lies the real explanation of the fact that, although the United Nations has been able to agree on the definition of most human rights, it has not, like Western Europe, been able to agree on effective measures for their international implementation.

The conclusions just set forth have the benefit of hindsight. I was only just beginning to learn something about what the Europeans were trying to do and why, when on the morning after M. Teitgen's speech, I had to leave Strasbourg for London, where I had people to see.

Next day over lunch in the Strand, I read an account in the *Times* of the Strasbourg meetings. "There was a feeling," the newspaper said, "that the Assembly could have found more urgent things to do than discuss a convention of human rights for Western Europe where they are in general well observed." After digesting that perspicacious comment, I made a pilgrimage to Runnymede to prepare myself for a talk I was to have the next day with John Grierson, who had once been the head of the Canadian film board and was now the controller of film activities in the British central office of information. I wanted him to talk the British government into sponsoring a film on human rights in British history. He seemed to be interested, but the film was never produced.

I booked on the *Aquitania* because she was going to Halifax. A great ship before the war, during which she had done distinguished service, she now shared the fate of the aristocratic old lady who had to take in boarders, and passengers were packed into the cabins like sardines. I shared one with an elderly man who, having emigrated to Canada where he had lived for forty years, had returned to Britain only to discover that he was now a Canadian and was on his way back home. We were at Halifax on 31 August. Jeanne, both of her arms still in slings, was waiting for me on the wharf with Joseph and Elizabeth Nisot, who were also holidaying in Nova Scotia. The Nisots drove us to Chester, where Jeanne had rented a little cottage on the Back Harbor.

The Nisots came to lunch the next day. When United Nations people are together they talk only about the United Nations. We talked long into the afternoon. Our friends said that Western European countries had everything to lose and nothing to gain from membership in the United Nations and remained in the organization only to please the United States. Although he was a member of the Sub-Commission on the Prevention of Discrimination and the Protection of Minorities, Nisot did not like the human rights program which, he said, would give certain groups and certain countries the right to interfere in the internal affairs of the Western democracies without any counterpart. The international machinery for the protection of human rights, to which I was so committed, would inevitably become a propaganda instrument in the hands of people who wanted to destroy our democratic liberties. There was some truth in what he said, and I had to admit that proper safeguards would have to be devised against the danger, but some risks are worth taking. Arguing with people like Nisot—and I knew many of them at the United Nations—helped to keep me in touch with reality.

Apart from arguments with Nisot our Nova Scotia holiday was as uneventful as a good holiday should be. We went for long walks and I had a supply of good books. Schwelb, my assistant director, sent me a packet of papers from headquarters, including the proofs of part of Lauterpacht's new book on human rights. Although I did not like what he said about the Universal Declaration of Human Rights, I could not help comparing the bitterness of this idealist, who wanted too much too quickly, with my other friend who wanted nothing.

It was getting late for swimming in the cold Nova Scotian water. I did swim every day, but as the days got shorter I was glad to warm up afterwards before a well-stocked fireplace. I asked our landlord about trout fishing. When he replied that this kind of information was not usually given to foreigners, I told him that I was born across the Bay of Fundy in New Brunswick, but he never directed me to a brook. It was obviously time for us to return to New York.

The General Assembly was already in session when we arrived in New York. Schwelb had bad news: the Third Committee had decided to postpone consideration of the draft convention on freedom of information. Since it had already decided that the Convention on the Gathering and Transmission of News (which it had approved at its last session) would not be opened for signature until work on the convention on freedom of information had been completed, neither convention could come into force in the foreseeable future. Freedom of information was in a bad way in the United Nations. Several days later, in the Fifth Committee, the Belgians moved to suppress the budget item covering next year's session of the sub-commission. Although only two delegations supported it, their motion was a harbinger of things to come.

The advisory committee on administrative and budgetary questions had recommended drastic cuts in the Secretary-General's budget for 1950—a threat to the Division of Human Rights, because sixteen of the twenty-four new posts the Department of Social Affairs had asked for were for us. But I was encouraged by a rumor that this year Trygve Lie would defend his budget more energetically than he had in the past. For a few minutes I thought that the Canadians were going to help us. In the Fifth Committee, one of the advisers to the delegation beckoned me to his side to say that Paul Martin, who was representing Canada, wanted to do something to help the Human Rights Division. But when the vote was taken a few minutes later, Canada voted with the minority against restoring the estimates.

I had lunch that day with Roberto Fontaina, the Uruguayan member of the Sub-Commission on Freedom of Information, who wanted to discuss arrangements for the next session of the sub-commission, which was to be in Montevideo. Everyone knew that Montevideo had been chosen because, across the Rio de la Plata, the Peronistas had closed down *La Prensa*.

The fourth session of the General Assembly was a relatively easy one for the Human Rights Division and I had more time to devote to my office work which, in the light of my long absences from headquarters, was just as well. There were now two new senior people in the Division, Hilding Eek from Sweden and Lakshmi Menon of India. Eek, whom I had met at the information conference in 1948, later became the chief of the section on freedom of information. He left us in 1952 to return to academic work and later became the Swedish member of the European Commission of Human Rights. Lakshmi Menon, who replaced Amanda Labarca as the chief of the section on the status of women, had represented India both on the Commission on the Status of Women and in the General Assembly. She was a good speaker and had a colorful personality but was not interested in office work and was inclined simply to pass on to me without revision papers which had been prepared in her section. Not many months after her arrival she wrote to Laugier to complain that Schwelb and I were interfering with her work and to threaten to resign. She did leave us in 1950.

I was looking around for other candidates to fill the new posts just approved by the General Assembly, but I no longer had the freedom in recruiting I once had. I was not impressed by the lists provided by the personnel bureau, the chief criterion for inclusion in which was geographical balance. There must be something wrong, I thought, if sixty countries could not provide better material. I thought it quite an achievement when, after much argument with the personnel officers, I was able to bring in some good people. These included King Gordon, whom I had known in Montreal. Once the managing editor of the *Nation*, he was now with the Canadian Broadcasting Company. I also brought in Mehdi Vakil from the Iranian delegation, who later became the Secretary of the Economic and Social Council and still later the permanent delegate of Iran to the United Nations. Another recruit was Enrique Garcia Sayan who had been the foreign minister of Peru before a recent coup d'état. Francisco Cuevas Cancino, who had studied law at McGill, came to us from Mexico. On his retirement from the Secretariat some years later he returned to the Mexican foreign office and eventually became the head of the Mexican mission to the United Nations.

An international secretariat expresses itself chiefly in writing. It was essential, therefore, to have people who could write in at least one of the working languages, English and French, both of which I fortunately knew. It was natural, however, that all member states should want to be equitably represented on the Secretariat, and indeed the Charter provided that "due regard shall be paid to the importance of recruiting the staff on as wide a geographical basis as possible." And, while the Charter also says that "the paramount consideration in the employment of the staff . . . shall be the necessity of securing the highest standards of efficiency, competence and integrity," geographical distribution was already becoming the major criterion. The two criteria were often incompatible. If a man could not write—and our standards were high—in one of the working languages, he was not of much use, however brilliant he might be, in the Human Rights Division. But ability to express oneself in one of the working languages was not, of course, enough. We also needed people who could undertake serious research. We fortunately had some first-class scholars who could also write, and in my time all the research for which we were responsible was done in the Division. Much of this work is now done, I understand, by outside consultants. I also learned that diplomats and politicians do not always make good bureaucrats: the qualities that make the one may handicap the other.

I had lunch with Paul Martin, who talked about St. Laurent (then the prime minister of Canada) comparing him with Mackenzie King. St. Laurent, he said, had a deeper understanding of events than Mackenzie King ever had and was more sincere. King had not believed in either the League of Nations or in the United Nations, but under St. Laurent, the United Nations had become the cornerstone of Canadian foreign policy. I had no difficulty believing all this; but I could not help remembering a conversation I had had with St. Laurent during the first session of the General Assembly when, without any visible success, I had tried to interest him in the human rights program. I also remembered that it was under St. Laurent's administration that Canada had abstained in the voting in the Third Committee on the Universal Declaration of Human Rights.

At its summer session, the Economic and Social Council had asked us to prepare plans for a service, either within the Secretariat or as a high commissioner's office under the control of the United Nations, for the protection of refugees and displaced persons. We recommended the latter course since it seemed desirable that the officer in charge of the operation should have sole responsibility, within whatever directives he might receive from the General Assembly, for program decisions. The French delegation incorporated this recommendation in a draft resolution which, after much discussion and some amendment, the General Assembly adopted on 3 December. The debate in the Third Committee was bitter with charges and countercharges of violations of repatriation agreements, the use of war criminals and quislings in positions of authority in refugee camps and of propaganda to discourage repatriation, the barring of repatriation officers from the camps and the use of refugees as cheap labor. The communist countries energetically opposed the creation of the office which, they said, could not solve a problem that was one of repatriation, not of resettlement. My division also prepared the first draft of the statute of the office, which the General Assembly adopted on 14 December, 1950. The office of the United Nations High Commissioner for Refugees came into existence on the first of January, 1951.

I also had something to do with the appointment of G.J. van Heuven Goedhart as the first high commissioner. I had worked with him when he was chairman of the first session of the Sub-Commission on Freedom of Information; he had also chaired one of the main committees of the Geneva information conference and, in 1950, the Third Committee of the General Assembly. Van Heuven Goedhart was a man of strong opinions and this sometimes got him into trouble with the Russians, particularly after he became high commissioner. A journalist by profession—during the war he had been the editor of the underground newspaper, *Het Parool* —he had many talents. Amongst other things he played the piano very well and once told me that, as a young man, he had wanted to be a concert pianist. While still in office he died of a heart attack after a set of tennis.

In the fall of 1949, the Human Rights Division was working on a draft convention for the protection of refugees. The International Refugee Organization also had a draft. When Laugier saw the latter, he became very excited over provisions giving the contracting parties the right to oblige refugees to take their nationality after fifteen years of residence and also restricting their political activities, both of which, in Laugier's opinion, violated fundamental human rights. I agreed with him on the first point but not on the second. I could not see any valid reason why a refugee should be obliged to accept the nationality of the state in which he had taken refuge. But, in the interests of the refugees themselves, it seemed desirable that the host government, which did not have to admit them in the first place, should have the right to limit political activities aimed at the countries from which they came; otherwise, governments might be unwilling to admit refugees to their territory.

Laugier was now talking about changes that should be made in the structure of the Secretariat. All kinds of rumors were going around, including one that the departments of social affairs and of economic affairs were to be merged. An official close to the Secretary-General's office told me that the motive was to get rid of Laugier, who was not popular at the summit. I do not know whether this rumor ever came to Laugier's attention, but he was himself talking about his retirement. When that happened, he said, a new department of human rights should be created, all the other functions of the Social Department going to a new department of economic and social affairs. When Dag Hammarskjold became Secretary-General, the two departments were merged with the Human Rights Division as part of the new department, much to the disadvantage of the Division, which became the prisoner of a department where the methods employed and many of the goals sought were quite different from our own, and where, indeed, there was little sympathy for us. I suppose most of the economists by whom we were then surrounded must have felt that we were an exotic group of impractical do-gooders. Eventually, Laugier's idea came to partial realization; for when Sir Humphrey Trevelyan came to the Secretariat in 1958 as one of the two under-secretaries for special political affairs, the Division was transferred to his jurisdiction, and we became, in effect, an independent unit. Had this happened earlier I would have been saved the frustration and grief of my worst years in the Secretariat. But, at that time, I did not take Laugier's talk about a department of human rights too seriously, partly because we were too small, but that might have been remedied. The inspection service had recently recommended that the two sections on social defense and immigration in the Social Division be transferred to the Human Rights Division. But thinking, perhaps mistakenly, that this addition might divert us from our main objective, I resisted the move and nothing came of it.

The work of the special board of inquiry on anti-Semitism in the Secretariat, on which I had spent so much time, was now coming to an end. Sutch had prepared a draft report which I considered unfair to the defendants. I, therefore, decided that unless I could bring both him and Weintraub around to my view, I would write a minority report. That there had been irregularities, and that the complainants had suffered from them, I had no doubt; but I could find no evidence of discrimination on racial or religious grounds. After much argument at meetings which often went on late into the night, my colleagues asked me to draw up the conclusions as I thought they should read. I did so, and after still more meetings, Weintraub began to see the point. Whatever we might think of the way in which the defendants had run their service, the board could not find them guilty of anti-Semitism without evidence. They were, I argued (citing Article 11 of the Universal Declaration of Human Rights) entitled to be presumed innocent until they had been proved guilty. Although Sutch remained petulant, even melodramatic, it was decided that he and I should rewrite the report along the lines I wanted. It was forthright in its criticism of the defendants, but there was no finding of anti-Semitism. Sutch and Weintraub said that I had imposed my will on the board, but this was not true; I had made many concessions, some of which I regretted.

I look back to my membership on this board as one of my most unpleasant experiences at the United Nations. Several days after the publication of the report, one of the defendants cut me cold. Some three months later, the chairman of the staff association asked me whether I would allow my name to be put forward as the chairman of the joint appeals board which advised the Secretary-General on disciplinary matters, adding that I was the only person in the Secretariat on whom the administration and the staff were likely to agree. I thanked him for the compliment and declined the invitation. In the summer of 1951, I was appointed, without being consulted, the chairman of the Secretariat committee on discipline. Remembering my experience on the special board of inquiry, I wrote to Assistant Secretary-General Byron Price suggesting that the appointment might be incompatible with my responsibilities as director of the Human Rights Division, that I was too busy to take on another job and that I was often away from headquarters. I heard no more about it.

The fourth session of the General Assembly ended on 10 December, the date of the first anniversary of the adoption of the Universal Declaration of Human Rights. There was a concert that night in Carnegie Hall to mark the anniversary. Leonard Bernstein conducted the Boston Symphony Orchestra in a performance of Beethoven's Ninth Symphony and special music which Aaron Copland had written to honor the Declaration. Yehudi Menuhin played a Bach partita and Sir Laurence Olivier read the preamble of the Declaration. So began a tradition which lasted until Hammarskjold decided there would be no more human rights concerts. After his death, I was able to revive the series. According to his biographer, Hammarskjold "established the tradition of playing the last movement of the Ninth on each U.N. Day (24 October)." But this symphony had in fact, been played at human rights concerts long before Hammarskjold came to the United Nations. I wanted to have it played at all the concerts in the hope that it would become associated in people's minds with the Declaration in the same way that the Fifth Symphony had been identified with the cause of freedom during the war. But it was not always easy to bring about the necessary combination of orchestra, choir and conductor. The 1949 concert was marred, I thought, by a citation which the Department of Public Information gave, without consulting Laugier or me, to General Sarnoff of the Radio Corporation of America for his contribution to freedom of information and human rights. I had nothing against General Sarnoff, but the Secretariat had no business giving such awards and the Secretary-General could have been put in an embarrassing position had the choice been questioned by some member state.

The character of the concerts has now changed. Shortly before my retirement from the United Nations, C.V. Narasimhan (who was then my immediate superior in the hierarchy) told me that the performances were too Western in character, and that something would have to be done to make them more representative. This has been done, but at a price. The 1973 concert, which I attended while in New York to address the General Assembly on the occasion of the twenty-fifth anniversary of the adoption of the Declaration, was a good variety show with excellent folk dancing; but the original idea had been quite lost; for a variety show however good does not lend itself to world-wide participation through radio broadcasting, which was a feature of the traditional concerts. In sharp contrast to the days when a human rights concert was a world event and tickets extremely hard to get, in 1973 the Assembly Hall was not filled and most of the audience was from the Secretariat.

Laugier's Speech (1950)

When the third session of the Sub-Commission on the Prevention of Discrimination opened on 9 January 1950, the Russian member objected to the presence of P.C. Chang, whom he described as the representative of the "Kuomintang clique" and who, he said, had no right to represent the Chinese people at the United Nations. He then moved that Chang be excluded from the meeting. The chairman ruled the motion out of order on the ground that the members of the sub-commission were acting in their personal capacity and not as representatives of governments. He also said that the sub-commission was not competent to decide on its own composition. This ruling was challenged and when the majority upheld it, the Russians and Polish members left the meeting. Similar scenes took place that year in other United Nations bodies, including the Security Council, the voluntary absence of the Soviet Union from which (where it could have exercised its veto) made it possible for the United Nations to respond to the aggression in Korea.

A week after the opening meeting of the sub-commission, I found myself in the chair at the opening meeting of the ad hoc committee on statelessness and related problems and had to make a ruling on the same question. As the committee was a new one and did not yet have an elected chairman, I made a short speech and then called for the election of officers. Anticipating trouble on the China question, I had asked Abraham Feller, the legal counsel, to sit behind me. We both hoped that the issue would not be raised until the officers had been elected and I was out of the chair. But before I could get a chairman elected, the representative of the Soviet Union asked for the floor and proceeded to move that the Chinese representative be excluded from the meeting. A procedural debate could not be avoided. Most of the delegates took the view that the committee had not yet been properly constituted, and that no decision on the quesion should be taken until all the officers had been elected. I was in a tight spot. Not only did I have to be fair, I had to seem to be fair. I could not follow the precedent set in the Sub-Commission on the Prevention of Discrimination, because the members of my committee represented governments; and the solution urged by the majority was obviously wrong, since I had myself declared the session open. Feller advised me to rule the motion out of order on the ground that the committee was not competent to decide the issue. I thought that this was arguable and, in any event, did not want to appear to be the instrument of an anti-Soviet majority. I, therefore, decided to ignore Feller's advice and to put the Soviet motion to a vote. The motion was lost, whereupon the Soviet and Polish members left the room. The Russians had been unfair in putting a Secretariat official on the spot in this way, especially since it would have made no difference if the issue had been postponed until a proper chairman had been elected; but I had the satisfaction that the precedent I set was later followed in other bodies.

Although I did not follow Feller's advice in this instance, I admired his ability as a lawyer. His tragic death in 1952 was a great loss to the Secretariat and to me personally. He was dedicated to the United Nations and one of the very few people in the higher echelons of the Secretariat who seemed to understand the importance of the human rights program. Shortly after the incident in the statelessness committee, we drove together from Lake Success to Stamford, Connecticut to discuss human rights on a radio program. If he was nettled by my failure to follow his advice, he did not show it.

At its first session the sub-commission had done some very useful work drafting provisions for the Universal Declaration of Human Rights; but notwithstanding the high caliber of its membership, it was now doing very little chiefly because, I thought, it still had no well-thought-out work program. I suggested informally to some of the members that it draft a convention on the prevention of discrimination. But attention in the United Nations was still so firmly fastened on a covenant that would include all human rights that the idea that there could also be conventions on particular rights had not yet taken root. In 1946, the sub-commission did do the preliminary drafting of the International Convention on the Elimination of all Forms of Racial Discrimination.

Not only did the sub-commission not have a well-thought-out work program, but the fact that its mandate covered both the prevention of discrimination and the protection of minorities was still a source of confusion; its members did not know what was expected of them. The General Assembly had refused to include an article on minorities in the Universal Declaration, but it had also asked the sub-commission to continue its study of minority rights. I was afraid that it would, in the circumstances, dissipate its energies pursuing a road which led politically to a dead end and that further work now on the protection of minorities could become a kind of red herring which would prevent it from getting ahead with the prevention of discrimination, where it could be reasonably expected to make some progress. And this is what happened—at this session in any event. For it decided to continue its study of minority rights. It began by agreeing, after much discussion, on a definition of minorities, which it sent to the Human Rights Commission for approval. It was a good definition; subject to a number of "exceptions and complexities" set forth in the resolution, the term minorities was to include "only those nondominant groups in a population which possess and wish to preserve stable ethnic, religious or linguistic traditions or characteristics markedly different from those of the rest of the population." The sub-commission also recommended that the General Assembly adopt as its own the recommendations for interim measures that the sub-commission had made at its second session, but which had not yet been studied by the commission. And it drafted an article on minorities for inclusion in the covenant. Sixteen years later the General Assembly adopted an almost identical text as Article 27 of the Covenant on Civil and Political Rights. This article was recently used to find Canada in default of her obligations under the covenant in a case relating to an Indian woman who, having married a non-Indian, lost her status as a member of an Indian band and her right to live on an Indian reserve. A weaker statement than the one in Article 27 could, however, be hard to imagine. For the article, which is drafted in negative terms, gives persons belonging to minorities only a right "in community with the other members of their group, to enjoy their own culture, to profess and practise their own religion, or to use their own language," without putting any duty on the state to provide any special treatment of minorities, for example, in the matter of schools, without which most minorities cannot survive.

The sub-commission's two resolutions on minorities, the one with the definition and the other on interim measures, never got beyond the Human Rights Commission which, at its next session, decided it would be premature to send them on to the Economic and Social Council—an obviously political decision that confirmed my diagnosis that governments had no intention of doing anything in the United Nations to help minorities retain their identities.

I was dividing my time between the sub-commission and the ad hoc committee on refugees, the officers of which I had finally succeeded in getting elected. Its members were experts who knew not only what they were talking about but also what they wanted; and, in the absence of the Russians and Poles, the work on the refugees convention was moving quickly forward. It was a pleasure to work with them. I noted the contrast in my diary; while the committee was making progress the sub-commission was still groping for solutions. Paradoxically, the very brilliance of some of the members of the sub-commission made it more difficult for them to work as a team. The committee also had the advantage of having a concrete job of work to do and a draft convention, prepared by the Secretariat, on which to work.

The committee had been asked to draft a convention on the status of refugees and stateless persons and to consider how statelessness might be eliminated; but, in view of their great numbers and the urgency of the problem, it decided to address itself only to the problem of refugees, whether they were stateless or not; the question of the elimination of statelessness would have to be dealt with later. A difficult question was how to define the refugees who were to be protected by the convention. Because the majority of its members were worried by the financial implications a more generous definition might have, the committee rejected a proposed definition in general terms in favor of one defining refugees by categories—an unnecessarily conservative approach, since the purpose of the convention was not to provide material assistance but only diplomatic and legal protection. I was shocked by the attitude of the observer from the International Labor Office who objected to the committee's discussing anything relating to labor; he also suggested that the convention be sent to the I.L.O. for final drafting—a particularly blatant example of agency imperialism which was sharply criticized by the chairman, Leslie Chance of Canada, and by other members of the committee. The sub-commission adjourned on 27 January, but the refugees committee continued meeting for another three weeks. On the thirteenth I had opened the session of the committee of experts on slavery. It continued to meet until 23 March.

Laugier returned to his office that day, after a long absence. He and Marie Cutolli had both been badly hurt in an automobile accident in Great Neck, but he was looking better than I had seen him for months. I remember that he was annoyed because I had not been able to accept an invitation from the Haitian government to attend the bicentenary exposition in Port-au-Prince. The theme was human rights and I would have liked to go, but the Department of Public Information was sending several people, and there was no money left. Without consulting me, the Social Department protested to the Secretary-General; but when Martin Hill spoke to me about it, I told him not to press the matter. We had had enough jurisdictional rows.

The four members of the slavery committee were acting in their personal capacities. They were Moises Poblete Troncoso of Chile, C.W.W. Greenidge of the United Kingdom, Bruno Lasker of the United States and Jane Vialle of France. They had been asked to review the whole problem, not only of slavery, but also of practices resembling slavery; and they did a remarkably good job, thus confirming my opinion of the usefulness of committees of experts acting in their personal capacities. The members gave one of the most remarkable press conferences I ever attended at the United Nations. Spades were called spades and situations identified; and the talk was so frank that I expected a howl from governments. The correspondents stayed for over an hour. You could interest them in concrete examples of violations of human rights, but they apparently thought that building institutions for protecting those rights had no news value.

The Economic and Social Council, which had opened on 7 February, was discussing forced labor. There were many charges and countercharges. An African observer from the World Federation of Trade Unions made a spirited attack on French policy in the Cameroons. That evening I met and talked to the governor of the colony at a dinner party. Next day, Corley Smith of the United Kingdom attacked the Soviet Union, repeating the substance of a speech he had made a year earlier. But this time the defendants were absent. The Secretariat had been asked to ascertain if governments would cooperate in an inquiry into forced labor. Some governments had not replied, and the point was being made that a commission of inquiry could not operate effectively. I liked the way Sir Ramaswami Mudaliar dealt with the objection: to refuse to cooperate simply because other governments would not was not convincing. Governments which said there was no forced labor in their countries should have nothing to hide and no reason, therefore, not to welcome an inquiry. Sir Ramaswami became the chairman of the ad hoc committee on forced labor when it was set up in March, 1951. My division was involved in the inquiry and I assigned one of our people to the committee's secretariat; but the bulk of the responsibility—and I quite agreed with this arrangement—went to the I.L.O.

Hernan Santa Cruz came to me with the suggestion that, since the next session of ECOSOC would have such a heavy agenda, the Human Rights Commission should be asked to by-pass it and send the draft covenant directly to the General Assembly. I talked him out of it. Remembering that the commission had not been able to agree on giving a right of petition to individuals, I was afraid that any covenant adopted in 1950 would be a weak one. Some days later, I talked to Abe Feller, who agreed with what I had done: the best strategy was to refrain from pushing the covenant too hard, in the hope that governments might later agree on a stronger instrument. In the meantime, we should concentrate on strengthening the authority of the Universal Declaration while encouraging the adoption of conventions on particular rights. In retrospect, I now think that the advice I gave to Santa Cruz may have been bad and that I may have been wrong in thinking that 1950 was a bad year for adopting the covenant. As the years went by, the chances of getting a good instrument became progressively worse, for it was becoming more and more a vehicle for achieving irrelevant political ends. But my opinion, good or bad, had no impact on events. As things turned out, there was no question of getting the covenant before the General Assembly in 1950; and, in fact, the commission did not complete its work on the instrument until 1954, by which time there were two covenants, one on civil and political and the other on economic, social and cultural rights.

The sixth session of the Human Rights Commission opened on 27 March. After the Russians had moved for the expulsion of P.C. Chang, whom they called "the representative of the Kuomintang," Mrs. Roosevelt read a statement, which had been prepared by the state department, ruling the motion out of order. That was the chairman's privilege, but it was quite improper to give the impression that she had been so advised by the Secretariat. Abe Feller, who was present, was so incensed that he wanted to take the matter up with the state department. I had lunch with Mrs. Roosevelt after the meeting. We did not discuss the incident, but I wished I could have warned her that some people thought the chair was being exploited for political ends.

At lunch next day I discussed with Paul Weiss of the International Refugee Organization the possibility of the Human Rights Commission's doing something about the right to asylum. The Universal Declaration of Human Rights recognizes only the rights of everyone "to seek and to enjoy" asylum; there is no recognition of a right to be granted asylum. Under international law no foreigner has the right to enter the territory of a state without its permission; and, while some countries have been very generous in granting asylum to refugees, few if any governments are willing to give up their right to judge each case on its merits. I therefore thought it unlikely that the commission would take any action which would result in the recognition of a real right of asylum; and in fact it did not. Weiss was a stubborn fighter. It was partly due to his efforts that the Refugees Convention of 1951 (and, in stronger terms, the Declaration on Territorial Asylum of 1967) prohibits the rejection of refugees at frontiers or their compulsory return to any country in circumstances where they may be subject to persecution.

I was becoming more and more pessimistic about the fate of the covenant. My colleague, Mousheng Lin, quoting Confucius, warned me that I would have to adopt a more philosophical attitude towards my work, but this I was never able to do. Perhaps I was too zealous, as Hammarskjold later said of me. If my zeal sometimes got me into trouble, this time it was Laugier whom I got into hot water. Early in April, I told an American diplomat, quite brutally, that the covenant was being ruined by the excessive prudence of Mrs. Roosevelt's state department advisers. Although shocked, he was interested and asked to see me again. Having gone this far, I decided to talk to Andrew Cordier, the executive assistant to the Secretary-General, who I knew was in close touch with the state department. Amongst other things I suggested to him that it might be better if the whole operation was postponed until some more propitious time. I was still working on the mistaken assumption that time was on our side. At Cordier's request for a memorandum, I sent him eight pages, leaving out, however, any criticisms of Mrs. Roosevelt's advisers. Laugier, to whom I had first shown the memorandum, liked it so much that he wanted to circulate it to delegations. It so happened that he had been invited to speak the following week to the observers from nongovernmental organizations. We decided to put some of the ideas I had expressed in my memorandum into his speech. Abe Feller, whose good judgment I was coming more and more to respect, also liked the memorandum, but doubted whether Cordier would do anything. Later, he told me that he had himself discussed it with the American mission.

Laugier made his speech on 13 April. It was a courageous statement in which he raised most of the controversial issues then before the Human Rights Commission—whether human rights should be defined in precise or in general terms, whether states should be expected to surrender some of their sovereignty, whether individuals and groups should have a right of petition, and whether the covenant should include economic, social and cultural rights—all questions on which most of the members of the commission had already taken positions. Not only did he discuss the issues, but "en pleine conscience au péril auquel je m'expose," he took a strong stand on each of them. The rights should be precisely defined, states must give up some of their sovereignty, the right of petition should be extended to individuals and groups, and the covenant should include economic and social rights. Better have no covenant than a weak one. "De même que la mauvaise monnaie chasse la bonne, de même un pacte dénué de force dépouillera la Déclaration de l'immense autorité morale dont elle est actuellement dotée. Ce serait là, à mon sens, un évènement désastreux." In his own inimitable style—for he had rewritten the text that had been prepared for him—Laugier had given voice to the ideas set down in my memorandum. The speech was generally well received and Laugier was delighted. But it had an unexpected result, the negative reaction of Mrs. Roosevelt. When the commission met the next morning, she announced that there would be a closed meeting at 12:45. Although she had not consulted me, I guessed that the closed meeting would have something to do with Laugier's speech, and, as he was not in the room, I wrote him a note suggesting that he be in the conference room at the appointed hour. I still have his reply ending with the words, "lève-toi accusé."

We cleared the room and Mrs. Roosevelt brought up the matter of the speech; but since the other members had not read the text, it was decided to postpone further discussion until the afternoon. Mrs. Roosevelt was furious. After the adjournment, her eyes flashing, she scolded Laugier in the presence of a number of people. He had, she said, compromised the future of the covenant. I admired his restraint. When the meeting reconvened in the afternoon, it was soon obvious that the chairman's strategy would misfire. Charles Malik, Max Sorensen and others came to Laugier's defense and even congratulated him on his speech. This time they were speaking as individuals and from their hearts. Marguerite Bowie and H.F.E. Whitham (the father of a future prime minister of Australia) mentioned the British civil service tradition of complete objectivity but were otherwise sympathetic to Laugier. Miss Bowie even said that she agreed with much of what he had said. The outcome was a complete victory for the Secretariat. Later that afternoon, Laugier sent me the following note:

"Mon cher John,

Je suis très content de ce qui s'est passé ce soir. Vous devez considérer que c'est votre victoire; je vous en félicite. Et dans la mesure où votre victoire rejaillit sur moi, je vous en remercie personnellement.

Le seul problème sérieux qui subsiste est de décider s'il faut circuler le memorandum. Il y a du pour et du contre, je ne suis pas encore décidé. Réfléchissez. Nous en parlerons lundi.

Amitiés. Henri."

We decided not to circulate the memorandum, but I had had my day in court and I am glad that I wrote it. The fuss soon died down; and, contrary to what might have been expected—for they knew very well that the ideas expressed in the speech came from me—it apparently did not harm my relations with either the American delegation or with Mrs. Roosevelt. I had lunch with her tête-à-tête and an opportunity for a frank talk at the end of the week, the day before I left for Montevideo. She asked me for my uninhibited opinion about the work of the commission, and I told her what I thought. She then said that her government was now ready to have the commission recommend that a right of petition be given to certain nongovernmental organizations as an optional measure of implementation for governments which were willing to accept it; but she warned me that this did not necessarily mean that the United States would itself accept it. No one could have been more friendly. But Cordier was annoyed, and the incident did not improve my relations with him. He called me to his office and, although he mentioned only Laugier's speech and not my part in it, he was obviously upset. It was easier for him to confront me than Laugier, who was his superior in the hierarchy.

There was an element of comedy in the affair, which gave it wider currency than it might otherwise have had. For, while Laugier's trial took place in a closed meeting, the conference officers forgot to turn off the loudspeakers in the pressroom so that everyone in the Sperry plant knew what had happened. In the Human Rights Commission the routine was scarcely interrupted. The Americans and the British continued to do battle over the best way to draft the articles of the covenant, a question which had come up again in connection with the article on arrest and detention. Only Australia and Lebanon voted with the United Kingdom in its effort to get precise definitions, France and Denmark having abandoned the fight since the last session. The article speaks of freedom from "arbitrary" arrest or detention, without specifying any permissible limitations. The qualification "arbitrary" was insufficient, since the word has various meanings: it has even been argued that it means only "illegal," but the law itself may be unjust. No definition of a right is satisfactory unless it is precise and indicates all permissible limitations. It is only when you know all the limitations to a right—and most if not all rights have limitations—that you can know what the right is. Part of the human rights problem is how to bring them down from their high level of abstraction. The Americans were happy about their victory, but I thought they had weakened the covenant.

The commission examined the draft covenant article by article in the light of comments received from governments. One of the most controversial issues was, as already mentioned, whether, like the Universal Declaration of Human Rights, it should include economic, social and cultural, as well as civil and political rights. In 1949, Australia and the Soviet Union had so proposed, but no decision had been taken. It was now decided not to include economic and social rights in a "first" covenant, and to consider, at the commission's next session, the possibility of drafting another covenant dealing with them. But by the time the commission met again, the General Assembly had taken the matter out of its hands by deciding that the covenant should include both kinds of rights. Later, in 1951, the General Assembly reversed its own decision and decided that there would be two covenants, one on civil and political, and another on economic, social and cultural rights, a decision which, taken largely on ideological grounds, notwithstanding the rationalization that the two kinds of rights needed different measures for their implementation, split the United Nations down the middle.

Although the commission devoted nine meetings at this session to implementation, the results were even more meager than they had been in 1949, when, by a tie vote of eight to eight, it had rejected a proposal that a right of petition be given to individuals and private organizations. A proposal to give the right to such organizations was now defeated by a vote of seven to four with three abstentions, and one to give the right to individuals by eight votes to three, also with three abstentions. Some delegations envisaged the possibility of the right being given by a separate protocol, but it was clear from the voting pattern that opposition to an effective right of petition was hardening. It would continue to harden. And in 1966, when the Covenant on Civil and Political Rights was approved by the General Assembly, even the right of states to bring complaints was put on an optional basis. Somewhat ironically, it was in 1950 that the European Convention for the Protection of Human Rights and Fundamental Freedoms was signed. This regional convention, which came into force in 1953, does give a right of petition—on an optional basis it is true—to individuals, nongovernmental organizations and groups. But Western Europe is a more cohesive community than the United Nations, the membership of which reflects many different economic and social systems. It has already been pointed out that states with radically different economic and social systems can often agree on statements of aims and objectives while having radically different ideas as to how these objectives should be realized in practice. It is therefore not surprising that what was a relatively easy achievement in Western Europe should be vastly more difficult in the United Nations. But the commission did take one decision in 1950 which, while nothing came of it immediately, would be taken up again and become the basis for a short-lived periodic reporting system which could have become a useful technique for the international implementation of human rights law. It recommended that the General Assembly instruct the commission to draw up a plan (in connection with the Yearbook on Human Rights) for reporting by states on the manner in which they were promoting respect for human rights. But when the matter came before the Economic and Social Council, it was referred back to the commission for further study; and it was not until 1956 that a system of periodic reporting was set up, and then only because the United States was looking for alternative procedures after the Eisenhower administration had decided to withdraw its support for the covenants which, Secretary of State Dulles promised, it would never bring before the Senate for ratification.

Reporting is the implementation system with which the international community has had the longest and most successful experience—witness its use for well over a half of a century by the International Labor Organization—and had there been a will to make it work, the system set up by the Council in 1956 could have become an effective means for implementing United Nations human rights standards. In 1981 the system was abandoned on the initiative of the Secretariat for the specious reason that it had been overcome by Article 16 of the Covenant on Civil and Political Rights, by which the state parties undertake to report on the measures which they have adopted and the progress made in achieving the observance of the rights recognized in the instrument. But the covenant binds only those states which have ratified it, whereas the 1956 Council resolution was directed to all member states.

Also disappointing was the commission's failure to back up its Sub-Commission on the Prevention of Discrimination, whose difficulties it did nothing to help solve. Not only did it not forward to the Economic and Social Council the proposals for the protection of minorities on which the sub-commission had labored at the request of the General Assembly, it even failed to take any action on the sub-commission's definition of minorities. The commission thus contributed to a growing dissatisfaction with the work of its sub-commission and helped prepare the ground for the attempt which the Council would soon make to liquidate it.

On 22 April, my wife and I embarked on the S.S. *Uruguay* for Montevideo and the fourth session of the Sub-Commission on Freedom of Information and of the Press. Not long before this, I had learned that a committee of the Canadian Senate had been appointed to study a proposed Canadian Bill of Rights and that I would be invited to be the first witness. But, when Senator Roebuck telephoned to confirm the invitation, I had to tell him that I would be on my way to Montevideo on the date the hearings were to begin and would not be back at headquarters until late in the summer. Two of my colleagues went in my place. I mention the incident because, many years later, C.V. Narasimhan, who was then my immediate superior in the hierarchy, refused to allow me accept a similar invitation.

First Mission to Latin America   (1950)

It was at Laugier's bidding (saying I needed a holiday) that I made the long trip—over two weeks—by ship to Montevideo for the freedom of information conference. It was the gayest and altogether most pleasant sea voyage I have ever made. The weather was mostly perfect, and my wife and I spent our days stretched out in deck chairs or joining in the many activities, including Spanish lessons, learning the rhumba and the samba, cocktail parties and fire drills, that were arranged to amuse the passengers. In the dining saloon, we sat at a table presided over by the chief engineer, and our dining companions included two wealthy American widows bent on sharing their enjoyment with everyone near them. Another passenger was the pianist, Alexander Brailowski.

The Big Dipper disappeared over the horizon and the Southern Cross came into view. King Neptune came on board, and we became shellbacks. Two days later, my forty-fifth birthday was celebrated with all the trimmings, and that night we saw Recife in the distance. On May third, the ship docked at Rio de Janeiro where we stayed for the best part of two days.

We would have liked to see more of Rio, but we were tied to the ship's itinerary. It was raining when she steamed out of the harbor so that, just as at Naples a year and a half earlier, the splendid view was spoiled. By the time we woke up the next morning we were already approaching Santos. I slipped a raincoat over my pajamas and went on deck to watch the docking operations. Other ships were being loaded with huge sacks of coffee. We disembarked at nine and went by train to São Paulo. The railroad was an engineering marvel, running through exciting subtropical country.

For two more days the ship steamed along the seemingly endless Brazilian coast. We finally arrived at Montevideo on 8 May. Roberto Fontaina, who was to be the chairman of the conference, met us at the dock and drove us to the El Parque Hotel, where the conference was to be held and where we were also to live. I was soon at work. One of the first things I had to deal with was a report from headquarters that Mrs. Menon was saying (in the Commission on the Status of Women, which had just opened its fourth session) that I was sabotaging its work. There was not much that I could do about this at the other end of the Hemisphere, but I wrote to Laugier, Myrdal and Schwelb. Another letter from Schwelb told me that Myrdal was siding with Menon; but, in still another letter, he wrote that the members of the commission now understood the situation. Laugier cabled from Geneva that he had cabled Myrdal. I wondered whether I had been wise in leaving headquarters while the commission was in session; but, on further reflection, it occurred to me that it was just as well that I was not at Lake Success: better have someone else fight that kind of battle for me than to try to fight it myself.

That first evening, after a late dinner, Jeanne and I went for a walk on the Avenida 18 julio. At first we did not particularly like what we saw, but the city took on more interest as we saw more of it. Before going to bed we dropped into the casino, which was part of our hotel; Jeanne won eight pesos. Later, one of our interpreters lost a sizeable sum there. The next day was pretty much like a day at Lake Success: meetings with my colleagues who had arrived by air, working on documents and dictating letters.

I was worried about this session of the sub-commission and very anxious to keep its work on a technical level and away from political controversy. The choice of the site had itself been political: there was no freedom of information across the Rio de la Plata in Argentina. Amongst other things, the Peronistas had closed down the great Buenos Aires newspaper, *La Prensa,* and the choice of Montevideo was a kind of challenge. I knew from past experience that this sub-commission, whose members were mostly professional journalists, some of whom were also diplomats, preferred political debate to some of the more mundane items on the agenda. But politics was not our real business, and I also knew that, as with the other sub-commission, there was dissatisfaction with its work, both in the Human Rights Commission and in ECOSOC. It was important, therefore, that the sub-commission improve its image by doing a good professional job. There were two items on the agenda which lent themselves to this purpose, a code of professional ethics and a court of honor. I decided to encourage the sub-commission to concentrate on them; and when I visited Fontaina to discuss the conference, he agreed with my suggestions and asked me to incorporate them in a speech which he was to deliver on his election as chairman.

On my desk I had a paper on monopolistic practices which had been prepared for us by a New York professor. Because I did not like it, and the sub-commission had never asked for it, I decided not to circulate it. This was used against me later in the summer when the sub-commission was under attack in the Economic and Social Council. One of the sub-commission's members, who had learned about the existence of the paper, mentioned my failure to circulate it as proof that the Secretariat had not prepared proper documentation for the session.

I was suffering from a physical handicap. On the morning of our departure from New York I had wakened with a pain in my hand (my only one!), and by the time we reached Montevideo it was so bad that I could not shake hands, a very real embarrassment in a country where ceremony is so important. Fontaina sent me to a doctor who prescribed electrical treatment. I went every day to his office, but the pain was still there when I left Montevideo. It disappeared as quickly as it had come on the sea voyage which my wife and I later made from Buenos Aires to Genoa. In the meantime I had to do something about shaking hands: there were a number of receptions and I was often in the receiving line. I let it be known that I had a bad hand and, for the big parties, had it wrapped in a large bandage. The chamber of deputies gave a reception for the sub-commission and also held a special session in our honor. As a manifestation of solidarity with the Soviet Union and Poland, whose experts were boycotting the sub-commission, the communist deputies refused to come to the reception. We were also received by the foreign office and by the president of the republic. I gave two receptions myself, one for the local press and the other, as usual on such missions, for the members of the sub-commission and local personalities.

The session opened on 15 May. We went through the now familiar comedy of the communist walkout, but I did not have the embarrassment of being in the chair. The next day, Carroll Binder, who had replaced Professor Chafee as the American member, introduced a resolution on radio jamming which was, of course, aimed at the Soviet Union. It looked as if the Cold War would again be the leitmotiv of the session, notwithstanding the absence of the communist members. But the next day the sub-commission turned to the proposed code of ethics, a draft of which had been prepared by the Secretariat.

Thursday was a national holiday, in honor of the Battle of Las Piedras, and we were all invited for an outing at the vacation colony of the Usinas Teléfonos del Estado, near Minas. Our hosts must have wanted to give us some idea of how the welfare state operated in Uruguay. After a drive through rich farming country, we were enthusiastically received by the vacationists whose charming good will and spontaneity contrasted with the polite formality with which we had so far been received in Montevideo. We had a good lunch and were back at the El Parque Hotel in time for dinner which, by our North American standards, was always very late.

The next day the sub-commission returned to the code of ethics. Philip Jordan (United Kingdom) argued that journalism was a trade and not a profession. In a far-fetched statement, Binder agreed with many references to the corporate state, uniforms and so on. My own opinion, unexpressed, was that the trouble with journalism was that it was becoming a trade whereas it should be a profession, which was one of the reasons why I wanted a code of ethics. The sub-commission then deleted a provision in the Secretariat draft which said that the reporting of news should always be distinguished from comment. After that I did not expect much from them.

We were all invited to spend the next weekend at Punte del Este, having been told to have an early lunch on Saturday so as to make an early start. But only two members of the sub-commission turned up at the appointed starting place. Even Fontaina, for whom we waited a full hour, did not turn up. It was therefore nine o'clock in the evening before we arrived in Punte del Este, where we were taken to pleasant, individual bungalows and told to repair to a club house for cocktails. Jeanne and I took them at their word and went there immediately, only to find that our hosts had not yet arrived. Notwithstanding our very early lunch, it was eleven thirty before dinner began, and it was nearly three o'clock in the morning before we got to bed. There was a *contretemps* at the dinner party. Binder, who must have been as fed up with the business as we were, decided that it was the duty of the guests to give the signal to leave the dinner table, which he did. He saved us from getting to bed later than we did, but, in the result, Senator Payse, one of our hosts, was not able to make his speech, for which I was duly thankful because Uruguayan speeches can be very long. There was more of the same the next day. We were told to be ready for lunch at noon so that we could see something of the countryside on our way back to Montevideo; but it was two o'clock before we sat down, and without our host. He strolled in before the meal ended, but without his wife, who never did join us. The weekend had done little to promote international understanding. On Monday the sub-commission completed its first reading of the code of ethics. They had produced a weak document, but it was at least something concrete which would, I hoped, serve as the basis for discussions in other bodies and by the profession. In fact, nothing came out of it, partly because the days of the sub-commission were numbered. We then worked on a resolution by which the Economic and Social Council would have convened a conference of professional journalists to consider the draft code, but nothing came of that either.

One of the many advantages in holding conferences away from headquarters is that there is more opportunity for informal contacts. In this case, we were all living at the same hotel and taking our meals together. I had several walks in the Parque Rodo with P.H. Chang. Like "P.C.," to whom he was not related, he had intellectual power and long experience, but he seemed very young, which he was not—one reason perhaps for his charm. The member from India was Devadas Gandhi, the son of the Mahatma. I can remember very little about him except his praise of Stockholm's good vegetarian restaurants. Two of the most capable members were Karim Azkoul of Lebanon, who was a professional diplomat, and Stephen Dedijer of Yugoslavia. I knew Azkoul well from other United Kingdom meetings. He had a good sense of humor and made good company. He was also a loquacious speaker and could go on at great length. One night he took my wife and me to a reception given by the local Lebanese colony, of which there is apparently a counterpart in every city. I thought the affair would never end. Azkoul made a long speech in Arabic which had to be translated into Spanish. Dedijer was a rare person—an apparently authentic liberal who was, nevertheless, the spokesman of a communist country. Together with his brother, Vladimir, he represented Yugoslavia at many United Nations meetings in the early fifties. André Géraud of France, better known as Pertinax, was not a particularly effective member, but he was a good conversationalist and well informed about what was going on in the world.

Missions abroad also help to cement friendships within the Secretariat. One of the people I got to know better on this one was Enrique Garcia Sayan, a recent recruit, who had been the minister of foreign affairs of Peru before a coup d'état had forced him to leave his country.

On 25 May, Devadas Gandhi, William Farr who was representing UNESCO at the conference, and I all gave speeches at the Instituto Cultural Anglo-Uruguayo. My speech very nearly got me into trouble. Some Argentinian women who apparently liked it, asked me to make a similar one in Buenos Aires, where my wife and I were going after the conference. Without giving it any thought, I agreed.

The sub-commission wound up its session the next evening. Its performance had not been brilliant, but it was better than I had expected. The report even looked impressive considering that the session had lasted for less than two weeks. Apart from the draft code of ethics and the proposal to convene a conference of professional journalists to consider it, the sub-commission had adopted resolutions on radio jamming, freedom of information in a state of emergency, the free circulation of newsreels, the access of accredited news personnel to United Nations meetings and to countries where such meetings were being held, government intervention in the sale and purchase of newsprint, and discriminatory treatment and mistreatment of foreign information personnel. But the report was badly received in the Economic and Social Council, and for the sub-commission it was the beginning of the end.

We left Montevideo on the Sunday following the adjournment of the session, crossing the Rio de la Plata by the night ferry. I had no official business in Buenos Aires, our purpose being simply to see the city and to enjoy ourselves. We spent most of the first day on the Calle Florida looking at crocodile bags, ponchos and so on. Some of the shops were very smart. There was obviously a tradition here of good living for people who could afford it. But we noticed that there were hardly any imported articles. I could not find a battery for my American-made portable radio. After dark, the shop windows were quite dark because there was not enough electric power. And there were very few cars on the streets. Later, an Argentinian friend told us that she could not use her car because she could not find a needed part. There were other visible signs of Peronismo. Like their homologues in fascist Italy before the war, the customs and other public officials were noticeably arrogant in their treatment of foreigners, and there were other signs of ultranationalism. Nationalism was exploited everywhere and à propos of everything. It was de rigueur that every shop window display a picture of San Martin. The government adorned itself with all the vestments of power, and its arrogance was not limited to organizing manifestations before the Jockey Club. One day, all traffic was stopped on the road to Rosario—the second city of the republic—so that Perón and his Eva could have it to themselves. One of the largest buildings housed the department of war. Because Argentina had no external enemies, it was obvious that the role of the big army was chiefly domestic, and therein lay much of the trouble. The situation was much the same, Garcia Sayan said, in Peru.

The country was a paradox. One of the most fertile countries in a world clamoring for everything that it could produce, its economic and social life was nevertheless in a shambles. I could understand the social ferment which had brought Perón to power. His was a bad government which could never solve the country's problems. But much of the blame lay with the regime that he had overthrown. That regime may have been more respectful of the traditional political freedoms, but it had done little if anything to alleviate the social and economic injustices which made the revolution possible. I soon realized that real democracy would not come to Argentina, even if Perón were overthrown by the kind of liberals I met in Buenos Aires, well meaning and personally agreeable as most of them were. But the explanations later given to me by the Canadian ambassador were too simple. He said that most of the people who were criticizing the government were simply jealous and that any regime that replaced the Peronistas would be equally bad. This was the reason, he said, why the United States had decided to bolster up the regime until elections could be held: Perón had mellowed in office, and the Americans knew who they were dealing with. But the ambassador was probably nearer the truth than my *porteño* friends whose liberalism was largely a function of their wealth and privileged position, and who lived in a kind of nineteenth-century dream world. Who was I to tell them that they had abused their great privileges and that the root of the trouble in Argentina was the tremendous gap between the rich and the poor?

We had lunch that first day in a restaurant in the railroad station recommended by Devadas Gandhi, where we had the best chateaubriand I had ever eaten. In the evening we dined with Garcia Sayan at a restaurant on the Avenida de Mayo. Returning afterwards on foot to our hotel, we passed in front of the famous Jockey Club. I bought half a dozen oranges at one of the stands which the government had caused to be erected on the sidewalk in front of the club, in protest against everything that it stood for. The next day I went to the Canadian embassy to talk to Ambassador John Kearney, whom I had known slightly in Montreal, and that evening we reestablished contact with the other members of the Secretariat who were also in Buenos Aires.

The next morning Ambassador and Mrs. Kearney took us to a reception and later for lunch at the Jockey Club. What a fabulous place that was and what an oligarchy once made its headquarters there! I could understand the symbolic importance of the stands which encumbered the entrance. I then visited the modest quarters of the *Fundación Ana M. Berry para el Conocimiento de las Naciones Unidas.* This was the only voluntary organization in Argentina devoted to support of the United Nations. There had once been an Argentine Association for the United Nations, but it had been dissolved because its officers had preferred to wind it up rather than give the police a list of its members; they were afraid that membership in the association might be considered a reason for refusing the certificate of good character which one had to have in Argentina for so many purposes. The *Fundación Ana M. Berry* operated as a study group, and was tolerated because it engaged in no public activities whatsoever. Two of the women at the meeting, Mrs. Robert Salmon, wife of the president of the Argentina branch of Imperial Chemicals, and Señora Christina de Aparicio, wife of a university professor who had been forced out of his post because of his political opinions, often came to United Nations meetings representing nongovernmental organizations, and I came to know both of them well. It was refreshing to meet such a courageous group of women in a country where there was so much talk about *libertad* and *liberadores,* but so little freedom. I visited their association again before leaving Buenos Aires to see a film strip on human rights, which they had just obtained with great difficulty from Lake Success. These were the women I had met at the Instituto Cultural in Montevideo; and, pursuant to my promise, they had arranged for me to speak at the Twentieth Century Club the following Tuesday.

The next evening, after a drive to Tigre with Mrs. Salmon, my wife and I were entertained at a reception and supper at the Canadian embassy. I talked with the South African minister, who was upset by the possibility that the new I.L.O. fact-finding and conciliation commission on freedom of association might want to inquire into whether the blacks in South Africa had the right to form and join trade unions. I was pretty sure that it would, but pursuant to the rules adopted for the new commission, it would have to have the agreement of the South African government. The meeting of the Twentieth Century Club, at which I was to speak on human rights and the United Nations, had been advertised in the *Buenos Aires Herald* and there was some buzzing about this on the diplomatic circuit. Several of the diplomats at the party warned me that a United Nations official could not possibly, in the light of what was happening in the country, give a speech in Buenos Aires on human rights. I agreed that I would probably be sticking my head into the tiger's jaw, but pointed out that I was now publicly committed. Some of the officers of the Twentieth Century Club were also at the party and some pressure must have also been brought on them, because, later in the evening, one of them asked me if I would speak on some other subject. I refused. If they really wanted an incident, I said, the best way to bring it about would be to have the director of the Division of Human Rights speak on some innocuous subject—I mentioned bird life at Lake Success—to an audience expecting a talk on human rights. The result was that the invitation was withdrawn and the meeting cancelled. In retrospect, I think I could have handled the situation, but what the newspapers would have made of my speech I cannot imagine.

But I had not finished with the business. We were invited to a reception the next evening in the apartment of Señorita Larguia, a member of the study group mentioned above. Professor de Aparicio called for me in his car, Jeanne following with Mrs. Salmon. This was a strange procedure, but I gave it no thought. All I knew was that I was expected to talk informally about the United Nations and its human rights program. Miss Larguia's apartment was large and luxurious and it was packed with, I gathered, the top crust of the liberal elite, including the editor of the suppressed *La Prensa*. I gave my talk, after which Karim Azkoul and Azmi Bey, the Lebanese and Egyptian members of the subcommission, also spoke. Azmi made a brutal attack on the United Nations. "Les Nations Unies, c'est une farce," he said—a remark that was very much resented by an audience which was looking, somewhat pathetically, to the United Nations for help.

When the party broke up at a very late hour, the guests departed in couples and at intervals. Jeanne and I were driven to our hotel, again in separate cars. When I asked for an explanation, I was told that, under Argentine law, the gathering might be considered an illegal assembly.

On Thursday, 8 June, we regretfully said goodbye to Buenos Aires, embarking on the Motonave *Paolo Toscanelli* for Genoa and on to Geneva and the summer session of the Economic and Social Council. There were hundreds of excited, waving people on the dock when the ship pulled out. But it was not a joyous occasion, because, as I later learned, many of the passengers were Europeans who had come to Argentina hoping to improve their condition and were now returning, broke and disillusioned, to their former way of life.

The ship had already docked at Montevideo before we were out of bed the next morning. After a light breakfast we walked up to the Avenida 18 de Julio and took a taxi to the El Parque Hotel, where the Economic Commission for Latin America was in session. I had a few words with Pierre Mendès-France. Mrs. Salmon, the loyal and indefatigable observer of United Nations meetings, was also there. We brought her back to the ship for lunch. That afternoon we sailed again and were soon settled down to a quiet, relaxing routine. I had a good supply of books, including some supplied by Señora de Aparicio. One of them was Rodo's *Ariel*. Ariel turned out to be the European tradition, Caliban American materialism. Superbly written, the book had poisoned the minds of a whole generation. The proof of the pudding is after all in the eating, and Argentina has a lot to learn from the United States.

As the ship steamed out to sea the weather turned cold and grey like the north Atlantic, but the next day the skies cleared and I could see an occasional lighthouse. The stars were very bright, brighter, I thought, than in the north, but this was only because, living a city life, I had not seen them very often lately. A day and a half out of Montevideo we came close enough to the Brazilian coast to pick out details—cliffs, what looked like good beaches and, in the background the Sierra Geral. We lost sight of the coast again before reaching Santos. It was now quite warm and the sea calm. It was seven in the morning when the ship docked at Santos and we would be sailing again in the afternoon. We hired a taxi and drove around the city for two hours seeing the aquarium, the House of Birds and an orchid garden; but the best part of the excursion was the drive through the colorful streets, and the stop at a tiny harbor where we watched four or five small boats unloading fish and bananas. We had missed all this on our first visit to Santos.

We were in Rio the next morning. I watched the approach from the porthole of our cabin, getting a fine view of Copacabana and the Sugar Loaf. An official from the foreign office had promised to meet us at the dock, but he never turned up. So we hired a taxi and drove up to Corcovada and back by the Tijuca Forest. The view from Corcovada was breathtaking, but it was no place for someone suffering from vertigo, as I then did. We were warned not to leave the ship in the afternoon, but the last bag of coffee was not loaded until after four. As the ship steamed out to sea, the sun set behind the Sugar Loaf.

I returned to *Ariel*. Some weeks later, I read Count Keyserling's *De la pensée aux sources de la vie*. It was full of the same kind of criticism of American materialism. I had some other Spanish books with me, including Gregorio's *El Conde—Duque de Olivares*. I also had Bergson's *La pensée et le mouvant* and Gide's *Feuillets d'automne*. But the masterpiece that I read on that voyage was Joyce Cary's *The Horse's Mouth*.

We were now well into the tropics. The Southern Cross sank towards the horizon. The sea was a deep blue. And there was nothing to do but sleep, read, eat and swim in the pool. On Sunday, 18 June, we crossed the equator and, a few hours later, sighted the Island of São Paolo, which is nothing more than some rocks with a broken down lighthouse—the most desolate place I have ever seen. The ship blew her whistle to stir up the seagulls but not one was to be seen.

On Friday, 23 June, the ship docked at Las Palmas in the Canaries. She was late and we had only the evening to see the city. The wharf was crowded with hawkers selling giant dolls, shawls and cigarettes. A taxi took us into the city—bougainvillea, palms and banana plants, all in the most arid setting imaginable. Apparently it had not rained for months. But the place was clean, and the streets shone like a well-polished country stove. We had time to visit the cathedral, where many young people were attending a service, after which we had an indifferent dinner at the Gran Parque Hotel, the fashionable resort of the city, where the orchestra played American jazz, which took some of the edge off the adventure.

There is something to be said for travelling on a ship filled with people whose language you do not understand. But there were also drawbacks: I hardly knew anything about what was going on in the world. There was a news bulletin, but it was in Italian and, although I can now read an Italian novel with the help of a dictionary, my knowledge of the language was then nonexistent. But there were enough words in that bulletin with Latin, French or Spanish roots that I could pick up the gist of what it said. One day as we neared the end of our voyage, I was deciphering it as usual when I came across something about an invasion of South Korea. Could it be that we were on the eve of a Third World War? One thing was certain, the crisis would be a challenge for the United Nations. When we got to Geneva, I found that people at the Palais des Nations thought it would strengthen the organization. In retrospect, I do not think this was the case, but in 1950 we were all excited by the fact that the United Nations was finally responding to an act of aggression.

We were to leave the ship at Genoa, but she would first dock at Naples, which we were happy to visit again. We passed near Ischia at dinnertime and were in Naples not long afterwards. There was a full moon, but a slight fog on the surface of the sea shrouded the panorama as we came into the bay. Soon the lights of Naples were sparkling like stars. By ten o'clock we were able to disembark. Our plan was to walk along the via Caracciola, but a cabby persuaded us to drive to Posillipo. There were flowers everywhere and umbrella pines stood out against the sky. The streets were full of people. Our cabby, a cripple, and as much in love with Naples as he was with his horse, treated us as if we were his guests. It made us feel good just to be with him. It was half past one when we got back to the ship and still later when we got to bed, but we were up again at five thirty to see the view as the ship sailed out of the harbor and along the coast. The mist played tricks again, but there was another good view of Ischia and the other islands on that side of the bay. Next morning we were in Genoa. We said goodbye to the Motonave *Paolo Toscanelli,* went through customs and immigration and had time for a walk as far as the Piazza di Ferali before boarding our train to Geneva.

The first person I met on arriving at the Palais des Nations on Saturday morning was Laugier. He was in good form and we had a good talk. Because the International Labor Conference was winding up its session and in occupation of most of the Palais, no office had yet been assigned to me. There being, therefore, little prospect of doing any work that afternoon, Laugier took Jeanne and me for lunch in a restaurant in the Jura.

Four Questions of Policy (1950)

Although it was not on the agenda or its business, there was some discussion of the Korean crisis when the eleventh session of the Economic and Social Council opened on 3 July. The Council then turned to the draft covenant which the Americans wanted referred to the General Assembly without further discussion. It seemed to me, however, that the draft was not ready for the Assembly and that, unless it could be somehow beaten into shape at this session of the Council, which was unlikely, it would be better to send it back to the commission. I was pleased, therefore, when the question of what to do with the draft was referred to the Council's Social Committee.

My wife and I were the guests on the weekend of Moral Rearmament, which had taken over a big, luxurious hotel at Caux, high in the mountains at the other end of Lake Leman. The place was run cooperatively, there being no servants—some of the people prepared the meals, others washed the dishes and so on. I liked that. I could also agree that suspicion and mistrust are at the root of much evil and that love should be the overriding principle of social action. But I was repelled by an emotionalism which had lost touch with reality, and was reminded of James' *Varieties of Religious Experience,* which I had recently read. Most of the people there were from the privileged classes, and much of what I saw and heard at Caux followed the patterns described by James. I particularly disliked the public confessions and noted that the sins confessed were always polite ones. But I liked most of the people I met at Caux and would have liked to return, had it been possible to do so honestly. On Sunday, we sat at Dr. Buchman's table. It was significant that no one at Caux had heard of the Universal Declaration of Human Rights and that the only man with whom I talked who had ever heard of the United Nations Economic and Social Council, which was meeting at the other end of the lake, was an ex-communist trade unionist from Germany. Caux was high in the clouds in more ways than one.

The Council having decided to take up the report of the Commission on the Status of Women earlier than had been expected, I cabled to Mrs. Menon, the chief of the responsible section of the Secretariat, asking her to expedite her arrival. She replied that for personal reasons she could not be in Geneva until over a fortnight later. The Social Committee discussed the report in her absence. It was very badly received and would have had even more severe treatment had the predominantly male committee not been afraid it would be accused of prejudice. The treatment reserved for the report of the Sub-Commission on Freedom of Information and of the Press was even worse. Jacques Kayser had warned me that the French delegation would be very tough. It was a question, he said, whether the mandate of the sub-commission should be continued. I thanked him and reminded him that it was the Commission on Human Rights that had elected the members of the sub-commission. But, although forewarned, I was not prepared for what followed.

I had never heard, nor was I to hear again, such harsh criticism in the Council of one of its organs. Kayser led off with a devastating speech. Although supposed to be experts, the members of the sub-commission had, he said, spent their time discussing political questions which were beyond their competence. This was my own opinion and he may have got some of his ammunition from me, but I would never have been as harsh in my criticism. He then went on to say that the sub-commission had had the benefit of excellent documentation prepared by the Secretariat, which it had apparently never seriously considered. Coming from Kayser this was particularly serious because he was by far the most knowledgeable man in the Council on information matters. The debate was interrupted by the weekend. By the time it resumed, Azmi Bey, the Egyptian member of the sub-commission, had arrived in Geneva, sore as a boil. He was blaming everything that had happened on the Secretariat and wanted to address the Social Committee; but, because he was not accredited to the Council—Egypt was not a member—the committee quite properly refused to hear him. But he raised such a fuss that the members agreed to hear him at a private, unofficial meeting after the adjournment that afternoon. This gave me time to prepare myself for the attack I knew was coming. I remembered Azmi's bad-tempered remarks at Miss Larguia's apartment in Buenos Aires. He accused us of three things: the documentation prepared by the Secretariat was poor, we were late in getting it to the members, and the director of the Division had suppressed a working paper on monopolistic practices. I offered no defense on the first charge. Whether the documentation was good or bad was a question of opinion. The documents were in the record and I knew that some of the members of the Social Committee had read them. Kayser, the most knowledgeable member, had praised them highly. But I did make a vigorous defense on the other two charges. Some of the recent files dealing with the sub-commission had fortunately been brought to Geneva, and I was able to show that all the documents which the Secretariat had been asked to prepare had been mailed to members a reasonable time before the Montevideo session. I admitted that some documents had only become available at Montevideo, but everyone of these—including the draft code of ethics—had been prepared, *ex gratia* as it were, to help the sub-commission, but without any request that they be prepared. As for the paper on monopolistic practices, the sub-commission had never asked for it, and if it had not been circulated, it was because the director of the Division had thought that it did not come up to United Nations standards. I then asked the Bey how it was that he knew about the existence of the paper. He did not reply, but I knew the answer. He had stopped off in New York on his way from Buenos Aires and had been poking around the Secretariat where an overzealous member of my staff had told him about the paper. The Secretariat came out of the incident with its reputation enhanced, but I was afraid that I had made an enemy. This did not happen. My future relations with Azmi could hardly have been better. Membership on the sub-commission—he was a journalist by profession—was his first United Nations experience. Later he represented Egypt on the Human Rights Commission and still later became the permanent representative of his country at headquarters.

The French were not alone in censuring the sub-commission. Other delegations joined in criticizing its failure to concentrate on practical problems. But the decision that neither this sub-commission nor the Sub-Commission on the Prevention of Discrimination would meet in 1951 was partly based on other considerations. As Jacques Kayser later said (when the matter came up again in the General Assembly), the decision was taken in response to the Secretary-General's request that, for purely administrative and budgetary reasons, the number of meetings of commissions and sub-commissions should be reduced. The Secretariat itself was, therefore, partly responsible for what happened later when the Council decided to abolish the Sub-Commission on Freedom of Information. The administrative services in the Secretariat often made suggestions like this without even consulting the substantive service concerned, in this case the Division of Human Rights; or, if we were consulted, very little attention was paid to our objections. I still think that the decision to liquidate the sub-commission was a great mistake. Its performance may not have been brilliant, but potentially it had an important role to play. After its liquidation, there was no expert body in the United Nations responsible for freedom of information; and this is undoubtedly one of the reasons why, notwithstanding the hopes engendered by the information conference in 1948, the work of the organization on freedom of information has been so frustrating and has produced so little. The Council, and the Secretariat, played right into the hands of those member states which have no respect for the freedom and where the information media are instruments of political power. I have no doubt that, had the sub-commission been given a reasonable opportunity to develop an effective work program as the Sub-Commission on the Prevention of Discrimination (whose reputation in 1950 was no better) subsequently did, the story would have been different. I did everything that I could to revive it. When, in 1953, the Council's rapporteur on Freedom of Information, Salvador Lopez, made his report—much of which was written by my colleague John Male—one of his recommendations was that a small continuing body be created which would be an international coordinating center and a liaison agent between the profession and the United Nations. And, much later, in 1964, I was able to get the Rome seminar on freedom of information to recommend that the sub-commission be revived. But nothing came of either initiative.

All the bodies for which I had responsibility, except the Human Rights Division itself, came under attack at this session of the Council. The Sub-Commission on the Prevention of Discrimination had also had rough treatment by its parent body, the Commission on Human Rights, which had refused to send its principal recommendations on to the Council. There was also criticism of the commission even though, like the Council, its members were states. I had been disappointed myself with its performance at its last session, but I knew quite well that what it had been asked to do was probably impossible: produce a draft covenant in time for the next session of the General Assembly, a task which, as it turned out, was not completed until 1954 and after both the Assembly and the commission itself had taken decisions on a whole series of questions of principle, most of which were highly controversial.

Much of the Council's criticism was unfair and some of it uninformed. And all of it failed to take into account the fact that final responsibility lay with the governments themselves which were responsible for policy and the quality of representation on the organs they were criticizing. The United Nations was going through a period of retrenchment, and the human rights program, which although they paid lip service to it had a low priority with most governments, was an easy target. More fundamental perhaps was the fear of some governments that the program might be made to work. But whatever the reasons, what was happening was of the utmost importance—more important than I realized at the time—for it foreshadowed an attempt, not only to liquidate some of the machinery which had been created by the United Nations for the promotion of respect for human rights, but also to slow down the whole program.

Criticism is easy. My diary is full of criticism of the Council's own performance at its 1950 summer session. The Council discussed points of procedure, fine points of drafting and administrative matters at great length, but important questions of principle were raced over with a few generalities. When I was in law practice, I learned that it is easier to argue a point of procedure than the merits of a case. This is also true of conference diplomacy; and in the United Nations there are many delegates who owe their reputations and influence to their knowledge of and experience with the rules of procedure, although these delegates are not necessarily the most productive. It was a measure of the importance which governments attached to human rights and other social matters that they sent their youngest and least experienced people to the Council's Social Committee, just as the weakest members of delegations to the General Assembly were apt to find themselves in the Third Committee (Social, Humanitarian and Cultural). Mrs. Roosevelt was fond of telling how she came to be assigned to the Third Committee when she was on the United States delegation to the first session of the General Assembly. Her colleagues on the delegation were appalled by the fact that she was to be one of them, and when the question of assigning members to the various committees came up, Senator Connally suggested that she go to the Third Committee where she would do the least harm. The delegates sitting in the Council's Social Committee were not Mrs. Roosevelts. My friend and colleague Mousheng Lin called them the sophomores of the Council. There were, however, some very good people at the eleventh session of the Council and some of them sat in the Social Committee. When I look at the list now I wonder at their performance.

After spending the whole of a Saturday morning discussing what to do with the draft covenant, the Social Committee decided that, although there would be no detailed examination of the articles—something that was probably quite beyond its competence—all the main questions would be discussed. It was becoming more and more obvious that, even if the draft were sent to the Assembly, there would be no recommendation that the covenant be adopted that year.

That evening, the French gave a big party at the Chateau de Larringes where there were great quantities of champagne and good things to eat. The French liked to have the Council meet in Geneva, and it was part of their strategy to make the Geneva sessions more pleasant for the delegates than meetings in New York, but Geneva had so many advantages that their efforts were hardly necessary. Apart from the better summer climate, it was an international center with a long tradition, and there was something about the place, including its small size and the absence of the many distractions of a metropolis, which was conducive both to sustained effort and to developing an esprit de corps. I always looked forward to the summer sessions of the Council and to other United Nations meetings in Geneva. It might have been different had the headquarters been there: one of the chief attractions from my point of view was to be away from headquarters and its many interruptions and to be able to concentrate on the work in hand.

The Social Committee returned to the covenant on Monday. I was shocked by the position some delegations were taking on the question whether it should include economic and social rights. It was hard to understand why the Western democracies, including the United Kingdom and the United States, should be opposing their inclusion. To put the matter on its lowest level, this was hardly good strategy at a time when the Russians were absent from the Council. If the Cold War was being waged for the minds of men, the West was not doing a very good job.

That night Jeanne and I dined with Hernan Santa Cruz, who was the president that year of the Council. On Tuesday, the Social Committee discussed the implementation of the covenant. The debate could hardly have been thinner. The recommendations of the Human Rights Commission, weak as they were, weren't supported even by some of the governments which had supported them in the commission. I was disgusted. Better have no covenant than this one. I recovered my temper in time for a dinner party in our apartment at which we entertained Laugier, Marie Cutolli, George Davidson (of the Canadian delegation) and Jacques Kayser. The debate was more animated the next day. An American delegate was foolish enough to ask the chairman to sum up the discussion on implementation. Dehousse's summing up soon became a devastating attack on the American position. But by Friday, the committee was near a compromise on what to do with the draft covenant. The General Assembly would be asked to give certain policy directions on the general adequacy of the articles, whether the covenant should include special provisions on its application to federal states and non-self-governing territories, whether articles on economic and social rights should be included and whether the provisions envisaged for implementation were adequate. The draft would then be returned to the Human Rights Commission. I had made this suggestion informally a few days earlier. But Dehousse very nearly upset the applecart. In his haste to adjourn the meeting—Laugier said that it was because he was going to Brussels for the weekend—he very nearly prevented an agreement's being reached; but we managed to get a small committee appointed to draft an appropriate formula. It met on Saturday morning, by which time the spirit of compromise had very nearly dissipated. But there was now very little difference between the two main positions and, if the members of the committee had not been so tired and consequently cranky, agreement would have been reached that morning. Everyone now agreed that the General Assembly should be asked for the policy decisions; but the Americans still wanted the draft referred to the Assembly, subject to the possibility (this was already a change in their position) that it would be sent back to the commission, whereas the French were insisting that a decision be taken then and there to refer it back. On Monday, after a weekend of rest, the Social Committee decided, without too much difficulty, to send the draft back to the commission after the Assembly had taken the policy decisions, and this was later confirmed in plenary. This decision was one of the most important the Council ever took on the covenants, because the Assembly did reach a number of decisions which helped clear the air and make it possible for the commission to work more effectively at its next session.

The committee then turned to the protection of refugees. There were two questions to be considered: the report of the ad hoc committee on refugees which had met earlier in the year, and arrangements for the functioning of the new office of United Nations High Commissioner for Refugees, which was to begin operations at the beginning of the next year.

The definition of "refugee" in the draft convention prepared by the ad hoc committee, which was based on categories, was still controversial. A few delegations, including Canada and the United Kingdom, felt that it and hence the protection of the convention, should extend to all refugees; but the majority, including France and the United States, wanted the narrower definition which, they said, would be more generally acceptable to governments and easier to implement: the wider the definition, the narrower the protection that governments would be willing to give. The Council decided to retain the definition by categories, and this was confirmed in the final text of the convention as it was adopted by the conference on the status of refugees and stateless persons in July 1951. In particular, the convention only protects persons who became refugees "as a result of events occurring before 1 January 1951," a limitation which was removed for countries which ratified it by the protocol of December 1966. The Council then asked the ad hoc committee to meet again between the adjournment of the Council and the opening of the General Assembly to revise the draft convention in the light of the comments of governments and the specialized agencies. This meant that my wife and I would have to forgo a holiday which we had planned in northern Europe; but the business was urgent and I welcomed the decision. We were then hoping that the convention would be adopted before the high commissioner took office, for it was to be the principal instrument through which he would exercise his functions. A second instrument through which he was to work was the statute of his office (adopted on 12 August) a draft of which had also been prepared in my division.

This was a Saturday. The ad hoc committee on refugees reconvened on Monday. Robert Rochefort made his usual long speech about the great sacrifices France was making on behalf of refugees. If ever a tune were played to death, it was this one. Everyone in the committee room knew about and appreciated what France was doing, but Rochefort talked too much about it. He wanted very much to be the high commissioner. But he apparently became convinced that the post would go to an American, and when he called on me later in the week to discuss the matter, he said that he wanted to be the deputy commissioner at least. General Du Barr also wanted the office and invited me to lunch to discuss it in his house across the French border. My own candidate was van Heuven Goedhart. Later, during the General Assembly, when Rochefort had become the official French candidate for the post, he called on me again. He said that the British, who were supporting van Heuven Goedhart, had interests to protect that had nothing to do with refugees, but he did not say what they were.

The membership of the committee had changed since its first session, and Knud Larsen of Denmark was now its chairman. When the committee had met earlier in the year, I had thought that it was one of the most competent bodies I had ever worked with, but at this session I had difficulty controlling my impatience. I could discover no spark of generosity or of imagination in its members. It is only fair to add, perhaps, that the mandate under which it was now working did not give the committee much scope either for generosity or for imagination.

The ad hoc committee finished its business on 25 August. Although we had missed our holiday in northern Europe, there was still time for a week in Stresa before returning to New York. We chose Stresa, partly because Laugier and Marie Cutolli were taking a cure at a place near there, and partly because we had so admired the Lago Maggiore on our way up from Genoa. Laugier and Marie had left Geneva immediately after the adjournment of the Council. I had had one of my very few rows with him just before they left. It was something that had been stewing for a long time and concerned the editor of the Yearbook on Human Rights, one of Laugier's many friends, who had been employed as a consultant to edit the volumes. The arrangement had been questioned by the department of administrative and financial services and I had agreed that we could not justify keeping Laugier's friend on the manning-table. It was another case of his good heart getting us into trouble. A decision now had to be taken whether the man's contract would be renewed. I explained my position, but Laugier insisted on continuing the arrangement. His temper was easily aroused and we exchanged some harsh words, words which were all the harsher because Laugier knew that he was wrong. I was angry myself because the man had begun to attack me personally: Fernand Dehousse had shown me a scurrilous letter which he had written to the members of the Human Rights Commission in which I was described as the "enemy." Laugier must have been as upset as I was by our quarrel, because as soon as he arrived in Italy he sent me a friendly letter in which he said that he would leave the decision to me.

The Milan express was a train in a hurry. As it approached Stresa, I began to worry whether I would have the time to get all our luggage off. I moved it near to the door, but the stop was so short that I could not get the bags off the train and I was soon speeding off towards Milan with Jeanne left standing alone on the station platform in Stresa. All she had with her was a portable typewriter. Not without difficulty, she persuaded the station master to have the express stopped at the next station, which was a place called Arona, and I returned to Stresa on a local with the luggage. The next morning we telephoned Laugier in nearby Pallanza and he brought Marie over for aperitifs, but they wouldn't accept our invitation to dinner because they were on a detoxication cure. On Sunday they took us for a drive, and on Monday afternoon Laugier drove us to Orta for dinner. He had given up the cure, but Marie, who I suspect had stronger will power, remained in Pallanza. Our holiday came to an end only too quickly and on Sunday, 3 September, which was the twenty-first anniversary of our marriage, we took the Orient Express to Paris, where we arrived the next morning. Our five days there were not a holiday. I had meetings at UNESCO headquarters and had other people to see on United Nations business. The UNESCO headquarters were in the old Hotel Majestic, just across the street from the Hotel de la Perousse where we were staying. I spent the whole of the first day talking to various officials, including Alva Myrdal who, having left the U.N. Secretariat, was now the head of UNESCO's Social Department. I wanted UNESCO to put more effort into making the Universal Declaration of Human Rights known everywhere in the world. There was a meeting on this in the afternoon. I put all my heart into the discussion and came back to the hotel dead tired. The next morning I talked to G.W.W. Greenidge who had come over from London to see me. The Economic and Social Council had decided that there would be only one more session of the ad hoc committee on slavery and I wanted to make arrangements for the preparation of its report. I spent the rest of the day at UNESCO headquarters, and there was more of the same the following day. I also spent an hour and a half at the Palais Royal, talking to René Cassin about the human rights covenant. That evening we had dinner with Laugier and Marie. The detoxication cure was a thing of the past.

On Thursday, I returned to UNESCO headquarters to talk to the legal counsel, Hanna Saba, about the controversial question whether the covenant should include articles on economic and social rights. Saba took me to see the director-general. I found Torres Bodet a man of great enthusiasm and dynamic personality and came away from his office convinced that UNESCO would do everything it could to help me.

We returned to New York on the S.S. *Veendam*. My first impression on arriving was the heavy traffic, mainly trucks, rushing through Holland Tunnel. We drove on to Great Neck, where our luggage was unloaded, and I immediately returned to Manhattan. During my absence, the Secretariat had moved to the new building on Turtle Bay, where the Division of Human Rights was temporarily located on the twelfth floor, but we soon moved to the thirty-first, where I had a big, comfortable office at the northeast corner with a fine view over the East River. But many of the other offices were small and some had no natural light. Some of the junior officers had to share offices, and the secretaries were grouped together in a kind of corridor. Not long after we moved to the thirty-first floor, I had to deal with a petition complaining about the conditions under which my staff had to work. So much for the great new building which was supposed to revolutionize modern architecture. Psychologically, one of the chief drawbacks was the fact that all the movement was up and down, with the result that most members of the Secretariat saw only those colleagues who worked on the same floor. There was something to be said for the long corridors at Lake Success and in the Palais des Nations.

Since the committee rooms were not ready yet in the new building, and the General Assembly's Third Committee was therefore to meet at Lake Success, I also kept my office in the Sperry plant, where most of the other offices were being demolished and it was so noisy that it was practically impossible to work. The fifth session of the General Assembly opened on 19 September and the Third Committee had its first meeting the next day. Van Heuven Goedhart was elected chairman. I enjoyed working with him, but he did not turn out to be the strong chairman I had expected. On 14 December he was elected the first United Nations High Commissioner for Refugees.

I had returned from Paris full of the idea, which I had been trying to get UNESCO to adopt, that the United Nations and the specialized agencies should undertake a world-wide educational program for the promotion of human rights. The Americans with whom I talked about it were interested, and I drafted a resolution for adoption by the General Assembly. Nothing came of it, but on 20 October, I did succeed in getting the Secretary-General to address a letter to member states, asking them to set aside 10 December every year in commemoration of the proclamation of the Universal Declaration of Human Rights. This was reproduced in a memorandum for the Assembly on the steps which forty-two states had taken in 1949 to celebrate the anniversary. It was about this time that Mrs. Roosevelt asked me if I could suggest some initiative that her delegation might take in the Third Committee. I suggested a resolution designating December 10 as Human Rights Day. She was delighted with the idea, and her delegation moved the resolution which, passed on 4 November, invited all states and interested organizations to adopt 10 December of each year as Human Rights Day.

I talked to the Assistant Secretary-General in charge of the Department of Public Information, Benjamin Cohen, about my conversations with UNESCO, but his department was unhappy about what I had done, and later, when I wanted to send one of my people to Paris to work out the details of a program, they tried to prevent him from going. Tor Gjesdal, the top-ranking director, said that we had no right to be dealing with such a matter, but

I stuck to my guns and my man went to Paris. Notwithstanding our rivalries, my personal relations with Cohen and Gjesdal were always good. A few days after this talk, and after the Soviet Union had announced that it would veto the reappointment of Lie as Secretary-General, Gjesdal, who was very close to him, told me that Lie thought the Soviet Union wanted to destroy the United Nations but that he would carry the fight into the General Assembly.

The Division had prepared a paper for the Assembly on the policy decisions the latter was being asked to make in connection with the covenant. Because of its importance, Laugier thought that it would be wise to have Cordier's approval, but all I got from him was a series of grunts. Before discussing the covenant, the Third Committee had first to consider the report of the Economic and Social Council. Azmi was now a member of the Egyptian delegation and this was his chance to defend the Sub-Commission on Freedom of Information and his role in it. One of the first things I had been told on my return to headquarters was that he was preparing to do battle against both ECOSOC and the Secretariat; and I had warned Jacques Kayser whose speech in the Council had especially angered him. But Azmi's bark turned out to be worse than his bite, for he did not even mention the Secretariat. His intervention was even useful, because the Assembly adopted his suggestion that the Council be asked to reconsider its decision not to schedule a session of the sub-commission in 1951, a resolution that was supported by Kayser himself, the chief critic of the sub-commission, who referred to the "great task" it had to perform. But this was only a reprieve; the sub-commission was doomed, and it held its last session in 1952. On the initiative of Hérard Roy, who was the Haitian member of the Sub-Commission on the Prevention of Discrimination, the Assembly also invited the Council to reconsider its decision cancelling the 1951 session of that body, which has continued to meet ever since.

Most of the Latin American delegations attacked the ad hoc committee on slavery, accusing it of bias. The representative of Colombia said that his delegation "could place little confidence in experts who apparently were engaged in investigating cases of slavery in an area, namely Latin America, where it did not exist." Peru moved that the ad hoc committee be replaced by a new committee of twelve members of the Economic and Social Council, a decision which, if it had been adopted, would have replaced an expert body of individuals acting in their personal capacity by a committee of representatives of governments. He referred to the committee's questionnaire which mentioned institutions in Latin America analogous to slavery, which, he said, "bore out his contention that the investigation was not objective." The truth was, of course, that there were institutions in Latin America analogous to slavery and that the terms of reference of the committee were not limited to chattel slavery. The Latin Americans had been cut to the quick, but the Peruvian motion was rejected.

Notwithstanding the indifferent performance of the Sub-Commission on Freedom of Information and the Council's reaction to it, I still believed that freedom of information would continue to be a major concern of the United Nations. The recent criticisms made it even more important that something be done to improve the services of the Secretariat. I, therefore, pleaded with Jacques Kayser to join us and help put the sub-commission on its feet. Eventually, he did—on a temporary basis as a consultant—but he refused to work in New York. Kayser told me that he heard that the Human Rights Division would be attached to the legal department in a reorganization of the Secretariat. Anything but that, I said. Although a lawyer, I did not want the human rights program to become part of a predominantly legal operation. We were in the business of making new law, and too close association with professional lawyers might be a restraint. I soon heard the same rumor from other sources. I talked to Laugier who agreed that the move should be resisted. In retrospect, however, I think it would have been better had the Division gone to the legal department rather than to the combined Department of Economic and Social Affairs, which is what happened after Hammarskjold became Secretary-General. Hindsight is often better than foresight.

Laugier told me that he had definitely decided not to stand for reappointment at the end of his term of office. Under no circumstances would he, he said, continue to serve under Trygve Lie. But not long after this, when in the Security Council the Soviet Union vetoed Lie's own reappointment, Laugier rallied to his support. If Lie's mandate were not extended, it would be solely because of the stand he had taken in the Korean crisis. Was it fair, Laugier asked, that he should now be punished for his loyalty to an ideal? And would any other candidate worth his salt accept the post if Lie were dropped? But Lie had apparently decided not to keep Laugier. I heard that he would be the Secretary-General's candidate for the new post of high commissioner for refugees. When I mentioned this to Laugier, he was visibly disturbed. The truth was that he did not want to leave the United Nations and was still hoping, notwithstanding what he had told me about his intention to retire, that Lie would ask him to stay on as Assistant Secretary-General; and he was upset by a rumor which seemed to confirm that he would be retiring in the spring.

The Third Committee began to discuss the covenant on 18 October, when the British again criticized the loose drafting. Later, the Assembly decided that the drafting would have to be improved and that the rights and permissible limitations on their enjoyment should be defined with the greatest possible precision. This would end, I thought, the long fight between the United Kingdom and the United States, which was one of the reasons why the Assembly did not have a final draft before it at this session. But I was being carried away by my optimism.

One of the policy questions referred to the General Assembly was whether the covenant should include a federal states clause, the purpose of which would have been to relieve a federal government from responsibility for matters which, under the constitution, were beyond its jurisdiction. Professor Bokhari of Pakistan made a brilliant speech opposing the inclusion of the clause, and it looked as if a majority would agree with him. This would create serious difficulties for countries like Canada and the United States, where many human rights matters fall within the jurisdiction of the constituent units. In the past, federal states clauses had been included in multilateral treaties almost as a matter of course; but the argument was now being made that they were not fair to unitary states on whose treaty obligations there was no limitation. The argument was hard to answer, but I thought that it was specious in a human rights context where the objective should have been to get as many countries as possible to sign and ratify the convention. There was even greater opposition to the inclusion of the traditional territorial application or colonial clause. The expressed reasoning behind this opposition was the desire to have the protection of the covenant extend to all parts of both metropolitan and colonial territories; but it ignored the fact, which I as a Canadian could understand, that, in the process of political emancipation, a point could be reached where the metropolitan power no longer had the right either to enter into treaties on behalf of or to legislate for the colony. In other words, a very strong argument could be made that a colonial application clause was necessary if local autonomy was to be respected. But the feeling against the colonial powers was running so high that arguments like this fell of deaf ears.

The Assembly instructed the Human Rights Commission to prepare recommendations which would secure "the maximum extension of the covenant to the constituent units of federal states," and also meet their constitutional problems. This was interpreted by the commission as a decision to exclude any federal state article, and the final text of both covenants provides that their provisions shall extend to all parts of federal states without any limitations or exceptions. The position of the Assembly on the inclusion of a territorial application clause was peremptory; for it instructed the commission to include an article worded as follows: "The provisions of the present Covenant shall extend to or be applicable equally to a signatory metropolitan state and to all its territories, be they non-self-governing, trust or colonial territories, which are being administered or governed by such metropolitan state." This was much more than the exclusion of a territorial clause; it was a new kind of territorial clause with a different purpose. The commission was also asked to study ways and means which would ensure the right of peoples and nations to self-determination. These decisions marked the beginning of the politicization of the covenants. The developing countries were in revolt, and new voices were beginning to be heard. My own reaction was ambivalent. I welcomed the new impetus that was being given to the human rights program as a result of the importance that the developing countries were now attaching to it. But, although I believed in self-determination as a political principle in the sense in which it is mentioned in Article 1 of the Charter, I did not think it should or indeed could be made into an enforceable legal right; and I was worried by the politicization of the covenant, which was becoming a pawn in the fight against colonialism. In 1950, it seemed quite unlikely that any of the colonial powers would ratify an instrument which made self-determination into a legal right. The proponents of that proposition were intent on scoring an immediate victory, even if it were only in words, and apparently quite indifferent to the fate of the covenant. When the real test came—the creation of effective machinery for its international implementation—they would back away. They would also invent their own definition of the right to self-determination. Notwithstanding the clear language of the two covenants as they were finally adopted, it would be understood in United Nations doctrine as a right belonging only to colonial peoples, which once it had been successfully exercised could not be invoked again, and it would not include a right of secession except for colonies.

René Cassin complained to me about these developments, forgetting perhaps that he was representing a country which was partly responsible for what was happening. About a week later, Mrs. Roosevelt gave a reception for the members of the Third Committee. We had a short talk about the new turn that the debate was taking. She agreed that the Third Committee was in revolt, a revolt, she said, of dark-skinned peoples against the whites; she had told her colleagues on the United States delegation that it would be wise to study the mood of the Third Committee: "if you want to know what other countries really think of us, come into the Third Committee." This committee was supposed to be nonpolitical, and a sharp distinction was always drawn between it and the First and ad hoc political committees. In the latter, where the issues were more often than not drawn on Cold War lines, a delegate had to stand up and be counted in the knowledge that the position he took might later be used against his country. Because it was thought to be less important, delegations in the Third Committee were less inhibited and said what they really thought.

The next policy question to be decided was whether the covenant would include economic, social and cultural rights. The consensus first seemed to be that, if they were not included in a first instrument, another covenant would have to be drafted forthwith. One of the very few delegations opposed to including them in any covenant was the Canadian. I was also struck by the negative attitude of the International Labor Organization. The speech which its observer, Mr. C.V. Phelan, made on the afternoon of 30 October could only be interpreted as a warning to the United Nations not to tread on I.L.O. territory. Referring to this speech, René Cassin said that "a unilateral warning against encroaching upon the sphere of action of the I.L.O. was not enough," and he asked its observer for a complementary statement indicating concretely how his organization envisaged cooperating with the Commission on Human Rights. Phelan then said that his organization believed the drafting of the articles should be a joint operation.

The Assembly decided that the covenant should include articles on economic, social and cultural rights and that the specialized agencies, including the International Labor Organization, should help draft them. But, at its next session, by a resolution that split the Assembly down the middle, this decision was reversed; there were now to be two covenants, one on economic, social and cultural rights and another on civil and political rights. The views of the specialized agencies were heard and acted on at the commission's seventh session in 1951 when the I.L.O., bent on protecting its jurisdiction, succeeded in watering down the articles—a task made easier for them by the instructions I had from Trygve Lie not to oppose their demands.

The last of the policy questions related to implementation, the big issue being whether individuals and groups would have a right of petition. The Assembly instructed the commission "to proceed with the consideration of provisions, to be inserted in the draft covenant or in separate protocols, for the receipt and examination of petitions from individuals and organizations with respect to alleged violations of the covenant," an instruction which the more conservative Human Rights Commission chose to ignore.

A proposal sponsored by Uruguay, which was not adopted, contemplated the creation of an office of United Nations Attorney General for Human Rights which would receive complaints, including complaints from individuals and groups, and act on behalf of the complainants as plaintiff in proceedings before a standing committee. He would also be responsible for the general supervision of the covenant, would undertake investigations ex officio and attempt to secure amicable settlement before referring disputes to the standing committee. The idea had been given to the Uruguayans by Moses Moskowitz, the observer at the U.N. for the Coordinating Council of Jewish Agencies. Had it been adopted, the plan would have effectively dealt with the argument often advanced against an individual right of petition that, if granted, the United Nations would be swamped by petitions. But the plan was never seriously considered. Many years later, a proposal of which I myself was the author was made for setting up an office of United Nations High Commissioner for Human Rights. Often confused with the Uruguayan proposal, it was really quite different.

Jean Lesage, then a junior minister in the Canadian government, but who was later to preside over *la révolution tranquille* as premier of Quebec, was representing Canada in the

Third Committee. I took him to lunch, thinking that he might help move the Canadians away from their negative position in the matter of the international protection of human rights. He told me that the leader of the conservative element in the Canadian cabinet, which was so chary about human rights, was C.D. Howe. Later I gave him some notes for a statement which might be made in plenary to help correct the bad impression Canada had made in the Third Committee, but they were never used.

About this time the newspapers were carrying accounts of trials of "collaborationists" in South Korea. It was shocking that this kind of thing should be going on under the auspices of the United Nations. I suggested to Laugier that he ask the Secretary-General to make a statement drawing attention to the Universal Declaration of Human Rights. Laugier said that I should go to Korea. There was a meeting in his office, at which Alfred Katzin, the Secretary-General's personal representative in Korea, was present. Katzin assured us that proper procedures would be followed in the proposed trials, but we remained skeptical and the Division prepared a letter for Laugier to send to the Secretary-General.

It was during this session of the Assembly that I had a quarrel with Andrew Cordier, who was not only the executive assistant to the Secretary-General but also the officer in charge of the Assembly and the most powerful man in the house after the Secretary-General himself. My relations with him were never good and this may be one of the reasons why I had so much trouble with the Secretary-General's office, particularly under Hammarskjold. I had already had one unpleasant experience with him over a picayune incident in 1947, when he was personally criticized in the Third Committee for some arrangements he had made as the officer in charge of the Assembly. Some of the committee's items had been disposed of in plenary while the committee was in session, with the result that the delegates responsible for them were not in their places. The committee spent the whole of a morning protesting these arrangements, after which the Secretariat was asked for an explanation and Cordier's personal attention. As the senior officer at the meeting, I thought it was my duty to go to Flushing Meadows, where he had an office, to report the incident. Cordier kept me waiting for two hours, received me very badly and gave me exactly two minutes. The matter, he said, should have been arranged between the chairman of the committee and the president of the assembly (which was nonsense) and there would be no explanation from the Secretariat.

What now happened was more serious. A new member of the Secretariat had prepared a paper for circulation in the Third Committee. Instead of following normal routine and clearing the paper, which was of minor importance, at the departmental level, he sent it to the office of the Secretary-General for approval. I wrote him a note suggesting that this was unnecessary. The officer then sent my note to Cordier who came down to the conference room in a temper. He could not understand, he said, reprimanding me, that a director who had been in the Secretariat since 1946 could be ignorant of the coordinating role of the office of the Secretary-General. He then sent me a sharply worded note repeating the rebuke. I knew all about the role of this high office, but I also thought that it was good administrative practice to protect it against a proliferation of paper concerning matters which could and should be dealt with at a lower level. Unwisely perhaps, I made an issue of the matter—for I knew that his intention must have been that his letter would remain in my dossier—but although other people in the Social Department took up my defense, Cordier could not be moved to apologize or to withdraw the letter. It was like arguing with Jehovah.

Many years later, in 1957, I was again the target of a similar outburst of temper. I was about to go on a mission to the Far East and the Chinese delegation wrote to the Secretary-General asking him to have me visit Taiwan. In his heavy handwriting, Cordier scrawled a comment on the letter to the effect that, in his opinion, I had solicited the invitation. In fact I had not, although I can imagine circumstances in which it would have been quite proper for me to do so. Cordier must have known that his insulting comment would be seen by other people, including myself. I did go to Taiwan and when I got there I discovered the real reason for the invitation. The government was being pressed by complaints that overseas Chinese were being persecuted in various Southeast Asian countries. There was very little they could do about this, but to have the director of the Division of Human Rights receive a delegation—which I did—was at least the appearance of action.

Fortunately, I had other things to worry about. In 1950, one of these was whether there would be a second human rights concert. Sir Thomas Beecham had been asked to conduct the Brahms Alto Rhapsody, but he was insisting that someone he considered his equal conduct the rest of the concert. It was not easy to find such a person at short notice and the Department of Public Information wanted to cancel the concert. I talked to Benjamin Cohen and Peter Aylen, a Canadian friend who was the director of the Radio Division. We decided to ask Fritz Busch to conduct the whole concert, which was held in the Metropolitan Opera House. As it turned out, Busch conducted Beethoven's Fifth and Sir Ernest MacMillan led the Schola Cantorum in a performance of the Halleluja Chorus from Handel's *Messiah*. Marian Anderson sang a Brahms rhapsody, and Claudio Arrau played Chopin's First Piano Concerto. Judith Anderson read the preamble of the Universal Declaration in English, and Charles Boyer read it in French. The president of the General Assembly made a speech and so did Mrs. Roosevelt.

Laugier was in a bad humor and scolded me during the intermission. He said that the concert should have been a popular manifestation in the Madison Square Garden, forgetting, I suppose, that it was a United Nations affair and not meant for the population of New York. He fulminated against the German music and German conductor. This was the occasion mentioned earlier on which he scolded me because the invitation called for black ties. I attributed his bad humor to his impending retirement, which he deeply resented.

The Third Committee was now discussing the revised draft convention on the protection of refugees and a draft protocol on statelessness which the ad hoc committee on refugees had prepared at its second session. A proposal to convene a plenipotentiary conference to complete the drafting of these instruments and open them for signature was adopted. Australia wanted the work of the conference referred back to the General Assembly for final approval; but this was fortunately rejected. The mistake made for the 1948 information conference would not be repeated. After one of these meetings, I saw Paul Robeson in the delegates' lounge. He had brought a group of youngsters to stage a "sit-in" protesting against President Truman's statement on the possible use of the atomic bomb in the Korean War. The youngsters were sitting on the cold floors of the corridors, but the great singer was comfortably seated in the lounge. All my sympathy was with the demonstrators, but I thought Robeson's proper place was in the corridors on the floor with the youngsters. Not long after that I heard him sing at a Soviet reception.

The last business of the Third Committee was a complaint that the U.S.S.R. had failed to repatriate or otherwise account for large numbers of prisoners of war still in the Soviet Union. The Soviet delegation insisted that all prisoners had long since been repatriated. The debate was acrimonious, and when the chairman said that he intended to circulate communications received from three nonmember states, the Russians accused the Secretariat of belonging to the Anglo-American bloc. The Assembly called on governments to respect the recognized standards of international conduct requiring that all prisoners of war be repatriated on the cessation of hostilities, and requested the Secretary-General to appoint an ad hoc commission to help settle the question. The members of this commission were Countess Bernadotte, Judge José Gustavo Guerrero and Judge Aung Khine.

My work with the Assembly was now over, and Wednesday, 13 December, was, I thought, my last day in the Sperry Plant at Lake Success. I was glad to leave the noisy office and get into my new quarters in Manhattan; but I had to return to Lake Success in the New Year for a new committee which had been asked to prepare a new draft of the Convention on Freedom of Information.

ECOSOC Session in Santiago (1951)

I spent most of 1951 away from headquarters. The Economic and Social Council held its spring session in Santiago de Chile and its summer session in Geneva. The Human Rights Commission also met in Geneva and the General Assembly in Paris. It was a good year to be abroad. I did not have to live through some of the events that nearly tore the Secretariat apart, when the thing history knows as McCarthyism began to rear its ugly head in the United Nations. The trouble had already been brewing in 1950, but I had been too busy with the General Assembly and other matters to give much attention to it. I was pretty sure there were no "communists" in my division, and would not have been upset had there been, unless it could be shown that they were plotting against a member state. But like many of my colleagues, I was shocked when I learned that the independence of the Secretariat was being threatened by a host state which did not respect its international character.

Lie never consulted me about the witch-hunting, nor did anyone else in the "administration." During the General Assembly that fall, a member of the United Nations administrative tribunal told me something which I found hard to believe: in one of the dismissal cases, it was argued on behalf of the Secretary-General that he was not bound by the Universal Declaration of Human Rights. I would not want to suggest that Lie was insensitive to the human rights issues involved; but it was quite obvious that he did not want any advice from the Division of Human Rights. He may even have thought that I was a "security threat" myself. I have no way of knowing. There was as much reason for thinking that I was subversive as that many of those were who were dismissed in violation of their basic human rights. Lie spoke to me only once about the matter. A passing remark that I had made to his friend, Judge Paul Berg, in Geneva came back to him, distorted and out of context. On my return to headquarters, Lie said to me coldly: "I understand that you have been talking about me to Judge Berg." I was so dumbfounded that I made no appropriate reply. If I had wanted to attack Lie, I would never have chosen Judge Berg as my confidant. Like most of my colleagues in the Secretariat, I had no doubt that Lie was wrong in capitulating before American pressures. If the Universal Declaration of Human Rights had any meaning, it at least established standards for the organization which had adopted it; and a stronger Secretary-General would have resisted the pressures and, if his position then became impossible, resigned.

The first United Nations body to meet in 1951 for which I had responsibility was the new fifteen-member committee on freedom of information, just appointed by the General

Assembly. It had hardly been elected when the members began to complain about having to meet at Lake Success, where the facilities were now poor and there was no local transportation. The business of the committee was to find some way out of the impasse that had developed over the draft Convention on Freedom of Information. But the protagonists were maintaining their positions and seemed to have ruled out any possibility of compromise. The one man who might have brought one about was Jacques Kayser. Not only was he the most knowledgeable member of the committee, but the French came nearest to bridging the two radically opposed positions. I invited him to lunch with a member of the British delegation, but we found no solution. Later, a compromise text for Article 2, which listed permissible limitations and sanctions, was worked out; but, largely because of the stand taken by Jamil Baroody of the Saudi Arabian delegation, it collapsed. Baroody had become a real power in the Third Committee and was responsible for some of its most controversial decisions, including the one that the covenant should contain an article enunciating self-determinatinon as a human right. He was a good speaker and spoke often and at great length, and more often than not had the last word. He held very strong opinions on nearly everything and could be bitingly sharp in his exposition of them, with the result that he made many enemies; but he represented a point of view which was gathering strength in the United Nations. Personally he had great charm. Although I disagreed with him on most things, he often consulted me before taking some initiative. He was amongst other things, I discovered, a very good poet.

On Tuesday, 13 February, my wife and I boarded an Eastern Airlines Constellation for Miami en route to Chile and the spring session of the Economic and Social Council. At Miami we changed to a Panagra DC-4 and flew on to Panama, from whence we flew through the night to Lima. I awoke at about six o'clock to the sight of the Peruvian desert below and the Andes in the distance. The world would look something like this, I reflected, after the final atomic blast; but there would be no oases or river beds. Emile Vaillancourt, who was now the Canadian ambassador in Peru, was at the airport to meet us and drive us to the embassy, where we were his guests for the next three days. The day after our arrival I was taken to the Chancery, where a large number of letters were waiting for me, including a petition signed by all the apristas incarcerated in the central prison. How they managed to get it out of the prison I do not know.

On Friday we flew on to Santiago, where we first put up at the Carrera Hotel—a big American establishment with "made in the U.S.A." stamped all over it—in which the conference was to be held; but the next day we moved to a quieter hotel which we liked better and which had the advantage of being several blocks away from the conference. Waiting for me in my office in the Carrera Hotel was a letter from the South African government protesting against the intention of the Secretariat to publish the text of that country's discriminatory Asiatic Land Tenure Amendment Act in the United Nations Yearbook on Human Rights. I had been discussing the matter with the South Africans before leaving headquarters and, in the light of their objections, wanted to bring our quarrel to the attention of the Human Rights Commission; and, before leaving New York, had so advised the Secretary-General. Martin Hill, a director in the office of the Secretary-General, who was also in Santiago, told me that he had been talking to Cordier over the long distance telephone. Cordier's view was that we should attempt to win the South Africans over and not push the matter too hard. I finally had to agree not to put the question on the commission's agenda. The Asiatic Land Tenure Act was a gross violation of human rights to which the widest possible publicity should have been given; and it would have been a useful precedent to have the Human Rights Commission confirm the right of the Secretariat to publish it, which, as a matter of fact, we eventually did.

In the afternoon, Professor Poblete Troncoso (the chairman of the ad hoc committee on slavery) drove Jeanne and me to the airport to welcome Trygve Lie, who was coming to Santiago for the opening of the Council. Laugier and Marie Cutolli arrived the next day. On Tuesday, we were all received by the president of the Republic, and ECOSOC got down to business in the afternoon. The communists were back, and Katz-Suchy of Poland bitterly attacked P.C. Chang, challenging his right to sit on the Council. We saw a great deal of Chang in Santiago. Jeanne gave him some good advice when he was suffering from "Chilean tummy." When I had the same complaint, Hernan Santa Cruz, the president of the Council, took me to a drugstore and had me drink a glass of water well laced with tincture of iodine. Jeanne's remedy, Epsom salt, was better.

Jeanne and I took Ambassador and Mrs. Kearney, who had come over from Buenos Aires to represent Canada at the Council, for dinner at the *Danubio Azul.* The next night, some of the other directors and myself gave a dinner party for Mr. and Mrs. Lie at the same restaurant. Lie was at his hearty best. If he was preoccupied by the witch-hunt that was going on in the Secretariat, he did not show it. But there had been some question whether he would come to the party, because Laugier and Marie Cutolli were to be there and he did not approve of their "irregular" relationship. I remember another dinner party—not so intimate as this one—which Lie himself gave at his Forest Hills home to celebrate the fourth, I think, anniversary of his appointment as Secretary-General. The house had about the same character as a well-kept hotel; the furniture looked as if it had come straight from a department store and the pictures on the walls reminded me of some hotel bedrooms. Lie, who was in very good humor, made a speech. Amongst other things he said that the directors were the most important cogs in the Secretariat machine, or words to that effect. If he really believed this, I had no further evidence of it.

The Council had begun to discuss the draft covenant in the light of the policy decisions handed down by the General Assembly. But, although the communists said that they wanted to discuss the substance of the articles, all the Council did was to arrange for the specialized agencies to participate in the work of the Human Rights Commission when it drafted articles on economic, social and cultural rights which, it will be remembered, the General Assembly had now decided should be included in the instrument. There were some fireworks when Corley Smith of the United Kingdom, replying to Katz-Suchy of Poland, said that all the latter wanted was an empty can which he could rattle. Katz-Suchy had such a sharp tongue himself that it was refreshing to hear a good reply. The Russian motion that all references to international implementation be deleted from the covenant (because they would constitute interference in the domestic affairs of states) was defeated; but that did not mean that the other powers wanted an effective implementation system.

The Council then turned to trade union rights, and Corley Smith and Katz-Suchy excelled themselves in their search for adjectives. Both sides in the Cold War were making a tremendous propaganda effort for the benefit of Latin America. A number of communications alleging violations of trade union rights in specified countries, some of which were and some not members of the International Labor Organization, had been received. A question to be decided was which, if any of these communications, should be forwarded to the I.L.O., in accordance with the decision taken in 1950, for possible consideration by its fact-finding and conciliation commission on freedom of association. Over the objections of the communists, all the communications relating to states members of the I.L.O. were sent to that body; and the Secretary-General was invited to report on the conditions under which the other communications could also be referred to it, after inviting observations from the governments concerned. One of the communications was from the communist World Federation of Trade Unions, protesting against the closing of its headquarters in Paris. France was a member of the I.L.O., and this communication should therefore have been referred to that body; but the Council took no action in the matter, an omission which was tantamount to taking a substantive decision contrary to the 1950 resolution.

The Council then turned to the fate of the survivors of the so-called medical experiments in Nazi concentration camps, on which my division had prepared a report in which we suggested, amongst other things, that the German authorities be asked to compensate the victims. With the help of Garcia Sayan, I also wrote a speech for Laugier to make on the item. Later in the session, the Council adopted a resolution which incorporated most of our suggestions. It was under this resolution that I went to Bonn that summer to negotiate a scheme for the compensation of the victims.

The Council had now settled down to its normal routine; and, when it was meeting, it really made little difference to me whether I was in Santiago or New York, for there was not much opportunity to enjoy the exotic surroundings. We made up for this on weekends. The Chileans could not have been more hospitable. Jeanne and I had our first opportunity to see something of the Chilean countryside when, on our first Saturday, we were driven to the Fundo Carmen Bajo in Melipilla to spend the day with Amanda Labarca. The next day the whole of the conference was taken to Viña del Mar and Valparaiso as guests of the government. On the following Saturday, we were royally entertained at the *bodegas* of the Undurraga Wine Company. Chilean wines cannot compete with the great wines of Europe, but as ordinary table wine they are as good as any in the world. That day we sampled them generously. There were also Chilean songs and dances and, of course, the colorful *huasos*. On Sunday, we went to the *fundo* of Enrique Bernstein (a member of the Chilean delegation and his country's ambassador to France) in Aculeo. For reasons of prestige rather than security, our buses were escorted by a score of *carabineros* on motorcycles. As we sped through the villages to the shriek of klaxons, people came out of their homes to see what was up. At the *fundo,* which was more like a fief than a ranch and where everything seemed to grow, the Bernsteins received us with pisco sours and great dishes of salted almonds. We were then taken to an island in a lake for an outdoor meal of *casuelo de ave* (a kind of chicken stew) and *asado al palo* or barbecued sheep, prepared by the *carabineros*. I could not help being impressed by the contrasts that we had seen this day between poverty and great wealth. When I spoke to Bernstein (who was himself obviously a very wealthy man) about this, he said that there had been a great improvement in the condition of the people over the last twenty years, and that the chief reason for this was the fear of socialism. But of all the South American countries I have visited, Chile seemed the most stable and the last I would have expected ever to elect a communist government or indeed to fall under the heel of a military dictatorship.

On Wednesday of that week, I took the morning off to visit the *rotas* or slums of Santiago with a captain of the *carabineros*. The slums were not quite as bad as I had expected. I had seen worse in Naples and in Buenos Aires, but conditions were pretty bad. It was degrading that anyone should have to live like that, and I was ashamed to be there under the protection of the police, examining these hovels simply to satisfy my curiosity. The new housing development to which I was then taken failed to take away the bitter taste.

We were overwhelmed by hospitality and soon satiated with food and people. So much so that we were seldom free at meal time; but when we were, it was a luxury to lunch or dine in the quiet of our hotel room on bread and cheese and the good Chilean wine. But the most elaborate entertainment was yet to come. On Saturday, 10 March, the whole of the Council and the Secretariat was taken by special train for a long weekend to Villarica and the Chilean lakes. Leaving Santiago late in the afternoon, we arrived at Villarica at eleven the next morning. We then crossed the lake of the same name by launch, from which there was a fine view of a volcano. After checking in at the hotel in Pucon, we visited the town, which was poor, primitive and unattractive. What a contrast when, in the afternoon, we walked on the beautiful peninsula with its magnificent trees, Merino sheep and fine views of the lake and mountains. I tried my hand at trout fishing but did not get even a bite.

Before the weekend, the Council had been discussing freedom of information and I had had a passing hope that the decision taken in Geneva not to have a session of the sub-commission in 1951 would be reversed. But the United Kingdom now suggested that the sub-commission be abolished and its functions taken over by UNESCO. The debate continued after our return from Villarica. Walter Kotchnig, thinking, I suppose, that the Secretariat would not have the time to prepare for a 1951 session and wanting to strengthen the American argument against convening one, began putting questions to me about documentation. He did not like my answers, because I could not honestly say that documentation would be a real problem; so he went on to attack the Secretariat. He knew as well as I did that the trouble was not with the Secretariat or the documentation but with the members of the sub-commission, including the American member. The Council decided to defer the question to its next session, which seemed to mean that there would be no session of the sub-commission in 1951. But, in the light of the position taken by the General Assembly, it did convene a session of the Sub-Commission on the Prevention of Discrimination to meet at headquarters later in the year.

One of the last items on the Council's agenda was forced labor. At one meeting the Soviet delegate spoke for two and a half hours. The upshot was that, on 19 March, the International Labor Organization was invited to cooperate with the Council in the creation of a joint ad hoc committee on forced labor. Its report, published in 1953, was a remarkable document and resulted in, amongst other things, the adoption of the I.L.O. Convention on Forced Labor. A short time after the publication of the report, some of the forced labor camps in the Soviet Union were closed. Many years later, Alexander Solzhenitzyn published a letter thanking the American Federation of Labor for its part in bringing about the inquiry.

I was again suffering from the Chilean complaint, perhaps because Jeanne had left Santiago. She would be with me for the rest of the year in Europe; but I had to return to headquarters before going on to Geneva and there was no reason why she should have to make the trip to New York. I therefore encouraged her to travel to Europe by ship: she might just as well have the benefit of the long sea voyage and the chance to visit some exotic ports on the west coast of South America and in the Caribbean.

Laugier made a farewell speech on the last morning of the session. He was obviously deeply moved, and his speech was strong and sincere, even passionate. At one point I thought that he might break down. One of the things he said was that he would continue to fight against any ''stabilization'' of the United Nations, the conventional wisdom of the time in some delegations and the higher echelons of the Secretariat being that the budget and operations of the organization must be stabilized lest they become unmanageable. I went to the airport immediately after he finished his speech and boarded a plane for Lima, where I joined Martin Hill, with whom I went next morning to Cuzco. The flight over the Andes was spectacular and, although we flew at times at an altitude of over 20,000 feet—which was so high for an unpressurized DC-4 that for part of the trip we had to take oxygen—the mountains seemed perilously near below. Looking down at the expanse of rocky peaks below us, Martin remarked that this was an unnecessary risk, which I suppose it was.

Cuzco is over 11,000 feet high. There were no lifts in our hotel, and it was a real effort to climb the stairs to my room on the second floor, but I soon adjusted myself to the altitude. We spent the morning inspecting Inca ruins in the countryside near Cuzco, and in the afternoon visited some of the many churches and other fine old buildings in the city. We had the luck to see a *parada* in honor of the *Christ of the Earthquakes,* a sight well worth the trip to Cuzco. It helped compensate for the fiasco the next day. We wanted to see the ruins at Machupicchu, a long trip for the one day that we had at our disposal. We were awakened at 3:45 in the morning to take the little train to Machupicchu. But after travelling for nearly two hours, we were forced by a landslide ahead to turn back. Our little train then stopped at a junction where a long, more conventional train had also stopped. The passengers, all of them Indians in traditional dress, were buying food from the villagers, who were preparing it on little stoves by the right of way. It was a kind of compensation for having missed Machupicchu. Everything I saw confirmed the impression I had had some weeks earlier that outside of Lima, Peru remained an Indian country, and that, unlike what has happened in Mexico, the process of integration had hardly begun. But yet in the United Nations, the almost purely Spanish Peruvian delegates were arguing that there were no minorities in South America. The Peruvian Indians may be technically a majority but they were certainly the kind of nondominant group contemplated by the definition of the Sub-Commission on the Prevention of Discrimination and the Protection of Minorities.

When we returned to Lima, the ambassador's daughter, who was waiting for me at the airport, drove me to the Canadian embassy. That night I boarded a plane for Panama. There was, as far as I could see, only one empty seat on the plane and seated beside it was P.C. Chang. I was glad to occupy it. We talked until the plane arrived in Panama after two o'clock the next morning. He told me all about his famous brother, Chang Po-ling, the great educator who founded the Nankai School in Tientsin, which later grew into a university. P.C. had himself been a student at the school and later a professor. Among other graduates of the school was Chou En-lai, who flew to Tientsin to pay his respects when Chang Po-ling died. P.C.'s brother was such a great man in China that both the nationalists and the communists claimed him as their own.

I was taking my time returning to New York, so I left the aircraft and Chang at Panama and went to the fine new El Panama hotel, where I got to bed at about three thirty in the morning. But I was up bright and early that morning to see as much as I could of the Canal Zone in the short time I would be there. Travelling to Colon by train, I expected to see a long structure in steel and concrete, but what I saw was more like a series of lakes. Colon, at the other end of the canal, was a conglomeration of bazaars, the most prosperous of which were run by East Indians. There were whole streets lined with brothels, little shacks hardly big enough to contain a bed. It was the most blatant display of vice I have ever seen, much worse than the licensed red-light district in Tokyo, which a Japanese official later drove me through only a few weeks before it was closed, and which looked very much like other poor sections of the city. They were equally uninviting.

My plane left after two o'clock the next morning. Before leaving Lima, Emile Vaillancourt had given me a handful of sleeping pills. I was now so tired that I was afraid I might not sleep, so I took one of them. I dropped off into a deep sleep and did not awaken until the plane was about to come down at Miami and all the other passengers had had their breakfasts. I was so frightened that I threw the rest of the pills into the toilet. At Miami I changed planes and shortly after lunch was at La Guardia, where a United Nations car was waiting for me.

I was back in my office early Monday morning. A member of the American delegation who came to see me in the afternoon said that the United States was now ready to accept the inclusion of economic and social rights in the covenant, adding that this would be innocuous. There was a pleasant letter waiting for me from Senator Roebuck, the chairman of the committee of the Canadian Senate studying the proposed Canadian Bill of Rights, whose invitation to testify before the committee I had had to refuse. He was happy, he wrote, that the General Assembly had decided to include economic and social rights in the covenant, not knowing perhaps that the Canadian delegation had voted against the decision. It was, he said, only lack of courage which had prevented his committee from recommending the inclusion of these rights in the Canadian Bill of Rights.

I was disturbed by a decision which had been taken in my absence regarding invitations to the forthcoming conference on the protection of refugees. As a result of American pressure and the wishes of the high commissioner for refugees, it had been decided that East Germany would not receive an invitation, although the Federal Republic would. The decision was politically motivated and, I thought, a mistake. In a humanitarian matter like the protection of refugees, we should have tried to get whatever cooperation the East Germans might be willing to give. I prepared a memorandum to the Secretary-General and spoke to several delegations, but I was, of course, fishing in troubled diplomatic waters. I doubt that the invitation would have been accepted even if it had been extended; Yugoslavia was the only communist country to attend the conference.

I was getting ready to leave New York for Geneva. Charles Malik telephoned from Washington to tell me that he was coming to Geneva for the Human Rights Commission. From something he said I gathered that Mrs. Roosevelt was giving up the chairmanship and that Malik would replace her, which proved to be the case. On 2 April, I saw Laugier for the last time in his capacity of Assistant Secretary-General and had lunch with him, Marie and the Chief Pilot of Air France. I did not know it then, but this was the end of an era in my United Nations experience. Things would not be so easy for me from then on.

Economic and Social Rights (1951)

It was a pleasant crossing. I had a volume of essays by Ortega y Gasset (which Santa Cruz had given me) but I spent most of my time in a deck chair relaxing or walking on the deck with my colleague, Ezekiel Gordon. The *De Grasse* arrived at Le Havre early on Friday morning, 13 April. The first thing I did after arriving in Paris was to walk across the street from my hotel to the UNESCO headquarters for talks with officials there. I then interviewed two candidates for posts in the Human Rights Division. That night, Jim Hendrick, who had been one of Mrs. Roosevelt's first advisers at the Human Rights Commission, gave a dinner party for me at the Marshall Plan "embassy." I had Saturday to myself and used it to go twice to the theater and for a long walk on the boulevards and up to Montmartre. On Sunday, I drove to Geneva with Hanna Saba, UNESCO'S legal counsel.

Next day, Malik was elected chairman of the commission. I already knew him well as a chairman, having worked with him when he was the chairman of the Third Committee in 1948 (when the Assembly adopted the Universal Declaration of Human Rights) and in the Economic and Social Council. In many respects he was a better chairman than Mrs. Roosevelt and, of course, there was no more state department interference in the conduct of the meetings. The Secretariat had always worked very closely with him and continued to do so. Representing a small country, he did not have rigid instructions and usually welcomed a good idea. When I or someone else in the Division had one, I often took it to him, and more often than not he picked it up.

The first item on the agenda was the question of the inclusion of economic, social and cultural rights in the covenant. It would be hard in the light of the attitude of the General Assembly for the commission to refuse to include them; but there were still people who apparently hoped to make concessions with words only. By far the cleverest and the most adamant of these was Wilfred Jenks of the International Labor Organization which, together with UNESCO and the World Health Organization had been invited to assist the commission in this part of its work. The I.L.O. was opposed to the inclusion of economic and social rights in the covenant, presumably because they felt that this would impinge on their jurisdiction; but realizing that their inclusion was now probably inevitable, they wanted the articles to be as general and as weak as possible. Jenks therefore wanted the drafting to be done by a small working party, on which the commission and the specialized agencies would be equally represented, and which he could control because some of the commission members had the same position as the I.L.O. He was supported by the United

Kingdom, which could usually be counted on to back up the I.L.O. in any jurisdictional conflict with the United Nations. If adopted, the proposal would have prevented the commission from taking a decision by majority vote; and since I was pretty sure that there was now a majority in it for economic and social rights, I suggested to the French that the commission transform itself into a committee or working group of the whole, which would work with the help of experts from the specialized agencies. This was adopted. That night, to celebrate my victory, I took Jeanne to hear the Munich Philharmonic Orchestra. Her long sea voyage had been a great adventure and, because she told a story so well, I soon felt as if I had made the trip myself.

Pending the arrival of the experts from the specialized agencies, the commission began to discuss provisions for the implementation of the covenant. I was not too hopeful about the result. At the most, they might agree on an optional clause recognizing an individual right of petition. But I was being overoptimistic, because the commission never did recommend a right of individual petition, even on an optional basis. At a cocktail party given by Mrs. Roosevelt at the Hotel des Bergues, I talked with P.D. Morozov, who was representing the Soviet Union on the commission for the first time. He later became a very important person in the Soviet hierarchy at the United Nations and, after that, a judge on the International Court of Justice. Our relations became cordial and remained so until he discovered, just before my retirement from the Secretariat, that I was the author of the plan to create an office of United Nations High Commissioner for Human Rights, a proposal which the Soviet Union energetically opposed.

I called on Jenks to discuss the organization of the ad hoc committee on forced labor, which was to be the joint responsibility of the United Nations Secretariat and the International Labor Office. We had no difficulty reaching agreement on the composition of the committee, the members of which would be Sir Ramaswami Mudaliar (India), as chairman, Judge Paul Berg (Norway) and Felix Fulgencio Palavincini (Mexico) who was later replaced by my colleague, Enrique Garcia Sayan who, by that time, was back in his law practice in Peru. But the committee's secretariat was another matter. Because the United Nations was the senior organization and had taken the initiative in setting up the committee, I suggested that the secretary should come from its staff. But Jenks said that there could be no circumstances under which his director-general would accept such an arrangement, even if there was a deputy secretary from the I.L.O. That evening Jeanne and I had dinner with Brock Chisholm, the director general of the World Health Organization, in his beautiful home overlooking Lake Geneva; and several days later I had a long talk with him about the victims of medical experiments in Nazi concentration camps. He promised to canvass the medical profession through the World Medical Association in an effort to discover the names of all the surviving victims. Compared to my difficulties with the I.L.O., my relations with the W.H.O. and UNESCO were always excellent.

In a rare gesture of strength, Trygve Lie refused to bow before the I.L.O. demand that the ad hoc committee on forced labor have joint secretaries, one from the I.L.O. and the other from the United Nations. Some weeks later, Jenks wrote a strong letter in which he suggested that the committee's secretariat be detached from both the I.L.O. and the United Nations. If he was afraid of my interfering, he need not have worried. For political reasons, Trygve Lie wanted to dissociate himself from the committee's work, and I never even attended its meetings. The I.L.O. even objected to the use of the United Nations crest on the committee's documents. The petty row over the office of secretary was settled by a compromise: the secretary would come from the United Nations, but there would be a technical adviser from the I.L.O.

In the Secretariat we were working on a plan for machinery to help implement economic and social rights which, based on reporting by governments, was inspired by the technical assistance program and the idea that it was better to help governments to fulfil their obligations than to penalize them for violations. I talked to Malik who agreed to sponsor the draft articles. Although I had no such intention, I was preparing another quarrel with Jenks. That evening, Malik gave a dinner party so that the members of the commission could meet the I.L.O. experts, who were now all in Geneva. They had brought their biggest guns, including Sir Guildhaume Myrrdin-Evans, Leon Jouhaux and G. Bergenstrom, all members of their governing body.

The working group met the next morning, 26 April. We had had difficulties with the I.L.O. even over the seating arrangements. The impression I had gained at Malik's dinner party that the I.L.O people might not speak with one voice seemed to be confirmed. Jouhaux, who apparently wanted a strong covenant and was only incidentally interested in protecting the jurisdiction of the I.L.O., was way out in front of his two colleagues. The commission itself was still hopelessly divided on fundamental issues; but there were some signs that, with the exception of the British, they were all moving forward. "The commission cannot turn back now," I said to Mrs. Roosevelt after the meeting. We had circulated, under Malik's name, the Secretariat proposal for implementation. René Cassin, who now seemed to be coming round to the I.L.O. position, said that it did not sufficiently recognize the role of the specialized agencies. I discussed this with Malik: the problem, as I saw it, was to find some formula which would permit us to make a reasonable concession to the specialized agencies without surrendering everything to them; and I undertook to reconsider the plan.

It had been decided that the meetings of the working group would be closed to the public; but that comedy ended when the press quite properly complained. There was indeed no reason why we should be meeting in secret: the commission had never done so before. A whole week elapsed before the working group adopted a text, the first part of an article on the right to work. In that first week, it was beginning to look as if the I.L.O. would cooperate in the drafting of the articles defining the various rights; and we were glad to have their help and the benefit of their long experience. But why should they not cooperate at this stage? For, essentially, their position was that, once the articles were drafted, the part of the covenant which dealt with economic and social rights—or still possibly a separate covenant—would operate as an I.L.O. convention. The real difficulties would come when we began to discuss implementation. On Saturday they made a proposal under which the United Nations would have had practically no role in the implementation of the articles; and there was a very real danger that the commission, which was itself divided, would be engineered into accepting it.

As it turned out, I was mistaken in thinking that the I.L.O. would cooperate in defining economic and social rights. What they wanted, and this soon became quite obvious, was that these rights should be defined in the vaguest and most general terms possible. UNESCO and the World Health Organization, on the other hand, wanted detailed provisions stipulating explicit obligations. There was a difference between an established organization, with its traditional interests to protect, and the two new agencies, which felt that they needed all the help they could get from the United Nations in furthering their programs.

On the first day of May, we took the afternoon off, although it might have been a better tribute to the workers of the world had we remained in session. That morning there had been some haggling, and Morozov was beginning to make long and provocative speeches. Later in the week the working party adopted a fairly detailed text on the right to health, the basic wording for which was supplied by the World Health Organization. Malik drew the attention of the working group to the difference in the quality of cooperation the commission was getting from this agency as compared to the I.L.O. An American text on trade union rights, which was then adopted, did not mention the right to strike, but neither had the Universal Declaration of Human Rights. When, however, the General Assembly approved the Covenant on Economic, Social and Cultural Rights, Article 8 recognized this right "provided that it is exercised in conformity with the laws of the particular country."

On Saturday morning, I had a long walk with Roger Baldwin, then the director of the International League for the Rights of Man, who had come to Geneva from New York, partly on my insistence. He was lobbying in the corridors and I was encouraging him. I had lunch with Malik, to whom I gave new and simplified articles on implementation. Jacques Kayser, who had finally succumbed to my pressing and had come to Geneva to help with the documentation on freedom of information, then drove Jeanne and me to Saint Germain du Joux to have dinner with Laugier. It was the first time that I had seen my old chief since his retirement.

The issue whether the covenant was to include economic and social rights was still far from settled. The British tried to get the commission to ask the General Assembly to reconsider the matter and, in point of fact, the Assembly eventually did reverse its decision. But at this session the commission adopted some fourteen articles, not including, however, any article on the right to property. The reason for the omission was not ideological—private property exists even in communist countries, and the right had been recognized in the Universal Declaration of Human Rights—but because no agreement could be reached on when and in what amount compensation should be given in the event of expropriation.

There was difficulty with a so-called umbrella clause which was to precede the articles on economic and social rights. As Morozov pointed out, what the commission was now trying to do was to write a covenant within a covenant. He was, of course, right. For if the covenant were to include economic and social rights, the instrument would have to have two parts, with distinctive implementation procedures for each. For procedures appropriate for the implementation of civil and political rights are not necessarily applicable to economic and social rights, most of which are program rights which can only be progressively implemented. This difficulty, which did not worry Morozov, who was opposed to any kind of international implementation, turned out to be academic, because, as already mentioned, the General Assembly subsequently reversed its 1950 decision and decided that there would be two covenants, one on economic and social and the other on civil and political rights.

Malik's proposal for machinery to implement the rights was fairly well received. Even the Americans were sympathetic. But there was also strong support for the I.L.O. proposal which would have given sole responsibility to it. Malik's most dangerous opponent would, I thought, be Cassin, who either did not understand the issue, which I could not believe, or was now in the pocket of the I.L.O., notwithstanding his big words—Laugier once said that he was in love with his words—about the role of the United Nations.

Miss Bowie wanted to know what we were thinking in the Secretariat; but although we had dinner together so that I could tell her, she was so preoccupied with her own problems that we never got beyond them. The person responsible for the conservative—I think she said "reactionary"—position which the United Kingdom was taking in the commission was, she said, Sir Gladwyn Jebb, the head of the British mission at U.N. Headquarters. She said that, after what she described as the British defeat in the General Assembly (when it decided to include economic and social rights in the covenant), the government was considering not only abandoning the covenant but withdrawing from the commission. They later decided that Miss Bowie would attend the session but take no part in the proceedings; but she refused to come on these terms, so the position was changed; however, she now had the most detailed instructions on every question, and her voting was closely watched by the foreign office. She did not think, she added, that Herbert Morrison, whom she knew well, was aware of what was happening; but she would brief him on her return to England. Our conversation ended there, for there was a night meeting, and we had to return to the Palais. Later in the session she told me that she could no longer stomach the instructions she was getting from the foreign office and would resign. She was replaced at the next session by Samuel Hoare who was the under secretary at the home office.

I had a letter the next day from Martin Hill. He was the director in the Secretary-General's office responsible for coordination with the specialized agencies, and was in Paris attending meetings of the administrative committee on coordination. Jenks, who had guessed that the Lebanese proposal for implementation was the work of the United Nations Secretariat, had been talking to him. If adopted, Jenks said, the proposal would result in overlapping and proliferation, which were dirty words in the United Nations family. Jenks said that the director general of the I.L.O. would discuss the matter with the Secretary-General and, if necessary, bring it to the attention of the administrative committee on coordination. In other words the Secretariat should be spanked for defending the interests of the United Nations. Martin's letter ended with an admonishment to be neutral. I immediately telephoned Paris. The Lebanese proposal would not, I explained, result in proliferation, because it did not contemplate the creation of any new machinery. This, therefore, could not be the reason for the I.L.O. opposition, which could only be concern for their jurisdiction as they interpreted it; and the proof was their own proposal which was quite unacceptable to the commission. I did not hide the fact that the Secretariat had indeed prepared both the original and revised texts of the Lebanese proposal, but only we and Malik knew this. Jenks was therefore fishing. What we had done, moreover, was quite proper; and, if we had not done it, the only text before the commission would be the quite unsatisfactory one from the I.L.O. Finally, I could hardly believe that the Secretary-General really wanted us to remain neutral as Hill had implied, when the I.L.O. was openly lobbying for a text which would divest the United Nations of powers which it possessed under its Charter. But if he were speaking in the name of the Secretary-General, I would of course obey orders.

I spent the whole of Saturday afternoon closeted with Malik, discussing various objections that had been made to the proposal standing in the name of Lebanon. My impression was that he would stand firm and fight. I had another meeting with him on Sunday night to which I brought three of my colleagues. We gave the proposal a good going-over, combining some of the articles to make it shorter and omitting some expressions to which objection might be taken; but there were no changes in substance.

When the commission met on Monday morning, it had three texts before it: a new version of the Lebanese proposal reflecting our work over the weekend, a text sponsored by Pakistan and Sweden but obviously inspired by the I.L.O., and one submitted by France. A drafting committee was appointed to prepare a new text on the basis of the three proposals: it produced a text which, with one important change, the commission adopted on Thursday. One of its articles would have obliged the states parties to the covenant to report on their performance to the competent specialized agency. Azmi Bey of Egypt moved an amendment requiring reports to be made to the United Nations as well and, with the help of the Soviet Union and the Ukraine, this was adopted. The final result as approved by the General Assembly was not substantially different from the Secretariat plan: reports were to be made to the United Nations unless a state party preferred to draw by precise reference the attention of the United Nations to a report which it had already made to a specialized agency.

The experts from the specialized agencies now departed. Turning to the implementation of civil and political rights, the commission decided that the proposed Human Rights Committee (the conciliation body contemplated by the covenant) would be elected not by the states parties to the instrument but by the International Court of Justice, and that the committee could ask the Economic and Social Council to request advisory opinions from the Court on legal questions relating to cases before the committee. Both references to the Court were later deleted. A proposal to give a right of petition to individuals was again rejected. Realizing, as I had in 1950, that this was an almost fatal defect, I suggested to some friendly delegations that a reporting system similar to the one just adopted for economic and social rights should also be adopted for civil and political rights. If this were done, it would be possible for the Human Rights Committee to compare the law and practice of contracting states with their obligations under the covenant, even if no state was prepared to take the initiative in making a complaint. The suggestion was not adopted at the seventh session; but Article 40 of the covenant on Civil and Political Rights as finally adopted says that ''the states parties . . . undertake to submit reports on the measures they have adopted to give effect to the rights recognized herein and on the progress made in the enjoyment of these rights.''

Because the procedures contemplated for the international implementation of the covenant were quite inadequate and would not, in any event, apply to states which did not ratify the convention, I was anxious to repair the damage that had been done in 1947, when the commission had decided that it had no power to take any action on the many thousands of communications alleging violations of human rights that the United Nations was receiving. I therefore talked to Hansa Mehta who, as the representative of India, had wanted these communications circulated at the first session, and who had remained an advocate of effective implementation. On 17 May she moved that the confidential list of communications be forwarded to the Economic and Social Council. But on Malik's suggestion, it was decided only to draw the Council's attention to the fact that the commission had, ever since its inception, been receiving these communications. He apparently thought this would be a sufficient indication of the commission's continued interest in an unsatisfactory situation—a situation which was of course, of the commission's own making. I had heard that the Chileans were considering asking that the list be produced at the next session of the Council, because they wanted to make an issue of the closing down of *La Prensa* by the Peronistas, but this never happened.

The night the commission adopted its report, I was on my way with Schwelb to Bonn for negotiations with the West German government regarding the claims of the victims of medical experiments in Nazi concentration camps. We were received by the minister of justice, Herr Dahler, in his home, who then took us for dinner. The next morning there were meetings at the foreign office and the ministry of justice. The minister of finance promised to recommend that Chancellor Adenauer write to the Inter-Allied Commission and undertake to compensate all victims coming within the definition of "persecutees," irrespective of their residential qualifications or of the fact that, under Laender legislation, the time limit for filing claims might have expired. What still needed to be decided was what was meant by "persecutees," which, in German law, apparently only included persons who had been persecuted for political, racial or religious reasons. I was afraid that this might not include all the Polish girls whose names we had and it certainly would not include common criminals; and I suggested a different formula. The minister of justice agreed, and I was now confident that the government would compensate all the victims; but I asked for another meeting to consider the matter further. This was arranged for the following day. In the meantime, the next morning, the government having put a Mercedes at our disposal, Schwelb and I drove to Swarzheimdorf to see a thirteenth century church, after which we drove up the Rhine valley as far as Drachenfels. When we returned to Bonn, we were told that our formula would be accepted and that all the victims would be compensated, whatever the reasons why they had been in the concentration camps. Well satisfied with the success of our mission, we returned to our hotel and had the time to draft a report to the Secretary-General before boarding the *schnellzug* to Cologne, where we spent the evening. Back in Bonn, the ministry car called for us again the next morning, and, our mission now being completed, took us for a long drive into the Eifel Hills. Schwelb, who was returning to New York, took the evening train to Paris; but my own train for Basel and Geneva would not leave until after midnight. I went for a long walk, reviewing in my mind the results of our mission. The Secretariat had given reality to a rather platonic resolution which the federal government would probably have ignored had it not been for our insistence; and we had prevailed on them to compensate all the victims. Some of the people with whom we talked had seemed surprised that we should want to help the "unworthy" victims and that we were interested not only in the fate of foreigners but also of German nationals. The reasons seemed pretty clear to me: even a common criminal has a right not to be a guinea pig.

I was back in my Geneva office early the next afternoon, where so much work was waiting for me that I had to postpone for a week the holiday that Jeanne and I were planning in Spain. My next assignment was to represent the Secretary-General at the UNESCO general conference in Paris; but that was two weeks away. It was Jeanne's doctor who had suggested Sitges: the weather in Geneva had been cold and clammy and he wanted her to be somewhere where there would be plenty of sun. I needed some myself, for the rheumatism in my hand that had been so embarrassing in Montevideo was coming back. We left Geneva by night train on Friday, 1 June, and were in Sitges the next afternoon.

A fortnight later I was in Paris for the UNESCO conference; it would last into July, but I was spending only a week in Paris, after which I had to return to Geneva for the plenipotentiary conference on the protection of refugees. One of the first things I did in Paris was to go to a big reception at the home of UNESCO's director-general, Jaime Torres Bodet. Afterwards I took the *metro* to the Palais Royal and went for a walk along the Seine. The next morning I listened to Torres Bodet's speech to the plenary session and then had lunch with Hanna Saba. The other guest was Andrew Cordier, who told me that Lie was going to ask Laugier to return to the Secretariat and that I could prepare him for the offer; but when I spoke to him over the telephone, Laugier was noncommital.

At a dinner party in Laugier's rue de Babylonne apartment, the guests included the Secretary-General and Mrs. Lie, Georges Bidault—until very recently the prime minister of France and still a member of the cabinet—and Sir John Maud. The purpose of the party was, I understood, to bring together Lie and Bidault, between whom there was apparently some coolness. But Lie spoke no French and Bidault no English. After dinner, therefore, when the guests moved into the large *salon* to admire one of the best private collections of modern French painting in Paris, I was asked to interpret. The three of us retired to the other end of the room; but the two statesmen had nothing to say to each other and, after a few banalities, they separated. Both of them seemed embarrassed by the encounter. When Laugier made what appeared to be a gaffe like this—inviting personal or political enemies to the same party—it was usually a studied attempt to heal a misunderstanding. When the difficulties between the Soviet Union and Yugoslavia were at their worst, he invited the Russian Assistant Secretary-General, Arkady Sobolev, and Joza Vilfan of the Yugoslav delegation to dinner. The evening passed without incident, but the next day, when thanking Laugier for his hospitality, Vilfan remarked that it had been a most imprudent thing to invite a Russian and a Yugoslav the same evening. And Sobolev: "What a strange idea to invite me to dinner with a Yugoslav."

Laugier told me later that Lie had asked him to return to the Secretariat. As Laugier described the offer, Lie had asked him to return on a "day-to-day" basis which, I understood, meant at pleasure. I did not think that there was anything extraordinary about this, and thought that Laugier should have accepted. But there had been a heated discussion during which Laugier had accused Lie of undermining the authority of the assistant secretaries-general and using other officers like Cordier and Feller as his effective cabinet. Lie then lost his temper, although, Laugier said, they parted on good terms. There was truth in what Laugier had said to Lie, but the assistant secretaries-general were themselves partly responsible for what had happened. However, it had not been very diplomatic for Laugier to raise the question when Lie was offering him an olive branch. Laugier also told me that Lie was contemplating a reorganization of the Secretariat which would reduce the number of assistant secretaries-general to three and give more authority to the top-ranking directors.

I returned to Geneva on Sunday, 24 June, and on Monday morning was back at work in the Palais. I spent most of the morning going over papers on freedom of information with Jacques Kayser, whose contract expired a few days later. Before leaving, he wrote me a wise and friendly letter about the role of the Secretariat. It completely endorsed my view that, in this highly controversial area, there were very few if any initiatives that we could take which we had not already tried. This made me feel better, because I had been asking myself whether the Secretariat might not have been partly responsible for the failure of the sub-commission.

The Protection of Refugees (1951)

In July I opened the conference of plenipotentiaries on the protection of refugees and state-less persons in my capacity as its executive secretary, after which I had lunch with its president, Knud Larsen of Denmark. I had thought this would be an easy conference. The draft convention and protocol had been gone over twice by an ad hoc committee and the General Assembly had already agreed on how refugees were to be defined. But there were many difficulties that remained to be ironed out. The conference even reopened the controversial question of definition, and there was much heated debate whether the protection provided by the convention should be limited to persons who had become refugees by reason of events occurring only in Europe and before 1 January 1951. The chief advocate of this limited definition was Rochefort, whose bad-tempered but sometimes brilliant interventions enlivened the conference. The compromise finally reached was that, when ratifying the convention, states could declare whether, as regards them, the definition would include only persons who had become refugees by reason of events occurring in Europe or whether these events might also have occurred elsewhere. I was shocked by the position the Americans were taking. Although represented at the conference, they had already served notice that they would not ratify the convention. There were, they said, no refugees in the United States and immigrants in that country already had all the rights contemplated by the instrument. If that were so, there was no good reason why they should not encourage other countries to ratify by doing so themselves.

I have mentioned Rochefort's bad temper. At a meeting of the credentials committee, we found that very few of them were in order, a not unimportant detail when it is remembered that we intended to open the convention for signature at the end of the conference. The president so reported to the conference, whereupon Rochefort who, up until that time had no credentials whatsoever, began to attack the Secretariat. He later returned a letter we had addressed to the plenipotentiary representative of France on which he had written ''Absent, retour au Secretariat.'' During the heated debate on the definition, he went so far as to accuse the Belgians of smuggling refugees into France on moonless nights. Another disgraceful incident occurred on 17 July, when the conference was discussing an article by which the states parties would undertake to cooperate with the high commissioner for refugees. Rochefort was against the article, perhaps because he had not been appointed the high commissioner; but knowing that it would certainly be adopted, he announced that France would make a reservation when ratifying the convention. But an article already adopted prohibited this. So he moved an amendment to the article on reservations and insisted that it be voted on before the article on cooperation with the high commissioner. The conference first refused to submit to this kind of bullying, whereupon Rochefort said that he would take no part in the voting and stalked out of the room. It was a delicate situation. No country was more important than France when it came to refugees and it would be a serious matter if that country did not ratify the convention. The other delegates knew this and so did Rochefort. He finally had his way and his amendment to the reservations article was adopted so that, under the convention as adopted, it is possible for a contracting state not to undertake to cooperate with the high commissioner. The only possible explanation for his success is that the conference did not want to give France any possible excuse for not ratifying the convention. During all this time, van Heuven Goedhart, who was now the high commissioner for refugees, was in the conference room. At a luncheon which the latter gave for the delegates, I was sitting next to George Warren, the representative of the United States at the conference, who said that the Secretariat was not doing enough preparatory work on human rights and, as an example, cited the case of the survivors of medical experiments in Nazi concentration camps. It was not easy to tell the representative of a member state that he did not know what he was talking about.

The conference finished the first reading of the convention on 20 July, after which it turned to the draft protocol on the protection of stateless persons; but, after a discussion which did not last for over half an hour, it decided to take no action on it. In 1954, another plenipotentiary conference, of which I was also the executive secretary, adopted a convention relating to the status of stateless persons.

The day the refugees conference adjourned, Larsen had tears in his eyes when he responded to the speeches of thanks. He made a reference to me that I could have interpreted as a left-handed compliment. "Professor Humphrey," he said, "has always been helpful both when he was active and when he was passive." He came to my office the next morning to explain his meaning. He was afraid, he said, that under Rochefort's attacks, I would get into the fight to defend the Secretariat, further provoke the Frenchman and make a difficult situation worse. Hence his mention of my passivity, which he had meant as a compliment. Two days later there was a ceremony at which the convention was signed on behalf of twelve countries. It came into force on 22 April, 1954, and has been widely ratified.

The thirteenth session of the Economic and Social Council began two days after the signing ceremony. Laugier, who was in Geneva to address the World Federation of United Nations Associations, turned up for the opening but, unfortunately, not as Assistant Secretary-General. It was nearly a month before we reached the report of the Human Rights Commission. In the meantime there was much informal discussion and lobbying about the covenant. I now favored sending it to the General Assembly, not because I thought that the text was ready for adoption or that the Assembly was the proper place for making desirable drafting changes; but I did not think that we would get much more out of the commission except under the impulsion of the Assembly. Its best work on the covenant had been done after the full debate in the Assembly on the four policy questions, and another Assembly debate might provide the stimulation that was needed. A year earlier the Assembly had decided to include economic and social rights. This time it might do something about an individual right of petition. The commission was a relatively small body where conservative influences were overrepresented, whereas the General Assembly reflected the aspirations of the United Nations as a whole.

On 2 August, the Council's social committee began to discuss the report of the Commission on the Status of Women. The one redeeming feature was the performance of Mary Tenison-Woods, the Australian who had replaced Lakshmi Menon, and who was turning out to be a first-class chief of section. At its last session, the commission had recommended, amongst other things, that the Council approve a convention on the political rights of women, a draft of which it had forwarded to the Council; but, nearly two more years were to elapse before the draft convention would be ready for signature; it came into force in 1954. There was some sharp debate on a Soviet motion, which was defeated, to have the commission study a "peace" proposal sponsored by the Democratic Federation of Women.

Jean Lesage, a future premier of Quebec, was the head of the Canadian delegation. On 10 August, we had him, Mrs. Lesage and Mrs. Salmon (our Argentinian friend) for dinner at the Vieux Bois. Two days later, there was a Swiss national holiday and Lesage invited Jeanne and me to watch the fireworks from his apartment in the Hotel de la Paix. Lesage was a jolly fellow who liked parties. I enjoyed his company but never imagined that he would ever play the important role in Canadian politics that he later did.

The Council rejected the recommendation of the fifteen-member committee on freedom of information that a new information conference be convened to complete the work on the Convention on Freedom of Information and open it for signature. But there were some sharp speeches about the closing down of *La Prensa* in Argentina and the incarceration by the Czechs of the American journalist, William Nathan Oatis. Walter Kotchnig, speaking for the United States, made a devastating case; the Czech reply that Oatis was a spy convinced no one. The Poles then attacked Jacques Kayser, who made a brilliant reply. Enrique Bernstein, whose ranch I had visited in Chile, told me that his delegation would oppose the liquidation of the Sub-Commission on Freedom of Information. But as I was now pretty sure that this would happen, I talked to him about my idea (about which I had been talking to the UNESCO people) that the Council should appoint a rapporteur to prepare an annual report on the state of the freedom. This was subsequently tried, but Salvador Lopez, who was the rapporteur, did such a good job that governments were frightened and the experiment was never repeated. It was in this same week that Kayser told me that Guillaume Georges-Picot, the French minister in Buenos Aires, would succeed Laugier as the Assistant Secretary-General in charge of the Social Department in the Secretariat.

On 29 August, the Council decided to send the draft covenant to the General Assembly and to ask it to reconsider its decision that the instrument should include economic, social and cultural rights. Among the delegations supporting the recommendation were the American, the Belgian and the Canadian. Much as I wanted policy questions to be decided by the Assembly, I thought that it was most unwise to reopen this one. The decision to include these rights had already acquired a symbolic value; for while the beneficiaries of the rights were to be individuals and not states, the issue had become conflated with the aspirations of the developing countries to share in the benefits of modern industrial civilization. I recognized the technical difficulties that would result from including two quite different categories of rights in the same instrument, for each of them required different procedures for their implementation; but these difficulties could be overcome. I knew, moreover, the real reason why some of the delegations were so anxious not to include the rights in the covenant; for, while their governments might ratify a covenant on civil and political rights, they did not want to be internationally bound to respect economic and so-cial rights which had, for some of them, a socialistic flavor. If there were two instruments instead of one, it would be possible to ratify the one and not the other.

On 30 August, the Council's social committee began to discuss the report of the ad hoc committee on slavery. At one point in the boisterous debate, Corley Smith of the United Kingdom interrupted the Polish representative and later challenged a ruling of the chairman, who was Jiri Nosek of Czechoslovakia. Nosek's objectivity was challenged more than once, but he was personally popular and everyone agreed that his position was difficult. The ad hoc committee had come to the conclusion that slavery still existed, even in its crudest form, in certain parts of the world. There were also many practices which were analogous to slavery and because the Slavery Convention of 1926 only covered chat-tel slavery and the slade trade, the committee had recommended, amongst other things, that a supplementary convention on slavery and other forms of servitude be prepared. It was now being suggested that the Secretariat prepare a new report and make suggestions to the Council on the action that might be taken by the United Nations. There were at least two reasons why I thought that this was not a good idea, one of which I could not mention in a public debate. We had ourselves written most of the ad hoc committee's report, and I was not clear as to what we could add to it. But what worried me most was that such a mandate might be an unwelcome political responsibility. We were ready to do any work that might be involved, I said in my intervention, but the Council should appoint a rappor-teur who could act as our political umbrella. The Secretariat was given the mandate over my objections, but in 1954, the Council did adopt my suggestion and appoint Ambassador Hans Engen of Norway as rapporteur. We wrote practically every word of his report, which came before the Council in 1955, but the diplomatic niceties were preserved. The president of the Council gave a ball at the Palais des Nations the night following the slav-ery debate. After it was over, Jean Lesage invited Jeanne and me to his hotel suite for more festivities, but we had to refuse because I was going to Istanbul the next day. He told me later that his last guest left at six o'clock in the morning.

I had been asked at the last minute to represent the Secretary-General at meetings of the Inter-Parliamentary Union in Istanbul. The slavery debate had kept me in Geneva lon-ger than had been expected and I would now be late for the meetings; but I left Cointrin airport late on Saturday afternoon for Rome, where I spent most of the next morning in a cafe on the Piazza Colonna working on a speech to give at the conference.

In Istanbul I put up at the Konak Hotel which, I hoped, had seen better days. There were some I.L.O. people there attending a seminar on social security, to which I agreed to make a speech if I could work it in. On Monday morning, I went to the Yildiz Palace, where the Inter-Parliamentary Union was meeting, chiefly to pay my respects to its Secre-tary-General. The conference was discussing procedure, so I returned to Istanbul to make my speech at the opening session of the I.L.O. seminar. After the meeting, a young Italian doctor who was the representative of the World Health Organization in Istanbul wanted to talk to me about human rights. When I explained that I had to be back at the Yildiz Palace in the afternoon, that I only had two days in Istanbul and that I wanted to use this noon hour to see Santa Sophia and the Blue Mosque, he offered to drive me there and back. Dr. Mochi turned out to be an excellent guide and arranged for me to see a number of important things in the short time I had for sightseeing. I had lunch the following day in his apartment, and Mrs. Mochi took me for a quick visit to the bazaar, where I made some extravagant purchases. I did not have to make a speech to the Inter-Parliamentary Union after all, because the tribune was restricted to delegates; but I would have liked to say something when they began to discuss refugees. I thought the speeches were below United Nations standards.

Returning to Geneva, I stopped for a day in Athens, most of which I spent on the Acropolis. The Council, which was still in session, approved the recommendation of its social committee that the Secretariat be asked to prepare a new report on slavery. We were also given new responsibilities relating to freedom of information and the prevention of discrimination. There was now a tendency to rely more and more heavily on the Secretariat, which I might have interpreted as an expression of confidence had I not known that governments wanted to eliminate as many as possible of the Council's subordinate organs and, with the help of the Secretariat, have the Council take over their work. Retrenchment was in the air. The coordination committee had recommended that the two sub-commissions be liquidated and that the Commission on the Status of Women meet every two years instead of annually. The latter recommendation was, I thought, especially inept: everyone was saying that what the United Nations needed more than anything else was public support; had they forgotten that women make up more than half the world's population? As for the Human Rights Commission, it was to be allowed to complete its work on the covenant, after which its future would be considered. Corley Smith said that the British delegation "would view the winding up of the Human Rights Commission with mixed feelings." I remembered my conversation earlier in the year with Elizabeth Bowie, when she had said that the United Kingdom was thinking of withdrawing from the commission.

The Council adopted all of these recommendations. It was a crisis through which only the Human Rights Commission and its Sub-Commission on the Prevention of Discrimination would come through unscathed. The Human Rights Commission was too important a part of the United Nations structure for the Council ever to be able to carry out its threat. But the Commission on the Status of Women would henceforth meet only every second year and, having no support in the General Assembly, the Sub-Commission on Freedom of Information and of the Press was discontinued after one more session. When the report of the Council came before the next session of the more representative General Assembly, where the western countries were in a minority, the Council's decision to discontinue the Sub-Commission on the Prevention of Discrimination was challenged; and by a roll call vote of 31 to 10 with 13 abstentions, the Council was invited "to authorize the Sub-Commission to continue its work so that it may fulfill its mission." The only western country to vote for this resolution was Denmark. Stimulated by the attempt to liquidate it and the support that it had received in the General Assembly, the sub-commission very soon settled down, under a new lease of life, to a new and useful work program.

On Saturday, 22 September, the long session having finally ended, we moved out of our comfortable Swiss chalet and drove with friends to Antibes, where we spent a few days with Laugier and Marie before going on to Spain for a short holiday before the opening in Paris of the sixth session of the General Assembly.

At dinner on Monday night, Laugier asked us if we would like to meet Picasso. Since we so obviously wanted to, we drove to Vallauris next morning, where we stopped in front of a small villa set back in a large lot. Lying on the lawn was a kind of scarecrow made of all kinds of vegetables: it looked very much like one of the painter's more playful compositions. Marie had warned us that Picasso did not always take kindly to strangers; so it had been agreed that she would go into the house first to see how things stood. The painter's mistress, Françoise, then came to the door and beckoned to Laugier to come in. Jeanne and I waited in the yard, wondering whether we would be admitted to the great presence and consoling ourselves by eating the very good grapes that grew on his wall by the road. Just as we were resigning ourselves to the prospect of returning to Antibes without meeting the painter, Picasso came down the steps with a cordial greeting. Laugier had told him that we were on our way to Barcelona and this interested him; for notwithstanding his many years in France, he remained passionately Spanish. He did not look his seventy-one years. His black eyes shone with intelligence and he seemed to have the vigor of a young man. Even if I had not known that he was a great painter, I would have immediately identified him as a remarkable man. That evening we were driven to Cannes for dinner. Jeanne lost a poncho which she had bought in Buenos Aires, and was so upset about it that I wrote to Mrs. Salmon asking her to buy another. When Laugier's successor, Guillaume Georges-Picot arrived in New York, he had it with him.

Laugier drove us to Nice the next morning and we boarded a plane for Barcelona, where we discovered that the motor bus, which was to take us on our trip around Spain, would not leave for another week. There did not seem to be much point in waiting in Barcelona, so we decided to visit Mallorca and next day boarded a ship for Palma. One day while we were there, we fell on a military parade moving towards the Capitanea General, where there was some ceremony in honor of the fifteenth anniversary of Franco's assumption of power as *caudillo*. We followed the surprisingly few people who were attracted by it. There were officers from the three services and many priests, but notwithstanding all the colorful pageantry—soldiers dressed in medieval costumes and great banners—practically no one else. In Palma in any event and notwithstanding all the ballyhoo in the newspapers, the ''glorious'' anniversary passed with very little evidence that I could see of any popular enthusiasm.

Returning to Barcelona we started out on our trip around Spain, driving as far as Valencia the first day through country some of which we had already seen in June. There were miles and miles of olive trees, some vineyards and, as we came nearer to our destination, orange groves, but the villages were poor and dirty. Valencia was drenched with sun and the temperature was mild. That night we admired the façade of the Lonja. At Granada we were taken to see some gypsies dance in a cave in the Albaicin quarter. The dancing was superb, but the artists were as tough a lot as I have ever seen. Next we visited the Alhambra and the Generalife, after which everything that we saw in Granada came as an anticlimax.

We drove on to Cadiz and Seville. At first blush Seville had little in common with the romantic idea I had long since formed of the place. If you want to keep such ideas intact it is sometimes better not to travel. But I changed my mind the next day after we had visited the Alcazar and the cathedral and walked in some of the neat white streets of the Santa Cruz district. This was more like the Seville I had expected to see. It was against our instincts and better judgment that we went to a bullfight, where we enjoyed the crowd and opening pageantry but could not stomach the butchery. I can understand that some people may like to watch this kind of thing, but how it ever became the national sport of a proud and cultured people is beyond me. Out of politeness we tried not to display our emotions, but they must have been patent to the people sitting near us, because, when we got up to leave after the second bull had been killed—there were seven more to come—Jeanne noticed that the big burly fellow dressed in the traditional Sevillian costume, next to whom she had been sitting, had shown his disgust by spitting on her shoes. Before we could get out of the arena, an attendant insisted on taking us through the butchery where they were cutting up the bull that had just been killed—a special favor granted to foreigners perhaps, but from the expression on his face I guessed that it was simply his way of expressing his disgust at our extraordinary conduct. Twice before I had sworn that I would never see a bullfight again. I swore another oath, but I regret to record that I did not keep it, because in Madrid four years later, I obliged a colleague by accompanying him to another bullfight—my last.

Our last stop before Madrid was Cordoba, where the great attraction is the mosque which has been a cathedral since the early thirteenth century. It was after dark when we arrived in Madrid. The city looked gay and metropolitan in the neon lights; but next day in the hard light of the sun it seemed almost drab. What I wanted to see most was the Prado, where we spent most of our time on this visit. Later I came to know it quite well, because I stopped off several times in Madrid on my many subsequent trips from New York to Geneva or on my way back. We then moved on to Burgos, where our short stay was one of the most rewarding experiences of the trip. The city has great character, and its fine gothic cathedral is one of the most beautiful I have ever seen.

We left the tour at San Sebastian, where the weather had suddenly turned cold. Glad to be free from the routine of the tour, we relaxed for three days before going on to Paris.

Second Paris Session of the General Assembly (1951)

On the morning after our arrival in Paris, I was at the Palais de Chaillot when Robert Schuman presented the keys of the building to the Secretary-General, after which I met Guillaume Georges-Picot for the first time. He was, I guessed, the exact opposite of Laugier and probably as cold as a fish; one of my colleagues once said that he had ice water in his veins. Georges-Picot was certainly not given to enthusiasms. He never smiled once during our first talk, which lasted for over an hour. His lips, I noticed, were so thin that they were hardly discernible. I discovered later that he suffered from liver problems, which was probably why he was so abstemious in his habits, another thing that made him quite different from my old chief. There were times when he would shut himself in his office, refusing all visitors, and he went to Vichy every year for a cure. Born into a wealthy family, he was a professional diplomat, was married to a Russian refugee and had three handsome daughters.

It took me a long time to penetrate this cold exterior; but once I did, my respect for the man grew and our relations, while never warm, were good and even close. When Hussein Mohammad Asfahany resigned as the principal director of the Social Department in 1953, I took over the post in an acting capacity and moved into an office next to the Assistant Secretary-General, who often called me into his office simply to talk about anything that was bothering him. In the last months of his tenure—before he resigned because he quarreled with Hammarskjold about his role as Assistant Secretary-General—he used these talks with me to let off steam, and I would hear first-hand an account of some row that he had had with the Secretary-General. They revealed not only the deep emotion behind Georges-Picot's cold exterior but an aspect of Hammarskjold's character that belied the popular image. Georges-Picot later returned to the United Nations as the permanent representative of France. Knowing as much as I did about his relations with Hammarskjold, I wondered how this would work out. On the surface their new relationship was smooth enough, but by that time I was no longer the ambassador's confidant. Unlike Laugier, Georges-Picot had no special interest in or enthusiasm for the human rights program. I can remember only one sign of real interest: during the troubles in North Africa he was interested in the possibility that the United Nations might provide some protection for the rights of French colonists, if they had to be abandoned by the mother country.

One of the first business matters I discussed with Georges-Picot was the department's budget for 1952, and I went over the speech—his first at the United Nations—which he was to make in the Fifth Committee defending this budget. He put up a good fight but he might just as well have remained silent, because, as usual, most of the delegations had instructions to vote for the recommendations of the advisory committee, which had already cut the budget. As for those parts of it relating to human rights, I suspected that some governments were afraid of the program and wanted to slow it down. Carl J. Hambro of Norway practically said so. Sir William Mathews of the United Kingdom criticized the Secretariat with such fervor that I wondered what his real motives could be. Our best friends that day were Valenzuela of Chile, Machado of Brazil and Ganem of France. The Canadians were coldly efficient and contributed generously to our defeat. As Pollack, who was representing Canada in the committee, put it to me after the meeting, the human rights program did not have high priority in Ottawa. A few days later, Tor Gjesdal complained to me about the role the Canadians were playing in bringing about the even more drastic cuts in the budget of the Department of Public Information.

The sixth session of the General Assembly did not open until 6 November. In the meantime, I had an office in the Palais Rose and represented the Secretary-General at meetings of the UNESCO executive board. I was concerned about the position it might take in the matter of economic and social rights. When the board discussed the question on 30 October, all the speakers but two wanted a single covenant which would include both economic and social as well as civil and political rights. I noticed, however, that both Sir Ronald Adam of the United Kingdom and Luther Evans of the United States remained silent. Hanna Saba, UNESCO's legal counsel, then prepared a carefully worded paper for a working party which met in the afternoon; but, on the initiative of India's Sir Arcot Mudaliar, this was replaced by a much more strongly worded document. I was delighted. Jeanne and I had lunch with the Cassins in their apartment on the Boulevard St. Michel. We had been in this apartment before, but today it seemed particularly old-fashioned, dark and cold. I could imagine Cassin living there many years earlier as a young professor. In the evening we went to a play in Montparnasse. The General Assembly had not yet begun, but we were already busy every day with some kind of social activity. On Sunday afternoon, we went to see Laugier and Marie. There were many people there, most of them strangers, and we found the party dull; but it was always worth visiting 55 rue de Babylonne, if only to see the unique collection of pictures. On Monday, we dined at the home of Hélène Lefaucheux, the chairman of the Commission on the Status of Women. Her husband was the president of the Renault Motor Car Company and most of the guests were apparently his business friends. Jeanne got into an argument with one of the women. She had made some remark about thinking internationally and not as a Canadian since we had come to the United Nations. The Frenchwoman commented that while this might be easy for a Canadian it would be impossible for a Frenchwoman. Jeanne made some reply, still trying to be polite.

"Mais enfin, vous êtes française," said the Frenchwoman.

"Non, madame, je suis Canadienne."

"Allez donc, vous parlez français et vous ancêtres étaient français."

By this time, Jeanne exclaimed, thoroughly aroused, "Il y a trois cents ans de ça et je m'en rappelle à peine." The Frenchwoman, furious, shot from her chair and moved to the other side of the room. She had deserved what she got.

Mrs. Roosevelt had arrived in Paris and was staying at the Hotel Crillon, where she invited me for lunch. The Americans, I learned, were apparently ready to proceed with the final drafting of the covenant at this session of the Assembly. Mrs. Roosevelt said that she was convinced the British no longer wanted a covenant; but she had not yet talked to anyone in the new Conservative government; she would, she said, talk to Churchill.

Cassin came to my office to talk about the French position on the covenant. He was insisting that the complaints system, which had been devised for the implementation of civil and political rights, also be made applicable to economic, social and cultural rights. I knew that this was impossible. Most of these rights are nonjusticiable program rights, the implementation of which can only be achieved progressively; and, I was afraid that if Cassin continued to insist that the complaints procedure also apply to them, he might compromise what little progress the commission had made on implementation. "Vous coulerez toute l'affaire," I said. He must have been convinced, because, before leaving my office, he promised to drop the matter if the Americans would agree to extending the reporting system (which the Human Rights Commission had recommended for the implementation of economic and social rights) to civil and political rights. This made sense, and I had been advocating it ever since the commission had decided not to give a right of petition to individuals and nongovernmental organizations. It was unlikely that governments would use their right to complain unless they were politically motivated; but if they were under an obligation to report periodically on the progress they were making toward the realization of the rights, the United Nations could exercise some degree of supervision. I told Cassin that I had already raised the question in my talks with the Americans and that I thought that they would agree.

It was only on 30 November that the Third Committee began to discuss human rights. Cassin gave a luncheon that day at which, in addition to Jeanne and me, the guests were Trygve Lie, Georges-Picot and Boustra (of the Quai d'Orsay). The chairman of the committee was Anita Figueroa of Chile, the first of many women to have the place. An unfortunate tradition developed that, if a woman were to be chairman of one of the main committees of the General Assembly, it had better be the Third—on the insulting assumption, I suppose, that she would do the least harm there, just as Mrs. Roosevelt was relegated to the Third Committee in 1946. But this was the most difficult of all the committees because the most uninhibited politically and procedurally the most unruly. Anita Figueroa was a woman of considerable ability and great charm, but even a strong and experienced chairman would have been in difficulty in that committee in 1951. It was at this session that the Arabs began to make their voices heard in discussions on human rights. They quickly became the militant spokesmen of the developing world which was still underrepresented at the United Nations. If they and the communist countries were beginning to take the initiative in human rights matters, the Western democracies, which were no longer providing dynamic leadership, had only themselves to blame. A vacuum had been created which other countries hastened to fill.

I was now fully occupied with the Third Committee where, after some procedural maneuvering, the general debate on the covenant had begun. The long general debate that takes place in the plenary sessions (when anything can be discussed and which sometimes attracts heads of government, foreign ministers and other important personalities) probably serves a useful purpose. This cannot be said of the general debate with which, in the Third Committee, the discussion of almost every agenda item was begun and which was usually a waste of time. At the sixth session, the general debate on the covenant lasted until after the Christmas adjournment. It is true that the future of the covenant was still in doubt and that a number of controversial issues, which the General Assembly was supposed to have decided in 1950, were being reopened. One of them was whether, as already indicated, there was to be only one instrument including both civil and political and economic and social rights or whether there were to be two separate instruments. Early in the debate, Mrs. Roosevelt made a suggestion which was a certain advance in the American position; there should, she said, be two instruments but they should both be approved and opened for signature at the same time. I still preferred one instrument divided into two parts, but the American suggestion, which was the one adopted, had at least the merit of treating the two categories equally. The other controversial issue related to the self-determination of peoples about which the Human Rights Commission had done nothing, notwithstanding the instructions the Assembly had given it in 1950. The Arab delegations in particular were crying up the issue again and it seemed pretty obvious that, at this session, the Assembly would decide that there should be an article in the covenant stating that self-determination is a human right.

Judge Guerrero, who was the chairman of the ad hoc commission on prisoners of war, wanted to talk to P.D. Morozov about the possibility of repatriating the prisoners still in the Soviet Union. I tried several times to arrange a meeting, but Morozov could not be budged. He said that the position of the Soviet government had been definitively stated in their last letter to the Secretariat; the matter was therefore exhausted and no purpose would be served by the meeting. The vice-president of the International Court of Justice deserved more courtesy than this; and, it was just as well perhaps that Guerrero had retired when, nearly two decades later, Morozov was elected to the Court. During all this time, I was as sick as I have ever been in my life. My doctor thought I had jaundice—a thing I attributed to an excellent lunch of oysters and Alsatian wine with an international lawyer friend, E.H. Loewenfeld, and Prince Henri of Liechtenstein.

About this time I also had lunch at the home of M. Boustra, who was the head of the international organizations division at the Quai d'Orsay. The countess of something or other who was on my right explained that it was very difficult for foreigners to know ''les gens bien'' in Paris. There was one man at the party whom she probably would have described as ''un homme bien'' although he did not have the advantage of being a Parisian. Thanassis Agnides was the chairman of the advisory committee on financial and administrative questions. Addressing himself to Selwyn Lloyd, but obviously intending me to overhear, he said that whenever his committee touched the human rights budget, the director of the Division raised the cry that human rights were being attacked. He was pulling my leg, but I was not in the mood for banter on that subject because only a few days before the Fifth Committee had cut our budget on the recommendation of his committee. But the encounter may have done some good, because a few days later I was called before Agnides' committee. It was already after twelve o'clock when my turn came to speak and the members were impatient to get away to lunch. In the circumstances I hardly expected to make much of an impression, and was therefore surprised when the Fifth Committee restored, on the recommendation of the experts, part of the cut that had been made in our 1952 budget.

There were difficulties with the third human rights concert. Because our own Department of Public Information was being anything but helpful—they seemed to think the Universal Declaration was already old hat—I had turned to UNESCO. The event was particularly successful. Not only was there a brilliant performance in the theater of the Palais de Chaillot, but orchestras and choirs in other countries, including the Danish State Radio Orchestra, the Symphony Orchestra of Radio Italiana, the Orchestra and Chorus of La Scala, the BBC Symphony Orchestra, the Vienna Philharmonic Orchestra and the Chorus of the Gesellschaft der Musikfreunde all cooperated and the programs were broadcast to international audiences.

Exceptionally, this session of the General Assembly was to run into the New Year and last until 5 February 1952. But there was to be a break over the Christmas holiday. The French government had invited a party of foreign journalists to spend a week in Cannes, and my wife and I were asked to join them. I am not sure to what I can attribute this act of favoritism; we were the only people in the party who were not journalists and the only ones from the Secretariat. It was a welcome holiday. We arrived in Cannes on a Monday morning, 24 December, in time to attend a reception at the Hotel de Ville. That afternoon we went to Villauris. This time we did not see Picasso, but I very well remember admiring his *Homme au mouton*. It was Christmas Eve and there was a *reveillon* at the Casino. On Christmas Day we went by boat to St. Honorat and St. Marguerite, islands just off the coast; and the next day were driven for a change of climate up to the skiing resort of Aurons. There were also drives along the Riviera to the Italian border and to Grasse.

We returned to Paris on the 29th. I left the next day for London to make a speech at a meeting organized by the Council for Education in World Citizenship. London was shrouded in a thick, yellowish fog, and the cold penetrated even the warmest clothing. I was to make my speech on New Year's Day, so I had a day to roam around the city, which I can enjoy even in the fog. In the evening, I watched a good-humored crowd celebrate the arrival of the New Year in Picadilly and Trafalgar Square. I could not help remarking on the contrast with what I had been seeing in France. A journalist to whom I talked in Cannes had said that the French people had forgotten how to laugh.

There were some three thousand students at the meeting on New Year's Day. I spoke after Sir Benegal Rau, after which the chairman gave a platform luncheon. I then went for another walk and spent over an hour in the National Gallery. But the picture I took back to Paris was the living view of the Victoria embankment from the new Thames bridge. The fog had disappeared and it had been a bright, brisk day and a delight to be in London.

Going through immigration that evening at Victoria Station I produced my United Nations laissez-passer. "Is that all you have?" asked the official. "Well no," I replied and showed him my Canadian diplomatic passport. "That will still be good," he said, "when the other has been forgotten." The channel crossing was so rough that the ferry practically stood on her head; but I am a good sailor and managed to get some sleep.

Van Heuven Goedhart, the high commissioner for refugees, had been impatiently trying to get the Third Committee to interrupt its discussion of other human rights questions to deal with his report, and, for no good reason, the committee had acquiesced. The interruption lasted for a week. The debate was highly political and van Heuven Goedhart came in for some sharp criticism. Much of this was occasioned by a book, *The Refugee in the Post-War World,* which had been written by independent researchers and financed by the Rockefeller Foundation, but published by the United Nations under an official document symbol. A number of delegations said the book was biased, the Russians going so far as to say that it smelled of fascism. The committee devoted five meetings to the incident, which was disposed of only when the high commissioner undertook to issue a press release stating that the book was not a United Nations document, that he was not responsible for its contents, that the United Nations symbol would be removed from all copies of the work still in the possession of the organization, which would cease to circulate it, and that a notice would be inserted in all copies still available to the effect that its authors were alone responsible for the opinions expressed in it. What really happened, it seems, was that van Heuven Goedhart had signed the preface without reading the book. I was in close touch with him all the time the hounds were at his heels. We had dinner together the night his father died in Holland. Van Heuven Goedhart had great qualities, but he was not a good administrator and was sometimes carried away by his zeal, shortcomings that did not make him any the less sympathetic as a man. While all this was going on, the committee was being chaired by its vice-chairman, Fernand Dehousse of Belgium. Dehousse delighted in controversy and sometimes provoked it. In spite of his brilliance, he was therefore a poor chairman and was partly responsible for the long unproductive debate on refugees.

The report of the high commissioner was out of the way, but we were now pressed for time; the session would last for only two more weeks, which meant that there would be Saturday and night meetings. Four delegations—Chile, Egypt, Pakistan and Yugoslavia—moved that the decision taken in 1950 that the covenant include economic and social rights be reaffirmed. There were a number of amendments and sub-amendments, including one with strong American backing proposing reconsideration. The latter amendment was adopted by a small majority, but the question was reopened in plenary session, when Chile moved that that part of the Third Committee's resolution which recommended that there be two covenants be deleted and that the Assembly decide that there would be a single covenant including both kinds of rights. After a bitter debate, the Chilean amendment was defeated by a roll call vote of 29 to 25 with 4 abstentions. The largely ideological controversy and decision split the United Nations down the middle. It could have been avoided, for it would have been possible to draft an instrument in two parts with a different system of implementation for each category of rights, which would have recognized their essential unity as the Universal Declaration had done, satisfied the socialist and developing countries, and in no way prejudiced the interests of the others.

It was at this session that the Third Committee began to earn its bad reputation. At one evening meeting so many points of order, most of them unfounded, were raised, that Anita Figueroa, who was now back in the chair, lost her temper and precipitously adjourned the meeting. Most of the trouble was coming from a small but vociferous group of delegations which were beginning to use the committee for political ends that had little to do with human rights or anything else on the agenda. The committee was called the social, humanitarian and cultural committee, but it was fast becoming as political as any in the General Assembly. Politics came in through the back door, and that was one of the reasons why its meetings were so hard to conduct. It was relatively easy for a small delegation or an ambitious man to play an important role in a committee that was not supposed to be discussing the great political issues that were the stock in trade of the Cold War. In the First and ad hoc political committees, countries had to keep in line and stand up and be counted; in the Third Committee there were no inhibitions. All this was compounded by bad manners, bad temper, fake points of order, irrelevant speeches and ambitious men who wanted to play a role in the international arena. After the session was over, Trygve Lie said that it was the Social Department of the Secretariat which had had the toughest time at the Assembly. Sitting in the Third Committee and trying to advise its chairman was certainly one of the toughest jobs I had at the United Nations.

It was a relief to worry about something else. One thing that I could always worry about was freedom of information. It had occurred to me that there should be a high commissioner for freedom of information who would be a kind of international ombudsman, with power to investigate complaints against governments and the media. Jacques Kayser and Fernand Terrou, whom I invited to lunch to discuss the idea, were so enthusiastic that I thought the French might take it up; but, like my later idea that there should be a United Nations High Commissioner for Human Rights, the time was not ripe for it. Back in the Third Committee that afternoon, we seemed to be making better progress, until the chairman, who was gaining confidence, crossed swords with Jamil Baroody, the representative of Saudi Arabia. She dined with my wife and me and Laugier and Marie Cutolli that evening. She needed to let off steam and did so with great gusto.

Much more controversial even than the decision to have two covenants instead of one, was the decision, approved by the majority, to include in each covenant an article stating that self-determination is a legal right. In the Third Committee the resolution was sponsored by thirteen countries and adopted, after the committee had voted on ten amendments and sub-amendments, by a roll call vote of 33 to 9 with 10 abstentions. The question was reopened in plenary, where the vote was even more conclusive—42 to 7 with 5 abstentions. My own reaction (which turned out to be wrong) was that the decision would wreck the covenants because it would prevent many countries from ratifying them. That it should be possible for all peoples to determine their own destiny may be a desirable political principle and a good guide for statesmen. It had, for example, been an underlying principle of the Treaty of Versailles. But to say that it is a legal right without qualification comes near to madness, particularly when there is no agreement on what is meant by a "people." One wonders how so many countries could have voted for the resolution. Perhaps they never intended to ratify the covenants. The decision was an incident in the fight against colonialism; and, as is now clear, the articles are not meant to mean what they clearly say. In the philosophy of the United Nations, self-determination is now understood to be a right that can be exercised only by a colonial people against a metropolitan power and, once it has been exercised, it cannot be invoked again. Nigeria could invoke the rule against Great Britain but Biafra had no such right against Nigeria. Since most of the former colonies are now independent states and members of the United Nations, the rule as so defined no longer has much meaning.

The Third Committee wound up its business in the evening of Saturday, 2 February. It was at this meeting that the Egyptians, to whom I had been talking about the matter, moved that the Economic and Social Council be asked to request the Human Rights Commission to make recommendations regarding the treatment of communications addressed to the United Nations alleging violations of human rights. The adoption of this resolution was, from my point of view, one of the most encouraging developments at the sixth session of the Assembly; and had the Economic and Social Council acted on it, which it did not, an implementation system, not related to the covenants but based on powers possessed by the United Nations under its Charter, might have been developed nearly two decades before the Council finally adopted a resolution under which such communications can be looked at to discover whether situations exist which reveal consistent patterns of gross violations of human rights.

Self-Determination of Peoples (1952)

My wife and I had decided to return to New York on the S.S. *Constitution*. I worked hard to dispose of all the things that had accumulated on my desk and we were able to take the train to Cannes on Thursday, 7 February. After three days there basking in the sun, we took a lighter to board the *Constitution,* which was lying off the coast. We did very little on that trip except sit in our deck chairs and read. In a display of exceptional energy, we were up one morning before daylight to watch the approach to Gibraltar, but the ship did not dock and we were not allowed to go on shore. It was the fourth time I had passed that rock without touching it, nor have I yet. There were a number of United Nations people on board, including the American member of the advisory committee on administrative and budgetary questions, who referred to Laugier as his worst enemy, whereupon I said that he was my best friend.

We docked at New York on Monday morning, 18 February, and I was in my office that afternoon. I had only to look at the calendar to see that I had a busy time ahead. There would be sessions that spring of the Commission on Human Rights, of the Commission on the Status of Women, and of the Sub-Commission on Freedom of Information; ECOSOC would meet in special session and again in the summer, and the Sub-Commission on the Prevention of Discrimination would meet in the fall. All of these, except the Commission on the Status of Women, would meet at headquarters, which was probably just as well for my reputation in the Secretariat, for I was being criticized (perversely, because it was quite beyond my control) for my long absences from New York.

My morale had reached a low point, and I had been turning over in my mind the possibility of returning to academic life. It happened that the day after my return to headquarters, Frank Scott, who had just accepted a U.N. technical assistance post in Burma, came to see me. He strongly advised me to return to McGill. My disenchantment was not with the United Nations, in which I believed as firmly as ever, but with my life and role in the Secretariat. Laugier's departure had taken much of the sparkle out of my work. By comparison Georges-Picot was a cold fish. I sometimes wondered whether he really believed in what we were trying to do. He said to me about this time that public discussion in the United Nations merely increased the tension between the Soviet Union and the United States, and that the Soviet Union was using the United Nations to stir up resentment in the economically developing world against the Western powers. There was a great deal of truth in this but I did not like to hear it said. Georges-Picot was a professional diplomat and by nature a cautious man; he would be a prudent and probably efficient chief of the department; but he would give us little if any leadership. The chief reason for my depression, however, was the experience I had just gone through in Paris and the dark view that I had of the future of the covenants. My pessimism was summed up, perhaps, in the advice I gave to a Canadian civil servant who came to see me about a post he had been offered in the U.N. technical assistance administration. If he took it on, I said, he should do so in the same spirit that he would accept a fellowship and make sure that his job remained open in Ottawa.

The Sub-Commission on Freedom of Information and of the Press opened its fifth and final session on Monday, 3 March. Its performance did nothing to boost my morale, although I felt a little better once we began working on the draft code of ethics which was at least concrete. The sub-commission adopted the code on 14 March with Basily Zonov of the U.S.S.R., Carroll Binder of the U.S.A. and Robert Waitham of the United Kingdom all abstaining. I had lunch the day this vote was taken with a man from the U.S. state department, from whom I gathered that Binder thought I was a sinister influence and largely responsible for the fact that the sub-commission was making so little progress. The truth of the matter was that this last session of the sub-commission had been convened for the express purpose of completing the work on the code. If Binder wanted to debate Cold War politics, he should have had himself named as the U.S. representative on the Security Council. When the code came before the Economic and Social Council in June, that body decided to send it to national and international professional associations and information enterprises and to inform them that, if they thought it desirable, the United Nations would cooperate in organizing an international professional conference for the purpose of adopting the code. This decision was later confirmed by the General Assembly, but the "profession" was apparently uninterested and the conference was never convened.

On 18 March, the sub-commission adopted a resolution condemning the closing down of *La Prensa* by the Argentine government. This must have been the first time an organ of the Economic and Social Council ever condemned a member state of the United Nations for a specific violation of human rights. The sub-commission met for the last time on Friday, 21 March. It expired without a whimper, and the people responsible for its demise must have felt that they had done the right thing. But potentially it had an important role to play, and its disappearance has left a gap which is partly responsible for the frustrating story of freedom of information in the United Nations. I did everything I could to revive the sub-commission with no success. I also considered alternative ways of doing the work. In Paris I had talked to Kayser and Terrou about the possibility of setting up an office of High Commissioner for Freedom of Information and, later in 1952, talked to friendly delegates about an international commission of inquiry without, however, very much conviction that either idea was politically feasible. More practical was the proposal that ECOSOC appoint a special rapporteur on freedom of information. This was tried, as already mentioned, but the rapporteur did his work so well that governments were frightened and the experiment was not repeated.

On 24 March there was a special session of the Economic and Social Council for the sole purpose of transmitting the instructions of the General Assembly concerning the drafting of the covenants to the Commission on Human Rights. It was the first meeting ever to be held in the new Council chamber and interesting only for that reason. A week later my wife and I were in Montreal. We were going to have a short holiday in the Laurentians, but my real reason for visiting Canada at that time of the year was to sound out people at McGill about the possibility of returning to academic life. I had lunch with Principal James on Monday and the next day talked to Dean Meredith at the Law Faculty. I gathered that the decision was for me to take.

We were back in New York in time for the opening on Monday, 14 April, of the eighth session of the Human Rights Commission. The officers were elected, the agenda was adopted and the commission was already discussing the first item, the right of peoples to self-determination, all within fifteen minutes. As instructed by the General Assembly, the commission adopted the text which, as amended by the Assembly, is now Article 1 of each of the two covenants. If anything, the commission's text was even more radical than the one finally adopted; for, in its third paragraph, after saying that self-determination includes permanent sovereignty over natural wealth and resources, it said that "in no case may a people be deprived of its own means of subsistence on the grounds of any rights that may be claimed by other states." The author of this paragraph, which was later softened down in the General Assembly, was Hernan Santa Cruz of Chile, and I remember how annoyed Mrs. Roosevelt was when he introduced it. In addition to the articles for the covenants, the commission also recommended two resolutions for adoption by the Assembly. One would have recommended that member states:

(1) uphold the principle of self-determination of peoples and nations and respect their independence; (2) recognize and promote the realization of the right of self-determination of the people of Non-Self-Governing and Trust Territories under their administration; and (3) grant this right on demand for self-determination of these peoples, the popular wish being ascertained in particular through a plebiscite under the auspices of the United Nations.

This text already contained the essential features of the Declaration on the Granting of Independence to Colonial Countries and Peoples which the General Assembly adopted on 14 December, 1960.

Most of the session was devoted to self-determination, but, on the basis of work done at previous sessions, the commission also drafted several other articles for inclusion in the covenants. It did not have the time, and perhaps no desire, to consider measures for their implementation, nor did it discuss the report of its Sub-Commission on the Prevention of Discrimination and the Protection of Minorities. While the Council had not asked it to do so, it did discuss the procedures for dealing with the many communications alleging violations of human rights which the United Nations was receiving; but a proposal that these procedures be changed was rejected. The commission also included in its report—and this was quite new—an analysis, prepared by the Secretariat, of the 25,279 communications received between 3 April, 1951 and 7 May, 1952. Of these, 24,294 alleged persecution on political grounds, 305 alleged genocide, 119 related to freedom of assembly and association, 64 to discrimination and the rights of minorities, 83 to trade union rights, and 478 to various other matters; 36 raised general principles without alleging any violations of human rights.

The session ended early Saturday morning, 15 June. We had scheduled Friday evening for adopting the report to ECOSOC, which is usually a routine matter; but the meeting was used to fight the Cold War and lasted all night. That morning I saw the sun rise over the East River.

In the meantime the Economic and Social Council was also meeting, but it did not reach the human rights items on its agenda until the end of July, when, after a lively debate which lasted through three meetings, it forwarded the commission's two controversial recommendations on self-determination to the General Assembly, but "without comment," which could be taken to mean that it accepted no responsibility for them. The Soviet Union reopened the question of the division of the covenant and moved a resolution which would have recommended that the General Assembly again reconsider its decision, but this was defeated by a vote of 10 to 6 with 2 abstentions.

It will be remembered that on the initiative of Egypt the General Assembly had asked the Council to request the commission to study the procedures for dealing with communications alleging violations of human rights. The Egyptian and Uruguayan delegations now moved that the commission be asked to make recommendations to the Council based on those communications which, in the commission's opinion, merited the Council's attention. The commission would also have been asked to recommend modifications in the existing procedures for dealing with the communications. The two delegations put up a good fight, but the Canadians had already moved that the Council take no action on the matter; and since their motion had priority under the rules of procedure, it was voted on first; it was adopted by a vote of 11 to 3 with 4 abstentions. I was disgusted that the delegation of my own country should have taken the lead in thwarting an initiative which might have helped give some reality to the great words of the Charter.

By the time the Council adjourned it was becoming uncomfortably hot in New York, and we were glad to get away for a short holiday. On our return to New York, we moved into our new apartment on Sutton Place, which we had chosen because it was only a few blocks from United Nations Headquarters. Not only could I walk to and from work, which is a rare thing in New York, but living there made my working day shorter, particularly when there were night meetings or receptions that I had to attend.

The Economic and Social Council had bowed to the wishes of the General Assembly and reconsidered its decision to abolish the Sub-Commission on the Prevention of Discrimination and the Protection of Minorities, which now had a new lease on life; it opened its fifth session on 22 September. But a new lease on life would be meaningful only if we could develop a useful work program. In the past, by devoting so much time to the protection of minorities, concerning which it was obvious that the United Nations did not intend to take any action—for the simple reason that most governments wanted to assimilate their minorities—the sub-commission had largely neglected a field where action was politically possible; namely, the prevention of discrimination. The protection of minorities had therefore become a kind of red herring. It must be added in defense of the sub-commission that it was not entirely to blame for what had happened; for the General Assembly had expressly asked it to continue its work on minorities. But this was to be the last session at which this comedy was to be played. The man responsible for the change was the sub-commission's secretary, Edward Lawson, who thought up the program of studies of various aspects of discrimination that kept the sub-commission busy for many years to come and made it one of the most useful organs in the United Nations. The new program was very nearly compromised when an internal working paper (on which there was no official symbol) containing a draft resolution was prematurely circulated. A member asked for an explanation and the paper was hastily withdrawn, but it nevertheless became the basis for the future work program. It is no exaggeration to say that the increasingly good reputation of the sub-commission dates from the incident.

The first study in the new program was to be on discrimination in education, and its rapporteur Minoo Masani; but, because the Indian government would not allow him to continue as a member of the sub-commission, he was replaced by Charles Ammoun of Lebanon whose study, completed in 1956, was an important contribution and became the basis for the UNESCO Convention on the Prevention of Discrimination in Education, one of the brightest stones in that organization's crown. UNESCO was at first frightened by this study, would not undertake it itself, and was opposed to our doing it. It happened that Ammoun was also representing his country at UNESCO and, in that capacity, he tried to get its secretariat to cooperate in the preparation of the study; but Luther Evans, its director general, refused to have anything to do with it because it might have meant criticizing governments. It was characteristic of Henri Laugier, who was then a member of the UNESCO executive board, that, at one of its meetings, he took Evans to task for his refusal to cooperate.

The sub-commission later made or initiated studies in a wide area of subjects including, in my day, discrimination in employment and occupation (by the International Labor Office on the suggestion of the sub-commission); in the matter of religious rights and practices; in the exercise of political rights; the right of everyone to leave any country including his own and to return to his country; and discrimination in the administration of justice. The success of the program, which was later copied by the Human Rights Commission, although less successfully, was due in great part to the method followed in preparing the studies. The sub-commission first adopted a questionnaire which was sent to governments. With the information thus obtained and other information at its disposal, the Secretariat then prepared a series of country monographs, theoretically one for every country, although, because of the magnitude of the research involved, we usually settled on a representative selection. The monographs were then sent to governments for comments and suggestions. It was in their interest to cooperate because they knew that the monographs would be used in any event. They also had an opportunity at this point quietly to correct any practice that fell below acceptable standards. The country monographs were usually more revealing than the completed study; but because the cost of translating them would be considerable, they were not circulated as regular United Nations documents and were not readily available to the public. The failure of the Secretariat to circulate them became a fruitful source of conflict between it and the sub-commission. The completed study, which was prepared on the basis of the monographs, might contain recommendations; and the sub-commission also usually adopted a series of principles which might, as in the case of the study on discrimination in education, become the basis for a convention.

Human Rights in the Secretariat (1952)

The sub-commission adjourned on 10 October and the General Assembly began to meet four days later. We were still having human rights problems of our own in the Secretariat. The day after the Assembly opened, there was a meeting of directors in Georges-Picot's office to discuss the investigations by American authorities of alleged communists in the Secretariat. The directors agreed that, if there were to be any investigations, they should be conducted by the Secretary-General, and that no one should be dismissed unless there was definite proof that he had been engaged in some activity directed against the United States government; membership in the Communist Party, much less political opinion, should not be a ground for dismissal.

When the General Assembly was in session, I spent most of my time in its Third Committee and, unless I had business there, seldom had the time to go into the rooms where other committees were meeting. Their debates on the great political issues I followed mainly in the columns of the *New York Times*. But at this session I did follow closely the debates in the General Committee and in plenary on the racial situation in South Africa. The South Africans were arguing that the item should not be included in the agenda because, by Article 2, paragraph 7 of the Charter, the United Nations had no right to intervene "in matters which are essentially within the domestic jurisdiction of any state." This argument was never accepted by the United Nations, although member states shifted their position on the question to suit their convenience. It was a nice point of international law whether the adoption of a resolution on such a matter or even its discussion was intervention in the technical legal sense. Intervention seemed to require an element of coercive interference in the affairs of a state, impairing its independence. But consistent patterns of gross violations of human rights, like those occurring in South Africa, were certainly not matters essentially within the domestic jurisdiction of a state.

The Third Committee held its first meeting on Monday, 20 October. Georges-Picot made a short statement explaining that it would be impossible for him to attend all the meetings, but it never occurred to him to welcome the delegates or to make some other friendly remark. The contrast with Laugier could hardly have been greater, but he was already becoming one of the most influential assistant secretaries-general and I was beginning to learn that there was a great deal behind that cold exterior.

The McCarthy witch-hunt had finally reached the Human Rights Division. I had been congratulating myself because none of my people were implicated; but one of them was now subpoenaed to appear before a federal grand jury and would also have to appear before the senate investigating committee. I knew nothing about her political persuasion, but I was reasonably sure that she had never been disloyal to the United States. Over my protest, another American member was later discharged because he was suspected of being a homosexual, the rationalization being that he had become vulnerable to blackmail. I pointed out that he knew no secrets—very few members of the Secretariat did—but no one listened. Martin Hill, who was in the Secretary-General's executive office, consulted me about the officer who had been subpoenaed to appear before the grand jury. Lie, he said, would be taking a decision on the matter that very day. I repeated to him what the directors had said at the meeting in Georges-Picot's office. If there had to be an inquiry, the Secretary-General should conduct it himself and there should be no guilt by association; but, if it could be proved that any member of the staff had been engaged in any activity against a member state, he should be discharged. Martin said that Byron Price, the American Assistant Secretary-General in charge of administrative and financial services, wanted to fire anyone who refused to say whether or not he was a communist. Price was the first American in the Secretariat to present himself to be fingerprinted. The Americans were about to go to the polls to elect a new president, and some people were saying that the current hate campaign against the United Nations was part of an attack against the state department. I listened to some of the speeches over the radio. How could any intelligent person believe the things that Senator McCarthy was saying? All of this had its impact on the morale of the Secretariat. But much of the resentment was reserved for Lie, who had been weak in resisting the American demands.

It was no great surprise when, on 10 November, Lie submitted his resignation. The determining factor in bringing this about was certainly his increasingly bad relations with the Soviet Union and the other communist countries which, ever since the extension of his tenure by the General Assembly in 1951—illegally they said—had refused to recognize him as Secretary-General. The boycott was complete. Even correspondence was no longer addressed to the Secretary-General but to the Secretariat, and he was harassed in many other ways. He was not invited to their social functions, nor did they attend his. More important, he could no longer perform one of his essential political roles, which was to act as an intermediary between the powers. There was a good deal of sympathy for Lie who, as Laugier had once said, was being punished for the stand that he had taken in the Korean crisis. But I have no doubt that his handling of the witch-hunt in the Secretariat was also a factor in his resignation; for he had quite lost the confidence of the staff, and, I suspect, of many governments. I remember talking to Georges-Picot about this shortly before the event, when he said that the time had come for Lie to go.

Lie's announcement immediately gave rise to a series of rumors. The favorite candidate of the West for the succession was Lester Pearson, the president that year of the General Assembly; but the Soviet Union, which had prevented his election in 1946, vetoed the choice. Pearson could have performed the political functions of the office with great ability; what kind of administrative chief he would have made, I do not know. Amongst the other names mentioned or proposed were several—Nasrollah Entezam, Charles Malik and Carlos Romulo—who had been or still were representing their governments on the Human Rights Commission. I would have been happy with any of them. But it was not until the following March that agreement was reached on a successor, a man who had never been mentioned as a possibility.

On Thursday 13 November, I was in the ad hoc political committee where I heard Professor Ahmed Bokhari of Pakistan—who later became the head of the Department of Public Information in the Secretariat—make a forceful speech on the racial situation in South Africa. It was the day that Abe Feller committed suicide by throwing himself out of his apartment window. I have no doubt that Abe was a victim of the witch-hunt, at least indirectly. He was not being investigated himself, but some of his colleagues and friends were, and his position as one of Lie's principal advisers must have been very difficult. Like many very intelligent people, he was highly strung and he worked too hard; the emotional strain of recent events was too much for him and he broke. There were rumors of a quarrel with Lie, but I knew nothing of this at the time. But many years later, just before my retirement from the Secretariat, Andrew Cordier told me in the presence of Jacob Blaustein that Lie had been very tough with Feller. At a meeting at which Cordier was present, Lie had turned to him and said, "Feller, you are no longer of any use to me." Abe Feller had one of the best minds in the Secretariat, and his death left a gap that was never filled. I went to his funeral, held in one of the Council chambers. It was a great tribute which would have pleased him.

Subjects debated in the Third Committee that year included a proposed protocol to the Convention on the Status of Refugees, freedom of information, the status of women and the self-determination of peoples. When the Convention on the Political Rights of Women was approved and opened for signature, eleven countries, including five Molsem countries and all the communist countries except Yugoslavia, abstained in the vote. The convention came into force in 1954 and has been widely ratified. After a lively debate which lasted for three weeks, during which there were scenes reminiscent of the Paris Assembly a year earlier and Baroody of Saudi Arabia and Pazhwak of Afghanistan began to assume the leadership stance in the committee they would retain for many years, the committee adopted by large majorities the substance of the controversial resolutions on the self-determination of peoples that had come up to the Assembly from the Human Rights Commission.

The chairman of the Third Committee in 1952 was Amjud Ali of Pakistan whose great white turban gave color to the proceedings. At a dinner party, at which our other guests were Paul Martin, Georges-Picot and Frank Scott, he said that the headquarters of the United Nations should be removed to Cyprus—not a bad idea. Frank Scott told me that he had just turned down an offer to become Haile Selassie's adviser on constitutional matters and wanted to know whether he could suggest my name for the job. It seems that the emperor wanted a Canadian, but I let the opportunity pass.

It happened that some Haitian members of the Secretariat had arranged for a group of United Nations people to visit Haiti over Christmas and the New Year; and since, once the item on self-determination had been disposed of, I had no more business in the Assembly, my wife and I decided to go along. We paid our own air fares and hotel bills, but much of the elaborate entertainment was provided by the government. It was our first visit to the Caribbean, and we were so enchanted by the experience that we returned to the islands nearly every year thereafter. But our holiday in Haiti was the most exciting, the most exotic and altogether the most pleasant of all our experiences in the tropics. We would have returned there often, but the political climate changed and Haiti was no longer a pleasant place to visit. We put up in the small Hotel Oloffson which overlooked Port-au-Prince. Only a Graham Greene could do justice to the attractions of this hotel, the owner of which spent most of his time hunting alligators. I remember the night watchman, a very old man dressed in a kind of cotton shawl like a biblical figure, who carried a great long sword and roamed around the place from dusk to dawn. Our adventures began the night of our arrival, when four of us were taken to Mission de la Croix to see a voodoo ceremony. I like to think the performance was authentic and not put on just for our benefit. The women who danced in their long white robes and the man filled with rum, who whirled his cutlass perilously near our heads before killing the cock, were certainly real. One of our next excursions was to Cap-Haitien, where we were taken by a military plane. After the climb up the mountain on mule-back to visit the Citadelle Laferriere, my thighs were raw for days and when, on New Year's Eve, we attended the brilliant reception given by President Magloire, I could neither sit down nor dance.

Jeanne and I were entertained at the homes of several families, including the Legers and the Roys. Jeanne said the big family Christmas party at the Roys (Hérard Roy was the chairman that year of the Sub-Commission on the Prevention of Discrimination and the Protection of Minorities) reminded her of big family parties in Quebec. But if part of Port-au-Prince was prosperous and a small minority lived well, the poverty and illiteracy on the island was appalling. Here was a place to test the United Nations technical assistance program. We visited projects at Marbial, Lafond and other places, an experience which left large questions in my mind. I could not understand, for example, why the International Labor Office was importing complicated machinery to teach Californian pottery techniques in a place where there was no proper clay. At a World Health Organization clinic there was not even a trained nurse. And for UNESCO to be using a phonetic alphabet to teach a creole patois to peasants seemed the height of folly. Questioning the students at some of these places, I discovered that some of them had been moving from project to project, like some students in advanced countries who live on government grants. And why was the Food and Agriculture Organization not doing something about soil erosion, which, with overpopulation, was probably the most urgent problem of the country? On my return to headquarters I discussed some of these matters with David Owen, the executive chairman of the technical assistance board.

There were other excursions: to the submarine gardens where, stretched out on inflated tires with our goggles pointed to the bottom of the sea, we admired a strange new world; to the Etang Saumatre, where we went ostensibly to see alligators but did see flamingos; and the weekend at Jacmel on the other side of the island with d'Artique (once Haitian minister of commerce and now an official in UNESCO) and Gabriel, the director of one of the UNESCO projects. The beach near Jacmel was one of the finest I have ever seen. Superlatives come easily in Haiti.

New Directions: The Action
Program (1953)

The pattern of both my work in the Secretariat and our life in New York was changing. Georges-Picot's ideas as to how the department should be run were different from those of his predecessor. Laugier had given me carte blanche, but Georges-Picot, notwithstanding the fact that he was the head of both the Social Department and the Department of Economic Affairs, maintained a close control over everything that was happening in the divisions, and everything I sent to him was scrutinized to the last comma. I welcomed this as long as he did it himself, because it meant that he was being educated in the business of my division; but it did consume a great deal of his time and mine. The trouble began when he took in Emile Giraud, who had been one of my own people, as his assistant. Giraud and I were still close personal friends, but it was trying to have to deal with all the minutiae that emanated from his fertile mind. As long as the situation lasted, which was not for long, it was as if he were the director and I the assistant. There was also a new principal director of the Social Department, Hussein Mohammad Asfahany, an Egyptian. My personal relations with him were friendly, but I had very little to do with him professionally. My impression was that he was given very little authority, and this is perhaps why he soon resigned from the Secretariat.

The witch-hunt was still going on. Shortly after returning from the West Indies, I had to appear before the appeals board to testify in the case of one of my officers, the man who was suspected of being homosexual and therefore, it was said, vulnerable. I did my best, but he was dismissed; for, after I gave my testimony, the case was pursued by the personnel bureau, which now argued that the reason for the termination was budgetary; the work that the officer was doing could, they said, be better done in another department to which, however, there was no question of transferring him. It was obvious that they were determined to have him fired and were using the crisis in the Secretariat to achieve their ends. How glad I now was that I had refused to become the chairman of the appeals board. I sometimes think that I do have a guardian angel.

Not long after this, Mrs. Roosevelt invited me to be one of her guests at a dinner given by the Americans for Democratic Action at the Waldorf-Astoria Hotel. She made a splendid speech, coming out against the wave of fear that was spreading across the United States. Now that the Democrats had been defeated in the presidential elections and she was no longer a member of the American delegation at the United Nations, she could speak her mind more freely. Trygve Lie was still in office. When I called on him, in my capacity as the chairman of a Secretariat committee which was collecting funds—we collected over twenty thousand dollars—in aid of the victims of devastating floods in northern Europe, I asked him if we could use one of the conference rooms to show a moving picture. "Yes," he said, "but do not show any subversive films." It was the last time that I was to see him in his role as Secretary-General. Marlene Dietrich was the guest of honor at the performance. It was the nearest I ever came to that kind of greatness.

The Commission on the Status of Women met from 16 March to 3 April. Its chairman was Minerva Bernadino, the fiery representative of the Dominican Republic who had been responsible for the reference to women in the United Nations Charter. At this session the commission prepared a text for a convention on the nationality of married women, the chief purpose of which was to prevent the automatic loss or acquisition of nationality by a woman who married a man of another nationality, which came into force in 1958. The Human Rights Commission met in Geneva, where I learned that the United Nations had a new Secretary-General. I met Dag Hammarskjold for the first time two weeks later, when he came into the Council chamber where the Human Rights Commission was meeting and sat at the table for a few minutes.

Before leaving New York, Francis (later Sir Francis) Vallat who was then the legal adviser of the British foreign office, had asked me whether I would be interested in becoming the registrar of the International Court of Justice. He said that Edvard Hambro was retiring from the post and that the United Kingdom would be happy to sponsor me if I were interested. The post had no attraction for me and I thanked him, saying that I was not interested. But in Geneva, Judge Guerrero, who was the vice-president of the Court, invited me for lunch and urged me to accept. I again refused. I then had a telegram from Judge John Read, the Canadian judge, saying that he had put my name forward, and I had to ask him to withdraw it. I was not very happy about my work in the United Nations, but my relations with Georges-Picot were good and becoming much closer and, like most other people in the Secretariat, I had great hopes for the new Secretary-General. I also thought that, while the post in the Court would be a promotion and carry a much higher salary, my duties there would be essentially administrative; accepting it would be tantamount to retirement from active involvement in affairs. The reasons for my refusal were confirmed a year later when I spent some time with Hambro at a Quaker conference for young diplomats in Clarens on the Lake of Geneva and he told me why he had resigned. The post, he said, no longer had the challenge that it had had in the early history of the Court when, in an advisory capacity, the registrar could play an important role in the preparation of judgments. The registrar no longer even sat with the Court, having been moved to a less conspicuous place; this, he said, was only one sign of his decreasing importance. Hambro also told me about his troubles with some of the judges. In the few days in which I had had to make up my mind, I had sent a cablegram to Georges-Picot asking him whether, in case I accepted the post, the United Nations would give me three years leave of absence, which was perhaps an unreasonable request. Georges Palthey, the director of personnel, telephoned to say that they would give me a year, but by that time, my mind was made up. Some months later, Georges-Picot told me that when he spoke to Hammarskjold about the matter, the new Secretary-General, whose uncle had been the first registrar of the Court, said that he was confident Humphrey had never had any such offer. I was never quite able to figure this out. Hammarskjold hardly knew me at the time; we had talked together for less than three minutes.

A much more exciting prospect soon presented itself. Laugier was now the French member of the executive board of UNESCO, which on the resignation of Torres Bodet was looking for a new director-general. There were many candidates for the post but little prospect, it seemed, of any early agreement being reached on any of them. Laugier, who was spending a short holiday at Gex, asked me if I would allow him to put my name forward. While I had no illusions about my chances I told him to go ahead; but I did nothing to further my candidature, except to go to Paris at Laugier's insistence, "to put in an appearance." The man chosen for the post was Luther Evans, the American member of the executive board.

Mahmoud Azmi, who was now a good friend, was the chairman of the Human Rights Commission. Although it met for over five weeks, it was unable to complete the drafting of the covenants. It adopted seven new articles for the Covenant on Civil and Political Rights: on the right to vote and to be elected and to hold public office; on the treatment of persons deprived of their liberty and on the penitentiary system; on the rights of minorities; on the equal rights of men and women; on the protection of privacy, the home, correspondence, honor and reputation; on incitement to hatred and violence; and on the right to marry and found a family. But it never could agree either at this or the next session on an article on the right to own property, a right which had been included in the Universal Declaration. The right itself is hardly controversial and is indeed so fundamental that it is even recognized in communist countries; but it proved quite impossible either in the commission or at the General Assembly to agree on whether and how owners of property should be compensated in the event of expropriation, with the result that this fundamental right is mentioned in neither covenant.

The defeat of the Democrats in the American presidential elections of November had far-reaching consequences for the United Nations human rights program. Not only was Mrs. Roosevelt replaced as the American representative on the commission by a Republican, Mrs. Oswald Lord, but there was a radical change in American policy. On 6 April, only one day before the opening of the session, the new secretary of state, John Foster Dulles, had promised the Senate judiciary committee that the new administration would never bring a human rights convention before the Senate for ratification; he was opposed, he said, to "treaty coercion." Dulles had surrendered to the forces behind Senator Bricker, the American Bar Association and other elements in the United States which had been opposed to the United Nations human rights program since the beginning; but in taking this decision he must have felt that it was politically necessary to make some gesture to more liberal elements both at home and abroad. For Mrs. Lord and her advisers were instructed to develop some new program which the United States could support in the United Nations as an alternative to the covenants. James Green, who was one of Mrs. Lord's advisers, told me that the new American proposals were worked out on board ship when the delegation was on its way to Europe and the Geneva session of the Human Rights Commission. The so-called action program, as I later called it when I began to see its possibilities, contemplated three things: a request from the Economic and Social Council to member governments to report to the United Nations annually on developments relating to human rights; the initiation by the commission of a series of global studies on specific aspects of human rights, like the studies on which its sub-commission was already engaged; and a program of advisory services similar to those already offered to governments under the technical assistance program. These suggestions, especially the one about advisory services, were received with a good deal of skepticism not only in the commission and other U.N. bodies but later, when I tried to implement them, in the higher echelons of the Secretariat. They could, of course, be no alternative to the covenants; and the Americans soon stopped describing them as such.

Psychologically there was something wrong about the proposed advisory services program. It was unrealistic to think that governments would ask the United Nations for technical assistance in a matter as politically delicate as human rights; to do so might be interpreted as an admission that human rights were not being respected; and, apart from nominating nationals for the few travelling fellowships that were available under the program, governments never did, at least in my time. But something could be salvaged if the program were stood on its head as it were and the original intentions of its proposers ignored. I was largely responsible for doing this. I quickly realized that the "seminars" which were to be part of the program could, with some juggling of ideas, become regional human rights conferences; and that is what happened, although the Americans had never planned it that way. They had assumed that the seminars would be organized in countries needing help; but we naturally received no invitations to organize them until I began to talk to governments in quite different terms. What I said to them was in effect, "Your record and reputation with respect to this right is good and you could at no political risk gain considerable kudos by sponsoring one of these seminars." I was not appealing to governments that needed help, although it was my intention that the latter should also be represented at the conferences. I wanted to start a series of regional conferences that would carry the debate on human rights far beyond the halls of the United Nations. The Americans gave me their support once they saw the point. In the light of the difficulties I was to have in the Secretariat, I needed it badly.

Despite all their considerable efforts the Americans could not get their scheme approved at the ninth session of the commission and it was not until a year later that it was adopted. In the meantime, I began to wonder whether they were serious, doubts which were confirmed when, after the plan was adopted, the United Nations budget for 1955 contained an allotment of only $50,000 for the implementation of the advisory services program, less than enough to pay for even one conference of the kind I had in mind. I was also beginning to encounter resistance from within the Secretariat. Even my compatriot and friend, Hugh Keenleyside, who was the director-general of the technical assistance administration, seemed to think that a human rights advisory serivces program would somehow contaminate his operation.

The only other business of any importance which the commission did at this session was to discuss the reports of the fourth and fifth sessions of the Sub-Commission on the Prevention of Discrimination and the Protection of Minorities, which it had not dealt with until now. The commission took no action on minorities, but there was a good discussion of the principles that should govern any international machinery for their protection. The majority of the speakers felt that the term "minorities" should cover only well-defined and long-established groups, and that the rights of persons belonging to them should not be interpreted as entitling any group settled in a country, especially under its immigration laws, to form separate communities which might impair the national unity or security of the state. This should have helped allay the fears of most governments. More important from the point of view of the immediate work program, the commission approved the sub-commission's plan to study various aspects of discrimination and the appointment of a rapporteur for the study of discrimination in education.

Looking back after many years I can say (although it was not realized at the time) that the ninth session of the Human Rights Commission was one of the most productive that it had held since it drafted the Universal Declaration of Human Rights. It was at this session that the two programs which were to have the most concrete results for over a decade—the program of regional human rights seminars and of studies of discrimination—were initiated or approved. But neither the one nor the other would have come to fruition had it not been for initiatives taken by the Secretariat. Edward Lawson had proposed the studies on discrimination, and I myself developed the series of regional seminars. The other important part of the "action program" related to periodic reporting by governments. Potentially this was the most important initiative taken at the session because it could have become the basis for an effective system of implementation; but it never really became operative, for, although many countries did in fact report, the commission never did—because it did not wish to—set up workable machinery for the critical examination of the reports. And in 1981, on the initiative, I am sorry to add, of the Secretariat, it decided to discontinue the system for the specious reason that a reporting system had been set up by the covenants which, however, are binding only on those states which ratify them.

The summer session of the Economic and Social Council met from 30 June to 5 August, also in Geneva. There were a number of human rights items on the agenda, but very little was accomplished. One controversial question was whether the two draft covenants should be sent to the General Assembly in the state in which they then were or whether they should be returned to the commission for completion, the Council having quickly decided not to discuss the substance of the articles. Some delegations argued that the commission had completed its assignment and that the outstanding issues, which they said were largely political, could be decided only by the General Assembly. Others wanted the draft covenants returned to the commission for completion. The compromise reached was that the commission was asked to complete its work on the instruments in 1954 (which it did) and the two drafts were sent, for information, to the General Assembly, governments, specialized agencies and nongovernmental organizations. The Americans, who had lost interest in the covenants because they did not intend to ratify them under any circumstances, took no part in this procedural debate.

In its debates on human rights, ECOSOC rarely touched on substance, and this was certainly true of the summer session in 1953. Indeed, although there was a great deal of talk, the Council took very few decisions. One that it did take related to slavery. The ad hoc committee had recommended, amongst other things, that the functions of the League of Nations under the Slavery Convention of 1926 be transferred to the United Nations and that a new supplementary convention on the elimination of forms of servitude other than chattel slavery be prepared. The Council therefore asked the General Assembly to invite states to agree to the transfer of the League's functions to the United Nations, and instructed the Secretariat to consult member states about the desirability of a supplementary convention. The protocol amending the 1926 Convention was opened for signature in December and came into force in 1955. The Supplementary Convention on the Abolition of Slavery, the Slave Trade and Institutions and Practices similar to Slavery was adopted by a diplomatic conference (of which I was the executive secretary) in 1956; it was widely ratified and came into force in 1957. Consideration of two other important human rights items on the Council's agenda, the report of the ad hoc committee on forced labor, which had now finished its business, and the report of the rapporteur on freedom of information was adjourned until the seventeenth session.

It had been a dull session and I was glad when it was over. My wife and I had planned a holiday in Yugoslavia before returning to New York and had therefore brought our car with us to Europe. But Georges-Picot wanted me back at headquarters to take over from Asfahany who had resigned as principal director of the Social Department. I occupied the post until December 1954, during all of which time I continued as director of the Human Rights Division, although I moved into an office next to Georges-Picot. My new assignment was frustrating, not only because as the acting incumbent I had very little authority, but because the duties of the office were so ill defined. There was really no job to be done between the level of director of division and assistant secretary-general. I was sure, indeed, that the real reason Asfahany had resigned was that he didn't have enough to do. In normal circumstances, I would have been confirmed in this post—and that was certainly Georges-Picot's intention and wish—but it disappeared from the manning-table when the two departments of social and of economic affairs were merged as part of Hammarskjold's reorganization of the Secretariat.

Although there was no question of the covenants being adopted at the eighth session of the General Assembly which began on 15 September, several questions relating to them were discussed at length. An attempt was even made to reopen the decision taken in 1950 that there would be two instruments instead of one. Another controversial question was whether they would contain a federal state clause, a treaty provision traditionally employed to meet the constitutional difficulties of federal countries like Canada and the United States, where the national government may not have the constitutional powers necessary to implement all the provisions of a treaty. It was argued that such a clause would be out of place in the covenants, since their purpose was to ensure universal respect for human rights, and that to include one would be to discriminate in favor of federal countries against unitary states. There would, it was said, be no equality of treatment, for while a unitary state would be bound to observe all the provisions of the treaties, a federal state would have to observe only those provisions which related to matters falling within the competence of the federal authorities. It wasn't easy to answer this argument, but the representatives of Australia, Canada and the United States, all countries with federal constitutions, warned that if the clauses were omitted it would be impossible for any federal state to ratify the covenants; and the delegation of India warned against forcing the hand of federal states. Other delegations felt that it would be premature to take any decision on such an important question, and it was finally decided simply to forward the various proposals that had been made to the Human Rights Commission for study. But the federal states were in a small minority, and it was already obvious that they would be outvoted when a decision was finally taken. When the two covenants were adopted in 1966 neither of them contained a federal clause. Listening to this debate, then and later, I was probably a prejudiced observer because my own country has a federal constitution, and many of the matters included in the covenants are within provincial jurisdiction; but I couldn't help feeling that the arguments advanced against a federal clause were more conceptual than practical. If delegations wanted federal states to ratify the covenants, they should have made some attempt to meet their difficulties, which were real and not imaginary. I also think that had the United States, the most important of all federal states, not taken the position on the covenants that it did earlier in 1953, the story might have been different; for the majority might have hesitated before taking any decision that could give the most influential country in the United Nations a reason for not ratifying. If the Americans had not already decided that they would not ratify under any circumstances, they might have used their great influence to bring about a result that would have made ratification easier.

Another attempt was made at this session to give a right of petition to individuals and groups, but although it had some support, it was not pushed to a vote. Delegations favoring an individual right of petition—all of them except the Danish representing economically less developed countries—argued very forcibly that unless this right were recognized, the value of the covenants would be in question. The point was made that, if only states had a right to complain, this could lead to international friction, for however well justified a complaint by one state against another state might be, it would never be interpreted as a friendly act and could generate a political response, whereas complaints emanating from private individuals would not ordinarily have diplomatic repercussions. These arguments were met by the familiar but specious claim that it would be intervention in the domestic affairs of states to give individuals and groups a right of petition. The argument is specious because, as some delegations pointed out, no state was under any obligation to ratify the covenants and, if it did, the possibility that it might be the object of a petition would be its own doing and by its own consent. It is probably idle to speculate as to what might have happened had the General Assembly voted on the issue in 1953, but the result could hardly have been worse than it was after the Human Rights Commission, to which the Assembly referred the draft resolution, dealt with the matter again in 1954.

The Americans were more interested in their three draft resolutions on periodic reporting, studies and the advisory services than they now were in the covenants, their implementation or a federal clause; and they worked very hard to convert other delegations, many of which were, as already indicated, skeptical about the proposed new program. When it was debated in the Third Committee, the spokesmen for Czechoslovakia and Poland recalled the recent statement of the United States government that it did not intend to ratify the covenants and said that to approve the new program, which was intended to be an alternative to them would, therefore, be to abandon the covenants. A significant change in leadership was taking place. A vacuum had been created and by Cold War logic, it was being filled by the other side. Henceforth, the communist countries would pose as the chief advocates of the covenants. But the Americans got what they wanted and, although many governments were obviously reluctant to vote with them, the Assembly instructed the Human Rights Commission to consider the three draft resolutions at its next session.

My work with the Assembly was now finished and it was time for the holiday my wife and I had missed that summer. On 15 December we flew to Cuba but, after two or three days, found the weather so cool that we decided to continue on to Jamaica. We spent most of our holiday at Montego Bay, a place we liked so much that we returned there several times. On our way back to New York we visited Ciudad Trujillo (as it then was) and San Juan.

Frustration (1954)

For me, 1954 was a bitter year, full of frustration—my worst year at the United Nations. Never in all my life have I felt more isolated or had to contend with such odds. Yet it began well. I was back at headquarters in time for the opening of the sixth session of the Sub-Commission on the Prevention of Discrimination and the Protection of Minorities, which was now shaping up well and, in fact, entering the period of its greatest usefulness. The Economic and Social Council had approved its new program of "studies" and most of the session was devoted to organizing it. At its last session the sub-commission had appointed Minoo Masani as its rapporteur for a study on discrimination in education; but, as already indicated, the Indian government had refused to allow him to continue as a member of the sub-commission. Charles Ammoun of Lebanon agreed to take on the job. It was an excellent choice. Ammoun was a bon vivant, a connoisseur of good food, wine and beautiful women, but he had other qualities that were not so obvious. He was also a member of the executive board of UNESCO, and that would be important notwithstanding its negative attitude towards the study.

The sub-commission then asked three of its members to report to its next session on how best to conduct studies on discrimination in the enjoyment of political rights, of religious rights and in emigration, immigration and travel. There was also to be a study of discrimination in employment and occupation, which the sub-commission wanted to undertake with the help of the International Labor Organization. And, notwithstanding the known coolness of the Human Rights Commission and opposition from the Secretariat (on instructions from the Secretary-General, Schwelb made a strong statement during my absence from the conference room), there was to be a study on "the present position as regards minorities throughout the world." Max Sorensen, the chairman and member from Denmark, said that it was the sub-commission's duty as an expert body to make this recommendation even though the commission might reject it, which in fact it did. After my retirement from the Secretariat, when I was one of its members, the sub-commission did with the approval of the commission undertake such a study.

It wasn't only the proposed study on minorities that ran into rough weather when the recommendations reached the commission and Council. In the commission the Americans said that it would not be appropriate to study discrimination in immigration; and when the matter came before the Council, the majority opinion was that, while there was a right to emigrate, there was none to immigrate, each country being free to decide how many and what kind of immigrants it could absorb. The sub-commission was therefore asked to limit this study to the right of everyone "to leave any country, including his own, and to return to his country," which is the language of Article 13 of the Universal Declaration of Human Rights. As for the study on discrimination in employment and occupation, the Council decided that it should be conducted by the International Labor Organization on its sole responsibility. As usual, the I.L.O. had a strong lobby in the Council, and its position was that it would not share any of its responsibilities with the sub-commission. Its hostility went so far that, when the study was completed, it snubbed the sub-commission by publishing its recommendations before giving the sub-commission or any other United Nations body an opportunity to comment on them. But the historical fact is that it was an initiative of the sub-commission that resulted in the study's being made and the subsequent adoption by the I.L.O. of its Convention and Recommendation on Discrimination in Employment and Occupation.

The sub-commission adjourned on 29 January. Georges-Picot left that day on a mission for the Far East, leaving me as the acting head of the Social Department. From several things he said before his departure, I hardly expected to see him back except to pack his bags. He was absent for nearly two months, and during that period I came closer to the high command in the Secretariat than I had ever been before. For one thing, I represented the Social Department at the regular Thursday morning meetings of assistant secretaries-general in Hammarskjold's board room, but I didn't learn very much at them because nothing of importance was ever discussed.

One of the first things Hammarskjold had done after taking office was to appoint a "group" to review the Secretariat with a view to its reorganization. Its six members were all officers in the Secretariat and, as Georges-Picot later said, most of them had an axe to grind. A director who was not in this group, which had some of the characteristics of a star chamber, was at a disadvantage; and I was not a member. But it was some time before I realized what was happening. In my diary for 29 February I even said that the review might be a useful operation, although I had added that Hammarskjold was an enigma:

That he is keenly intelligent there can be no doubt. I also find myself in agreement with him on specific issues. But I wonder about the direction in which he is going. I sometimes think that his purpose is to reduce the nonpolitical activities of the organization to a minimum.

A few days later Alfred Katzin, the South African army officer and businessman who was Hammarskjold's principal agent for carrying through the reorganization, told me that the Secretary-General wanted to relieve the Secretariat of some of its duties so that it could play a more important role in fixing policy. The more I thought about this remark, the more fantastic it seemed.

On 9 February I met with Roy Blough (the principal director of the Department of Economic Affairs), Martin Hill and Julia Henderson (who was the director of the Division of Social Welfare and a member of the "group") to discuss the organization of the top echelon of the new Department of Economic and Social Affairs into which the two existing departments were to be merged. My three colleagues wanted the Under Secretary (note the new title, Hammarskjold having decided that heads of department would no longer be called assistant secretaries-general'') to have two deputies: one a top flight economist and the other in charge of liaison with the specialized agencies, two jobs obviously tailored for Blough and Martin Hill. My experience as acting principal director of the Social Department since August 1953 had convinced me that there was no need for any post between the head of the department and the directors of divisions; but it might be different in a much bigger department, particularly if its head were an economist; and, if a deputy were needed for economic affairs, the same argument applied to social affairs. I was afraid that if the lopsided structure my colleagues were proposing were adopted, the social affairs and human rights programs would suffer. I was the odd man out and in the embarrassing position that if I pushed my point too hard, I could be accused of acting in my personal interest, because I was the obvious choice for the third deputyship. Julia Henderson, who insisted that there was no need for a deputy on the social side, later told me that she regretted the Secretary-General's decision; for, after Philippe de Seynes, who was an economist, became the Under Secretary of the new combined department, the social affairs program did suffer. Much more serious than the direction of the new department was the treatment reserved for the Human Rights Division.

On 13 March I wrote in my diary:

On Tuesday Hammarskjold called me to his office to acquaint me with his thinking about the reorganization of the Social Department. This thinking is not supposed to crystallize until Georges-Picot returns, he said; but it was obvious that the Secretary-General had already established the broad lines of his reorganization in his mind even before he began his review. The activities which will suffer most in the Social Department are population and human rights. The former all but disappears, becoming a unit in Julia Henderson's service, the only one in the department incidentally which shows any expansion. The Human Rights Division becomes an "office." When I later asked Katzin the significance of this, he said that it was to underline the fact that responsibility for establishing policy was to be at a higher level. The number of sections are reduced from five to three with a corresponding reduction in P5 officers. The deputy director will also be a section chief so that the post of three of the present section chiefs will be eliminated. The overall reduction in the Division's manning-table would be eighteen—ten professional officers and eight secretaries. Of course, says the S.G., this is only a target; the actual operation would take from two to three years to complete.

I warned him that as far as human rights at least are concerned, he is making a great mistake. The workload should in fact increase as soon as the commission finishes with the draft covenants. The S.G. will therefore merely expose himself to attack without being at all sure that he can achieve his objective. But I might just as well have saved my breath. He is very sure of himself and his mind is made up.

Two things that he said to me are worth putting down for the record. He would like, he said, to throw the Human Rights covenants out of the window. I checked him up on this and suggested that a better policy would be to put them on ice until there is an improvement in the political climate. Later when boasting about what he called "the successful elimination of the department of financial and administrative services," he said that he found that he could do everything that the A.S.G. had done in the past. This kind of activity he said, was more useful than seeing delegations—which was "a waste of time." In spite of his brilliant mind and his possible (but yet unproved) administrative ability, he lacks the qualities of statesmanship.

Georges-Picot returned to headquarters less than a week after I made the entry just quoted, and my first experience as Acting Assistant Secretary-General came to an end. It hadn't been very rewarding and did nothing to enhance my standing in the Secretariat. Hammarskjold himself treated me as if I had already become a kind of chief clerk in an "office of human rights;" but I noted that even the assistant secretaries-general (whose title he was changing to "Under Secretary" so that it would be clear that they did not share any of his political responsibilities) had scarcely better treatment. Even Georges-Picot, who had all the prestige of the French government behind him, told me that he rarely saw Hammarskjold alone; this was now one of his chief complaints and a reason for some of the emotional outbursts that I witnessed. Hammarskjold didn't like to share authority; he preferred to work alone with people who never questioned his judgment. That to do so was a cardinal sin, I very soon discovered. As far as I know, I was the only official at my level in the Secretariat who challenged the reorganization; and I suffered for it as long as Hammarskjold was the Secretary-General.

On the day he returned to headquarters, I spent most of the morning with Georges-Picot. When he left on his mission to the Far East I had expected that he would soon resign; he now said that he was going to tell Hammarskjold that he would not stay unless certain changes were made in the proposed reorganization of the Secretariat. I didn't expect much help from him in saving the Human Rights Division, for as I put it in my diary, "his conflict with the Secretary-General was too personal." It was about this time that Martin Hill confided to me that it was hard to be loyal to both Georges-Picot and the Secretary-General.

At a cocktail party I told Cordier that I didn't like the reorganization and that, in my opinion, the morale of the Secretariat was lower than it had been at any time when Lie was in office. This was strong language and I knew that he would pass it on to Hammarskjold. It wasn't very diplomatic of me to have used it, but I was stirred to the very core; the issues at stake were more important than my personal relations with the Secretary-General. I went to see Ralph Bunche, hoping that he would help me save the human rights program. His reaction can be summed up in his remark that "this is what the Secretary-General wants and we must cooperate with him." He also said that at the very first meeting of the survey group, of which he was a member, Hammarskjold had expressed his doubts about the Secretariat accepting any responsibility for a human rights program. Georges-Picot had already told me that the Secretary-General had suggested that the program be divorced in some way from the regular work of the United Nations. Julia Henderson gave me more details that summer at a luncheon party in Geneva at which Martin Hill was also present: Hammarskjold had said in her presence that he wanted to divorce the human rights program from the United Nations and intended in any event to replace the Human Rights Division by a commission secretariat of three or four people. In the light of the commitments of the Charter, the history of the program before he became Secretary-General, and subsequent developments, it is almost inconceivable that Hammarskjold could have been so openly hostile to the implementation under United Nations auspices of one of the stated principal purposes of the Charter. I leave the problem to his biographer.

On Friday, 16 April I was summoned to appear before the special survey group. Although Georges-Picot was with me, he left me to do the talking; I don't remember his opening his mouth. Speaking at this meeting as the acting principal director of the Social Department and not as the director of the Human Rights Division, I put up a fight for retaining the separate existence of the population division which, under the reorganization, was to become a branch of Julia Henderson's new Bureau of Social Affairs; but no one gave me any support. It is amazing, in the light of subsequent developments, that so little importance was attached at this time to population problems and the population explosion. One would have thought that the economists present, including Hammarskjold, would be the first to understand that there could be little economic development without population control. Reviewing the record over a quarter of a century later, it gives me some satisfaction to observe that there is again a Population Division in the Secretariat.

It wasn't until the following week that I had an opportunity to defend the Human Rights Division. One of the proposals was that its staff should be reduced by eighteen officers, which was about a third of our manning-table. There could be no justification for this, I argued, at a time when the Economic and Social Council was increasing our workload, and I referred to, amongst other things, the new programs of studies in discrimination and human rights. I was then told that the Secretary-General would be recommending changes in the program. I mentioned the great expectations to which the Charter had given birth and said that the reaction of public opinion would be unfavorable; the human rights program was an expression of the idealism and conscience of the United Nations. This was received with disdain. The conscience of the organization, said Hammarskjold, resided in the whole organization, not in its parts. He had, of course, distorted the point that I was trying to make; I was laboring under intense emotional strain and may not have expressed myself too well. Not one person at the meeting spoke up to give me any support. Some years later, Martin Hill, who was at the meeting, told me that Hammarskjold never forgave me for my remark about the conscience of the United Nations; he may have also thought that I was too involved emotionally, which was probably correct. But he was visibly stirred by my disagreement with his plans; he couldn't brook opposition by any member of his staff: if you didn't agree with him you weren't loyal. He had a "logical" answer to every one of my arguments, none of which he accepted, and was so wedded to his course that nothing I could say could divert him. I achieved only one thing at the meeting and that probably worked against the interest of my division; as a result of my objections, the recommendations of the group were better presented when they came before the Economic and Social Council and therefore more plausible.

The report of the survey group was published in September. In circumlocutions which would never have been tolerated in my own division, it said that

on the basis of the Division's present and immediately foreseeable workload and on the assumption that the views which the Secretary-General has conveyed and the specific proposals he has made to the Economic and Social Council (E/2598) and which he will be reaffirming and developing before the General Assembly are endorsed and acted upon by Member governments, the Survey Group concluded that a progressive reduction in the Division's presently authorized establishment by some ten professional posts could safely be entertained.

The rationalization revealed the bias behind the recommendation:

> In this field of the United Nations endeavor, the course of international action is inevitably slow and beset by political difficulties. . . . Consequently there is a constant danger, where agreement cannot be reached at the inter-governmental level, of the Secretariat being asked for compilations of studies involving efforts and funds quite disproportionate to the probable value of the results. . . . In this field there is a further danger of not taking sufficiently into account the proper limitations upon the scope of Secretariat action and the proper distribution of functions between the Secretariat and the specialized agencies. . . . It is desirable that wherever possible responsibility (for particular phases of work) should be placed squarely upon the specialized agencies concerned insofar as the work falls directly within their statutory competence.

The hand of more than one person could be detected in the drafting of this masterpiece; but, assuming that they were being intellectually honest, none of the draftsmen revealed any knowledge of the human rights program or its history. There was nothing in the report about the purposes and principles of the United Nations as enunciated by the Charter and its specific mention of the promotion of respect for human rights and fundamental freedoms and the corresponding duties of the organization, or to the many resolutions of the General Assembly and other bodies which presumably reflected the wishes of member governments. "The course of international action" might be "inevitably slow and beset with difficulties;" but this was true of nearly everything the United Nations had undertaken, including measures for the maintenance of international peace and security. By comparison, the human rights program had taken form relatively rapidly. The Universal Declaration of Human Rights had been drafted and adopted by the Assembly in less than two years, and the Human Rights Commission would that very year send its drafts of the two covenants to the Assembly. And the "compilation of studies involving efforts and funds quite disproportionate to the probable value of the results" would become one of the most concrete and useful activities of the Secretariat, an activity which would continue long after Hammarskjold ceased to be Secretary-General. It is not surprising, therefore, that his program recommendations were never accepted by member governments; but the staff of the Human Rights Division was nevertheless drastically reduced, and it was a long time before we could cope with an ever-increasing workload.

Although I was no longer the acting head of the Social Department, Georges-Picot continued to take me to the Secretary-General's Thursday morning meetings, at one of which Hammarskjold lashed out against disloyal members of his staff who, he said, were criticizing his reorganization outside the house. I sat through this harangue thinking that I might myself be a target, even though I had taken great care to say nothing outside the house. I later learned that the target was Benjamin Cohen, who was suspected of organizing the twenty Latin American votes in the interest of the Department of Public Information which was to become and did become an "office." I never attended another meeting of the survey group. Georges-Picot told me that at one of them, the details of which she reported to him, Julia Henderson raised the question of what was to be done about the manning-table of the Human Rights Division "in the light of Humphrey's statement." Would the Secretary-General revise his recommendations in the light of the resolutions of the Economic and Social Council to which I had referred? The reaction of the meeting was energetically negative and Hammarskjold himself said, "No. I will do nothing which might seem to give reason to the arguments and methods employed by Georges-Picot and Humphrey." Georges-Picot interpreted this as meaning that Hammarskjold thought that we had inspired the Council resolutions.

The concomitant of the recommendation that the manning-table of my division be reduced was that the Economic and Social Council would accept the Secretary-General's recommendations for changes in the program. On 28 April, Martin Hill invited me to a meeting to help prepare appropriate recommendations for the Council. The other people at the meeting were Bruce Turner (the Controller), Alfred Katzin, Roy Blough and Julia Henderson. The discussion reflected the worst kind of intellectual confusion; if this was the thinking of the survey group it was already bankrupt. It was significant that Hill's first draft didn't even mention changes in the program, although there were some abstractions in it about rhythm and emphasis in the work of the Secretariat. When I questioned him about this, Hill explained that the Secretary-General had now asked him to go easy on the program. He was apparently having second thoughts, and I wondered whether some of my arguments, unpopular as they had made me with the high command, may not have helped bring this about. But the recommendations for drastic reductions in my staff were retained even though part of the rationalization for them had disappeared. There was something else in the paper which I thought it most unwise for the Secretary-General to say. "There is," he said, "a limit to what can be handled effectively by the organization given the responsibilities that must be assumed by the senior staff." Did he mean that the future of the United Nations was to be limited by the physical capacities of one man and a small group around him? As well say that the activities of a national government should be limited by what the prime minister and his cabinet could personally perform or, in the words of Thomas Paine, as if "the world were a village in which everything that passed must be known to its commanding officer." Hammarskjold's position stemmed partly from his failure to understand that the sine qua non of good administration is the ability to delegate responsibility.

Katzin continued to push the Secretary-General to crystallize his policy. He asked me for a list of people in my division "who will become redundant under the reorganization target." Since he spoke with all the authority of the Secretary-General behind him, I had no choice but to comply, and the indicated number of officers were fired. A more brutal operation could hardly be imagined. I pointed out to Col. Katzin that some of the officers had given up careers in their own countries to join the Secretariat and that they might have nothing to return to; but he pushed my objections impatiently aside: he was a military man and used to having his orders obeyed.

The tenth session of the Human Rights Commission had opened on 23 February with

Mahmoud Azmi still in the chair. At this session the commission finished its part of the drafting of the two covenants—twelve years before they were approved by the General Assembly. Although it never changed its decision to refuse a right of petition to individuals, there was now an article in the draft Covenant on Economic and Social Rights requiring contracting states to report on "the progress made" in achieving observance of the rights defined by that instrument. Failing any individual right of petition, I wanted, as already mentioned, a similar provision in the other covenant. The commission so decided. But the reports were only to be made on the legislative and other measures taken to give effect to the covenant and not on "progress made;" and, except on the matter of self-determination, when annual reports were to be made, a government would be required to report only once when the instrument came into force for it and thereafter at the request of the Economic and Social Council. One of the very few improvements the General Assembly made to the Covenant on Civil and Political Rights was to extend the reporting system to "progress made in the enjoyment of these rights."

The commission also drafted the final clauses for both covenants. I thought the Americans were carrying their opposition to the conventions to unnecessary lengths when they announced that they would abstain in the voting on the federal clause, leaving Australia as the only member state with an interest in retaining it. Their abstention was interpreted in some quarters as meaning that the Republican administration wanted to make it impossible for the Democrats to ratify the covenants. Whatever their motive the end result was that there would be no federal clause. On the initiative of the Soviet Union the commission went to the other extreme; for it decided that there would be an article in each of the covenants specifically extending its provisions to all parts of federal states without limitation or exception, and this was later confirmed by the General Assembly.

The General Assembly had instructed the commission to prepare recommendations for the implementation of the right to self-determination. Mention has just been made of the obligation under which states parties to the covenant would report annually on the measures taken by them to implement this right, which significantly enough would be more onerous than their reporting obligations in respect to other human rights. This provision was not retained, however, when the General Assembly approved the covenant. Nor did the Assembly adopt either of the two other highly controversial recommendations which, by a vote of 11 to 6, the commission now made. One of them recommended that the Assembly set up a commission to survey the status of the right of peoples and nations to permanent sovereignty over their natural wealth and resources and to recommend measures for strengthening the right. The second proposed the creation of a commission to examine situations resulting from alleged denials or inadequate realization of the right to self-determination to which its attention was drawn by any ten member states; this commission would offer its good offices for the rectification of any situation and, if no adjustment were made to the satisfaction of the parties within six months, report the facts with appropriate recommendations to the General Assembly. When the matter came before the Economic and Social Council at its next session, a small majority refused to forward the resolutions to the General Assembly; but that was by no means the end of the matter.

The commission adjourned on 18 April. In the meantime both the Commission on the Status of Women and the ad hoc commission on prisoners of war had also been meeting, and the Economic and Social Council was in session. The General Assembly had asked the Council to give priority to the report of its rapporteur on freedom of information. This report, which contained a number of recommendations, had been drawn to Hammarskjold's attention, and he did not like it. The recommendations were, he said, impractical and wasteful and he was proposing to come down to the Council's Social Committee to oppose their adoption. It would have been a rash thing for him to do. Not only was the rapporteur, Salvador Lopez of the Philippines, a determined man who had been lobbying for support, but there was strong feeling on the issues, the developing countries being particularly concerned about the monopolistic practices of the great news-gathering agencies. I finally convinced Hammarskjold that it would be a mistake for him to oppose the recommendations himself; but he insisted on instructing Georges-Picot to make an oblique attack on the report, saying in effect that the Secretary-General would reserve his right to question any action that the Council might take on the recommendations when he made his own recommendations on program and priorities at its summer session.

As it turned out, the Lopez report, which criticized a number of governments, also came under attack from other quarters. The rapporteur's objectivity was commended by several delegations, including those of France, the United Kingdom and the United States; but the Czechs and the Russians said that his report was weighted in favor of Western concepts and therefore biased; other delegations said that the criticisms of governments were unfair and unjustified. The result was that some of its recommendations were rejected, including the one that a rapporteur be appointed for another period to perform a number of tasks. These tasks should, the Council said, be performed by the Secretariat, a result that Hammarskjold (who wanted to "streamline" it) did not welcome.

After one of our talks about this matter I had left Georges-Picot alone with Hammerskjold. From what Georges-Picot told me later, they must have had a real row. Hammarskjold said that he interpreted Georges-Picot's criticism of his reorganization and policies as being directed against him personally, to which Georges-Picot replied that the Secretary-General was surrounded by people who were only giving him the kind of advice they thought he wanted, and that the proposed reorganization of the Secretariat was ill conceived. As for the Human Rights Division, there was nothing new in the attacks that were being made against it; they had been led by the same people for over four years, and the reorganization was being used to bring them home. It was a very strange coincidence, Georges-Picot added, that none of the programs for which members of the survey group were responsible would suffer. I now knew that Georges-Picot was firmly on my side; but I didn't think this would help save the human rights program, because his relations with the Secretary-General were now so bad that Hammarskjold would probably only be confirmed in his determination to carry through with his plans.

Georges-Picot soon left for Europe and I was again in charge of the department, but it would not be for long, because the Council's summer session was opening on 29 June, and I would have to be in Geneva for that. Before leaving for Europe I made a speech at a congress of the United World Federalists in Springfield, Massachusetts. I talked about the United Nations, but what I said wasn't much appreciated and perhaps even resented. For to the earnest, middle-class people at the congress, world federalism was a religion, and they were impatient of any reference to what was actually happening at the United Nations, which they wanted to reform from top to bottom. It is easy enough to write a constitution even for the world; the trick is to make it work. Movements like world federalism are nevertheless useful, particularly in educating public opinion, and they should therefore be encouraged; but it would be more realistic to begin with what we have.

I had a booking on the S.S. *Liberté* and was looking forward to a few days at sea, but the advisory committee on administrative and budgetary questions was meeting and wanted the Social Department represented at the highest level when it examined our budget for 1955. Because I was the acting head of the department, I had to cancel my reservation and travel later by air. I also had to abandon plans for consultations with some UNESCO people in Paris. I had lunch the day before the meeting with the committee's chairman, Thanassis Agnides. This would have been an opportunity, had I wanted to avail myself of it, to lobby against Hammarskjold's proposed reorganization of the Secretariat. Instead I provoked Agnides into talking about the League of Nations secretariat. He also talked about the United Nations. He was outspoken in his criticism of Trygve Lie, but said that Lie had offered him a post as Assistant Secretary-General and indeed of Deputy Secretary-General. When I appeared before his committee on 23 June, only one question was put to me and I answered it by quoting from a document that the committee already had before it. I might just as well have sailed on the *Liberté*. The proceedings of the committee were ex-parte and every item was scrutinized with a view to cutting the budget regardless, I thought, of consequences. I had no mandate from Hammarskjold to defend it and knew indeed that he himself disapproved of some of the items. Had I been a free man, which I was not, I could have told the committee a few plain truths about this budget and the famous reorganization.

I had lunch the next day with King Gordon who told me that he had been offered a post as information officer with the United Nations Korean Reconstruction Agency, which he later accepted. I was sorry to see him leave the Human Rights Division and not a little resentful of the fact that he should abandon us in our most difficult period. As I explained to him, his departure at that time would certainly mean that, in the light of the impending reorganization, he would not be replaced and the Division would lose a post of chief of section. This is what happened. Other officers also saw the writing on the wall. Recasens-Siches and Walker both resigned, Shameen was terminated; Ranshofen-Wertheimer and Hamburger would reach retirement age at the end of the year and would not be replaced; and Ezekiel Gordon was looking for a post in UNESCO.

I also attended a meeting of the assistant secretaries-general in Hammarskjold's board room to discuss the introduction to his report to the next session of the General Assembly. I had received the draft a few minutes before leaving my office the night before, which was normal procedure: Hammarskjold didn't welcome serious discussion of such documents. He opened the meeting by saying that there would be no discussion of the policy content. There followed two hours of talk, most of which was devoted to praising what he had written, its style and semantics. Only Victor Hoo, the Assistant Secretary-General in charge of Trusteeship and Information from Non-Self-Governing Territories questioned a point of policy. There was a paragraph in the report elaborating the statement which the Secretary-General had already made in his report to the Economic and Social Council, and which I had questioned at the time; there is a point, it said, beyond which an international secretariat cannot grow, and that point is determined by what the Secretary-General and his immediate collaborators can personally supervise. Hoo said that it would be unwise to include this, but he got a quick answer and beat a hasty retreat. Hammarskjold leaned over towards Cordier who was sitting beside him. "We wouldn't give that up, Andy, would we?" he said.

Last Days of the Social
Department (1954)

I was in Geneva in time for the opening at the end of June of the summer session of the Economic and Social Council. Georges-Picot gave a luncheon for the officers the day after the opening, at which I found myself wedged in by two vice-presidents, Sir Douglas Copland of Australia and Jiri Nosek of Czechoslovakia; and a president, Juan Cooke of Argentina. The Social Committee over which Nosek presided met on 1 July with the report of the Commission on the Status of Women as the first item on its agenda. It included a recommendation that a revised draft Convention on the Nationality of Married Women (the chief purpose of which was to change the blatantly discriminatory rule obtaining in most countries that a woman's nationality automatically follows that of her husband) be sent to governments for their comments. Some delegations wanted it sent instead to the International Law Commission "for its use in developing proposals." I suspected that the Americans, who with the Belgians moved a resolution to that end (and who didn't want this or any other convention on human rights) thought that this would be a good way to bury it. But the women, who wanted to retain some control over the text and to have the convention adopted quickly, were able to defeat the stratagem; and, although the draft was sent to the law commission for information, it was also sent to governments for their comments, which were studied by the commission at its next session. The convention was adopted in 1957.

On Saturday afternoon, I went bird-watching and in the evening dined with Tom Hamilton, the U.N. correspondent of the *New York Times,* who said that Hammarskjold had been appointed Secretary-General for the express purpose of trimming down the United Nations. As it happened I sat next to the Secretary-General at a luncheon on Wednesday. In circumstances like this one could appreciate his social graces. I had dinner the same day at Gex with Laugier and Marie Cutolli. Laugier looked well but said he was "dead inside," a condition I put down to nostalgia for the United Nations. None of this "deadness" appeared in the rest of his conversation, which was as lively and controversial as ever. Of Hammarskjold's speech that morning in the Council, which he had heard, he said that the Secretary-General spoke with the voice of Byron Price, the retired American Assistant Secretary-General who had been in charge of financial matters and with whom Laugier had often quarreled. But I had heard the speech myself and knew it had been well received. Hammarskjold had won the first round in his battle to reorganize the Secretariat and would undoubtedly win the second in the General Assembly. His reply, after a number of delegates had spoken, was a masterpiece in dialectics. Here was an expert chess player, but the role he was playing was as unrelated to the real world as the game itself.

Several days later Pierre Mendès-France, who was now the prime minister of France, addressed the plenary session. I had not gone to the meeting, nor had I been invited to a luncheon the Secretary-General gave in his honor, but I happened to be in the long corridor of the Palais when all his retinue was conducting the honored guest from the Council chamber. I clung to the wall to let them pass, but Mendès-France saw me, stopped the procession and came over to shake hands. As I was in the doghouse, his gesture, I must confess, gave me a certain amount of satisfaction. I lunched alone and in the afternoon took my place in the Council, where a discussion of the two draft covenants was to begin. But just as in 1948, when the Universal Declaration of Human Rights was on its agenda, the Council did not discuss the articles and on 29 July sent the two drafts on to the General Assembly. It was always more at home discussing procedure. There was, for example, a byzantine debate on the question whether the Sub-Commission on the Prevention of Discrimination—which not long before it had wanted to abolish—would meet for three, four or five weeks at its next session.

Driving me back to the Palais one day after lunch with Laugier in Gex, Gunnar Myrdal, who was the executive secretary of the Economic Commission for Europe, said that the United Nations had not yet reached the bottom of its depression. I was certainly depressed myself, but I had my own ways of personal escape, including my bird-watching. There were also many receptions and dinner parties, including a French party at Evian where we saw a performance of *Amphitryon*. Helped along by these distractions, the eighteenth session of the Council came to an end and I went to Paris, where I arrived on a rainy Sunday morning. On Monday I had business with UNESCO and the next day was on board the S.S. *Flandre*.

The skyline of New York was subdued by haze when the ship steamed into the harbor late on Monday afternoon, 16 August, and it was without enthusiasm that I drove across town to the East Side. I had almost forgotten how dirty and mediocre the streets of New York can be. The temperature was well over ninety degrees, the air soaked with humidity and the taxi driver in bad humor. Fortunately, I would have only a day in the city before going on to Nova Scotia on my annual leave. I travelled by train to Boston, where I boarded the S.S. *Evangeline* for Yarmouth. Jeanne was waiting for me with the car and we drove to Sandy Cove where she had rented a small cottage. That summer, we investigated most of the west end of the province from Freeport to Annapolis Royal and at Granville very nearly bought a preloyalist house.

It was an almost perfect holiday, but our time ran out and on Monday, 13 September I was back in New York in time to open the plenipotentiary conference on stateless persons, of which I was the executive secretary. The conference was orderly and productive, a really rewarding experience. This was partly because the subject matter was relatively noncontroversial; another reason was the technical competence of the delegates, including its president, Knud Larsen; but I was inclined to think that the principal reason was the absence of delegations from either the Soviet Union or the United States. The Convention Relating to the Status of Stateless Persons was opened for signature on 28 September and came into force in 1960.

I was still the acting principal director of the Social Department. One day Georges-

Picot called me into his office to tell me that Hammarskjold had asked him to put another man in my place but that he had refused. I said that the post meant nothing to me because it had no future, but I was shocked by the callousness of the Secretary-General: the post was going to be abolished in any event, and the only reason for his gesture must have been that he wanted to humiliate me in punishment for the stand that I had taken on the reorganization. I therefore attached no importance to the fact when shortly afterwards I was invited to lunch in his private apartment with half a dozen heads of delegations, including Cabot Lodge and Henri Spaak: I put it down to an accident of protocol.

The ninth session of the General Assembly began on 21 September and its Third Committee got down to work a week later. Coming from Czechoslovakia, its chairman, Jiri Nosek, was clearly embarrassed whenever the representative of China asked for the floor, because he would not address him as such. Whenever possible he ignored the request or, when he saw the name of China coming up on the speakers' list, would hand the chair over to the vice-chairman.

The debate on the report of the high commissioner for refugees was always controversial, partly because van Heuven Goedhart, who was well known for his anti-communist sentiments, was himself controversial. The Russians attacked him bitterly—and I think rightly—for using the expression "free world" in his report. He was accused of courting the favor of the Americans, who were vigorously backing his proposals for "permanent solutions" through a United Nations Refugee Emergency Fund. On 7 October there was an uproar in the committee when Jamil Baroody tried to interrupt the refugees debate and have the committee take up the report of the Economic and Social Council, presumably because he wanted to discuss self-determination. I was with Nosek the next morning when Minerva Bernadino came up to complain about Baroody, who had referred to her in one of his speeches as "that woman from the Dominican Republic." "Your duty," Minerva said to the chairman, "was to call the son of a bitch to order." Baroody spoke often and at great length. Another loquacious speaker who could work himself up into a fine passion was Professor Enrique Fabregat of Uruguay. His eloquent Spanish was largely lost in interpretation, but I now knew the language well enough to appreciate his eloquence and always listened to him with pleasure, no matter how irrelevant what he was saying might be.

By far the most important business before the Third Committee in 1954 was the two draft covenants. Had there been a will to do so, they could have been adopted that year and the result would not have been very different from what it was in 1966. But governments were in no hurry. Rumor had it that the delegations had agreed that, to satisfy public opinion, several of the least controversial articles in each convention would be adopted at this session. If there was such an agreement it was not respected; for on 20 October the committee decided after a procedural discussion, which lasted for five meetings, that there would be a general debate, which lasted through seventeen meetings, to be followed by a first and then a second reading of the articles, with the result that none of them was adopted that year. But all the controversial questions were discussed, including self-determination, the inclusion of a federal state clause and implementation.

I still thought the inclusion of the articles on self-determination would prevent some of the most important countries from ratifying the covenants. The idea occurred to me that the General Assembly might be persuaded to delete the articles if the same principles were proclaimed in a solemn declaration. The anti-colonial countries might be attracted to the idea if it were pointed out to them that articles in the covenants wouldn't carry very much weight if the "administering" powers didn't ratify those instruments; while a declaration, although it might not be legally binding, would have great political authority. I talked to Roger Baldwin (who was the observer of the International League for the Rights of Man and one of the best lobbyists in the building) about this and also to several friendly delegates, including Mahmoud Azmi. He was still the chairman of the Human Rights Commission and, in that capacity, addressed a meeting of nongovernmental organizations. Amongst other things, he said that the purpose of all the procedural maneuvering about which many of the n.g.o.'s were so upset, was to give delegations time to think through some of the political questions. Baldwin asked him whether it might not be possible to have more than two covenants, including one on self-determination. Azmi did not dismiss the idea. Because he was representing one of the anti-colonial countries, I attached a good deal of importance to what he said; and when a year later the Secretary-General agreed on my urging to come down to the Third Committee to support a declaration on self-determination as an alternative to the articles in the covenants, the Egyptian delegation was one of those that I approached for support. My conversation with Azmi before the meeting of the nongovernmental organizations was the last that I ever had with him, for two weeks later he had a stroke at a meeting of the Security Council and died shortly afterwards.

Although seldom reflected in the press, there was great public interest in what the United Nations was doing or failing to do about human rights, and I was often invited to speak to voluntary organizations. On 13 October I addressed a group of two hundred New York teachers. After describing the United Nations human rights program, I said that the late Justice Oliver Wendell Holmes had defined human rights as things one was willing to fight for; if the nongovernmental organizations felt deeply enough about the program they should be fighting for it. The next day I met with the bureau of the conference of the nongovernmental organizations in consultative status with the Economic and Social Council to get their views on a conference of nongovernmental organizations on discrimination, the calling of which ECOSOC had authorized at its last session. I knew these people well and with some of them I had worked very closely, but a more difficult group collectively I had rarely seen. It was almost as difficult to get them to agree on anything as to bring about agreement between sovereign states. This stemmed partly from the fact that the individual members of the bureau could speak only for their own organizations and most of them had no mandate to speak on matters of substance. But the difficulties were finally ironed out and they helped us to plan the conference which, as it turned out, was a great success. The same day there was a meeting in my office of the Secretariat committee for the relief of the Haitian victims of hurricane Hazel, of which I was the chairman. Since nothing could now be done in the Secretariat without the express approval of the Secretary-General, I had to ask permission to organize an evening of entertainment in aid of the victims. The only answer I got was Cordier's message that the Secretary-General was "unresponsive to the idea." Why this permission was necessary and still more refused, I could never figure out because the affair was to have been held outside the United Nations building. The Haitians were discouraged by the Secretary-General's attitude and the entertainment was abandoned; but, on 28 December, I handed a cheque for $2,600 to the Haitian ambassador, which was considerably less than the $20,000 a committee also under my chairmanship had collected in 1953 for the victims of floods in northern Europe.

Krishna Menon came into the Third Committee on 23 November to propose the designation of a World Children's Day. His performance was mediocre, but I was impressed by the sharpness of his tongue and the easiness with which he made enemies. The Secretary-General had instructed me to make a statement opposing the Indian proposal, and I did so the next day, although I could see no reason why the Secretariat should be interfering. Hammarskjold had also asked me to make a statement opposing an American draft resolution on the use of technical assistance to promote freedom of information. There would have been hell to pay had I done so. Georges-Picot advised me to make the statement and let the Secretary-General take the consequences, but this was something I obviously could not do. I therefore sought out Hugh Keenleyside (the director general of the technical assistance administration) whose idea it had been that the statement be made and talked him out of it. My differences with Keenleyside on the appropriateness of using technical assistance to promote human rights, including freedom of information, never interfered with our friendship; only a fortnight earlier Jeanne and I had had dinner at his place in Larchmont. Some months later, after the Human Rights Commission had adopted the American plan to extend technical assistance to all human rights, and not only freedom of information, Keenleyside, who had always been contemptuous of the plan, wanted to take over its administration lock, stock and barrel. This never happened and, as I have already explained, the advisory services became the basis for the series of regional conferences on human rights which soon became an important part of the human rights program.

The Third Committee, the bad reputation of which I have already mentioned, came in for criticism at the Secretary-General's private meeting on 26 November. I mentioned three reasons for what was happening. The first was that governments had got into the habit of using this committee as a berth for politically important people whom they wanted to honor but didn't know how to use. Since most of these people had no United Nations experience, about all they could do was to read statements prepared by their foreign office advisers. The result was that a few capable people with long experience in the committee pretty well controlled it. At a recent meeting, Abdul Pazhwak of Afghanistan had intervened twenty-one times. The remedy was to get governments to send more experienced representatives to the committee. The second reason was that there was a general debate on nearly every item. In what national parliament, I asked, could a member make a half-dozen general statements at a single session? And, third, the committee met too often, with the result that the speeches were long and usually badly prepared.

There was a human rights concert in the General Assembly Hall on the Sunday following 10 December, at which Charles Münch conducted the Boston Symphony Orchestra. I did a short broadcast for the Canadian Broadcasting Corporation and later attended a farewell luncheon for Georges-Picot who was leaving the Secretariat. His speech was full of barbs. The Social Department gave him another dinner the next week and I had the pleasure of proposing a toast to his health. I was sorry to see him leave because our relations had become friendly, even close; but like my much closer relationship with Laugier, this had only worsened my relations with the high command. For Georges-Picot's relations with Hammarskjold were now even worse than Laugier's had been with Lie. He returned to the United Nations in 1957 as the head of the French mission. Either he patched up his differences with Hammarskjold or he was such a good diplomat that they never appeared on the surface.

On Wednesday morning, 22 December, I presided over the last directors' meeting in the history of the Social Department, after which I had lunch with Georges-Picot, Roy Blough and Martin Hill. The next morning there was mulled wine in the Secretary-General's apartment, and I met for the first time Philippe de Seynes, the new Under Secretary of the merged Department of Economic and Social Affairs.

A New Under Secretary (1955)

The Sub-Commission on the Prevention of Discrimination began its seventh session early in January, its main business being the progress report of the rapporteur on discrimination in education. Another item related to a study on minorities, for which the sub-commission had asked the Secretariat to assemble relevant material; but, in the light of the decisions taken by the Human Rights Commission, which did not favor the international protection of minorities, and the Secretariat policy of retrenchment, we had had to inform the sub-commission that we could not carry out its instructions. The sub-commission thereupon decided to defer any further work on minorities until the commission gave it specific instructions. Over ten years later, when I had retired from the Secretariat and I was myself a member of the sub-commission, we ignored this decision and again took up the problem of minorities.

On the instructions of the Secretary-General, I also had to inform the sub-commission that, because of their financial implications, the Secretariat could give no further assistance in the preparation of the three studies which it had decided to conduct, until the study on discrimination in education had been completed. My statement was so badly received that I immediately wrote a memorandum to the new Under Secretary, even though, assuming that he shared the views of the Secretary-General, I hardly expected a positive reaction. The next day, de Seynes instructed me to make another and tougher statement, which I did; but I felt like an accomplice in a plot to sabotage the work of the sub-commission. De Seynes later came to the conference room himself and flatly told the meeting that the Secretariat did not have the staff to prepare any further studies until the one on which the sub-commission was engaged had been finished. There was immediate protest, and that afternoon the members held a private meeting (which I did not attend) at which a strong resolution was prepared. It was to be formally presented on Monday, but over the weekend some of the fury abated and the formal reaction was much less energetic. It was strong enough, however, that it should have been a warning to the Secretary-General and his new Under Secretary; it was also the beginning of the conflict between various United Nations bodies concerned with human rights and de Seynes, which lasted until 1958, when the Human Rights Division was moved out of his department. Since it was assumed in the higher ranks of the Secretariat that I was responsible for most of the resistance to the Secretary-General's retrenchment policies, my position became progressively more difficult. It even began to affect my health. I have never been unhappier or more frustrated than I was in the period from 1954 to 1958.

De Seynes was carrying out the policies of the Secretary-General, but it is also true that, as an economist who had once been an *inspecteur general des finances* in the French civil service, he wasn't interested in human rights, didn't know anything about the program and apparently didn't want to know. We were soon at loggerheads. Georges-Picot had sometimes annoyed me because he wanted to see and approve every piece of paper produced in the department. De Seynes didn't want to be bothered by such details and often handed over dossiers, even on important matters, to his personal assistant, who was a young man who knew no more about the program than he did himself and with whom I often had to carry on a dialogue. My differences with the Under Secretary were thus unnecessarily increased and a difficult situation exacerbated.

On 26 January there was a meeting in de Seynes' office at which all my chiefs of section were present. Referring to the reaction of the sub-commission to his intervention, I said that we could expect more trouble at the next session of the Human Rights Commission. De Seynes said that the policy of the Secretary-General was deflation and that we had no alternative but to support it. It was also our duty, I replied, to warn the Secretary-General that his policy was being challenged, but I might just as well have saved my breath. My position was becoming impossible and perhaps I should have resigned from the Secretariat there and then; but that was what some people probably hoped that I would do and having a touch of obstinacy in my character I stayed on. By doing so, I probably saved the Human Rights Division, which Hammarskjold wanted to replace by a small secretariat of the Human Rights Commission.

The stand taken by the Secretariat did not prevent the sub-commission from adopting a resolution, moved jointly by all its twelve members, by which it decided that two further studies would be undertaken in 1956, adding that it hoped adequate staff would be provided for that purpose. This decision was approved by the Human Rights Commission at its eleventh session, which recommended that, in the event of its not being possible to begin both studies in 1956, one study should be authorized for that year and another in 1957. De Seynes made another statement when the matter came before the Economic and Social Council; it was the opinion of the Secretary-General, he said, that only one new study should be begun in 1956, a retreat from the position that he had taken before the sub-commission because the study on discrimination in education would not be completed by that time. The Council so decided adding that a third study should be begun, if possible in 1957; but a minority of members thought that since the Council had already approved its work program the sub-commission should be given the means to pursue that program without delay.

There was another incident on 13 January when Mohammed Awad, the member of the sub-commission for Egypt, criticized Hammarskjold for having referred, in his paper to ECOSOC on reorganization, to work on the protection of minorities as an example of useless effort by the United Nations. I had warned the Secretary-General through Martin Hill against this. Hammarskjold's comment was all the more uncalled for because it was quite unnecessary; it was obvious for anyone to see that the United Nations did not intend taking any action to protect the rights of minorities. Awad was perhaps the wisest and most experienced member of the sub-commission at that time. When, later, the Economic and

Social Council decided to undertake a second study on slavery, I arranged to have him appointed its rapporteur, but I had another reason for my choice: I conceived the new rapporteur as someone who could be a pivot, as it were, around which negotiations designed to bring an end to chattel slavery could turn; and because chattel slavery was now largely an Arab problem, a Moslem would be best suited for the job.

The sub-commission adjourned on 28 January, after which my wife and I left for a holiday in the West Indies. We were back in New York early in the morning on 28 February. It was depressing to be back at headquarters; all one heard was talk about the Secretary-General's deflation policy. After my long holiday I was in fine fettle and ready for a big job had there been one to do; but the possibilities of doing anything constructive were now so limited that I could not look forward to the future with any enthusiasm. I was being asked to implement a policy in which I did not believe and that was against my nature. One of the first things I had to do on my return to headquarters was to draft a statement which the Secretary-General wanted to make to the Human Rights Commission setting forth the consequences of his retrenchment policy, which I knew would be provocative and could only result in resentment. I raised the question with de Seynes at a meeting of his directors, but it changed nothing.

I was also preparing a speech to deliver at the opening in Geneva on 31 March of the conference of nongovernmental organizations on discrimination. I was rather pleased with it, but a message came down from the Secretary-General's office that I would not be making the speech. It seems that Ralph Bunche had raised the question of colored representation at the conference and, without consulting me, Hammarskjold had decided that Bunche would open it. I sent my draft to Bunche. I did make a speech of welcome the following Monday, 14 March, at the opening of the session of the Commission on the Status of Women. I had strong objections to the Secretariat's speaking when it had nothing to say, but a tradition had been created in this commission by other people and I thought it wiser to conform. I never made such speeches in the Human Rights Commission or other bodies for which my division was responsible. It was a different matter when, as always happened at diplomatic conferences, I had to open the session and get a chairman elected. In this case the outgoing chairman of the commission, Minerva Bernadino, was quite capable of doing the honors. She was reelected to the post and in her acceptance speech criticized the Secretary-General for failing to include any women in the top ranks of his reorganization. The next day, adjusting the loud speaker in my office so that I could listen in on what was happening in this commission, I chanced by mistake on the Population Commission, which was also sitting. The members were urging the same objections to the reorganization that I had made a year earlier when, as acting principal director of the Social Department, I had defended the population division. It helped my morale to learn that the experts agreed with me.

On 23 March I went to Geneva for the n.g.o. conference on discrimination and the eleventh session of the Human Rights Commission. To ensure the success of the n.g.o. conference we had sought and obtained the active support of the World Veterans Federation, and Vincent Auriol, its president, was to preside. Over lunch I found him a real meridional who displayed nearly every emotion in the short time we were together. After I had explained some of the difficulties, he even threatened to refuse the presidency. He reminded me of Laugier. I like such men of character and deep enthusiasms. There were ninety-eight organizations represented at the conference. It was a stimulating experience. Auriol himself was a delight to work with. He took his presidency as seriously and devoted as much care to our problems as, I imagine, he must have to important matters of state when he was the president of the French Republic. Amongst other things, he helped us bring about agreement between the Roman Catholic organizations, one of the representatives of which was my old friend and colleague, Emile Giraud (who had retired from the Secretariat), and most of the other organizations on the wording of a key resolution. Auriol's technique was a hearty meal with plenty of wine and good talk (he told me that once on a visit to Canada he had wanted to decorate Maurice Duplessis, the premier of Quebec, but that St. Laurent had refused to make an exception to the rule against Canadians accepting foreign decorations) and, in the last twenty minutes down to business over coffee. We spent all of a Saturday afternoon trying to iron out the differences and to find an acceptable wording for the resolutions that the conference would adopt on Monday. The nongovernmental people were as difficult as United Nations diplomats, and the most difficult of them all was my friend, Giraud, who worked himself into a position where he practically had a right of veto. But, thanks chiefly to the drafting skill of Jacques Kosciusko-Morizet, at one time Auriol's *chef de cabinet* and later the French ambassador in Washington, a compromise was reached on Sunday evening; and, the next day, encouraged always by Auriol's enthusiasm and driving force, the conference adopted without dissenting voice the four resolutions that had been drafted over the weekend. I saw Auriol again that spring in New York. He had been to see the Secretary-General, to whom he suggested that the heads of state of the four great powers be invited to attend the ceremonies soon to be held in San Francisco in commemoration of the tenth anniversary of the signing of the Charter. Hammarskjold had thrown cold water on the idea, and Auriol was upset. He returned to the subject again and again.

The eleventh session of the Human Rights Commission opened immediately after the conference. René Cassin, who had served several times as vice-president, was elected chairman. He wasn't a particularly good presiding officer; he was so preoccupied with his own point of view that, probably without realizing it, he wasn't always objective. The first day was spent in procedural debate precipitated by a Secretariat paper on priorities. The next morning I made a statement in the name of the Secreatry-General on priorities and the reorganization. It didn't prevent the introduction of a resolution by four delegations, including the United Kingdom and the United States, the purpose of which was to add new features to the Yearbook on Human Rights. Since this was contrary to Hammarskjold's wish to abandon the publication, I had to cable New York for further instructions. They were to oppose the resolution, which was nevertheless unanimously adopted. De Seynes returned to the battle at the twentieth session of the Council.

The commission then began to discuss the report of the Sub-Commission on the Prevention of Discrimination. A question to be decided was whether the commission would approve the decision of the sub-commission to begin two new studies on discrimination in 1956. I have already indicated the result. Only Samuel Hoare of the United Kingdom and Ralph Harry of Australia agreed with the Secretary-General, who wanted the studies postponed until the sub-commission had completed its study on discrimination in education. The recommendation that the Economic and Social Council be asked to approve the decision was adopted by seventeen votes to none, with one abstention. It should be remembered that these were governments voting. The message was therefore loud and clear, but Hammarskjold would not listen. Nearly everything the commission did at this session could be interpreted as a repudiation of his deflation policy. Against his express wishes it added a new feature to the Yearbook, which he wanted to discontinue, and it approved the decision of the sub-commission to begin two new studies in 1956. It also repeated its recommendations to the General Assembly (adopted at its last session) that two new commissions be set up on self-determination, recommendations against which Hammarskjold had taken a strong stand. And it adopted the United States proposal to extend technical assistance for the promotion of human rights, a proposal that he had ridiculed. Because it had been busy with the two convenants, the commission had taken no decision on this in 1954. It now recommended that the Economic and Social Council ask the General Assembly to set up the program. Under it, the Secretary-General would be authorized to provide technical assistance at the request of governments, in the form of advisory services of experts, fellowships and seminars. Apart from a few details, all these decisions were subsequently confirmed by higher bodies in the United Nations; and even if they had not been, Hammarskjold's policy would still have been repudiated by the organ principally responsible for human rights.

The session ended on 29 April. My impression at the time was that it had done very little. I hadn't yet come to realize how important one aspect of the new advisory services program would be and how much of my own time would soon be devoted to organizing the human rights seminars which, until they too became politicized, were to be one of the most visible expressions of United Nations concern for the promotion of respect for human rights and fundamental freedoms and important if only for that reason. As for the politicization of the commission, I reflected that while it might go too far, as it ultimately did, this was proof that some countries at least were taking the commission seriously. The delegations with the strongest positive convictions were now without any doubt those which represented the Third World. Hence the growing importance of issues like the self-determination of peoples and racial discrimination. Issues like this could not be dismissed by the legalistic arguments that were coming from the industrialized countries of the West or, indeed, by Scandinavian logic.

Saturday, 30 April, was my birthday and I reached the half-century mark, something I didn't like, but there wasn't anything I could do about it, so I took a bus to the Abbaye de Pomier, went for a long walk and had a good lunch. Back in Geneva I had dinner with Mousheng Lin and Paonan Chen, the latter the Chinese representative on the commission. On Sunday, I went to Nice for consultations with Judge Guerrero, the chairman of the ad hoc commission on prisoners of war. After a splendid view flying over the Alps, I was in Nice in time to take the lift up to the Castello, from which I could see most of the city and part of the coast. Judge Guerrero called for me the next morning and drove me to his house in Cimiez. It took us less than fifteen minutes to settle our business, which we did over an excellent lunch. I had no difficulty in persuading him on Hammarskjold's instructions that his commission should not meet in 1955. Instead the Secretariat would prepare a draft progress report and circulate it to the members of his committee for their approval. It meant, of course, that nothing would be done for another year.

Back in New York I reported to de Seynes on what had happened in Geneva. He seemed friendly enough when I talked to him, but I soon began to have difficulty seeing him and more often than not had to talk to his assistant. My relations with the Under Secretary were not improving, and it was partly my own fault because I couldn't always keep my cool. On one occasion when I did see him, I lost my temper and said something—I forget what—that I couldn't back up. Another time I read out to him with some heat the first article of the Charter, which says that one of the purposes of the United Nations is to promote and encourage respect for human rights and fundamental freedoms.

The Economic and Social Council was in session. Against my advice, Hugh Keenleyside insisted on making another statement opposing a resolution sponsored by the United States and six other delegations asking the Secretariat to put in operation the plan to use technical assistance to promote freedom of information. He went so far as to suggest that if the plan were implemented it should be known by some other name than technical assistance. He got an energetic reply from Walter Kotchnig of the United States delegation, but this didn't prevent him from returning to the attack the following day. There was a good deal of crowing in the higher echelons of the Secreatriat when the Americans made some minor concessions. An extraordinary thing about this obstinate position was that the Secretary-General maintained it even after the Human Rights Commission had recommended that the Council approve an advisory services program covering the whole human rights field, a program which the Council later approved. Hammarskjold said that if any resolution were adopted on the use of technical assistance to promote freedom of information he would limit its implementation to its purely information aspects, leaving aside those relating to human rights. But the Americans insisted that this was not their intention, and the resolution as adopted left no doubt as to what it meant. Yet de Seynes told me that the Human Rights Division would have only a consultative role in its implementation, with the result that the United Nations Secretariat did nothing to implement the resolution. Years later, after the controversy was forgotten, I was able to organize a successful seminar on freedom of information in Rome and another in New Delhi. After some maneuvering the Human Rights Division was given responsibility for the broader program of advisory services in human rights, a program which would have quite clearly come to nothing had we not been in charge.

Roger Baldwin invited my wife and me for a weekend at his place in New Jersey, where he owned a great slice of wild-looking country on the side of Suffern mountain. I had known him for some time and I thought well, but I didn't know that he was such a nature lover. The bond helped cement our friendship. Back in New York we went to a party at his Greenwich Village house, where we met Jules Romains and Adolf Berle. The next night we had dinner with the Lins. All the other guests were Chinese. P.C. Chang talked about the philosophy of Lao-tse and I promised to read *The Way and the Power*.

Minimum Flying Speed (1955)

Hammarskjold called me to his office, ostensibly to talk about the ad hoc commission on prisoners of war. He agreed to approach Arkady Sobolev, who was now the head of the Soviet mission, about getting more information on the fate of p.o.w.'s in the Soviet Union, but he wouldn't do it, he said, until after the San Francisco celebrations in commemoration of the tenth anniversary of the signing of the Charter; he didn't want to complicate other, more important negotiations by raising one which he considered of relatively minor importance. He then—and I am sure that this was really why he wanted to see me—mentioned the report of the eleventh session of the Human Rights Commission which, on the insistence of the rapporteur, reflected some of the current criticism of his policies. I explained the circumstances, adding that the report did not reflect the full extent of the criticism. I then said that it was my clear duty to say so if I thought that he was wrong; and I quoted from a speech he had just made at Johns Hopkins University, where he had said that loyalty implied the courage to disagree—a strange thing for Hammarskjold to have said because it was out of character. His attitude towards the human rights program was determined, he said, by his concern for bigger issues. He wanted me to keep it going at the slowest pace possible: "There is a flying speed below which an airplane will not remain in the air. I want you to keep the program at that speed and no greater." He then said that the Human Rights Commission was naive and politically uninformed. To that I replied that the initiative for the resolutions on self-determination, which he particularly disliked, had not come from the commission but from the Third Committee of the General Assembly. If that committee was sometimes irresponsible, it was partly because of the quality of representation. He could do something about that by pleading with governments to send better people. I went on to say that many of the debates in the Third Committee, including those on self-determination which he so disliked, were symptomatic of unrest in the economically less developed world and that they should be so interpreted; it wouldn't do any good simply to try to treat the symptoms. He said that I had the missionary spirit. I had been born with it, I replied, but I was also a lawyer and my methods were conservative. Before I left his office, he said that he was glad we had the talk, that we had to have it. The same day I also had a frank talk with de Seynes. I told him that his attitude towards the human rights program was too conservative and that his statements on the necessities of the reorganization had been too rigid: he always came back to the reorganization. The reorganization had become, I added, the joke of delegations and of the Secretariat. I realized that I was now attacking the holy of holies, but I kept it up. As for the Secretariat, its morale had never been lower, not even when Lie was capitulating before McCarthyism. De Seynes may have been a good economist—people who should know had told me that he was—but his job as the head of the combined departments of economic and social affairs was too big for him. A few days after our talk I sent him draft "position papers" on all the human rights items on the agenda of the forthcoming session of the Economic and Social Council. This was a new practice and I thought it very silly. An objective international civil service shouldn't have a position and certainly should not appear to have one. But preparing the papers was a useful intellectual operation because it forced me to think through certain problems. De Seynes substituted negative conclusions for the ones I had suggested, but it made no difference because the delegations had their own views.

There was a rumor going around that the Human Rights Division would be moved to Geneva, perhaps to deflate its importance. Personally I liked Geneva and would have been happy to live there; but if I were the Secretary-General I wouldn't allow such a politically important operation out of my immediate reach. Hammarskjold, of course, didn't think it was important even potentially.

It was time to go to Geneva for the summer session of the Economic and Social Council. The day after my arrival de Seynes read a paper to the Council on "financial implications," the political naivete of which shocked me. Couldn't they see that they were making the Secretariat the scapegoat for what some people were calling the failure of the human rights program? Only that day I read a document published by the International League for the Rights of Man which attributed what they called the failure to make any progress with the prevention of discrimination to the Secretary-General's lack of encouragement; and ten days later the Under Secretary's statement was criticized by the World Jewish Congress.

Laugier was in Geneva with Senator Bellegarde and Hernan Santa Cruz for a meeting of the committee on the racial situation in South Africa. He thought I was exaggerating when I told him about what was happening to the human rights program. However, he had heard de Seynes' statement which, he said, was "de l'ordure." Mehdi Vakil—the Iranian I had brought into the Secretariat who was now the Secretary of the Council—told me that René Cassin, the chairman that year of the Human Rights Commission, had sent a letter to Hammarskjold through the president of the Council, complaining about Hammarskjold's failure to provide adequate Secretariat facilities for the human rights program. The letter had been passed on to de Seynes, who had said nothing to me about it: they must have thought I had inspired it. Cassin had sent me a copy, but because it had gone to headquarters it was some time before I received it. In his letter to me, Cassin said that he had written to the Secretary-General at the request of the Human Rights Commission, but if this was so I had no knowledge of it; perhaps they wanted to protect me against a charge of complicity. I never did see the original of this letter, nor did Hammarskjold or de Seynes ever speak to me about it. De Seynes' personal assistant later sent me a copy without comment of the Under Secretary's reply to Cassin and, on my return to headquarters, I also saw a copy of the Secretary-General's reply. Reading them again now, it is almost inconceivable that they could ever have been written. From their tone and content it was clear that the Secretary-General thought it was his prerogative to decide what the future of the human rights program would be, and this irrespective of what the Charter might say or governments want. In his letter to me, Cassin complained that there had been no mention of human rights at the San Francisco celebrations: "au temps de Laugier, cela ne serait pas ainsi." He also said that Pierre Juvigny (who was on the French delegation to the Council) knew about the letter to the Secretary-General. When Juvigny spoke to me about it, he said that Cassin was furious because Hammarskjold had twice refused to see him. He added his own opinion about the role of de Seynes recalling that, when he was appointed Under Secretary, it was generally understood that he would neglect the social side of the department's work. I unwound that afternoon—it was a Saturday—by going for a long walk on the Sentier des Saules and watching the gulls and kites fishing in the Rhone. I then returned to my hotel to read *Leviathan*. In my bad moments I had the consolation of intellectual and other resources that made it possible for me to retire into a kind of personal castle.

It wasn't until Wednesday, 20 July, that the Council's Social Committee began to discuss human rights. The Secretariat's position was actively negative on all the items.

The committee devoted five meetings to self-determination. A majority obviously didn't like the recommendation of the Human Rights Commission (which in 1954 the Council had refused to forward to the General Assembly) that a commission be set up to survey the status of the permanent sovereignty of peoples and nations over their national wealth and resources, or the recommendation that a good offices commission be created to deal with situations resulting from alleged denial of or inadequate realization of the right to self-determination. The Council now decided to forward the recommendations to the General Assembly "without comment," together with a third draft resolution, sponsored by the United States, which would have requested the Secretary-General to appoint an ad hoc commission of five members to conduct a thorough study of the concept of self-determination, the American intention being that this body would take the place of the two commissions proposed by the Human Rights Commission. As I will explain shortly, Hammarskjold wanted to support the American proposal when it came before the Third Committee of the General Assembly.

The American-sponsored resolution on advisory services was adopted over the continued opposition of the Secretary-General by a vote of 14 to one with 4 abstentions. At a directors' meeting several days later, de Seynes said that his policy would be to play the resolution down as much as possible and that he would not countenance the Secretariat taking any initiative, for example, in the organization of seminars. I was boiling inside but I managed to control myself. Mousheng Lin was a great help to me during this frustrating time; by osmosis I may even have absorbed some of his Chinese philosophy of resignation.

Charles Ammoun came from Paris to discuss the general pattern of his report on discrimination in education. It was always a delight to work with Ammoun, and I was pleased with the way his report was shaping up. But the study was being threatened by the refusal of the Secretariat to publish the country monographs which described the situation in each country. Both the rapporteur and I felt strongly about this, because these monographs were much more revealing than the generalities that would be included in the report. I spoke to de Seynes, but he was adamant, and none of the monographs on which the many studies on discrimination or other aspects of human rights were based were ever published as official documents.

Shortly after this I had lunch with Judge Guerrero, who wanted to exploit the recent improvement in the international situation and suggested that the ad hoc commission on prisoners of war should meet in Geneva when the foreign ministers met there in October. The session would be a pretext for diplomatic negotiations, and he would himself approach the ministers in the hope that they would agree to some solution. I reported this to de Seynes, who later said that the Secretary-General was cold to the idea; Hammarskjold wanted, he said, to conduct the negotiations himself. Whether he ever did I was never told, but if he did, nothing came of them.

After the adjournment of the Council I went to Clarens at the other end of Lake Leman, where I was a consultant at a Quaker conference for young diplomats. The Clarens conference was an outstanding success, one of the best unofficial occasions for exchanging views I had ever experienced; and I kept it in mind later when I organized the program of United Nations seminars on human rights. The Quakers also provided good hospitality. The conference over, I returned to Geneva and boarded a Viscount for London, where I took a plane for New York. Sometime on that flight I decided to have it out with Hammarskjold and, on the very day of my return to New York asked to see him. He was surprised when I asked him to find me another job in the Secretariat, a job, I said, where I could make a significant contribution. I explained that I wasn't the kind of man he needed to implement his human rights policy. I had come to the United Nations to do what I had thought was an important job, and I had done it to the best of my ability whatever he might think of the program. I wasn't willing to share the fate of some of my colleagues in the Secretariat, who had become prisoners of insignificant work for which they drew fat salaries. His first reaction was to play on my reference to "a significant contribution." He was shocked, he said, that I of all people should be saying that work for the promotion of human rights was insignificant, but he was much too intelligent not to have understood my point. He then said that he needed my idealism in the place where I was. But when I insisted that I was serious he said that the next move would be his. What he had in mind I have no idea, but in any event he did nothing, unless our conversation inspired his later decision to move the Human Rights Division out of the Department of Economic and Social Affairs. He had great personal charm and our conversation was friendly. I couldn't help liking him even though I disagreed with him on so many fundamentals. I hardly expected anything to come from my *démarche* but I was glad that I had made it, for Hammarskjold now knew exactly where I stood. In retrospect, I think I can say that my relations with him now improved. Henceforth he was less visibly opposed to the human rights program, although I attribute this to the unfavorable reaction of delegations to his policies and not to any stand I had taken. My relations with de Seynes did not improve; they continued indeed to deteriorate until, two years later, responsibility for the human rights program was taken away from him and transferred to Sir Humphrey Trevelyan. My implied threat to resign was not an empty gesture. Before leaving Geneva I had written to Percy Corbett and Manley Hudson, seeking their help in finding a university appointment, for I hesitated to renew the conversations with McGill that I had broken off in 1952. Had there been an attractive opening, I probably would have taken it. Looking back, I think I was passing through a kind of crisis, and blowing off steam improved my morale. I had done what I thought needed to be done and, even though there had been no immediate result, I was better equipped psychologically to carry on with my work. As for leaving the Secretariat, the truth was that this was the last thing I wanted, for I was as firmly committed to my work as I had ever been.

An Idea Aborted (1955)

De Seynes told me that the Secretary-General wanted him to support the American proposal for a study on self-determination as an alternative to the two commissions recommended by the Human Rights Commission, when the matter came up at the tenth session of the General Assembly which was about to begin, and he asked me to prepare a statement. If such a statement were to be made it would, I pointed out, put the Secretary-General on the side of the great powers against the small. I also thought, but did not say, that if it were to be made, it should be done by Hammarskjold himself and not by a Frenchman whose country was then denying self-determination in North Africa. But I prepared a draft. Given the intention to intervene, which I still thought was a mistake, it was the best speech that could be made in the circumstances. I took it to de Seynes. Martin Hill, to whom I had sent a copy, was with him in his office. De Seynes began by saying that my draft wasn't what he wanted: the Secretary-General should simply explain what he could do in preparing the study. I replied that this would compromise the Secretary-General; he shouldn't take sides in such a controversial question. In my draft, I had suggested that the General Assembly undertake the drafting of a declaration on self-determination which would provide a normative background and therefore lines of discipline for the commission, the creation of which had been recommended by the Human Rights Commission and which I fully expected the Assembly would set up. If such a declaration were substituted for the articles on self-determination now in them it might also save the convenants. By now both de Seynes and Hill were obviously impressed by the reasoning behind the draft, and, as luck would have it, a message came through that Hammarskjold wanted to see de Seynes immediately. "Well," he said, "what are we going to do about this text?" "Take it with you," I replied, "and say that it is one of Humphrey's crazy ideas." He must have done so, because half an hour later, a message came that there would be a meeting the next day in Hammarskjold's office with Bunche, Hill, Tchernychev (the Soviet Under Secretary), Stavropoulos (the legal counsel), de Seynes and myself to discuss the speech.

The meeting lasted for an hour and a half. Hammarskjold began by saying that he agreed with my criticism of the two recommendations which had come from the Human Rights Commission. I said that I had tried to read his mind. The criticisms were not mine but his; I had nevertheless tried to tone them down because I thought that a legal argument to which he attached so much importance was untenable. Stavropoulos agreed with me on that point. The discussion then became confused, and it was impossible to know what

210

Hammarskjold wanted. At one moment he veered in one direction and at the next in another. He then said that his idea was simply to tell the Third Committee what the Secretariat could do to further the study proposed by the Americans. I repeated that if he did this, he would be taking sides and risk being defeated. The advantage of my draft was that it dissociated him from any of the proposals under consideration and suggested a quite different approach, which had the merit that it could help save the convenants; for there was little likelihood (and most people thought this in 1955) that they would be ratified by a number of important countries as long as they contained the controversial articles on self-determination. If these could be transferred to a declaration, there was some hope that the convenants would be universally accepted.

How much of my argument the Secretary-General accepted I could not be sure. I knew that he wasn't interested in saving the covenants; he had once told me that he would like to throw them out of his window. But the result of the discussion was that de Seynes and I were instructed to prepare a new speech. When I talked to de Seynes later he said that he thought we could salvage most of my draft. I had been pleasantly surprised by his attitude at the Secretary-General's meeting and his understanding and penetrating comments. But we were, of course, working for different ends—I to save the covenants and he to defeat the recommendations of the Human Rights Commission. Bunche took a most conservative line. I was annoyed by his references to the draft convenants and must have showed it. He said that the articles in them on self-determination presented no problem because the covenants would never come into force. Coming down the hall with me after the meeting, he also said that the Commission on the Racial Situation in South Africa—of which Laugier, Senator Bellegarde and Hernan Santa Cruz were members—was a waste of time. Tchernychev didn't open his mouth once. I was surprised that Hammarskjold could be so partisan and even flippant in his presence on issues on which the Soviet Union had expressed strong views.

I sat down to write a new speech, but there were a number of interruptions before I could finish it. Van Heuven Goedhart called to discuss the possibility of getting an article into the covenants on the right to asylum. I offered to help in any way I could, but I pointed out that when the Universal Declarationof Human Rights was being adopted in 1948, the General Assembly had been unwilling to go beyond recognizing a right to "seek and enjoy" asylum. It was unlikely that states would now agree to recognize a real right of asylum in instruments which were to become legally binding on ratification, because even the most liberal governments insisted on retaining their full sovereign discretion to decide what aliens they would allow to enter their territory. The high commissioner then left me to talk to delegations. Returning to my office the next day, he said that what he had heard from them confirmed my diagnosis. Charles Ammoun arrived to discuss his report on discrimination in education. Pressures were being brought on him to introduce certain Cold War elements, which I advised him to resist.

I gave my new draft of the speech to de Seynes, who passed it to Martin Hill for suggestions. I was afraid that Martin would squeeze all the life and fire out of it, but when I saw his suggestions I was pleasantly surprised. He had changed the order of some of the ideas, had taken out some of my strong language—which I had put in to express conviction—and had eliminated a passage in which I had tried to identify the Secretary-

General with the spirit prevailing in the Third Committee. Otherwise the speech remained as I had written it and the essential idea of a declaration was retained.

Hammarskjold worked on the speech over the weekend but changed only a few words. He also talked to delegations. Mary Tenison-Woods, my Australian chief of section, told me about a conversation he had with R.G. Casey and Sir Percy Spender (which she had overheard) in which he had repeated my arguments. But when I saw him next, Hammarskjold seemed to be having second thoughts about the wisdom of making any statement, which was of course my own original position. He asked me to sound out some delegations. Amongst others, I consulted the Egyptians and the Yugoslavs. Omar Loutfi, whom I had known fairly well when he was the representative of Egypt on the Human Rights Commission, doubted whether the colonial powers would agree to a declaration. Branko Jevermovic was so insistent on retaining the articles on self-determination in the convenants that I thought it wiser not to mention the declaration at that stage. I also talked to General Romulo of the Philippines, to the Australians, the British, the Canadians and the New Zealanders. Samuel Hoare, the British member of the Human Rights Commission, began by saying that it was probably too late to organize opinion in the Third Committee for such a radical change in policy. Moreover, the United Kingdom was opposed to setting up any commission on self-determination and would probably be fearful about the end result of a declaration. The prospects were anything but promising and I so reported to de Seynes, who told me the next day that the Secretary-General would probably make no statement.

But he did make it—on Tuesday, 11 October, the day the Third Committee took up the item on the covenants. The gist of his suggestion was that the General Assembly should appoint an ad hoc committee which would try to reach agreement on certain basic principles relating to self-determination. These principles would then be incorporated in a declaration which would be adopted by the Assembly. If this were done, it would help find "a way out of the political impasse in which the convenants now find themselves." Most of the delegations reserved comment until they could study the statement, but Jamil Baroody (Saudi Arabia), Abdul Ramam Pazhwak (Afghanistan) and Father Nuñez (Costa Rica) were immediately critical. The real fireworks began the next day. Baroody and Pazhwak returned to the attack and were joined by the Syrians. More serious, P.D. Morosov, speaking for the Soviet Union, criticized the Secretary-General, whom he accused of taking sides. There was a hopeful development when Krishna Menon of India came into the conference room and suggested that the debate on self-determination be postponed. A week earlier, I had suggested to both de Seynes and Hammarskjold that Menon might like to play the role of savior of the covenants and that he might support a declaration. I had also talked to Roger Baldwin, who knew Menon well. If he would talk to Menon, he could, I said, use the argument that the anti-colonial countries would gain nothing by having self-determination in the covenants if those instruments were not ratified by the colonial powers, but a declaration, even though not legally binding, could be invoked against any country whether it had voted for it or not. Baldwin later told me that Menon immediately saw the point. He wasn't concerned with saving the covenants but only with strengthening the right to self-determination, and he agreed that this could be done better outside than in the covenants; but he wasn't sure that he could carry the Arabs with him. Baldwin also saw the Arabs, but judging from the ensuing debate they were not impressed.

Hammarskjold decided to reply to the criticisms that had been levelled against him; and Per Lind, his personal assistant, showed me a draft of a statement. It was, I thought, weak and diffuse and had better not be made. That night—it was a Friday—I went to Cambridge, Massachusetts to see Manley Hudson who, in response to my letter from Geneva seeking his help in finding a university appointment, had suggested the visit. It was a wild goose chase. Hudson had even forgotten about our appointment, and when I finally did get to see him at his house, I found a bedridden, broken invalid, who was however as irascible as ever. He wrote me an encouraging letter several months later, but by that time the prospects of the human rights program seemed to be improving, and I replied that I was inclined to stick it out in the Secretariat.

I was back in the Third Committee on Monday, where the situation continued to develop. By Wednesday more delegations began to speak up, and it was soon quite obvious that the articles on self-determination would remain in the covenants. The *démarche* had failed miserably. I had the satisfaction, however, that I had prevented Hammarskjold from making a statement that would have brought him under still greater criticism, for if, as he had originally intended, he had come out in favor of the American proposal for a mere study on self-determination as an alternative to the recommendations of the Human Rights Commission, he would have been much more vulnerable. He admitted this to me when I met him in the corridor after the meeting and also said that I had been right all along in my sizing up of the situation.

Charles Ammoun, who was still in New York, was upset by the Secretariat's refusal to publish the country monographs on which his studies of discrimination in education were to be based. He invited de Seynes for lunch to discuss the matter. I had reports from both parties. De Seynes retired from the rigid position he had taken in the spring, and told me the next day that the Secretary-General had agreed that the decision would have to be reversed. Ammoun was pleased. But it was later decided that the monographs would be published only as "conference room documents," which meant that they would be neither translated nor given regular distribution, and the question remained a bone of contention between the Secretariat and the sub-commission.

The debate on the covenants continued on until 11 November, a whole month in all, and twenty-six of the meetings were devoted to self-determination. Neither of the commissions recommended by the Human Rights Commission was created, nor did the Assembly approve the study proposed by the Americans. But the article on self-determination remained in the covenants.

On 16 November the Third Committee adopted the advisory services program by a vote of fifty to none with four abstentions, and this was confirmed in plenary. But only $50,000 was allotted for the program in the budget for 1956. I couldn't do very much with that, and I became skeptical about the real intentions of the Americans. After all they had invented the program only as a substitute for the covenants. With the help of Minerva Bernadino, the chairman that year of the Commission on the Status of Women—to whom I promised that I would do everything within my power to ensure that there would be a seminar every year on the status of women—I was able a year later to get the budgetary allocation increased to a more realistic sum.

First Trip Around The World (1956)

When the Sub-Commission on the Prevention of Discrimination met early in January, the most important item on its agenda was a progress report on its study of discrimination in education. This study would not be completed for at least another year; but, notwithstanding the admonitions of the Under Secretary, the sub-commission decided to proceed forthwith with its studies on religious rights and practices and on political rights, and appointed Arcot Krishnaswami (India) and Hernan Santa Cruz (Chile) as rapporteurs. Also in session was an ad hoc committee of ten members of the Economic and Social Council that had been appointed to prepare a first draft of a supplementary convention on slavery.

Now that the General Assembly had approved the program of advisory services in human rights, I was anxious to organize some seminars. I didn't think governments were likely to come to the United Nations for help, but some of them might be persuaded to host seminars (which I envisaged as regional conferences) on subjects on which their record was good. Borrowing a term from bridge my idea was that they should be encouraged to lead from strength and not from weakness. I talked about this to several members of the sub-commission, including Santa Cruz, who agreed to sponsor a resolution I drafted. The resolution, which was unanimously adopted, asked the Secretariat to consider the advisability of holding seminars on the prevention of discrimination and the protection of minorities. Such seminars, it said, would be a particularly fruitful way for nations to exchange information and experience.

The twelfth session of the Human Rights Commission opened on 5 March. Hammarskjold had agreed to attend the opening, and I had written a speech for him in which he would explain and give his blessing to the new interpretation I was putting on the human rights seminars, namely, that the Secretariat would expect countries with strong records to take the initiative in sponsoring them. I showed this to several of my colleagues in the Human Rights Division. Both Lin and Tenison-Woods encouraged me to go ahead with it; but Schwelb, who was becoming increasingly impatient with the direction the work of the Division was taking and particularly disliked the advisory services program, challenged nearly every sentence in my draft. With a few stylistic changes, the Secretary-General accepted the text and, notwithstanding his earlier opposition to the advisory services program, made the speech. Later, both the Human Rights Commission and the Commission on the Status of Women also requested the Secretary-General to explore the possibility of holding human rights seminars; and at its next session the Economic and Social Council was even more specific when it requested him to undertake, if feasible during 1956, a seminar or seminars, preferably on a regional basis, along the lines suggested by the two commissions. I now had a clear mandate to develop the program. One of the first things I did was to prepare a *note verbale* addressed to all member governments, drawing their attention to the Council's resolution. Not long after this I wrote another speech for Hammarskjold, the one he gave at Williamsburg on the one hundred and eightieth anniversary of the adoption of the American Declaration of Independence. Preparing this speech gave me some personal amusement, because I happen to be a descendant of those early political refugees, the United Empire Loyalists (the Americans called them Tories) who left the United States after the Revolution because they preferred to live under George III even if it were in the wilds of New Brunswick.

The so-called action program, which the Americans had first proposed three years earlier, included two other features in addition to advisory services: annual reporting by governments and studies of specific rights and groups of rights, both of which were also discussed at this session of the Human Rights Commission. The studies, the first of which was to be on the right of everyone to be free from arbitrary arrest, detention or exile, were modeled on the studies being undertaken by the sub-commission, with the important difference that they were to be conducted not in the name of rapporteurs but of small committees appointed by the commission from amongst its members. It followed that all decisions on matters of policy would be taken by representatives of governments and not by individual experts. Because of pressure by the Americans, it was decided that supporting documents for the studies (including those undertaken by the sub-commission) would not include material emanating from governments of states which were not members of the United Nations or of the specialized agencies—a formula meant to prevent the Secretariat from communicating in any way with the government of Communist China.

The new program of studies and the reporting system were approved notwithstanding the efforts of the Secretariat to defeat them; the controller went so far as to ask for six new translators if the resolutions were adopted. Mary Lord, the new representative of the United States on the commission, told me that she wouldn't mind very much if the studies program was defeated on financial grounds. I knew, of course, that the only reason the Americans had sponsored the new program was that they had decided not to ratify the covenants and needed a program they could support, but I had thought they were now converted by their own suggestions. The studies and reporting system were also opposed by the United Kingdom, Samuel Hoare voting against both projects. By now the United Kingdom had become one of the most conservative influences in the commission.

But something else happened at this session that very nearly upset the applecart. As part of the Secretariat campaign to defeat the American plan for seminars on freedom of information, the Office of Public Information had suggested a year earlier that a seminar be convened of news personnel; and now that the Council had adopted the advisory services program, the O.P.I. was even more anxious to have its seminar and to have it paid for out of funds voted for the new program. I couldn't be enthusiastic about the proposal because I knew all about its history and also because the O.P.I. didn't intend that the emphasis would be on human rights. The Council approved the suggestion, and the seminar was held in July. De Seynes arranged to have it run by the Office of Public Information and I therefore had nothing to do with it, even though there had been agreement in the Council that "due emphasis will be given to freedom of information." I quote from my diary (26 April):

> The news-personnel program sponsored by the O.P.I. got a bad drumming and members insisted that the emphasis be brought back to human rights and freedom of information. The O.P.I. project always was a fake, having been invented by the Secretariat as part of a plan to kill the American plan for technical assistance in freedom of information.

But several days after I had written this, Walter Kotchnig, the American representative in the Council's Social Committee, made another speech in which he put a quite different interpretation on the resolution. It was his opinion, he said, that the seminar should be organized along the lines originally suggested by the Office of Public Information. I have no doubt that this statement was inspired by the Secretariat, but why Kotchnig should have been taken in by lobbying which was so obviously directed against the policy of his delegation still intrigues me. A member of the American delegation later came to complain that the Secretary-General's letter to governments about the proposed seminar did not give enough importance to freedom of information, to which I replied that I had not drafted the letter or even seen it. In the light of the interpretation that had been put on Kotchnig's speech, I explained, the Office of Public Information was in full control. He said he was disappointed that responsibility had been taken away from the Human Rights Division. As for Kotchnig's speech, the explanation was, he said, that Kotchnig thought de Seynes wanted to kill the seminar. This incident had another echo. De Seynes' personal assistant told one of my colleagues that de Seynes thought the Human Rights Division had misrepresented the situation in the Council's Social Committee. I was so incensed that de Seynes could entertain such an idea and say nothing to me that I resolved to have it out with him if it were the last thing I ever did at the United Nations. It happened that there was a meeting of directors the next day and I seized the opportunity to protest without, however, addressing my remarks specifically to the Under Secretary, but later I went to his office and read out the pertinent parts of the official record. I think I made my point, but his attitude towards the seminars never changed.

My wife and I had rented that spring a cottage on Roger Baldwin's Suffern Mountain property. It took me an hour and a half to drive to work in the morning and as long to return home at night, but it was well worth the effort. There were so many birds around the place that I no longer kept lists. We also had ground hogs, raccoons and snakes. You could see water snakes and copperheads almost any day, and there were even said to be rattlers which, fortunately, we never encountered. This wild country was only thirty-five miles from Times Square. We left it late in June for Nova Scotia, where Jeanne was to spend the summer. I returned to New York on 1 July en route to Paris (where I spent the best part of a week working with Charles Ammoun on his study on discrimination in education) and on to Geneva for the summer session of the Economic and Social Council.

We were beginning to receive some replies to the letters I had sent to governments about the seminars. Two of these came from the governments of the United States and Romania, both of which wanted to sponsor a seminar on the status of women. De Seynes dismissed the second out of hand, but this was the one that we did accept—after the Human Rights Division was moved out of his department.

Another part of the "action program" was to be periodic reporting. Following the recommendation of the Human Rights Commission, the Economic and Social Council invited governments to report to it on developments and progress achieved in the realization of the human rights proclaimed by the Universal Declaration and the right to self-determination. But, at the suggestion of Canada and Yugoslavia, the reports were to be made every three years instead of annually as recommended by the commission. Reporting is the implementation system with which the international community has had the most and probably the best experience and could become an important part of the United Nations system for the protection of human rights. I thought, therefore, that the Canadian-Yugoslav move was unfortunate and wasn't impressed by the argument that annual reporting would put too great a burden on governments. As already indicated, the Human Rights Commission decided in 1981 that it would no longer examine these reports. The Council also authorized the series of studies on specific rights and groups of rights which the Human Rights Commission had decided to undertake.

The plenipotentiary conference on the abolition of slavery, the slave trade and institutions and practices similar to slavery, which I opened on Monday, 13 August in my capacity as executive secretary, also met in Geneva. Because it took so long to reach agreement on the election of officers, I was still in the chair the next day when the Russians challenged the credentials of the Chinese delegation; but, since there was no formal motion, I did not have to make a ruling. It was a good conference and produced a good convention. Chattel slavery (the condition or status of a person over whom all or any of the powers of ownership are exercised) had already been prohibited by the League of Nations Slavery Convention of 1926. By the new Supplementary Convention of 1956, states parties would also undertake "to bring about progressively and as soon as possible" the abolition of certain practices which resemble slavery, including debt bondage, serfdom, bride-price and the exploitation of children. At the signing ceremony after the conference thirty-three states signed the convention; it has been widely ratified and came into force the following April.

I returned to New York. In the meantime we had decided to convene a meeting of experts in Bangkok to plan an Asiatic seminar on the status of women; and, because it was to be the first step in a new program, I decided to go myself—notwithstanding the fact that I had only just returned to headquarters after an absence of over two months—and Jeanne went with me. We traveled by way of Vancouver, Tokyo and Hong Kong, stopping at Vancouver long enough for me to give a lecture at the university and visit relatives. Flying up the British Columbia coast to Cold Bay in Alaska, I asked the captain why the route wasn't advertised for its extraordinary beauty. "Because," he replied, "there is usually so much fog that you can't see anything. You have been very lucky." We stopped at Cold Bay, one of the most desolate places I have ever seen, to refuel and then flew on over the Aleutians and the Kuriles to Tokyo, where we arrived in the middle of a rainy night. After a short rest, we set off to tour the city. Apart from one popular market and its temple, the experience left no strong impression. I hadn't yet learned that in Japan beauty is usually to be found in unsuspected places, perhaps some hidden garden. The next day we went to Nikko to see the Shinto shrines. There was a fine view from the train window of small farms and rice paddies and the great trees of the Japanese forest. Nikko itself was crowded with sightseers, including many school children, long lines of whom wound their ways through the crowds following the colored flags of their leaders. We left Tokyo that night for Hong Kong where, because we had chosen a hotel on the island, one of our first experiences was to cross over the harbor on a Star ferry, on which I could have spent the whole day, there was so much to see, not only immediately around us but in the harbor. We were soon on it again when we returned to Kowloon for a drive around the New Territories, which I couldn't have found more exciting had we been in China itself. Boarding our plane for Bangkok after four exciting days, we learned that some thirty people had been killed in a riot on Nathan Road while we were enjoying an exotic dinner only a few blocks away.

In Bangkok we were met by officials from the Economic Commission for Asia and the Far East, and the next morning I opened the meeting of the working party. The experts came from seven different Asiatic countries and spent a little over a week planning the seminar which, it was agreed, would be held in 1957. It only remained to find a host country. I had no difficulty getting an invitation from the Thai government, a job made easier by the fact that I was able to tell them that it would not cost them a penny because I already had the promise that we could use the facilities of the Economic Commission for Asia and the Far East, which had its headquarters in Bangkok.

I was busy most of the time with the working party and the round of official entertainment, and the heat was so intense that in my free time I was tempted to sit back in a chair and relax. But we managed to see quite a lot of the city, including some of the three hundred or more temples and, very early one morning, the famous floating market. The next time I was in Bangkok which was after my retirement from the United Nations, the city had lost much of its exotic charm; some of the klongs had even been cemented over.

We were on the point of returning to New York when I received a cablegram instructing me to attend part of the UNESCO general conference which was about to open in New Delhi, a stroke of luck which I owed to the fact that Martin Hill, who had been designated to represent the Secretary-General at the conference, was being held up by the Suez crisis. There were a few days remaining after the end of my business in Bangkok and the opening of the conference, and we decided to spend them in Rangoon and Calcutta. I belong to a generation whose romantic ideas were partly formed by Rudyard Kipling, Joseph Conrad and Somerset Maugham, and I will never get them out of my system. There were things in Rangoon that came up to my standards, including the exotic Malay sailors at the waterside, the turbanned waiters in the hotel where I shocked Jeanne by eating oysters, admittedly an unnecessary risk, and, notwithstanding the filth, the climb up to the Golden Pagoda; but generally the city was drab and poor. From Rangoon we flew to Calcutta, a city which displays its character on the drive from the airport to the center of the city. I had the impression that I was not in a great city but in a huge conglomeration of villages where, it seemed, the life and occupations of the people remained essentially rural. There were signs of great poverty everywhere and many people lived literally in the streets with all their small belongings.

My duties at the Delhi conference were almost purely representational, but they were time-consuming. We nevertheless managed to see something of the city in the few days before the conference began and on weekends. I have been in Delhi half a dozen times since, but never again did I find the place as enjoyable. For one thing the November weather was ideal. I could return to places like the Qutab Minar, and Red Fort and the Chaudni Chawk time and again. We stayed at the Maidens Hotel in Old Delhi and had hardly been there an hour when, going into the dining room, we spied Laugier (who was still a member of the UNESCO executive board) and Marie Cutolli.

Our best experience on this visit to India was the weekend we went to Agra. The hotel porter having given us the wrong information, we took a train that stopped at every station. We seemed to be the only first-class passengers on board and, presumably for our protection, the conductor locked the door of our compartment, leaving us prisoners in the heat. I amused myself during the long journey by watching exotic birds on the telegraph wires and, in the fields, great red-tufted cranes. Finally, we arrived at a station where there was a sign reading "Agra." The doors of our compartment were now unlocked, but the conductor had disappeared. We got off the train only to discover, after it had moved on, that we had not yet reached our destination. There must have been at least a dozen pedicabs waiting for the unlikely event that a fare would turn up, and when their owners spied us there was nearly a riot. There then occurred one of the most disgraceful scenes I have witnessed anywhere. A husky-looking policeman came up and began to thrash the men with a great bamboo staff. There isn't very much that a stranger can do in a situation like that, particularly when the brutality is coming from authority, but I felt like an accomplice. We grabbed the nearest pedicab and were soon speeding towards the real Agra. The chief attraction there was, of course, the Taj Mahal, about which it would be hard to say anything original. It is an exquisite gem particularly in the early evening. I have now seen it four times and hope to see it again; but our pleasure on this occasion was spoiled by the importunities of stupid guides—cultural sabotage, Laugier called it.

We had about two weeks in Delhi before Martin Hill came to replace me. I spent long hours at meetings in the Vigyan Bhavan and at official receptions, but I had very little to contribute. One day I was sitting in the seat reserved for the representative of the Secretary-General when a junior official asked me to move over because C.V. Narasimhan, the executive secretary of the Economic Commission for Asia and the Far East (who had been absent from Bangkok when I was there) had arrived. I wasn't going to stand on protocol and moved to another seat. It was just as well that I did, for he later came to headquarters to become my immediate chief in the hierarchy.

Our original intention had been to return to New York by way of Beirut and Cairo, but events in Egypt made this impossible and we were routed through Istanbul and Athens instead. I had already been to both places, but they were new to Jeanne. Istanbul was nearly my undoing. For one night, on my insistence, we decided to dine in an exotic restaurant in the Spice Market. Up until now we had followed the advice of Jeanne's New York doctor and taken the most extraordinary precautions in the matter of eating, and both of us had been remarkably well. But I figured that we were now in Europe and that I could cater to my tastes. It must have been the almond cakes which Jeanne had warned me not to eat. That night and all the next day I was violently ill.

In Athens, we had a stroke of luck. On our very first evening there we met a U.N. colleague on the street. Jean Romanos had just retired from the Secretariat, had time on his hands and was glad to do everything in his power to make our stay agreeable. Amongst other things he took us to see a Byzantine church in Daphne, which is something I will always thank him for. We also visited Delphi, this time alone; but we spent most of our short visit on the Acropolis and in the Athens museum.

We were back in New York on 19 November. The General Assembly had been in session for only a week and the Third Committee was only getting down to business. The committee continued its article-by-article discussion of the covenants that it had begun a year earlier, devoting some forty meetings to the Covenant on Economic, Social and Cultural Rights, to which it decided to give priority, a decision which reflected the human rights priorities of most governments. The committee approved six of the articles: on the right to work, to just and favorable conditions of work, trade unions and the right to strike, social security, the protection of the family, the right to adequate food, clothing and housing and the right to health.

At ECOSOC session, 1950, John Humphrey with Henri Laugier and George Davidson
(Courtesy: U.N. Association of the U.S.A.)

At session of the Third Committee, General Assembly, 1950, John Humphrey, Egon Schwelb, van Heuven Goedhart
(Courtesy: U.N. Association of the U.S.A.)

STATES

COMMITTEE SECRETARY

With Eleanor Roosevelt, first chairman of the Commission on Human Rights
(Courtesy: U.N. Department of Public Information)

Eleanor Roosevelt and John Humphrey
(Courtesy: U.N. Association of the U.S.A.)

At ECOSOC session, 1952: Dot Osborne, Georges-Picot, Jiri Nosek, John Humphrey
(Courtesy: U.N. Association of the U.S.A.)

Sub-Commission on Prevention of Discrimination, John Humphrey, Assistant Secretary-General Georges Picot, and Hérard Roy, chairman, 1952   (Courtesy: U.N. Association of the U.S.A.)

Eighteenth session of the Commission on the Status of Women, Tehran, 1965. John Humphrey with Madame Arimhol of Guinea

John Humphrey is received by abbot of Gandantehehingling Pagoda, Ulan Bator, 1964

Children's camp near Ulan Bator, 1965

(Courtesy: U.N. Department of Public Information)

John Humphrey and Pandit Nehru, 1962

(Courtesy: U.N. Department of Public Information)

John Humphrey and Haile Selassie at Seminar on the Participation of Women in Public Life, 1960

(Courtesy: U.N. Association of the U.S.A.)

Canberra Seminar on the Role of the Police, 1963, John Male, Sir Kenneth Bailey, John Humphrey

(Courtesy: Australian News and Information Bureau)

Meeting Secretary-General U Thant and Mrs. Thant

U.N. Commission on Human Rights

(Courtesy: U.N. Department of Public Information)

Working Party in Manila (1957)

Exceptionally, the General Assembly reconvened after the Christmas holiday and remained in session until 8 March. At this session it adopted the Convention on the Nationality of Married Women which was designed to change the traditional rule of law (based on the principle of the unity of the family presided over by the husband) to the effect that the nationality of a woman automatically followed that of her husband and could be changed by his act without her consent. The convention came into force in 1958 and has been widely ratified. It was typical of the United Nations that the most hotly debated issue related, not to the substance of the instrument itself, on which there was general agreement, but to a Byelorussian amendment, the purpose of which was to open it for signature by "any state," and not merely the restricted category devised to ostracize mainland China.

The ninth session of the Sub-Commission on the Prevention of Discrimination took place while the Assembly was still meeting. Its main business was Ammoun's final report on discrimination in education, on the basis of which the sub-commission drafted ten principles and proposals which were forwarded to the Human Rights Commission and later to UNESCO, where they were used in the drafting of its Convention against Discrimination in Education, adopted in 1960. This convention is still one of the brightest jewels in the UNESCO crown. It is therefore worth recalling that when the study on discrimination in education was first proposed, the UNESCO secretariat wanted to have nothing to do with it. Other business before the sub-commission included the progress reports of its two rapporteurs for the studies of religious rights and practices and of political rights. The sub-commission also recommended that another conference of nongovernmental organizations be organized for 1958. When the matter came up in the commission, a statement was made on behalf of the Secretary-General to the effect that he was not convinced the conference would be useful, but a second conference was nevertheless held in June 1959.

Missing part of the eleventh session of the Commission on the Status of Women, I had to go to Europe for meetings at UNESCO and the thirteenth session of the Human Rights Commission. I flew on one of the new fast airplanes direct from New York to Paris without the, for me, usual stop in Shannon or indeed the time for sleep. If this was progress, I could do without it.

In Paris, where I spent six days representing the Secretary-General at meetings of the executive board of UNESCO, I was chiefly interested in the discussion arising out of the Ammoun report on education. Ammoun himself was the permanent representative of Lebanon at UNESCO and he came to the meetings to defend his work. Awad, who was currently the chairman of the sub-commission, was a member of the board. Thanks to him the discussion was particularly well informed. I also had useful talks with people in the Secretariat, including Tor Gjesdal, who had left the United Nations Secretariat after Trygve Lie's retirement.

I had a long talk at the Palais Royal with Cassin, who wanted to be chairman of the Human Rights Commission for a third term. We also talked about a seminar which the French government was considering on the right to asylum. Pierre Juvigny had come to see me at headquarters, looking for ideas for some step that the French might take to develop such a right. Because we both thought there was no chance that the covenants would recognize such a right, I suggested that France might want to sponsor a United Nations seminar on the question. The French delegation was pleased by the suggestion and arranged for me to discuss the matter further at the Quai d'Orsay, where I went after my talk with Cassin. The conversation went particularly well, and I left the Quai d'Orsay convinced that we would soon have a formal invitation. But de Seynes, who was a Frenchman, told the French that the United Nations Secretariat wasn't interested in having such a seminar, thus cutting the ground from under my feet. I had, however, told him about my talks with the delegation, and he knew about my intention to discuss the matter further at the Quai d'Orsay. While I was at the Quai d'Orsay, the question of Cassin's chairmanship came up. Because he had already held the office for two terms and had not been a particularly good presiding officer, there was a feeling in the commission that he should be replaced by an Asian, and Felixberto Serrano, the acting foreign minister of the Philippines was a candidate. We thought in the Secretariat that Serrano had an easy majority, but on Cassin's insistence, the French had launched an energetic campaign to keep him in the office. I could now see that the Quai d'Orsay was beginning to have second thoughts. Was it worth risking the loss of Asian friends simply to satisfy Cassin's vanity?

I now thought that my plan for a series of human rights seminars was firmly on the rails. I fully expected that the French would sponsor one on the right to asylum; negotiations with the Filipinos had gone so far that arrangements had been made to have a working party meet in Manila in May; and I was talking to the delegations of Brazil, Costa Rica, Chile and the Dominican Republic. In nearly every case, I worked through some member of the country's delegation whom I personally knew. There was still a good deal of hostility to the program in the Secretariat and some skepticism even in the Human Rights Division, but I now knew that I had the active and enthusiastic support of the Americans. My determination to get the program started was partly influenced by my realization that, with the draft covenants stalled in the General Assembly, something had to be done to keep the human rights flag flying at the United Nations.

I was in Geneva on Saturday, 30 March. One of the first people I saw and had dinner with that night was Paonan Chen, the Chinese member of the Human Rights Commission. He said that his government wanted me to visit Taiwan on my way back to headquarters from Manila, where I would be going for the working party just mentioned. When this was followed up by a formal letter of invitation addressed to the Secretary-General, Cordier said that I had myself solicited it. I later saw his insulting comment crawled over the letter: "Let me say bluntly that I think that this was inspired." When I protested to de Seynes, he told me, after inquiry, that the reference was not to me, but to the Chinese, which was something I could hardly swallow. How could the Chinese inspire the Chinese to write the letter?

It took us the whole of the morning to get a chairman elected when the Human Rights Commission met on Monday. There were three candidates, Cassin, Serrano of the Philippines and Gunewardene of Ceylon, none of whom wanted to retire from the arena. Cassin was the first to do so; Gunewardene sat stubbornly for some time insisting that he was acting on the instructions of his government, but he finally yielded to Serrano, who was then elected by acclamation.

The commission devoted part of this session and the next to a draft declaration on the rights of the child, which had been prepared by the Social Commission and dated back to the very first years of the United Nations. The essential principles had already been enunciated in the Universal Declaration of Human Rights and in a declaration which had been approved by the League of Nations. I doubted whether the purpose it would serve could possibly justify the time and effort the United Nations was devoting to it. It was, I suspected, a stopgap which was being used to give the impression that the Human Rights Commission was doing something. There were certainly other more important matters that needed attention. The French, who were still very anxious to do something about asylum, now proposed that the United Nations adopt a declaration on the matter, but their draft gave rise to so many difficulties that it wasn't until 1967 that the Assembly adopted a Declaration on Territorial Asylum which, like the covenants and the 1951 Convention on the Protection of Refugees, does not recognize a right to asylum.

At its last session the commission had appointed a committee to make plans for the widest possible celebrations of the tenth anniversary of the adoption of the Universal Declaration of Human Rights, which would be in 1958. Surprisingly enough, the report of this committee gave rise to a great deal of controversy. One question that was hotly debated was whether all countries or only those that were members of the United Nations or of the specialized agencies should be invited to celebrate the anniversary. The chief advocate of a limited observance was the United States, whose policy of preventing any contact between the United Nations and nonmember countries like China, the German Democratic Republic and Mongolia (the existence of which it did not recognize) was becoming more ridiculous every day. The question came to a vote on 5 April, and it happened that the Italian representative was absent. The result was a tie and a defeat for the Americans who, however, recovered their lost ground in this battle of words when the commission's report was debated in ECOSOC. One obvious suggestion made in connection with the proposed celebrations was that the General Assembly should arrange to adopt the two covenants on 10 December, 1958. A resolution to this effect proposed by Poland was also opposed by the United States, but it was adopted. The negative attitude of the United States towards the covenants had, by this time, provided the communist countries with the unexpected opportunity to pose as their chief champions; and they lost no opportunity to advocate their early adoption, a policy that also appealed to the anti-colonial countries now that the instruments included the right to self-determination.

The thirteenth session of the commission wasn't one of its most productive. But in terms of intellectual capacity the commission still had the highest rating and could be compared favorably with any other United Nations body. People like Dayal of India, who was one of the best debaters in the United Nations, Sir Samuel Hoare of the United Kingdom,

Gunewardene of Ceylon, Morosov of the Soviet Union, Cassin of France, Calderon Puig of Mexico, Haim Cohn of Israel, Colban of Norway and Serrano of the Philippines were the intellectual equals of anyone at the United Nations. But the agenda was now so thin that at times it seemed they were playing games, and an uninformed observer would have found the debates trivial, if not incomprehensible. Like the United Nations itself there was nothing wrong with the commission or the people who came to the meetings; the trouble lay with governments and their policies. Probably the most influential member of the commission at this time was Sir Samuel Hoare. I sometimes thought he was also the most conservative, but his arguments were so well thought out and so well documented that he very often had his way. I heartily wished that I had him on my side. Our intimacy was such that I could talk to him frankly. One night over a bottle of *pinot noir* I told him I thought the role he was playing in the commission was doing incalculable harm to Britain. The fault, however, was not with him but with his instructions. On 23 April he nearly torpedoed the seminar program when he suggested that each participating country should pay the expenses of its own participants. I could never have got the program moving on that basis.

The session ended on Thursday, 25 April, and the next day my colleague, Kamalshwar Das, and I were on the first leg of the long trip to the Philippines and the working party to prepare for a seminar on the protection of human rights in criminal law and procedure. In Tehran the next day, A.H. Hekimi (my Iranian colleague who had now retired) was at the airport to meet us, as were the parents of a young man who had been to see me in Geneva looking for a job. The Ganjis presented us with a wreath of flowers that must have been at least three feet high. We had dinner at their house the next day. We had been asked to come at about five in the afternoon and found an elaborate tea waiting for us with all kinds of cakes and other dainties. Because we had been invited for dinner and I fully expected one to be served later, I limited myself to a cup of tea and a piece of fruit, but when an elder son came in and demanded to be fed with eggs I decided that this was indeed the meal for which we had been invited and began to satisfy my appetite. I did not know that it was Ramadan and that the man had been fasting all day. Not long afterwards, doors were thrown open, leading to another room in which there was a large table laden with an elaborate feast the like of which I have seldom seen—great platters piled high with rice and dressed with all kinds of meats. I regretted the tea.

We were just as elaborately entertained by Hekimi, who also wanted to take us to see the Caspian Sea on the other side of the mountains. But, once in the mountains, we had to turn back because it rained so hard. Hekimi belonged to the ruling class, his father having been a prime minister, and he was himself a member of parliament, which we visited. There was no party system, he said, and the elections were managed; otherwise the people would vote for the mullahs or the communists.

Our next stop was Singapore, where I put up at the Raffles Hotel, partly because of its colonial associations. For the same reason Das refused to stay there. Everything about the place, including the lotus tree in the garden, was pure Somerset Maugham. Singapore was a mosaic of races, and each race proclaimed its individuality in the most visible ways possible. They dressed differently—Malays in brightly colored sarongs, Chinese women in tight-fitting skirts and Indians in dhotis or turbans—and they ate different food. The colony was on the eve of independence. Would all these races ever form a united people? I was seeing for the first time concrete evidence of the extent of the minority problem in Asia.

On the last leg of our long journey, our plane stopped for an hour at the Saigon airport, where I was struck by what I thought was the unfriendliness of the Vietnamese, a reaction I find very strange in retrospect, because I found them very friendly in 1963 when I spent nearly two weeks in Saigon as the principal secretary of a United Nations mission of inquiry.

A delegation of officials was waiting to greet us when we arrived at the Manila airport. Martin Arostegui, the head of the United Nations information center, then drove us to the Filipinas Hotel, where an immense basket of exotic fruit from Serrano's farm was waiting for me. We had an appointment with Serrano and Eric Ward (the representative of the United Nations Technical Assistance Bureau) the next day. Carlos Ramos, who had once been an officer in my division, called for us early in the morning and took us for a drive around the city. The old Spanish section, which was the only part of the city with real character, had been pretty well destroyed during the war: one whole side of the river had been razed, and all that remained of the many fine old Spanish buildings was ruins. After our meeting with Serrano, who was the acting secretary of state, I returned to my hotel, swam in the pool and had lunch and a siesta. The working party would convene only the next day. That evening Das and I walked to the Manila Hotel and back. We were later warned that it was dangerous to go out at night; it was risky even to take a taxi. I never got out of one without the driver's showing me pictures of prostitutes whose favors he was advertising. Our hosts seldom left us alone. One night we saw a game of Jai Alai, the fastest sport I have ever witnessed. The goodlooking crowd of enthusiastic young people was almost as interesting as the game. The members of the working party were driven one morning to Tagaytay—high on the edge of a volcanic lake—for a traditional luncheon of roast pig, as Serrano's guests. I enjoyed seeing something of the countryside, which has real character and little evidence of the American veneer so obvious in Manila. Another morning I was taken to a place within the walls of the old city, where the Japanese had tortured and killed some six hundred Filipinos. I then attended a meeting of the Civil Liberties Union, a group of some twenty-five judges, lawyers and laymen whose association dated back to the Japanese occupation.

A feature of the seminars program was that we also encouraged governments to organize national seminars. One of these was in progress and I was invited to attend two of the meetings, at one of which I sat next to the president of the republic and at which I also made a speech. Our own working party went smoothly and quickly developed a formula which could be used, not only at the Philippine seminar on the protection of human rights in criminal law and procedure (which was to be held the next year), but for others in the series. The government thought the seminar should be in Baguio which is high in the mountains far from Manila and, after the adjournment of the working party, they wanted me to see the place. Baguio is about five thousand feet above sea level and has a good climate, but it is hardly typical of the Philippines. It took us five hours to drive to the place and much longer to return.

The invitation for me to visit Taiwan had been accepted, notwithstanding Cordier's skepticism. To get there, I had to change planes at Hong Kong. My heart missed several beats as the Convair came in through heavy rainclouds over the hills to the airport. I spent a day in Hong Kong before going on to Taipei, but it rained all the time I was there so that I did not see the Peak once. I had another bad landing coming into Taipei, with visibility near zero. A big delegation was waiting for me at the airport, after which the vice-minister of foreign affairs, Mr. Chow, took me to the Golden Dragon Hotel, which was one of the best I have ever stayed in anywhere. I could look down from the hotel to a war college, where there was a large scale outdoor map depicting, I assumed, part of the Chinese coast. Twice during my visit I watched groups of army officers listening to lectures illustrated by this map—in preparation, apparently, for the reconquest of the mainland. Many people to whom I talked seemed to think this would soon take place, and some of them even invited me to visit them on the mainland. Mr. Chow gave a dinner party for me the evening of my arrival at which my dexterity with chopsticks was much admired.

The next day, Thursday, I was taken to the department of justice. The deputy minister, Dr. Cha, who gave another dinner party for me that evening, then took me to visit the law courts. I noticed that most of the testimony of the witnesses had to be translated for the benefit of the judges who, like the elite in the administration, were obviously refugees from the mainland. Dr. Cha then took me to the Chinese bureau of investigation where, for nearly two hours, I had to listen to a lecture—amply illustrated by wall maps, pictures and charts—on communist atrocities on the mainland. It would have insulted the intelligence of any schoolboy and, not being a good actor, I did not react with the enthusiasm expected of me.

On Friday, I was taken for a long drive south of Taipei, ostensibly to inspect two factories, which were very much like factories anywhere; but I enjoyed the pleasant countryside, which was lush and prosperous. That evening the United Nations Association entertained me at dinner, but I didn't enjoy the experience, for although most of my hosts could speak fluent English they conversed mostly amongst themselves in Chinese, leaving me the odd man out. By contrast I was much too much the object of attention at another luncheon, which was meant to be a happy occasion and at which many toasts were drunk in rice wine. There must have been twenty guests at the big round table, and each one of them proposed a toast to my health. The trick was that only the proposer and I were expected to drink—twenty against one. I can handle alcohol fairly well and wasn't afraid of getting drunk, but I did think the rice wine, which can be pleasant in small quantities, might make me sick.

It was only on the last day that I discovered what I imagined was the real purpose of my visit, which was to receive a delegation of overseas Chinese from the Philippines and other parts of Southeast Asia, who came to complain about the way they were being treated. It was an embarrassing moment, and all I could do was to listen to what they said. The government obviously wanted to make some gesture to these people, and the presence of the Director of the U.N. Division of Human Rights provided an opportunity. Another reason for the invitation was that the government apparently felt they were being neglected at the United Nations and wanted a senior offical to visit the country.

I left Taipei on Saturday morning and after a short stop at Tokyo—long enough to buy cultured pearls for my wife and sister—flew on to Vancouver, where I spent most of Sunday. According to my watch it was only two hours since I had left Tokyo, but it had really been a long, tiring flight. We had come down for refueling at Shemyo in the Aleutians, where I had the time for a short walk. The place could hardly have been more desolate, but I did see some birds which might have been larks or buntings. A mechanic to whom I talked didn't know but thought that the U.S. Army had brought them during the war!

At headquarters several decisions had been taken during my absence with which I did not agree, one of which was that the meeting of the ad hoc commission on prisoners of war would again be postponed. I had this reversed and the commission did meet in September. Another was to cancel a proposed working party in Chile, which was also reversed. There were difficulties in the section on the status of women. Its chief, Mary Tenison-Woods, was to retire at the end of the year and in the meantime was so ill that she would probably be away from her job for some months. After considering a number of candidates for the job, I recommended Mrs. Agda Rossel, the Swedish member of the commission, who was that year its chairman. Whether this operated as a kind of catalyst I do not know, but she very soon became the permanent representative of Sweden at the United Nations, and I had to look for someone else. A more immediate problem was to find someone to replace Tenison-Woods at the Bangkok seminar in August, to which I attached considerable importance because it would be the first in the series, but which I knew that I could not attend myself. I asked Schwelb, but he did not want to go. We decided to send Edward Lawson and a Frenchwoman who was a member of the section on the status of women. When I spoke to her about it, she asked me whether the department would recommend her as Tenison-Woods' successor and said that if we did not, she would resign and not go to Bangkok. I didn't like being held up in this way, nor did I think that she would make a good section chief. I therefore sent her to see her countryman, Philippe de Seynes, but he also refused to commit the department. She did go to Bangkok, and later during my absence from headquarters was appointed chief of the section.

In July, after a holiday on Prince Edward Island, I went to Geneva for the summer session of ECOSOC. My first business there was in the coordination committee, where a Secretariat "streamlining" paper was discussed. Amongst other things it suggested that the Commission on Human Rights and the Commission on the Status of Women meet once every two years instead of annually. I was flabbergasted when the committee agreed. Minerva Bernadino, who was a vice-president of the Council and the chairman of its Social Committee, told me that the suggestion had originated with the American delegation. She had it, she said, straight from Mrs. Lorena Hahn, the American representative on the Commission on the Status of Women, and then she said that she intended to have the decision reversed insofar as it applied to the Commission on the Status of Women. I wished her luck; she might save the Human Rights Commission in the process. Things had really come to a pretty pass when the future of the human rights program in the United Nations could depend on the efforts of the representative of Trujillo's Dominican Republic. True to her word, Bernadino led a movement to have the decision reversed insofar as it applied to the Commission on the Status of Women, and, as I had hoped, this also helped save the Human Rights Commission.

Speaking before a meeting of the nongovernmental organizations I said that the twenty-fourth session of the Council was one of the most uneventful I had ever attended. The discussions in the Social Committee were certainly mediocre. I couldn't help comparing the level of representation there with the Human Rights Commission earlier in the spring. I was pleased, however, that most delegations seemed happy about the progress we were making with the seminars. Walter Kotchnig criticized what he called "these double-headers," and we soon abandoned the practice of having working parties to plan the seminars; they had already served a useful purpose and we could now get along without them. I nevertheless found that I still had to visit most host countries twice, because governments still wanted to discuss arrangements with me on the spot. De Seynes remained as hostile to the program as he had ever been. He told Gunner Myrdal that the advisory services program was a mere stopgap and not to be taken seriously, turned down out of hand a suggestion from Haiti that the United Nations might help in the presidential elections (on the ground that the program was not meant to be used in critical situations), and opposed holding seminars in either Romania or Costa Rica because of their bad records in human rights matters. The Romanians wanted to host a seminar on the status of women and the Costa Ricans one on electoral laws. I do not know how the Romanians reacted, but the Costa Ricans were annoyed and complained to the Americans, who came to see me. I could only refer them to de Seynes who, in the face of pressure, immediately capitulated. As a result I had to add Costa Rica to my forthcoming South American trip. Some months later, the Swedes were interested in hosting a seminar on capital punishment. The Under Secretary turned down the suggestion with the remark that a seminar on that question would be morbid.

Rio, Santiago and Costa Rica (1957)

When I left Geneva for Rio de Janeiro at the end of June, de Seynes had made it clear to me that he would be happy if I returned to headquarters empty-handed, with no South American seminar. I did my best to disappoint him and, in fact, came back with the agreement of the government of Chile to sponsor a seminar on human rights in criminal law and procedure and a request from the president of Costa Rica to have the United Nations send someone to observe the forthcoming elections in that country.

The first thing I did on arriving in Rio was to call on Georges Rabinovitch, the urbane director of the U.N. information center, who was as helpful as he was hospitable. He took me next morning to the foreign office, where the officials with whom I spoke said that, although the government wanted to host a seminar on racial discrimination, they preferred to have it organized on a global basis, with participants coming from different parts of the world and not only from the Americas. I said this could be arranged. They then said that they were worried by the attitude of the Americans, who were afraid the Russians could not be prevented from coming to such a global seminar at which, if they did come, they would exploit the opportunity to criticize the racial situation in the United States. None of this was very convincing, and I began to wonder whether the Brazilians weren't having second thoughts. American practice could be criticized just as easily in other forums as at a seminar, and the seminar didn't have to be organized on a global basis. A more likely explanation was that the Brazilians were worried that there might be repercussions in Brazil itself if the seminar were held there. Brazil had a good reputation for the way she treated her racial groups; it was for that reason that I wanted to have the seminar there. But it was quite obvious that there was racial discrimination in the country: in all the years I was at the United Nations I never saw a black member of the Brazilian delegation. I therefore suggested that they might begin by hosting a working party, not a very strong line, but there was little else I could say in the circumstances. I left the foreign office, convinced that there would be no seminar in Brazil, but I hadn't yet had a final answer. They would, they said, study the matter further and talk to me again after the weekend.

On Monday morning I went for my second interview at the foreign office. The Brazilians couldn't hide their embarrassment. Much as they would like to sponsor the seminar, they said, they didn't think a regional meeting restricted to participants from the Americas would have any real significance and, if they hosted a global seminar, they would risk displeasing the Americans; but, following my suggestion, they would sponsor a working party. I left them thinking it would be unlikely if they did even this and, as a matter of fact, neither the working party nor the seminar ever met. The seminar on apartheid, which was held in Brasilia in 1966 after my retirement from the Secretariat, was hardly the kind of thing I had in mind. In 1965, we did hold a successful seminar in Yugoslavia on the multi-racial society. I returned to the foreign office again on Tuesday, and in the evening had dinner at the Canadian embassy. Mrs. Irwin, the ambassador's wife and better known as P.K. Page, was a fellow New Brunswicker and a well-known Canadian poet.

The weather was so bad over the Andes, when I left for Santiago on Wednesday, that I had to spend a night in Buenos Aires, but the skies were clear the next day and I had a fine view flying over the mountains. It was winter in the southern hemisphere and, compared to Rio de Janeiro, Santiago looked drab. I went to the foreign office the next morning for talks with the acting under secretary and the chief of the political section. The latter was Diaz Casanueva, whom I had known at the United Nations, and who knew the human rights program well. With his help and that of Hernan Santa Cruz, I had no difficulty getting the Chileans to agree to host the seminar in 1958 on human rights in criminal law and procedure which, we had already decided, would be held somewhere in Latin America. It was to attend a working party to plan such a seminar that I had come to Chile. I then talked to the deputy executive director of the Economic Commission for Latin America, Louis Swenson, who agreed not only to allow the seminar to use the commission's Santiago premises but also to provide simultaneous interpretation and other facilities. My business in Chile could hardly have gone better. That night I had dinner with the Santa Cruzes. One of the other guests was Salvador Allende. Santa Cruz was politically eclectic; on my next visit to Chile I would meet another president-to-be of the country, Eduardo Frei, also at his house.

I can think of nothing duller than a cold, grey winter afternoon in Santiago. I didn't even dare to go to the cinema because there was an epidemic of influenza. The skies were still grey on Sunday, but I went for a long walk on the Cerro San Cristobal with Santa Cruz and his daughter Adriane, after which we went to his house for lunch on oysters and *empañadas*. The meetings of the working party began on Monday morning. By this time I knew that there would be a Latin American seminar and that it would be in Santiago, but there remained a number of other questions to be discussed, including the agenda and documentation. The participants at the working party were all expert criminologists, and I could tell from these preliminary discussions that the seminar would be a useful exercise. There was a good deal of entertaining, including a dinner party at the Casanuevas that lasted on into the next morning. I shocked my hosts by leaving at two thirty, which was early by Chilean standards. The working party ended on Friday afternoon. On Saturday morning I went for another walk on the Cerro Cristobal with Santa Cruz, after which he drove me to the home of an architect friend in the foothills of the Andes for lunch. At places the road ran along the top of high precipices; there was no protection of any kind, and Santa Cruz terrified me by his driving. One saw some signs of spring, including a few mimosas and flowering peach trees. On Sunday morning we went for another walk, this time on Santa Lucia, and after lunch, Santa Cruz drove me to the airport. I was sorry to leave this land of friendly people, good wine and good food.

To get to Costa Rica, I had to change planes at Panama, where I arrived early on Monday morning. It was four thirty before I had checked in at the El Panama hotel and was in my bed. After four hours of sleep, I was up and out for a walk on the water front, but it rained torrents and I had to return to the hotel. The doorman said that this happened only once a day. The sun did shine again and I was out in the afternoon and saw some churches and what seemed to be hundreds of pelicans feeding in the sea.

There was no one at the airport to meet me when I arrived at San José, and it was with some difficulty that I got to the Presidencia the next morning. When I finally got to the place and rang the doorbell, I was told that President Figueres was shaving but that he would receive me in the afternoon. In the meantime I was directed to Father Nuñez, the Costa Rican delegate on the Third Committee of the General Assembly, who took me to see the minister of foreign affairs, with whom I had a long talk. That night I had dinner with Father Nuñez at Coronado, a village about twenty kilometers from San José. He called for me again early the next morning and drove me to the Irazu volcano, but there were so many clouds at that height that we couldn't see down the crater. I enjoyed the drive immensely. The countryside was beautiful, neat and clean, and there were few if any signs of poverty. The houses were painted in gay colors and we passed several bullock wagons which were so gaily decorated that they looked as if they were on their way to a carnival. I made some remark about the homogeneity of the population. Father Nuñez explained that there were no Indians because they were so brave that they had all been killed. In Chile I had heard a similar remark about the Araucanians. We then had lunch with President Figueres at the Casa Presidencial, where we were received with great simplicity. I drank milk from the president's farm, of which he was very proud. He was a man with wide views and a good grasp of economic and social problems. We discussed the proposed seminar on electoral laws and practices, but I was soon given to understand that what he really wanted was to have the United Nations send someone to observe the presidential elections in February. He was not a little surprised when, remembering de Seynes' reply to a similar Haitian request, I explained that this might not be possible. We did send Professor Horace Reid of Dalhousie University, although I could never figure out why one request was accepted and the other refused.

The plane from San José to Mexico City (known locally as the milk train) landed in every country between Costa Rica and Mexico, and in each of these places the passengers were given coffee, the best that the country could provide, which was very good indeed. After one of these stops, my plane passed quite close to an active volcano, one whole side of which was a sulfurous mass, a great sight. I spent a night in Mexico City, where there had been an earthquake which had made great crevices in the sidewalks. But I saw none of the color that had so impressed us when my wife and I had visited the country in the summer of 1940. It was raining and cold, and it may have been then, if not in Santiago, that I picked up the bug which quite spoiled my few days' leave (most of which I spent in bed) in Nova Scotia, where I went to fetch my wife.

Back in New York after our spoiled Nova Scotian holiday, we moved into a new apartment on Beekman Place. For over a year we had been living practically in our suitcases, and had recently rented a furnished apartment in the Beaux Arts Hotel. When we found the apartment on Beekman Place, I sublet the hotel apartment to a member of the Libyan delegation, but he moved to Washington and didn't pay the rent. I couldn't sue him because he had diplomatic immunity, but Jamil Baroody, to whom I told the story, put pressure on the man's delegation, and I was paid. Beekman Place was even nearer to headquarters than Sutton Place, too close indeed for a good walk in the morning; but I could always walk in the United Nations' gardens, where there was usually something interesting to see, either in the gardens themselves or on the East River. The trees and green grass attracted the birds, particularly when they were migrating. I have even seen flickers and blue jays there, only a few minutes walk from Times Square.

There were no unpleasant surprises at my office. The Bangkok seminar on the civic responsibilities of women and their participation in public life had been a success and had apparently won new friends for the advisory services program, and the Americans were pleased with the results of my South American mission. Their original idea had been that, as already mentioned, the seminars would be small study groups linked to technical assistance. As I hoped the program would develop, and as it was in fact developing, they were becoming full-fledged human rights conferences. It seemed important, therefore, to divorce them from the regular technical assistance operations of the Secretariat. Not only were the technical assistance people skeptical about the usefulness of the seminars, but our too-close association with them was for us a political embarrassment; for the seminars had very little if anything to do with technical assistance, and I always had to play down this aspect when I was trying to get a government to act as a host. Governments didn't like the idea of asking for assistance in any matter pertaining to human rights. I talked to Hugh Keenleyside and his new program director, Myer Cohen, and thought that I now detected more understanding in that quarter than in my own department.

The human rights program seemed to be taking on new life: the seminars were taking shape; both the Human Rights Commission and its sub-commission were preparing studies on various aspects of human rights; and governments were beginning to respond to ECOSOC's request that they report on the progress they were making in the realization of human rights. These reports were not always revealing—governments could hardly be expected to condemn themselves out of their own mouths—but an important principle had been established and, if machinery could be created for a critical examination of the reports, they could become the basis for an effective implementation system. It is something of a paradox that most of this new activity was the direct result of the negative attitude the Americans had adopted towards the covenants, and that it had developed notwithstanding the active opposition of the Secretary-General.

The twelfth session of the General Assembly opened on 18 September. On the 23rd, the Canadian members of the Secretariat were lined up to meet John Diefenbaker, the new Conservative prime minister of Canada, who had come to New York to speak in the general debate. When he reached me he stopped and said. "Congratulations for the magnificent work you have been doing. I want to have a talk with you." But I never spoke to him again. I hasten to add that while he was prime minister, and for the first and only time while I was in the Secretariat, Canada became a member of both the Human Rights Commission and the Commission on the Status of Women.

The Third Committee devoted thirty-four meetings at this session to the covenants. It approved the articles in the Covenant on Economic, Social and Cultural Rights on education and the right to take part in cultural life, to enjoy the benefits of scientific progress and the protection of the moral and material interests resulting from authorship. It also adopted an article on the right to life for the Covenant on Civil and Political Rights, one major issue being whether the article should provide for the abolition of the death penalty. This was not done, and an amendment that would have protected the right to life "from the moment of conception" was defeated. A whole week was devoted to self-determination; but, although a resolution was adopted which called on member states to respect the right, and on states responsible for the administration of non-self-governing territories to promote its realization by the peoples of such territories, no action was taken on any of the three proposals that had come up from the Human Rights Commission two years earlier. Two resolutions were adopted on freedom of information, one of which invited the Human Rights Commission to keep the subject under constant review; the other invited member states to comment on the latest text of the ill-fated convention on freedom of information.

It occurred to me that it would be useful if the Assembly were to endorse ECOSOC's request that governments celebrate the tenth anniversary of the adoption of the Universal Declaration. When I mentioned this to Salvador Lopez, who was the chairman of the Third Committee, he asked me to draft an appropriate text, which I did. Because the Americans had sponsored a similar resolution in the Human Rights Commission, I showed my draft to Mary Lord, who was representing them in the Third Committee; but she was afraid that it would revive the controversy whether the invitation should be addressed to "all states" or only to those which were members of the United Nations and the specialized agencies (the formula invented to ostracize the Chinese communists) and the idea was dropped. The Americans had won their battle in the Economic and Social Council and she didn't want to run the risk of a defeat in the General Assembly. Her reaction reflected the kind of issue to which some delegates gave priority.

At the beginning of November, I heard the welcome news that under Hammarskjold's final plans for the reorganization of the top echelon of the Secretariat, the Human Rights Division would be transferred out of the Department of Economic and Social Affairs to one of the new Under Secretaries; and I understood that we would go to Sir Humphrey Trevelyan. Jeanne warned me to control my enthusiasm. The progress from Laugier to Georges-Picot to de Seynes hadn't been for the better. But I thought the situation of the Division could hardly be worse than it now was, wherever we might go. About a week later, André Ganem, the French member of the advisory committee on administrative and budgetary questions, and one of Laugier's closest friends, told me that the Division would go to Dragoslov Protitch, the Under Secretary for Political and Security Council Affairs, but that this would be "pour la forme" only and that we would be a relatively independent unit. Neither de Seynes nor the Secretary-General ever spoke to me about these plans. The first I heard about them officially was after a press conference when Hammarskjold said that one of the units that would be moved out of the Department of Economic and Social Affairs was the Human Rights Division; and at a champagne party which he gave before Christmas, de Seynes said that there would soon be fewer directors in his department. It wasn't until the last day of the year that I read a story in the *New York Times* which said that the Division would go to Sir Humphrey Trevelyan. The day before this, Jeanne and I had lunch with Mrs. Roosevelt, who wanted material for the third volume of her memoirs. I didn't think her ghost writer from Harper Brothers, who was at the luncheon, knew very much about the United Nations, and I wondered how the anecdotes which I recalled for his benefit would sit in the book. Late the following April she sent me for comment a copy of a manuscript. I made some suggestions.

Baguio, Santiago and a Tenth
Anniversary (1958)

The bright lights of Times Square shone like a string of rubies the night at the end of January 1958, when I flew over Manhattan on my way to the Philippines. The Sub-Commission on the Prevention of Discrimination, which had begun its tenth session on 13 January, was still in session, but it was now so well established in its new routine that I had no compunctions about leaving it in the care of my colleagues. Most of this session was devoted to Arcot Krishnaswami's study of religious rights. Other items on the agenda included an interim report on the study of political rights and the proposed study on the right of everyone to leave any country including his own and to return to his country.

I had planned my trip to include a weekend in San Francisco, where a visit to the Presidio confirmed me in my opinion that it had been a mistake to refuse the American offer to have the United Nations Headquarters there. I also had two days in Honolulu. Flying from there to Manila—it took twenty hours—we came down to refuel at Wake and Guam. Although it was quite dark I went for a short walk on the beach at Wake, where I saw more than one reminder of the war, including a wrecked fighter plane.

It was five o'clock in the morning by their watches when I arrived in Manila, but my colleagues, Mousheng Lin and Pedro Yap, were at the airport to meet me. I spent most of that day in conference with Serrano, Barrera (the deputy minister of justice who was to be the chairman of the seminar) and other officials. Lin, Yap and I took the train for Baguio the next morning. I found this long journey, some seven hours, even more interesting than the one I had made by road in 1957 because we stopped at so many small towns and villages.

I opened the seminar on Monday, 17 February, in the Pines Hotel, which was a kind of resort place on the outskirts of Baguio, where the participants also lived. Living together helped create the easy atmosphere of good fellowship that contributed so much to the success of the conference. Baguio itself had very few attractions, but there were two good bowling alleys that became evening haunts which helped to break the ice. None of the participants were diplomats or active in politics, but they were all important people in their own countries, and, as lawyers, were professionally interested in human rights whether they realized it or not. I came to know some of them quite well later, including Dick Wild (later Sir Richard and chief justice of New Zealand) and Arthur Hooton, the attorney-general of Hong Kong. One of the best of the participants was Sir Ernest Williams, the chief justice of Sarawak, who wrote most of the report. The language of the seminar was

English. The Philippine government had promised to provide interpreters in English and French; but the technical legal jargon was too much for them and they gave up after the first day. Fortunately, only one participant, the attorney general of South Vietnam, didn't understand the *lingua franca*. I had him sit next to me and undertook to interpret his interventions after he agreed that he would give me a rough idea of what he wanted to say before taking the floor. One day, when the seminar was discussing the use of violence by the police, he became quite excited and said that he wanted to speak. I asked him what he intended to say. "Il faut frapper," he replied: unless the police used violence there wouldn't be enough evidence to convict. Perhaps I should have allowed him to speak, for he badly needed a lesson; but I talked him out of it, pointing out that this was a conference on human rights. We had professional interpreters at all the other seminars.

The agenda covered the whole gamut of the law of criminal procedure, where many of the most effective guarantees of human rights are or should be found: Churchill once said that you can judge a country by the remedies and protections that its criminal procedure provides. Most people go through life hardly aware of the fact that the law is there, or should be there, to protect their rights; it is only when, for some reason, they come into conflict with the law that they begin to understand how necessary its remedies are. I have always thought it is more important to define these remedies than to proclaim the existence of a right, however solemnly. What I want to know is how that right will be protected. This was the spirit of the Baguio discussions. Topics on the agenda included safeguards against arbitrary or illegal arrest and detention, conditional release prior to and during trial, confessions and admissions, how to avoid delays in bringing an accused person to trial and concluding the trial and appellate processes, the right to counsel and legal aid, proof of guilt, language difficulties, public trial and exceptions thereto including trial in absentia, and detention without trial—questions, all of them, that went to the very heart of human rights.

The discussions were so good and so informed that, if I had had my way, we would have sat on weekends when, as it happened, there was little else to do. Our hosts did what they could to entertain us, but the possibilities of Baguio were limited. One Saturday morning they took us on a tour of the city and then to the military academy, which compared very unfavorably with Fort John Hay, the American base which I had already seen. Under threat by one of the Filipino judges to take me to the Convent of the Good Shepherd, I had slipped out of the hotel with no destination in mind and, finding myself at the entrance to the base, was allowed to enter. I walked for over an hour on the fine golf course. The contrast between this privileged American enclave and the poverty and drabness of Baguio was striking. Not long after this I had lunch in the home of a local doctor. Driving me back to my hotel afterwards, an American businessman (who was established in the Philippines) boasted that the Americans had handed this country back to the Filipinos as soon as possible, whereas the British had had to be kicked out of their colonies. He didn't know that I had seen their base, but he should have realized that I had only to look down the valley to see a large American-owned mine.

On 28 February the president of the Philippines came up to Baguio to close the conference. It was time to return to New York. My next visit to the Philippines, nearly twenty years later, would be in quite different circumstances. In the meantime, President Marcos had imposed martial law and his personal dictatorship in a country which, however badly it may have operated in practice, had been a democracy since the beginning of the century; and, together with William J. Butler of New York, I had returned to the Philippines to investigate the situation on behalf of the International Commission of Jurists. We were helped in our inquiry by both the civil and military authorities, which even allowed us to visit and question detainees—including Marcos' chief political rival, Benigno Aguino —in a number of prisons and military camps, both in Manila and in Mindanao. We concluded that, whatever justification there may have been for the imposition of martial law when it was first imposed in 1972, it was now being enforced to maintain the personal power of the president. Even more damning was the evidence we found that political prisoners, some of whom had been in detention for long periods of time without trial, had been tortured; nor was this the only violation of fundamental human rights for which the regime was responsible. Our report, which was published in the summer of 1977, was badly received by the government; but I think they were even more upset when I resigned as chairman of the human rights committee of the World Peace Through Law Center and refused to attend the big conference (the theme of which was human rights) that organization held in Manila in August of that year—on the ground that there would be no discussion of violations of human rights in the host country. I also resigned for the same reason as rapporteur of the human rights committee of the International Law Association, which held its biannual conference in the same city in 1978.

Returning to New York after the Baguio seminar, I broke my journey in Tokyo and Vancouver. The Imperial Hotel, where I stayed in Tokyo, was full of tourists. I escaped the day after my arrival, a Sunday, to Kamakura and Enoshima. It was a beautiful day and there were some splendid views of Fujiyama. I had taken the pains to inquire about a place to eat before leaving Tokyo, but was so confused by the Japanese calligraphy that I couldn't find the restaurant. Someone directed me to a place which looked like a private house where, after I knocked at the door, an old man took me up a flight of stairs and led me to a room in which there was only a mat and a miniature dressing table. I took off my coat and after a few minutes a young woman dressed in a kimono came in carrying a small earthen stove on which she prepared a very good sukiyaki. Back in Tokyo that evening I had another in a place on the Ginza.

My business in Tokyo was at the ministry of justice, where I met and talked to everyone of importance from the minister down, after which there was a luncheon in the office of the director of the Civil Liberties Bureau. The Japanese eventually hosted two seminars, one in 1960 on the role of criminal law in the protection of human rights and the purposes and limits of criminal sanctions, and the other in 1962 on the status of women in family law.

I stopped in Vancouver long enough to see Larry MacKenzie, the president of the University of British Columbia, who offered me a post where I would have straddled the arts and law faculties. But, although I found the offer attractive, I did not accept it, chiefly because I was cautiously optimistic about the future of the Human Rights Division once it left the Department of Economic and Social Affairs.

I was back in New York in good time for the opening of the fourteenth session of the Human Rights Commission on Monday, 10 March. R.S.S. Gunewardene presided over the opening meeting in his capacity as retiring second vice-chairman and declared himself elected chairman after a procedural incident that brought credit neither to him nor to the commission. Both he and Serrano, the outgoing chairman, had been nominated for the office. I quote from the summary records of the five hundred and seventy-seventh meeting of the commission:

> Mr. Maloles (Philippines) expressed the regret of the outgoing chairman, Mr. Serrano (Philippines) that he could not preside over the commission's opening meeting since he was detained by his duties at the SEATO conference. He proposed that Mr. Serrano should be reelected to the office of chairman explaining, however, that Mr. Serrano was prepared to accept reelection only if his candidacy met with general support.

Gunewardene ruled that the rules of procedure made no provision for conditional resolutions, which was true, and declared himself elected. I thought, as did others, that he should have ignored the condition—if it was one—and put the question to a vote. He was obviously very keen to be chairman. But he made a good presiding officer and the fact that he held the office helped me to arrange for a seminar in Ceylon.

The commission did very little at this session, a good third of which was devoted to an unproductive discussion of various administrative questions raised by the Secretary-General as part of his "streamlining" drive. Most of his suggestions were rejected. The Americans wanted to expand the advisory services program, but, realizing that this could not be done unless the staff of the Human Rights Division were increased, they asked for a paper showing all the projects for which we were responsible and the staff allotted to each of them. But the Secretary-General refused to allow any paper to be circulated on the ground that housekeeping information of this kind should not be disclosed to the commission. When the Americans complained, I told them that they would have to fight the battle themselves.

It was about this time that de Seynes told me that Hammarskjold had finally made up his mind, and that very shortly the Human Rights Division would be transferred to the responsibility of Sir Humphrey Trevelyan. Sir Humphrey then called me to his office and for two hours I briefed him on the work of the Division. He might have passed for a Mediterranean. His black thinning hair was brushed back in a pompadour and he had black intelligent eyes. In complexion he was sallow, the result, I guessed, of many years in the tropics. He struck me as a man of quick intelligence, and perhaps even quicker decision, nervous, possibly irritable, but probably considerate. I described all the various aspects of the human rights program. He listened attentively, interrupting me only to show that he had grasped a point. I gathered from this first interview that he would be mainly interested in the political aspects and leave the running of the program to me. The greatest danger was that he would make up his mind too quickly; I would have to take special care that he understood all sides of a question. He said only one thing that really worried me: he would, he said, react very conservatively to any suggestions to increase the staff of the Division. I had not raised the question, so I guessed that he had already been endoctrinated on that point; he was, moreover, an Englishman and probably shared the prejudices so common in British officials about the size of the United Nations establishment.

On Tuesday, 8 April, there were two long meetings with the new Under Secretary at which senior members of my staff explained their work programs, and we had another on

Friday morning. We were all impressed by his quick perceptions, his friendliness and apparently sympathetic interest. Several days later he showed me the draft of a memorandum to the Secretary-General evaluating the program. I was well pleased by the way he seemed to have digested our briefings, but I was disappointed when I learned that the administrative officer of the Department of Economic and Social Affairs would continue to act for us in that capacity. It meant that de Seynes' department would always be able to interfere at critical points, and I had to live with this unsatisfactory arrangement as long as I remained in the Secretariat.

De Seynes gave a cocktail party on the eve of the transfer. I was embarrassed when in a short speech, he referred to me as ''a man of vision and purpose,'' a remark that I hardly took as a compliment—although I am sure it was well meant—because I knew well enough that I wasn't the kind of man either he or the Secretary-General would have preferred to have as the director of the Division. What they really wanted was a bureaucrat who could be depended upon to do what he was told to do. My speech in reply to de Seynes was one of my worst efforts. I mumbled something about this marking an epoch in the history of the Human Rights Division and thanked him for the party. Privately, I hoped to God that this transfer would usher in a new day, but not long thereafter two things happened which dampened my enthusiasm. The first was a meeting in Sir Humphrey's office with two people from the American delegation. To my surprise, Sir Humphrey agreed to their request that the Secretariat steer away from any Soviet participation in the human rights seminars. I thought this was wrong and unrealistic and said so, and after Sir Humphrey left the Secretariat I did not respect his commitment. Russians and other communists did participate and I myself organized seminars in Hungary, Mongolia, Poland and Romania, and I tried very hard to have one in Moscow or Kiev.

The chief reason for my fourth trip to South America was to attend the Chilean seminar on the protection of human rights in criminal law and procedure (which had also been the subject discussed at Baguio), but I also visited Colombia, Peru, Argentina and Uruguay, looking for governments to sponsor other seminars. My first stop was Bogotá where I was greeted at the airport by a large delegation including the rector of one university, the secretary-general of another, officials from the foreign office and their señoras.

The director of the United Nations information center, Jorge Viteri de la Huerta, took me for a first visit to the foreign office the next morning, after which we found the time to visit the fine Museo Nacional and the church of San Ignacio. We then had lunch with Dr. Rueda Vargas who, I soon discovered, was an enthusiastic supporter of the United Nations, after which there were more churches and the Quinta Bolivar. It was now time to return to the foreign office, where I had an appointment with the minister; but something had gone wrong, and I was aked to come again the next day.

There was a big dinner party that night in the home of Señora de Aya, a charming hostess and, I soon realized, a very remarkable woman. I was pretty sure that she would be listened to before the government decided to sponsor any seminar on the status of women. Her house was almost as interesting as its owner. Most of the furniture, she told me, had come from Spain in colonial times and had been brought up from the coast on mule-back. There were at least twenty guests at the long table which, I remember, was decorated with orchids from end to end.

Next morning I talked to the minister of foreign affairs, after which the secretary-general of the *Universidad de los Andes* gave a luncheon at the Jockey Club. Not to be outdone, the rector of the *Universidad de America* entertained at dinner. I was sorry to have to leave Bogotá the next day and even sorrier when I was prevented from attending the seminar there on the participation of women in public life. No other Latin American city that I have visited, except Cuzco, has retained in the same degree its old colonial flavor. I felt that I was on the top of the world, but although I had some difficulty getting to sleep at night I was not otherwise indisposed by the altitude. The weather was balmy and springlike: my hosts said that it was like that all year. Great cumulus clouds hung over the city and I could hardly keep my eyes off the sun-washed white church at the top of Monserrate in the distance. My plane was three hours late leaving Bogotá, a lucky break because it gave Viteri de la Huerta the time to take me to see the fine collection of Inca gold at the Banco Nacional.

I regretted not having planned to spend the weekend in Quito, where my plane stopped for a few minutes after an impressive descent over the mountains; but I put it to good use in Lima, where, on Saturday morning, I went to the Magdalena, the unique anthropological museum which had been closed when Emile Vaillancourt had taken me to visit it on an earlier visit to Peru. On Sunday morning I rented a car and had the driver take me to Miraflores and out along the beaches to the Pachacamac ruins. In this country it never rains—"no lluve nunca", my driver said—and nothing grows, nothing lives, not even mosquitos. By the time we reached Pachacamac, a northwest breeze was blowing up clouds of dust: it was desert dirt, not sand, and it penetrated everything. I had made this drive seven years earlier with Jeanne and Helene Vaillancourt, but that time there had been no wind and, perhaps because I was seeing the coast for the first time, it had seemed more romantic. My real discovery was that I could carry on a reasonable conversation in Spanish. My driver explained at length every point of interest and to my surprise I was able to keep up my end of the conversation. In the afternoon I visited the Presidential Palace and marvelled to find such a pretentious monument in a country with a tradition for good taste.

In the light of the political context I thought it unlikely that the Peruvian government would sponsor a seminar on human rights, but one could never know until one tried. Albertal, the representative of the U.N. technical assistance bureau, arranged for me to meet some people who might be interested, including Judge Domingo Garcia Rada of the Supreme Court and dean of the law faculty in the Catholic University, who was to represent Peru at the Santiago seminar. They greeted my suggestion with caution; but Garcia Rada gradually warmed to the idea and said that the topic should be *amparo*, the Spanish American equivalent of *habeas corpus*. I left Peru without an invitation to organize a seminar, and, although I discussed the matter later with the Peruvian delegation at U.N. Headquarters, nothing came of it. As Albertal had explained over lunch at the Club Nacional, in Peru the Army was the government and, according to him, the only stable force in the country. Its officers were recruited from the lower middle class, with the result that its influence was weighted towards the left, and, he went on to say, in Colombia, where I had just been, the strongest influence was the Church.

I left Lima on Wednesday morning. Travelling down the coast seven years earlier, my wife and I had had a fine view of the Andes. But today all the seats on the port side of the plane were occupied and all I could see from starboard was empty ocean. Now, of course, the jets fly so high that one seldom sees anything no matter where one sits, and in a jumbo one might as well be in a movie theater. However, there was a fine view of the mountains as the plane came down at Santiago. My colleagues, John Male and Pedro Yap, were at the airport to meet me. I gathered from what they said that, although it was preoccupied with protocol, the host government wasn't being too cooperative. Fortunately, we had all the facilities of the Economic Commission for Latin America at our disposal, including simultaneous interpretation, and as it turned out the material arrangements for the conference were excellent. I spent the next three days ironing out difficulties that had arisen in connection with the opening session.

On Monday the minister of justice opened the seminar at the university; the other meetings were held the ECLA building. I also made a speech, as did Cousino MacIver, who was elected chairman. I was pleased by the high level of representation, but there were delays getting the seminar down to business. On Tuesday morning we were all taken to visit the minister of justice and, in the afternoon, the president of the republic. On the initiative of the participant from Uruguay, the president commuted the death sentence of a murderer—he had murdered a woman and two children—who was to have been executed that day. I was happy enough that the man's life was spared but not a little shocked by the hazard that motivated the decision, if hazard it indeed was. On Wednesday there was again no meeting because it was a national holiday and the opening of congress, which we all attended.

Notwithstanding these interruptions, the seminar was a success, although perhaps not as successful as the one in Baguio. The Latinos ran true to form; their speeches were usually brilliant and sometimes erudite and well documented, but they were inclined to skate around reality. I would have been happier to hear one of them say, for example, that the reason a particular institution didn't work was that the judges were poorly paid or that there was political interference. Baguio had been more prosaic but also more real. The chairman was inclined to be doctrinaire and at times inflexible. Like some other chairmen I have worked with, he seemed to resent advice coming from the Secretariat, and did not take us into his confidence. I began to worry whether the report would do justice to the discussion and, at a meeting of the steering committee, had to take a strong stand, much to the annoyance of the chairman. Nor do I think the report did do justice to the seminar. In this experimental period, the reports were written by the participants themselves, with some help from the Secretariat, largely because our staff was too small. At later seminars, the Secretariat took over this responsibility although, as with other United Nations meetings, the reports were always issued in the name of rapporteurs.

I remember that there was some good discussion on the meaning of the word "arbitrary" as it is used in several places in the Universal Declaration of Human Rights and in the covenants. In the General Assembly several delegations had taken the position that the word was synonymous with "illegal." I had no doubt that this was wrong because an action can be legal and yet arbitrary, witness the kind of thing that happened in Nazi Germany. To say that no one shall be subjected to arbitary arrest (Article 9 of the Declaration) means more than to say that no one shall be subject to "illegal" arrest, for the law under which a legal arrest is made may itself be unjust. It would have been useful had the seminar been able to agree on this interpretation.

The seminar ended on Friday, 30 May. On Saturday I drove far out into the Cordillerra for lunch with friends; and on Sunday again had dinner at Santa Cruz's, where I met

Eduardo Frei, who was running as the Christian Democrat candidate for the presidency of the republic.

On Monday night I was in Buenos Aires, having had to change my travel plans at the last moment because the Panagra plane on which I was scheduled to fly developed engine trouble. My much smaller plane flew quite low over the Andes—or so it seemed——and I had a splendid view of the forbidding peaks. My week in Buenos Aires was a busy one, but mostly in connection with things that had nothing to do with what I had come for. The first thing I did was to call on Mr. Mario Pico, the director of the Division of International Organizations at the foreign office, who told me that Argentina would be happy to sponsor a seminar in 1959 on either freedom of information (shades of *La Prensa!*) or the remedies of the citizen; but he wanted me to see the minister, and this wouldn't be possible until Friday. I then returned to the Plaza Hotel for lunch with Bertrand Ges, the director of the U.N. information center, and Señora Carmen Perkins, the Argentine member of the Commission on the Status of Women, who invited me to dinner later in the week at the Cabaña. Her other two guests were, like herself, ranch owners with English names. For some reason there was much talk about the British Commonwealth, and I gathered the two men regretted that the brief occupation of Buenos Aires by the British in 1806-07 had not been permanent. I was also entertained by Carlos Bertomeu, who represented Argentina on the Human Rights Commission, by the rotary club, and by Mr. Picard, the Canadian ambassador. The latter gave a luncheon at the Plaza, which was attended by a number of personalities, including the deputy minister of foreign affairs who received me in his office that afternoon. I gave a lecture on Wednesday afternoon to the Association Argentina Ana M. Berry, which arranged a press conference the next day. I also talked to a group called *Los Lideres por los Derechos Humanos*, took part in a round table at the law faculty arranged by Dean La Plaza (who had been at the Santiago seminar) and gave a speech at the Ateneo Ibero-Americano, where a Cuban revolutionary created an incident.

I had my interview with minister of foreign affairs Señor Florit at six o'clock on Friday afternoon. He told me that Argentina would definitely sponsor a seminar in 1959 and that the topic would be remedies against the state.

On Saturday I was taken to San Isidro for tea in the sumptuous house of the writer, Victoria Ocampo. Some fifty other guests had also been invited. I hadn't been told that I would be expected to make a speech, but after tea had been served, my hostess asked me to say a few words and to answer questions. It was fair sailing until someone asked me how the people present could contribute to promoting respect for human rights in Argentina. That wasn't an easy question for an international official to answer. But I had been reading Ortega y Gasset and, taking my cue from him, I replied that perhaps the most important thing they could do was to try to educate their masters, who were the great masses in whom political power now rested. I am not sure how this went down in a gathering of such privileged people. I could hardly say what I really thought, which was that their greatest problem was the gap between great wealth and abject poverty. That night I dined with Dr. Soler, who had been the attorney general in the interim government after the deposition of the Peronistas, a man of fine intelligence, good sense and liberal views. All of these people were sympathetic—in the Spanish sense—and they meant well, but they had had their day and it would never return. It is not for me to say that they had abused their privileges and that the kind of liberalism in which they believed was dead as the dodo.

I had trouble getting to Montevideo. The airport bus which was supposed to pick me up at my hotel arrived ten minutes before the scheduled time while I was paying my bill. The driver of the bus was in an ugly mood, said that he was late and refused to wait for me, leaving my luggage on the sidewalk. It was only after I complained to Pan American Airways that he returned to pick me up. But when we got to the airport, I was told that there was fog at Montevideo and that the plane wouldn't land. They offered to arrange accommodation on the night ferry. In the meantime I was to go to another hotel, where a Pan American agent would meet me. There was no agent at the hotel but only a message saying that I would fly the next morning by Aerolineas Argentinas. By this time I had joined forces with two businessmen—one British and the other a Dane—who were in the same case. Since it wasn't at all sure that the fog would clear by morning, we decided to cross the Rio de la Plata by ferry, the arrangements for which we had to make ourselves in spite of a series of promises by the Pan American people, none of whom ever turned up at the places indicated. It was a wet, miserable crossing, but on the ferry I chanced to meet Señor Migone, an Argentinian diplomat whom I had known in Montreal, where he was a consul general before the war.

In Montevideo I put up at the Victoria Hotel. Professor Caballo, who had been the Uruguayan participant at the Santiago seminar, had promised to introduce me to people in the government and late Monday afternoon, after several postponements, he took me to the foreign office and the supreme court. It was just as well that my Spanish was improving because Professor Caballo's French was purely theoretical. The visit to the court, where I met the president and two of his colleagues, was pure protocol; but at the foreign office I talked to the minister, Professor Secco Ellauri, and Francisco Forteza whom I had known at United Nations Headquarters. I left them thinking that the government would sponsor a seminar. This never materialized, but I would be returning to New York with firm offers from Argentina and Colombia. On Tuesday, the foreign office gave a lunch at the golf club. I then called on Dr. Rodolfo Mezzera, the dean of the law faculty, after which I gave a long interview, in Spanish, to the newspaper *El Dia*, but I never saw the printed result.

Returning to New York, my plane came down at São Paulo, Rio de Janeiro, when I had another fine view of the city, Caracas and San Juan. My first business at headquarters was to report to Sir Humphrey Trevelyan, who was pleased with the results of my mission. The seminars were now firmly established. During my absence an official invitation had come from Ceylon confirming my negotiations with Ambassador Gunewardene. Reports from Ceylon about the communal riots made me wonder whether we could go ahead with our plans, but on reflection I decided that this was an additional reason why the seminar should be held.

I had only a few days in New York before going on to Geneva and the summer session of the Economic and Social Council. The night is short, traveling east across the Atlantic late in June, and the woman sitting next to me insisted on having the blind open, with the result that I hardly closed my eyes. I was therefore tired when I arrived in Geneva on Tuesday morning, 24 June; but I went straight to the Palais, only to find that I had no office, no secretary, no documents—nothing. So I hurried back to town, boarded a train to Nyon, changed to another for La Cure and had lunch at a restaurant on the French border. I then walked to St. Cergues—two hours—and took the train back to Geneva. There were beautiful views of Mont Blanc and indeed of the whole range of the Alps.

Sir Humphrey came to Geneva to follow the discussions on the advisory services program in the Social Committee. I went to Cointrin airport to meet thim. We talked about the Ceylonese seminar and agreed to go ahead with it notwithstanding the communal riots. He agreed that, on my way to Ceylon, I should visit some countries in Africa and Asia and try to get other governments to sponsor seminars. After a few days he was called back to headquarters; there was a whole series of crises in the Near East on which his advice was needed: a political assassination in Iraq, the American military intervention in Lebanon, to name two. But I was glad he was in Geneva long enough to hear the best part of the debate on the advisory services program, for, with measured reservations from the Soviet Union, there was unanimous support for the program and praise for the way the Secretariat had developed it. It was better for him to hear these things himself than to listen to any account that I might give. We ran into some rough weather the day after his departure, but this was partly because the representative of the Soviet Union couldn't understand what was meant by remedies against the abuse of administrative power. A member of the Dutch delegation asked me whether this subject would not be too difficult for a seminar in Ceylon. I replied that the level of the discussions at the Baguio and Santiago seminars was certainly the equal of anything that could be heard in the Economic and Social Council. The program was also discussed in the Coordination Committee. I had never had much respect for this committee, but I now followed its discussions with some amusement, for there was great praise and even enthusiasm for the seminars. Two years earlier hardly a delegation had had a good word for them.

The performance of the Council on the other human rights items was indifferent and for the same reason that the last session of the commission had been so unproductive. Now that the Human Rights Commission had finished its work on the Universal Declaration and the covenants, governments were faced with some very difficult decisions. The next logical step was to devise some international machinery for implementation, and things like periodic reporting and the study on arbitrary arrest were all steps in that direction. Would governments cooperate? I was saying all this one day to Sir Samuel Hoare, who agreed that governments were embarrassed, but the difficulties about which he spoke were quite different from the ones that were bothering me. He mentioned the difficulties inherent in drafting conventions on such subjects as the right of asylum and the rights of the child. My own experience told me that it was relatively easy to draft a convention or a declaration. The real difficulty was how to make them work. What was the use of a whole series of human rights conventions if none of them worked in practice? We had, it seemed to me, reached a kind of political obstacle which has not yet been surmounted even today. In the meantime we needed some imaginative programs, if only to keep the human rights flag flying in the United Nations. Apart from their educational value, I considered that the seminars were such a program. Sir Humphrey Trevelyan understood this very well.

Not long before the end of the session, Laugier came to Gex for a vacation where I had lunch with him one day and dinner another. He looked tired and was suffering from the more or less chronic bronchitis that had laid him up for a month during the winter. He was now seventy and all his life he had practiced his hedonist philosophy. It was remarkable, I thought, that he was as well as he was.

Just before leaving Geneva I gave a lecture at a summer school organized by the World Federation of United Nations Associations but had to turn down invitations to speak in Brussels, in connection with the World Fair, and also in Berlin. I was back in New York on Wednesday, 30 July, after a delay of three hours in Geneva, waiting for the heir to the Spanish throne, who traveled with us as far as Lisbon. When I got to my office at headquarters, I found the section on the status of women in an uproar because, during my absence in Geneva, a new chief of section had been appointed who was so unpopular with her colleagues that two of them asked to be transferred out of the section.

I had been away from headquarters for nearly three months, which was much too long; but I was entitled to a holiday and if I didn't take one now I didn't know when I could. So after three weeks in the August heat I left for Nova Scotia to join Jeanne. We had some glorious days there before going on to Prince Edward Island. Back in New York for the opening of the General Assembly, I had a long talk with Charles Malik who had just been elected its president. I was now more optimistic about the future of the covenants; so many dependent territories were becoming independent that the political implications of the articles on self-determination seemed less important. And the level of debate in the Third Committee was higher than it had been in 1957. But the advisory committee on administrative and budgetary questions had cut the budget for the advisory services program, and I was doing everything I could to have it restored. The Fifth Committee reestablished the item. Because most delegations vote almost automatically for the recommendations of the advisory committee, the vote in the Assembly was a real victory; I hoped the Secretary-General would be impressed by the support the program was getting, particularly from the economically developing countries.

On Monday, 27 October, Sir Humphrey Trevelyan told me that he was leaving the Secretariat to become the British ambassador in Iraq. I was sorry to see him go. We had established a relationship based on confidence and respect, at least on my side, and I had been reasonably confident about working with him in the future. I never detected any special enthusiasm in him for the human rights program—Laugier was my only chief who had that—but his attitude towards it was intelligent, and he never created unnecessary obstacles. If he sometimes seemed skeptical about the program, this was a function of his honesty. He once said that he had never in all his experience seen so much cynicism and hypocrisy as governments showed in this matter, and there was a great deal of truth in what he said. His greatest fault was his tendency to jump to a conclusion before he could possibly know the whole story. I have never known a man who could say "no" faster, and once he had pronounced this sentence, the question was closed. But he was always courteous and friendly, even when this happened, and I never felt any personal resentment.

Sir Humphrey can speak for himself, but I thought that if he were leaving the Secretariat after only six months in office, it was because he didn't have enough to do. His title was Under Secretary for Special Political Affairs, but he didn't have a department, and the only divisions that reported to him were my own and the Division of Narcotic Drugs, which was stationed in Geneva. Hammarskjold made a great fuss over him at the beginning, as he did over anyone new, but my guess is that he made no real use of Sir Humphrey's talents and experience. Sir Humphrey left New York almost immediately after the announcement of his resignation.

On 10 December, the General Assembly celebrated the tenth anniversay of the Universal Declaration of Human Rights, an event which was also widely observed throughout the world. For over a year an ECOSOC committee had been planning these celebrations;

and earlier in the year its chairman, Hortencio Brillantes of the Philippines, had come to me suggesting that the General Assembly should adopt a resolution reaffirming faith in the Declaration, but I had talked him out of it because I was afraid that an attempt might be made to amend the Declaration, which could upset the consensus now behind it. The proceedings were therefore purely formal. The speakers included Mrs. Roosevelt, the first chairman of the commission, Charles Malik, who succeeded her as chairman and was the first rapporteur as well as the chairman of the Third Committee in 1948 when the Declaration was adopted, and was now the president of the General Assembly, and R.S.S. Gunewardene, the current chairman of the commission. Statements were also read by their delegations on behalf of René Cassin and Felixberto Serrano, both former chairmen, and from the foreign minister of the United Arab Republic in memory of the late Mahmoud Azmi who had been chairman in 1953 and 1954. At the request of the French delegation, but without consulting the Human Rights Division, the Office of Public Information displayed a document in Cassin's handwriting as part of the exhibition in the corridors. It was the draft of the declaration that he had prepared for the Drafting Committee on the basis of my own draft. It helped create the myth that Cassin was the father of the Universal Declaration.

The Kandy and Buenos Aires Seminars (1959)

The Sub-Commission on the Prevention of Discrimination met in January and devoted most of the session to its three studies of religious rights and practices, political rights and the right of everyone to leave any country including his own and to return to his country. The first of these studies was scheduled to be finished in 1960, and the sub-commission wanted the Secretariat to make arrangements for the completion of the study on political rights at the same time. But we had to tell them that this could be done only if we had more staff; and, at its next session, the Economic and Social Council instructed the sub-commission to readjust its program accordingly. The sub-commission was now working well; the session was relatively productive and, apart from some ideological clashes between the American and Soviet members, smooth-running, a result which I attributed to a minimum of interference from the Secretariat.

I had two other committees meeting in January, one of which was a committee of seven set up by the Human Rights Commission to recommend procedures for handling communications which would be "better calculated to promote respect for and observance of fundamental human rights." Hiding behind the controversial decision which the commission had taken in 1947, and which had been confirmed by the Council, that it had "no power to take any action in regard to any complaints concerning human rights," the committee made no recommendations which could, by any stretch of the imagination, be regarded as "better calculated to promote respect for and observance of human rights." The other committee was the one created by the commission for its study on arbitrary arrest, detention and exile. About the only thing it did was to authorize the Secretariat to forward certain country monographs which the Secretariat had prepared to governments for their comments and suggestions. This was a case where some "streamlining" would have been appropriate. If the commission had been willing to act through rapporteurs, like its sub-commission, the expense of an unnecessary committee meeting could have been avoided.

There was a struggle for the chairmanship at the opening of the committee, with Ambassador Gunewardene again the principal protagonist. In 1958 the chairman had been Serrano (who was now the secretary of state of the Philippines), but in his absence, Gunewardene had chaired the meetings on an ad hoc basis. This year he wanted to be the titular chairman. So did Francisco Delgado, Serrano's successor as head of the Philippine mission at headquarters. The Filipinos had worked hard on behalf of their candidate and obviously had a majority of the votes committed. But Gunewardene had the advantage that he had already opened the session in his capacity as retiring chairman of the Human Rights Commission and ad hoc chairman of the committee in 1958. The meeting was adjourned and the two candidates sat silent on opposite sides of the conference room. A compromise was finally reached. Delgado would be the chairman, but "in his capacity of chairman of the Human Rights Commission" Gunewardene would preside whenever he was in the conference room. He had shown the same staying power when he was elected chairman of the commission in 1958 and he would put on a similar performance at the seminar in Ceylon.

Sir Humphrey Trevelyan's successor, the new Under Secretary for Special Political Affairs, C.V. Narasimhan, arrived on Monday, 26 January, and on Tuesday came to visit me in my office, a courtesy which I thought augured well for the future. Although regretting Sir Humphrey's departure, I welcomed Narasimhan's appointment and the prospect of working with him. The main support for the human rights program was now coming from the developing countries, and I thought it would be good to have an Indian at the top. Like Sir Humphrey Trevelyan, he didn't have enough to do in the first months after he came to headquarters. He once told me that he was spending part of his time translating the Indian classics into English. As long as this continued, he took the human rights program very seriously and was always ready to back me up. But when he became the busiest and, next to the Secretary-General, the most powerful man in the Secretariat, his attitude changed. He once explained that it was now impossible for him to seem to favor the Division of Human Rights, and whether for this reason or because his interest had flagged, I sometimes thought that he leaned in the other direction.

On that first day of our relationship I formed a very favorable opinion of the man. He was, I thought, at least as intelligent as Sir Humphrey and probably more contemplative. He would be unlikely to come to a quick decision before knowing the whole story. In his book, *Back to Katanga*, Conor Cruise O'Brien paints a series of thumb portraits of top officials in the Secretariat. Narasimhan is compared to a Brahman priest jealous of the rites of his calling. I do not know whether he really was a religious man, but he certainly liked to convey that impression. In the early days of our relationship, when he didn't have too much to do, he sometimes told me that he had spent part of the day in prayer or reading the Vedic classics. He didn't eat meat of any kind, and at dinner parties special vegetarian dishes had to be prepared for him. Later he took to eating fish, explaining that he needed the protein. This distinction between cold-blooded and warm-blooded life was too difficult for me to grasp. He was proud of his sense of humor, which wasn't very subtle, and liked to tell bawdy stories punctuated with bad puns. I soon discovered that it wasn't easy to discuss a problem with him, for he spoke as one possessed of some mysterious knowledge that could not be questioned.

In the halcyon days of 1959 Narasimhan was the first to encourage me in my efforts to get governments to sponsor human rights seminars, and it was with his approval that at the beginning of April I left New York for one of my longest missions abroad. My last business before leaving headquarters on this mission was the fifteenth session of the Human Rights Commission, which met from 16 March to 10 April. Gunewardene was again the chairman. As in 1957 the commission spent most of its time on the Declaration on the Rights of the Child, a draft of which it sent on to the General Assembly. I had some reservations about the wisdom of adopting such a declaration: a proliferation of United Nations declarations would undermine the authority of the Universal Declaration of Human Rights. I also thought that there was something wrong with our priorities. It was easier to draft a declaration on the rights of children than to devise practical measures for the protection of human rights.

On Friday, 3 April, a week before the end of the session, my wife and I set out on our long trip to Ceylon and the seminar on judicial and other remedies against the illegal exercise or abuse of administrative authority. Narasimhan had encouraged me to visit a number of other countries en route for talks with governments. We first went to Egypt, where we spent ten days, but this was on my own time and deducted from my annual leave. There was no point in trying to have a seminar in Cairo. All the countries of the Near East, including Israel, would have to be invited to send participants, and that was something to which the Egyptian government would certainly not agree. It was our first visit to Egypt, our intention to spend a few days there in 1956 having been thwarted by the Suez crisis. We did all the things that tourists do: visited mosques, the great Egyptian Museum (which alone is worth a trip to Cairo) and, of course, the pyramids; and we had three days in Luxor which was, however, already much too hot for comfort. One day an Egyptian friend drove us to see a farm on the delta at some distance from Cairo. It was hot when we left the city and we were dressed accordingly, but by evening it had become quite cold, with the result that we both caught bad colds which we did not shake off until we reached Ceylon.

Our next stop was Khartoum, where I had business and which we reached on Wednesday, 15 April. I remember the fine view of the Nile—a bright green strip in the desert—from our small plane. We had only three days in the Sudan, which was much too short; but I had several interviews with heads of government departments, all of them colonels. They were polite but skeptical when I suggested that the government sponsor a seminar on the status of women. I realized that this might not be easy, because the Sudan was a Moslem country, but that was why I tried. I did not succeed. I had no better luck when, some weeks later, I visited the Malayan Federation; nor did I ever succeed in having a seminar on the status of women in a Moslem country. But I did do one useful thing in Khartoum. Making conversation with Chief Justice Abu Rannat at a garden party, I asked him whether he had ever been at the United Nations. He said something about the Sudan's being a poor country. I then asked him whether he would like to be a member of the Sub-Commission on the Prevention of Discrimination. When he replied that he would be interested, I said that I would see what I could do. In December I arranged to have him elected a member of the sub-commission, of which he became one of the most useful members, and the rapporteur of its study on discrimination in the administration of justice. There wasn't much time for sightseeing, but we did visit Omdurman—which is across the Nile from Khartoum, not far from where the Blue and White Niles join—where we saw a fine camel market (Jeanne made friends with one of the animals) and the house of the Mahdi, which is now a museum. Looking at the exhibits, and particularly the weapons of the tribesmen, one's sympathies naturally went out to them in their unequal struggle with the British lion.

We spent a week in Addis Ababa, and here I was able to get an invitation for the seminar on the status of women that was held there a year later. One day we hired a car and drove many miles into the country until we reached a lake nestled in a kind of crater. Here the vegetation was relatively lush and there were many birds, including little red-headed fellows who spent most of their time on the backs of cattle, but most of the countryside was arid. It seemed to be standing still and one had the impression that it had done so for centuries. There were scenes that were almost biblical in their antiquity, including a couple on a donkey who might have been Joseph and Mary. Addis Ababa itself was less attractive. I have never seen anything more degrading than the beggars in the markets. Some of them, condemned thieves from whom the offending member had been amputated, exhibited their stumps to the pity of passers-by; and some of them, we were told, kept their revolting sores fresh by rubbing them in salt. What was really needed in Ethiopia was a seminar on cruel and inhuman punishment.

From Addis we flew to Bombay by way of Djibouti and Aden. The very name of Aden spelled romance, but nothing could have been more humdrum than our hotel, which was disgustingly English and could have been anywhere except on the Arabian peninsula. We took a taxi to the Crater, where we walked in the streets for an hour. Here there was plenty of color: Arabs, Africans, Indians, Malays all in their national dress. But when the next morning we boarded our plane for Bombay, Aden still remained little more than a romantic name. We changed planes again at Bombay, stopping there for the best part of three days, long enough to see the Gate of India and the temples at Elephanta, but not long enough to get a real taste of the place.

We were in Colombo on Wednesday, 29 April. The seminar was to be in Kandy, but I had a round of official calls to make in the capital. Mr. Bandaranaike, the prime minister, invited us to a garden party at Temple Trees, his official residence. It was a stroke of luck that the representative of the U.N. technical assistance bureau in Ceylon was John Corry, who was a brother of James Corry—later principal of Queen's University—whom I knew back in Canada. I also knew Nik Cavell, the high commissioner for Canada. Corry drove us to Kandy. I remember the lush vegetation, the great flowering trees and the rice paddies. The Ceylonese say that Ceylon was the Garden of Eden and I can think of no more likely candidate. In Kandy we put up at a hotel on the lake, around which we walked at every opportunity. I sometimes got out of bed early to do the walk before breakfast, but the lake was as its best in the cool of the evening. Another beautiful walk was in the Peradeniya Gardens, about half-way between the city and the university where the seminar was held. We also liked to go to a pool on the outskirts of Kandy where elephants bathed in the evening.

The prime minister opened the seminar on 4 May. There was some maneuvering between Ceylonese candidates for the chairmanship. Gunewardene insisted that because he was the chairman of the Human Rights Commission he should act in that capacity at the seminar—not a very convincing argument—but he was finally designated by the government as the person to be elected. It was Gunewardene who arranged to have the participants visit the Temple of the Tooth to see the tooth of the Buddha. This was a great privilege because the relic is ordinarily exhibited only once a year at the Esala Perahera, when the event is celebrated by elaborate parades with elephants and dancers. We were taken into a room in the center of which was a large receptacle, the shape of a pagoda, which a priest opened. A great pile of jewels, apparently of great value, was then carefully removed to reveal a casket containing the relic. The tooth itself was big enough to have belonged to some animal. We also went on several interesting excursions, one of them to Eliya, high up in the mountains where, in colonial days, British civil servants found an atmosphere that reminded them of home. Another was to Sigiriya to see the frescoes. We also visited a tea plantation. There were several receptions and dinner parties, the most pleasant of which was an intimate dinner party for my wife and me at the home of the rector of the university, where we had some good talk and the rector taught us the proper way to eat a mango. The governor general came up from Colombo to receive the participants at a reception in Government House, which was a fine example of the comfortable official residences the British built for themselves in so many parts of the empire. The Kandy seminar was a success, and it had at least one concrete result. One of the institutions discussed, on which the Secretariat had circulated a working paper, was the Scandinavian office of ombudsman. Jonathan Robson, the New Zealand deputy secretary for justice, took the idea back to New Zealand, which became one of the first countries outside of Scandinavia to adopt the institution. When I was in New Zealand in 1961, the minister of justice publicly confirmed that the idea had come from Kandy.

We had planned to spend part of my annual leave in Ceylon after the seminar and someone advised us to make our headquarters at the Mount Lavinia Hotel, which is on the ocean not far from Colombo. I can't imagine anyone wanting to swim in the muddy warm surf; it was like tepid *cafe au lait*. A feature of the place was the crows and the cats. The crows were so bold that, when you were having tea on the terrace, they would swoop down and steal the sandwich out of your hand. The place was also infested with cats. Ceylon's being a Buddhist country, nobody would kill a kitten, but they didn't feed them either. When we did from our table in the dining room, we soon had a dozen around us, much to the annoyance of the waiters, who could not understand this kind of charity. Another feature of the place was the elephant that was paraded every morning not far from the hotel for the benefit, I suppose, of people like us, but we always enjoyed seeing him. One night, Julius Katz-Suchy, who was now the Polish ambassador accredited to both India and Ceylon, came to see us. We had a long friendly talk about the United Nations.

The day after we arrived at the Mount Lavinia, the government gave an elaborate dinner party for Gunewardene to which my wife and I were invited. The prime minister was there, but his name was not on the long list of speakers. It was nearly midnight when the master of ceremonies, having exhausted his list, turned to Bandaranaike. "And now, Mr. Prime Minister," he said, "wouldn't you like to say a few words?" Mrs. Bandaranaike, next to whom I was sitting, turned to me and said: "Now we will never get to bed." She had already questioned me about our experiences on the island. "You haven't seen much of it," she summed up. "Would you like to have a car?" I said that I would, and the next morning a large chauffeur-driven limousine drew up in front of our hotel. Mrs. Bandaranaike's suggestion was that we should drive that day to Galle, which is on the south west point of the island, but Jeanne was not well, so we decided to put off the trip until the next day. I therefore took the car and went alone to a place noted for its semiprecious stones. Nik Cavell told me later that I could buy them cheaper in Toronto. Our decision to postpone the excursion to Galle turned out to be a lucky one. For the day we went was Wesak, and in the long line of villages through which we passed there were elaborate celebrations with parades and decorations in honor of the Buddha, all of which we would have missed had we made the trip the day before. As Nik Cavell said, we had seen something unique even for Ceylon. This expedition was attended by one unexpected risk. For it seems that on Wesak the faithful offer hospitality to strangers in honor of the Buddha, and everytime our car was held up by a parade, which was often, glasses of sweet colored water were pressed on us by friendly people. We were of course being very careful about what we drank, and for Jeanne to accept the stuff was out of the question. But I felt that I had to rise to the occasion, and I drank I do not know how many glasses without, I am happy to record, any bad effects.

After three or four days at Mount Lavinia, we decided that a change in our plans would be in order and it would be better to move on. For one thing I was becoming too involved in the communal strife then rife in Ceylon. People were coming to see me at all hours, even while we were having breakfast; and I was afraid that, sooner or later, my name might be used in the controversy, to the embarrassment of the government and the United Nations. Also the monsoon had broken and Jeanne was suffering with intestinal trouble. According to my itinerary, my next offical visit was to be to Kuala Lumpur and to attempt now to change these arrangements seemed unwise. If we were to leave Ceylon, we would have to put in the intervening time somewhere between that country and the Malayan Federation. We decided on Singapore, which was certainly not the best place for a holiday at that time of year. I have always regretted that we did not go to some other place in Ceylon, far from the capital. Singapore was hot and humid, and by the time we got there Jeanne was ill enough to see a doctor. But there were some bright spots: we spent happy hours in the botanical gardens, did some shopping and enjoyed mingling with the people on the crowded streets.

We were glad to move on from Singapore to Kuala Lumpur. I had been led to believe at U.N. Headquarters that there was some possibility the government of the Federation would sponsor a seminar on the status of women. If there was anywhere in the world where the condition of women needed to be improved, it was in Asia. But just as my attempt to organize a seminar in the Sudan had been frustrated by the skepticism of the colonels, I failed here because of the conservatism of the mullahs.

After three days in Kuala Lumpur, we flew to Hong Kong, which was now becoming familiar ground. Arthur Hooton, the attorney general, who had been at the Baguio seminar, entertained us royally. Amongst other things, he arranged for a police escort to take us to the Chinese border. I would have given a lot to be able to continue on into Red China. On Saturday, 6 June, we were in Japan. My negotiations with the government were especially fruitful, for the Japanese eventually sponsored two seminars, one on the status of women and the other on the administration of criminal justice. When I said something about the possibility of having the seminar in some typically Japanese city like Kyoto, arrangements were made through the Japanese Tourist Bureau for us to see that city. I came back to Tokyo full of enthusiasm, but by that time the government had decided that they didn't have the proper facilities in Kyoto for a conference, and the two seminars were held in Tokyo. I never did get back to Kyoto, although it is one of the places in the world that I would most like to see again.

We left Tokyo on Thursday, 11 June, had a day in Honolulu and flew on to San Francisco. Jeanne stayed on in California for several weeks, but I continued on to New York in one of the new jets and was back in my office on Monday morning, 15 June, having been away for over two months.

On the first of July I was in Geneva for the summer session of the Economic and Social Council. There were relatively few human rights items on the agenda. With three member states abstaining, the Council expressed its satisfaction with the seminars and approved the holding of three in 1960. It also increased the membership of the Sub-Commission on the Prevention of Discrimination from twelve to fourteen, and there was some discussion of the proposed study on the right of everyone to leave any country including his own and to return to his country. An attempt to broaden the scope of this study to include immigration failed. At its session in March, the Commission on the Status of Women had recommended that the Council approve the drafting of a convention on age of marriage, free consent and registration of marriages. The Council felt that there should be both a convention and a recommendation, and instructed the Secretariat to prepare drafts of both instruments for the commission's next session. The commission had also asked the Council to adopt a strong resolution on the equal treatment of men and women under pension plans; but ECOSOC was not convinced that arrangements for the earlier optional retirement of women and therefore an earlier pensionable age infringed the principle that pension plans should not place women workers at any disadvantage, and consequently took no decision "at the present time."

At the spring session of the Council, the United States and three Latin American delegations had proposed the adoption of a declaration on freedom of information; and over the objections of Afghanistan, the matter had been put on the agenda of the summer session, which now had a revised draft before it, as well as a draft resolution under which the Council would send the draft declaration to governments for their comments. This was again opposed by Afghanistan and by the Soviet Union, which argued that to begin work now on a declaration would disturb "the atmosphere of political compromise" in the General Assembly on the draft convention dealing with the same subject. The resolution was nevertheless adopted by a vote of 13 to 3 with 2 abstentions. If there was any atmosphere of political compromise at the United Nations in the matter of freedom of information, I knew nothing about it.

The Council adjourned on 31 July, and on the same day I went to Vienna to make arrangements for a seminar on human rights in criminal procedure. The city was acting as host to a World Youth Festival and there were "young communists" there from all over the world. I watched the parade. My talks with the government did not take long, and I had time for a quick visit to Krems to see a fine exhibition of baroque art, which I found more edifying than the parade I had just seen in Vienna. I stopped at Estoril in Portugal for a long weekend on my way back to New York.

I was not long at headquarters before I had to go to Buenos Aires for the seminar, which began on 31 August, on judicial and other remedies against the illegal use and abuse of administrative authority—the same topic that had been discussed at Kandy. I was glad to be in Buenos Aires again. The city has a sophistication that can be found in very few other places in the New World. Built to rival Paris, it has retained a nineteenth century cachet, but one felt that somehow it had stopped growing at the turn of the century; and that may have been at the root of some of the social unrest. For a foreign traveller, living was cheap, but the *porteños* found it expensive enough. In 1959 a beefsteak could be had in a good restaurant (of which there were many) for less than a dollar, and there was good wine for the price of beer in New York. I now had some good friends in Buenos Aires, which helped to make my stay pleasant. One day Carlos Bertomeu, who represented Argentina on the Human Rights Commission, arranged to take me and two of my colleagues to see an *estancia*. But the ranch, although it was said to be an important one, did not come up to my romantic expectations. By Canadian standards it didn't look like a farm; there were hardly any buildings, and the cattle, apart from one old bull, were away in some remote place. But the owners, who were Irish, received us with old-country hospitality.

The seminar was held in the great building of the law faculty. Like the Santiago seminar in 1958 it did not come up to the standard of the Asian seminars; there were too many elaborate speeches filled with rhetoric and not enough down-to-earth discussion. But it was a useful exercise and helped make the U.N. human rights program better known in South America. Early one morning while I was still in bed, La Plaza, the chairman of the seminar who was also the dean of the law faculty, telephoned to say that no meeting could be held that day because there was a coup d'état, General Montero was driving his tanks into the city and the minister of justice had ordered all public buildings, including the university, closed. I protested, perhaps naively, that coup d'état or not, a United Nations conference should not be interrupted and made the point that, if there was going to be trouble, it would be better to have the participants all in one place. The meeting went ahead as planned. Shortly before this, the participants had been received by President Frondizi. Nothing in his attitude indicated that he expected any trouble. I had found him *muy simpatico* and was sorry that he should be humiliated by an ambitious general.

I stopped in Lima on my way back to New York. A damp cloud had settled over the city, but only a few miles away there was bright sunshine. The Peruvians speak of the revenge of the Incas who, it is said, advised the Spaniards where to build the city. I had the time, while in Lima, to see my old colleague, Enrico Garcia Sayan, who was back in law practice.

I was back in New York in time for the opening of the fourteenth session of the General Assembly, which as I remember was strenuous. I was now representing the Secretary-General in the Third Committee for all items, whether they touched on human rights or not, and had therefore to be in the conference room morning and afternoon whenever the committee was in session. Because I also had an office to run, I used to bring my paper work with me to the meetings; I had my secretary sitting behind me and a junior officer who was instructed to warn me when I should be listening to the debate, much of which was quite irrelevant to what the committee was supposed to be doing. The level of the discussion in the Third Committee was indeed inferior to what I was becoming accustomed to at the seminars. Except on the rare occasions when something sensational happened, the press wasn't interested in what was said in the Third Committee, with the result that delegates could get away with almost anything and decisions were taken which, if they had been reached in the parliament of a democratic country, would have caused a public uproar.

At this session the committee adopted three more articles for the Covenant on Civil and Political Rights: Article 12 on freedom of movement and residence, including the right of everyone to leave any country including his own—but not the right to return to his country, which is proclaimed by the Universal Declaration of Human Rights and was proposed by the Human Rights Commission for the covenant—and a prohibition of arbitrary exile; Article 13 which stipulates certain guarantees against the arbitrary expulsion of aliens; and Article 14 on the right to a fair trial, the drafting of which was one of the most difficult in the covenant. As a lawyer I was shocked by the decision to add the French civil law concept of *ordre public* to the list of permissible grounds for imposing restrictions on freedom of movement and residence in Article 12. The same expression, "ordre public," was later also used in Article 19 on freedom of information and Articles 21 and 22 on the freedoms of peaceful assembly and association. Unlike the English term "public order," which has no precise legal meaning in common law jurisdictions, and in ordinary English usage implies simply the absence of disorder, the civil law concept is so far reaching that it can be interpreted as including public policy and perhaps even *raison d'état*. Although an extreme view, and one that should be rejected because it would defeat the very purposes of the covenant, it is worth recalling what the representative of Spain said in one of the debates relating to this dangerous concept. "In every country," he said, "the established order could be endangered by the clash of different political, legal and philosophical systems; the state should therefore be able to invoke considerations of public order to safeguard its integrity and sovereignty." More topical, when the Soviet Union ratified the covenant in September 1973, the Soviet press, which can be taken as expressing the views of the government, said that the limitations clauses permitted all the restrictions imposed on the enjoyment of human rights in that country. These are extreme views, but they reflect the opinions of certain governments, which are important factors in the interpretation of international law. The committee also adopted the preamble and first article of the ill-fated convention on freedom of information. As adopted by the committee, this article provided that contracting states were to secure "freedom to *gather* [Italics added], receive and impart without governmental interference . . . information and opinions orally, in writing or in print, in the form of art or by duly licensed visual or auditory devices." When approved by the 1948 Conference on Freedom of Information, the text had read "to seek," which is the language used in both the Universal Declaration and the Covenant on Civil and Political Rights. The amendment to substitute the weaker expression "to gather" was sponsored by the delegations of Ethiopia, India, the Philippines, Saudi Arabia and Venezuela, who said that the change was aimed at journalists who offended religious sensibilities and national traditions, invaded personal privacy or threatened the security of the state. That such an amendment could be adopted in the full light of day explains what I mean when I say that, in the Third Committee, governments could get away with almost anything. One would have thought that in a matter that touched them so intimately, professional journalists would have reacted to protect their interests and freedom of information.

Behind the Curtain, Around the World, and an Ethiopian Coup d'Etat (1960)

The General Assembly behind me, my wife and I left New York for a short holiday in the West Indies. I was back at headquarters in time for the opening of the twelfth session of the Sub-Commission on the Prevention of Discrimination, most of which was devoted to the study of religious rights and practices. Presenting his final report, Arcot Krishnaswami pointed out that the study was based on information summarized in some eighty-six country monographs which were available to the members of the sub-commission as "conference room papers" but only in the language in which they had been prepared by the Secretariat. These monographs set forth the *de jure* and *de facto* situations in the countries with which they dealt; but the study itself only rarely mentioned particular countries. He therefore considered that the monographs were an integral part of his report and hoped that the Secretariat would give them the widest circulation possible, something that was never done, as I have already explained. The report also contained certain draft basic rules or principles which were intended to show how the goals proclaimed by the Universal Declaration could be achieved and suggestions for action that might be taken to eradicate discrimination. As amended by the sub-commission, these rules and suggestions were forwarded to the Human Rights Commission.

Very little progress had been made on the sub-commission's other study, on discrimination in the enjoyment of political rights. Hernan Santa Cruz, the rapporteur for the study, had become the regional representative in Latin America of the Food and Agriculture Organization and, because of that, asked the sub-commission to accept his resignation. He was urged to continue in office which, notwithstanding the fact that he was now an international official he decided to do, and, because the study on religious rights and practices was now out of the way, the Secretariat was able to concentrate on helping him prepare a final report in time for the 1962 session of the sub-commission, eight years after the decision to undertake the study. It could have been completed in half that time had the staff of the Human Rights Division not been cut down to a bare minimum.

It was a rare thing all the time I was at the United Nations for either the Human Rights Commission or the sub-commission to discuss, much less adopt, any resolution relating to a concrete case of alleged violation of human rights. At this session, however, when the International League for the Rights of Man drew attention to an outbreak of manifestations of racial and religious hostility reminiscent of National Socialism in a number of countries, including the Federal Republic of Germany, the sub-commission unanimously condemned such practices as violations of the Charter and the Universal Declaration of Human Rights. The resolution, which was later followed up by similar resolutions in the Human Rights Commission and the General Assembly, even made some provision for its implementation, for it instructed the Secretariat to obtain information on the manifestations from states which were members either of the United Nations or of the specialized agencies, a formula that included the Federal Republic of Germany.

The sub-commission adjourned on 30 January. Four weeks later I was in Geneva for the sixteenth session of the Human Rights Commission that began on 29 February. I crossed the Atlantic by ship (the first time I had been able to do this for years) and had a day in Paris. The extra travelling time was deducted from my annual leave, but the sea voyage was worth it, even though at that time of year the weather on the Atlantic wasn't too good and you had to be robust to enjoy a walk on the sun deck. Mousheng Lin, who was travelling with me, introduced me to Wellington Koo, with whom we had dinner.

In Geneva the primroses, snowdrops and crocuses were blooming in the parks, the trees were brushed with light green, and there were hundreds of birds of every kind. One of the first things I did after arriving in the city was to walk up to the Saleve hoping to see a wall creeper, which I never found, but I did see dozens of people scaling the steep rocks.

The first item on the commission's agenda related to the advisory services program. The interest of governments in sponsoring them was now so great that we had to plan seminars up to two years in advance. That year there would be three: one in Tokyo on the role of criminal law in the protection of human rights and the purposes and legitimate limits of penal sanctions; one in Vienna on criminal procedure, and another in Addis Ababa on the participation of women in public life. Arrangements had also been made to hold three seminars in 1961: one in New Zealand on criminal procedure, one in Romania on the status of women in family law and a third in Mexico on *amparo, habeas corpus* and related remedies.

The commission devoted most of the session to the draft declaration on the right to asylum. Like the Universal Declaration of Human Rights, it did not recognize any right to asylum, but only the right to seek and enjoy it. It was indeed only in its third article, which provided that no one should be rejected at or expelled over the border of a country from which he was fleeing or had fled in circumstances where his life or liberty might be seriously endangered, that the draft purported to give any real protection to persons seeking asylum. Similar provisions had already been incorporated in the Refugees Convention in 1951. An amended declaration was adopted by the General Assembly on 14 December 1967, as the Declaration on Territorial Asylum. Its chief purpose seems to be to protect states. That it does not grant any right of asylum is clear by its first article, which says, amongst other things, that "it shall rest with the state granting asylum to evaluate the grounds for the grant of asylum."

Two days after the commission adjourned I was in Prague on my way to Romania. Although I had now been a United Nations official for nearly fourteen years, it was the first time I had ever been in a communist country. A fortnight later, returning to New York by ship, I wrote down my impressions, beginning with a reference to the iron curtain, an expression which, as a conscientious international official, I had always hesitated to use. There really was, I wrote, a curtain. Occasionally they lift it high enough for someone to get through to the other side, but once you are there, you are in another world. During my two weeks in Czechoslovakia and Romania, the only English or French newspapers that I saw were the *Daily Worker* and *L'Humanite*.

My Czech hosts took me to the Alcorn Hotel, bourgeois and run down, and a kind of international enclave, the lobby of which was crowded with people from all over the communist and noncommunist worlds: Germans, Russians, Arabs, a few orientals, a few English and French, but as far as I could see, no Americans and no Canadians. The walls of an alley leading to the dining room were adorned with the coats of arms of the Communist countries: the Peoples Republic of China, the Peoples Republic of Germany, the Peoples Republic of Mongolia, and so on, as if this were the sum total of the known world. I already felt that, like Alice, I had ventured through the looking glass.

My first real impression of Prague came when I went for a walk on Wenceslas Square. What I saw was such a convincing confirmation of preconceived ideas that it came almost as a shock. For the people who crowded the sidewalks (there was very little vehicular traffic and you could hear the sound of feet on the pavement) seemed to be exclusively workers and peasants. This was apparent not only in their faces and bearing but chiefly in their dress, which added a note of drabness to the scene. A Czech acquaintance later told me that, until very recently, nonconformity in dress was not tolerated. Stock phrases like the dictatorship of the proletariat and the class war came to my mind. I felt conspicuous and not a little silly in my London overcoat and Homburg hat and continued to feel uncomfortable as long as I was in Prague, even though the shock of my first impressions began to wear off before I left the city. I never detected this same aggressive proletarianism in any of the other communist countries I later visited, certainly not in Romania.

I went for another walk the next day, this time with an official from the foreign office. The reason for all the cleaning of façades, he said, was that they were trying to brighten up the city for a sports festival that summer. It certainly needed cleaning up; Prague was as drab as any city I had ever seen and dirty too; but that could have been partly because so many factories burnt soft coal. Here and there a new shop or apartment building was going up, but most of the building was going on in the industrial suburbs, which I visited later. Here they were providing decent housing for the workers—one up for the Revolution. We visited a large department store and a supermarket, as well as some smaller shops. I was intrigued by the apparent abundance of goods they offered. My guide complained about standardization: everything is the same, he said. But luxury goods aside, there seemed to be a great variety. In Bucharest, even consumer goods were limited in quality, quantity and variety.

I was taken for another walk starting high up on Bradcany Hill where we first visited the Cathedral of St. Vitus. It was bitterly cold inside, but I remember the fine stained glass. We then walked down through the old city to Charles Bridge, which was exactly my idea of what a medieval bridge should look like. On the horizon to the left stood a colossal monument to Stalin. "I don't know what they will do with it now," said my guide. "It was criticized even during Stalin's lifetime. The designer committed suicide."

I had come to Prague in the hope that the government would sponsor one of our seminars. But, although I was received by one of the deputy ministers at the foreign office, with whom I had a pleasant conversation—he seemed glad to talk about the United Nations—nothing came of my suggestion.

My business in Prague now completed, I moved on to Bucharest, which was quite a different kind of place from Prague—and the Romanians very different from the Czechs. Prague may have been drab and grey (and the fact that I was there in March made it seem more so) but it was an old European city with a strong gothic accent. Bucharest looked new and relatively poor in historic monuments. Many new buildings were going up, including gaily colored apartment houses, which were a relief after some of the utilitarian architecture I had seen in Prague. I soon realized that Romania is a potentially rich country, even though the standard of living was still very low, particularly outside of Bucharest. Several weeks later, in an airplane over the Pacific on my way to the Far East, I found myself sitting next to a young man from the United States state department who was on his way to a posting in Hong Kong. I said something about what I had seen in Romania and the rapid economic development of the country. He turned to me in surprise. "But," he said, "how can that be possible if there is no profit motive?" He must have thought I was a communist.

My business with the government was quickly dispatched. They were taking the forthcoming seminar on the status of women very seriously, and the arrangements being made for it were, as far as I could gather, excellent. Partly I suppose because so few U.N. officials had up until that time visited Romania, my hosts wanted to make a good impression and were anxious that I should see something of Bucharest and the surrounding country. I visited factories, a hospital, a movie studio and the famous geriatrics institute, the director of which offered to give me one of the injections which, if I were to believe the photographs of old men who had had it, would make me young again, but remembering Balsac's *Peau de Chagrin*, I resisted the temptation.

On the weekend my hosts took me to Orasul Stalin in Transylvania, ostensibly to see the Black Church, so called because its walls had been blackened by fire. We stopped at Sinaia for lunch and a visit to Ferdinand's Castle, a Hohenzollern horror that must have cost the Romanian people the equivalent of a steel mill. My sympathy for the Revolution grew as I went through its pretentious halls. If Ferdinand could see Sinaia now, he would groan in his grave. His castle is a museum, the casino a health resort and rest house for workers, and a smaller palace a resort for writers and artists. "They come here to rest and, who knows, perhaps to create," said my guide. I looked around but could see no writers, let alone anyone in the process of creating. The thing was probably a phony. For how could anyone create anything in such surroundings? The casino-become-workers-holiday-resort was at least real, but I have seldom seen a more pathetic place. The now shabby ballroom and roulette rooms were filled with unhappy, bored-looking workers, some of whom were wearing hats and overcoats—it was so cold. Now the masters of the state, they had come to enjoy the privileges of their former betters. A few of them were playing cards or checkers, but otherwise there seemed to be nothing for them to do, and they sat there looking miserable. There was certainly no roulette or any of the other pleasures of the idle rich. They would have been infinitely happier on Coney Island.

My guide took me to the Black Church, as planned. It was Sunday, and the Protestant service was about to begin as we sat down in one of the pews. About twenty worshippers were already there and others were coming into the church. They looked hard and determined. As we left the church before the end of the service, I spied a little man dressed in black chasing two small boys who had been playing on the church steps. We could have been in Switzerland. I then asked to see an Orthodox church, but my guide apparently didn't know the difference and took me to a church that turned out to be Roman Catholic. The next was also Roman Catholic, but finally I found what I was looking for. The church was so crowded that it was difficult to squeeze into it. I moved towards the left, not knowing that only women stand on that side. Seeing only women around me seemed to confirm what I had so often heard, that only women and old men had kept their faith in communist countries. But, glancing to the right, I saw that half the church was filled with men of all ages. I moved to my proper place with them and began to listen to the service; I also watched the faces of the people. The beautiful chant of the Eastern rite filled the church. It was a religious experience of real beauty and it had happened in a communist country.

Coming out of the church I noticed some half-dozen beggars near the entrance.

"I didn't expect to see this in Romania," I said to my guide.

"They are gypsies."

"But I thought that everyone had to work in this country."

"They are artists," he replied. "They are tolerated."

My visit to Romania ended, I flew to Paris and after one night there sailed, on 31 March, from Cherbourg to New York. I was back at headquarters in time for the opening of the spring session of the Economic and Social Council. Over the objections of the communist and some other delegations that it would hamper work on the convention, it adopted the draft of the Declaration on Freedom of Information, which it sent to the General Assembly. The Commission on the Status of Women was meeting in Buenos Aires. I regretted not being able to attend, particularly since the Argentine ambassador later complained about the abrasive manner in which the representative of the Secretary-General conducted herself at the meetings. My schedule was very tight. I had only three weeks at headquarters before going to Tokyo for the seminar on the protection of human rights in criminal law.

Flying to Tokyo I broke my journey for a day's rest and some sun in Honolulu. Even in 1960 the city was an overdeveloped monstrosity, but it was a good place to break a long and tiring trip.

The Tokyo seminar was held in the Shinagawa Prince Hotel, far from the center of the city, where all the participants were lodged. It opened on 10 May, but before that there was a meeting of experts to prepare the agenda for a seminar that was to be held the next year in New Zealand.

I already knew something about Japanese hospitality. This time there were a number of exquisite dinner parties. At one of them in a Buddhist restaurant I counted sixteen dishes, but the only thing that I could identify with any certainty was the strawberries at the end of the meal. The minister of justice gave a reception at which there was some very fine Kabuki dancing. There were several excursions, including one to Nikko, where I had already been. The other was a weekend in a resort high in the mountains from which there was a particularly fine view of Fujiyama. Everyone else put up at the slick modern hotel, but my colleague John Male and I chose a traditional inn. Arriving there, the first thing we did was to change our Western clothes for light kimonos and, after a cup of tea, proceed down one of the corridors towards the bathhouse, not without some qualms because I knew that in Japan men and women bathed together, and I wasn't too sure how I would react in such a situation. I need not have worried; mixed bathing is apparently a privilege from which foreigners are excluded, and we had the bathhouse to ourselves. Nothing could have been less like the utilitarian Western facility. The pool was partly hewed from native rock into which warm water bubbled up from a spring. But we were not meant to wash in this, for on a kind of wooden platform were two pails of warm water and some soap. The clear fresh water in the pool was not meant to be polluted. We washed ourselves carefully and slipped into the pool. There are very few more refreshing or civilized experiences.

Another adventure came when a Japanese acquaintance invited Richard Wild, Jonathan Robson (respectively the solicitor general and secretary of justice of New Zealand) and me for a traditional Japanese dinner. After the dinner, saying that now that we had seen something of traditional Japan he wanted us to see something modern, he drove us to the center of the city and, after some difficulty (he had obviously never been there before) found the place he was looking for. We first entered a large room on the ground floor which was filled with prosperous-looking men in Western dress and as many women in kimonos. But we were quickly ushered out of this room and directed to another on a higher floor where there were, I suppose, about a dozen men, some of them foreigners, and a score of beautiful girls scantily dressed in Western fashion. We sat down at a table, after which a bottle of champagne was produced, and some of the girls joined us. It wasn't until the madam came up to me, however, and whispered in my ear, ''Wouldn't you like to retire now?'' that I realized that we were in a high-class brothel. We passed it off as if we had not understood, finished the champagne, thanked our host and did retire—but to the Shinagawa Prince Hotel.

The seminar ended on 24 May and I returned to New York for only a fortnight before I had to go to Vienna for the seminar on the protection of human rights by criminal procedure. One of the first things I did after getting there was to have dinner with Stephen Verosta, a well-known international lawyer who had been brought from his diplomatic post in Poland to chair the seminar. He made an excellent presiding officer, partly because he had a sense of humor.

I opened the seminar on 20 June and introduced the foreign minister, but I hardly heard his speech because I was worried by a rumor that the Russians (who were attending a human rights seminar for the first time) would make an issue of the absence of participants from the Democratic Republic of Germany which, not being a member of the United Nations, had not been invited to send any. The Russian participant was Lev Smirnov, a vice-president of the supreme court, whom I remember as a bon vivant. He opened the discussion on fact-finding and evidence. We also had participants from Byelorussia and the Ukraine. I had never seen the Russians more relaxed at a United Nations conference. They provided some very good fun—my colleague Tchernov acting as interpreter—at a reception I gave for the participants.

On the Saturday before the adjournment, the foreign office took us to Ypps-Persenberg to inspect a hydroelectric dam and to Melk to see the monastery and a fine collection of baroque art. For part of the time we drove along the Danube which, as I had already discovered in 1959, isn't blue; much of it looked like a canal. We stopped at Durnstein for supper and generous quantities of good green wine. The party became more and more joyful; songs were sung and the Deputy Procurator of the Ukrainian S.S.R. did a folk dance. But when the time came to return to Vienna, we discovered that one of our party, a young Austrian foreign service officer, was missing. We organized a search party down through the vineyard and found him asleep under a tree. I had the authorities promise that there would be no sanctions.

The seminar ended on 4 July. Like other seminars on criminal law and procedure it had dealt with a whole series of problems that were fundamental to any discussion of human rights and freedoms; for the criminal law not only defines the limits of permissible conduct, but also protects the rights of society and individuals. I was surprised to learn that in many European countries it was still possible to detain accused persons for long periods of time incommunicado without trial. We did not encourage the seminars to adopt resolutions for the simple reason that we did not want the participants to become wedded to rigid positions or to become bogged down in procedural debate, but in this case the violation of basic human rights seemed so serious that exceptionally the seminar did adopt a resolution by which it recommended that the Human Rights Commission undertake a study of the right of detained persons to consult counsel and friends, something the commission later did.

After Vienna, I went to Geneva for the summer session of ECOSOC. Narasimhan, who was there for a weekend, told me that the Secretary-General was annoyed about "members of the Human Rights Division travelling all over the world;" but he went on to say that he himself thought what we were doing was useful. He would, he said, seize the first opportunity to put Hammarskjold straight, but he wouldn't lecture him "because that put his back up and made him worse." A few years later Narasimhan would himself be taxing me with spending too much time on the seminars. I knew I was making myself vulnerable to easy criticism, but I had decided to take that risk because I knew there was a great deal of support for this program. Only two days after my talk with Narasimhan, the representative of New Zealand said in the Social Committee that the seminars were the most successful—singularly successful, she said—single factor in the whole current human rights program of the United Nations, and in 1960 this was probably true. The truth was (and this was something that Sir Humphrey Trevelyan had understood) that in those years there wasn't very much the Secretariat could do to further the human rights program apart from preparing "studies" and organizing seminars. Pending decisions to be taken by governments on the draft covenants and measures for their implementation, one of the most constructive things we could do was to help create the kind of climate of opinion which would further the objectives of the Charter. The seminars helped keep the human rights flag flying and were one of the best devices yet used to publicize the objectives of the United Nations in member countries, one proof of which was that the technique was soon copied in other parts of the organization.

The level of representation in the Council's Social Committee compared unfavorably with what I had just witnessed in Vienna. Apart from Sir Samuel Hoare and Pierre Juvigny, who had first-class minds and had done their homework, the delegates were an uninspiring lot. Most governments sent relatively junior or inexperienced people to represent them in this committee and the Third Committee of the General Assembly, but they usually sent their best people to the seminars. This was not only because the subjects discussed at the seminars required a degree of legal expertise and experience not possessed by most diplomats but because practicing lawyers didn't have too many opportunities to participate in the work of the United Nations and attending one of the seminars was a privilege sought after in the profession.

The Social Committee soon reached its normal level of discussion; a hotly debated question was whether the word "stimulate" should be used in drafting a resolution rather than "encourage." They finally decided on "favor." Some of the delegates were very clever in this kind of debate, but it wasn't very profitable. I noticed that weak delegates usually tried to speak at the beginning of a debate when a prepared statement could be read without the risk of repeating remarks that had already been made by other delegates and it would not be necessary to deal with difficult points raised in the debate.

I returned to headquarters at the beginning of August but left with my wife after a few days, on annual leave to Prince Edward Island. We were back in New York at the end of the month. On 10 September, Hammarskjold made a speech in the Security Council in which he referred to "flagrant violations of human rights" in the Congo. This was the first and last time that, to my knowledge, he ever showed any concern about human rights. The fifteenth session of the General Assembly opened on the twentieth. It was the session at which Nikita Khrushchev put on his great show. I very seldom went into the plenary sessions unless I had business there, but on the morning of 3 October I sat in the gallery and listened to Khrushchev, King Hussein and Nehru. Khrushchev's speech was one of several in which he attacked the Secretary-General, describing him as an agent of the imperialist countries and calling for his resignation. In the afternoon, Hammarskjold took the floor and made an impassioned reply. He would not resign, he said, because if he did the Soviet Union would insist on arrangements for the succession—the troika—which would make it impossible for the United Nations to maintain an effective executive. "By resigning, I would, therefore, at the present difficult and dangerous juncture, throw the Organization to the winds."

The storm in plenary hardly troubled the relatively calm waters of the Third Committee. By 1960, the committee had already approved the preamble and the first article (on the right to self-determination) of both covenants, all the substantive articles of the Covenant on Economic, Social and Cultural Rights, and Articles 6 to 14 of the Covenant on Civil and Political Rights. It now approved four articles of the latter instrument: on the retroactive application of criminal law, the right of everyone to be recognized as a person before the law, the privacy of family, home and correspondence and on freedom of thought, conscience and religion. It also approved Article 2 of the draft convention on freedom of information, but it did not even discuss the proposed declaration on the same subject or the draft declaration on asylum, which had come up to it from ECOSOC.

The General Assembly adjourned on 20 December, but a full month before that I was in Paris representing the Secretary-General at the UNESCO General Conference, the conference at which the Convention on Discrimination in Education was adopted. From there I went to Addis Ababa and the seminar on the participation of women in public life, which began on 12 December.

In the speech with which I opened the Ethiopian seminar I returned to a theme I often used at headquarters when I had to defend the Commission on the Status of Women. There is no better way to raise standards in a country than to improve the status and condition of its women, and the condition of its women is as good a test as any of the standards reached by its whole people and its place in the community of nations. The Haile Selassie Theater, a great mausoleum-like edifice in the centre of Addis Ababa, was packed for the seminar; it was the largest conference that we had yet had under the program, some thirty-two African countries being represented, mainly by women. They were a colorful sight in their national costumes. The princess royal gave a garden party in the afternoon; and the next evening I had dinner in the home of the chairman, Neizero Senedu Gebru.

Walking from the Ghion Hotel to the theater the next morning, I saw tanks patrolling the streets; and when I got there the place was buzzing with talk about an insurrection. Insurgents were indeed in control of Addis, but there were loyalist troops just outside the city. What would happen if, as seemed likely, the two armies came to blows? When I complained that nothing was being done to protect the many foreigners who were attending the conference, the vice-minister of foreign affairs assured me that there was no danger; the loyalists would, he said, soon join the revolution: "they don't want to be killed." Anything but reassured, I returned to my hotel for lunch and, although it was a fair distance, was planning to walk back to the theater. The city seemed quiet, but I had gone hardly a hundred yards when I was surprised by an outburst of gunfire, some of the bullets coming so near to me that I could hear them whistle. I hastened back to the Ghion Hotel, where I was marooned for the next twenty-four hours in a kind of no-man's land between the Jubilee Palace just behind the Ghion, which had been occupied by the rebels, and the loyalist troops not far away behind some hills. The fighting kept up all that afternoon, through the night and the next morning; but fortunately for us in our exposed position both sides were using light weapons. Later as the loyalists began to advance they used heavier hardware including bazookas and light artillery. The hotel must have been hit hundreds of times but there was no serious damage within the walls. When night came, the sky was lit up by tracer bullets. Some rebel soldiers set up a machine-gun nest just under my bedroom windows; and when they opened fire there would be an answering spattering of bullets on the wall outside; but none of them penetrated my room, although after it was all over I saw bullet holes within inches of my windows. In spite of the racket I actually slept soundly for part of the night—a result, I suppose, of nervous exhaustion. The next morning there was an artillery bombardment and some bombing, but we didn't seem to be a target. We thought it better, however, to retire to the hotel basement, where we were even served lunch. The artillery bombardment proved to be the prelude to a loyalist attack and, shortly after we had finished lunch, the hotel was surrounded by loyalist troops. By this time we had returned to the lobby; and one of our number, who was an employee of the Ethiopian Airlines and spoke Arabic, went out to parley with the commanding officer. The gist of the exchange was later retailed to me:

The commanding officer: "There are rebel sympathizers in this hotel and I have orders to demolish it."

Airlines employee: "I am so and so. My brother is an officer with the loyalist troops and most of these people are from the United Nations."

The commander, who was apparently only half convinced, ordered us all out of the hotel with our hands in the air above our heads and lined us up in the garden. The hotel was then searched for rebels. None were found and I would not have liked to be in their shoes had there been any. All kinds of atrocities were committed by both sides. At the beginning of the insurrection, the rebels herded a dozen or more cabinet ministers into a room and mowed them down with a machine gun. Only one escaped, the husband of the princess royal to whom I had talked at his wife's garden party.

The rebellion was just about over, although shooting could still be heard far off in the hills. I watched some airplanes dropping propaganda leaflets and picked up some that fell in the hotel garden. The rebels had made two very bad mistakes. They had failed to secure the cooperation of the Air Force, the final appearance of which in the skies over Addis signalled their defeat. And by allowing at least one loyalist general to escape at the beginning of the rebellion they had given the loyalists the leadership they needed.

It was now possible for me to renew contact with the other members of the Secretariat and the seminar participants who were at the Ras Hotel in the center of the city near the theater. They had also had a harrowing experience; for, while their hotel was not so exposed to gunfire as mine, it was in the thick of some bad street fighting. Some of them had been caught in the theater when the fighting began. Miss Fenwick, an Australian member of my division, led them to the relative safety of their hotel. She also commandeered a jeep to take a wounded man to a hospital. I commended her bravery in my report to the Secretary-General. Everyone indeed—Secretariat and participants—behaved very well throughout the crisis except the Egyptians, who drank to the success of the insurrection. I learned indirectly from the surgeon general of the Army that some two thousand people had been killed in the rebellion, including an Ethiopian member of the Secretariat of the United Nations Economic Commission for Africa (which had its headquarters in Addis). I had been given an office in their building but had had no reason to use it. Visiting it after the fighting I saw a great hole in the ceiling above my desk, and the office was filled with debris. Through the good offices of the British embassy, which had its own radio station, I was able to report to New York headquarters that none of the participants had been hurt and that we intended to carry on with the seminar.

Apart from an occasional shot—marking perhaps the end of some unfortunate rebel— the city was now quiet, but I was to have one more bad scare, so bad that I thought that my heart would burst. I had returned to the Ghion Hotel and was sitting down for my evening meal when there was a sudden outburst of gunfire. We did not seem to be the target but the hotel was hit several times and one bullet broke a window in the dining room. Were the rebels returning from the hills? I thought we were in for it, but the firing stopped after about five minutes. It was only later, in Nigeria, that I learned what had happened, when the Ethiopian ambassador (next to whom I was sitting at a dinner party) explained that, after the failure of the rebellion, many of the rebel soldiers, who were still in uniform, had taken refuge in the numerous gulleys in and around Addis Ababa. If these men were to be saved they had to be given an opportunity to return to their homes. The sudden outburst of gunfire was a diversion ordered by the rebel chief for that purpose.

Haile Selassie—whose absence in Brazil had provided the occasion for the insurrection—returned to his capital. From a distance, I watched a procession accompanying his motor car, including a number of white-robed women who were making a weird noise, like a kind of strange yodelling which was produced by an action of their hands against their lips. The emperor gave a splendid reception for us in the Jubilee Palace, where I talked with him. Perfectly calm, he showed no sign of having been upset by the challenge to his throne. I also talked to the crown prince, whom the rebels had set up as their puppet (I had heard his statement over the radio) but who had now been forgiven.

On Christmas Day I left Addis Ababa for Lagos, Nigeria, where I was to represent the Secretary-General at a conference of the International Commission of Jurists. Lagos was on the other side of Africa but to get there I had either first to return to Rome or travel by way of Johannesburg. Since I had over a week before the conference would begin and wanted to see as much of Africa as possible, I opted for the latter route, flying first to Nairobi. Kenya is one of the most beautiful countries in the world and has one of the finest climates. Little wonder that the British colonists did not want to give up their farms. I was fascinated by the great wild-animal park on the outskirts of Nairobi and visited it twice. One of the finest sights I have ever seen was a pride of lions we stopped to watch. The cubs had been isolated on one side of our car, but two or three growls were enough to bring them hurrying to their parents. The animals seemed quite unconcerned by the presence of a motor car; but we had to keep the windows closed to prevent the baboons from reaching in. And what a place for a bird-watcher!

I also visited the Mau Mau country. It happened that the chief of the section on the status of women was also in Nairobi, and a Catholic nun (who had been an observer at the Addis conference) had invited her to visit her convent. They asked me to come along. I remember seeing the long neck of a giraffe above the foliage on the beautiful drive to the convent. Zebras were more common; there were so many along the road to the airport that the taxi driver had to take care not to hit one. I was given a great welcome when we arrived at the convent. Two of the half-dozen nuns were French-speaking Canadians, one of whom took us after lunch to visit a neighboring village. This was in the very heart of the Mau Mau country and I would not have been welcomed there had it not been for the auspices under which I came. As it was we were welcomed into the huts, and some of the women even changed into their best clothes so that we could take pictures, but I had already used up my film on the drive from Nairobi.

In Johannesburg, where I spent two or three days, everything of interest seemed to be closed, perhaps because it was in the week between Christmas and New Year. Nor did I attempt to see anyone. I hadn't consulted the Secretary-General about my travel plans and I didn't want the newspapers inventing some sensational story about the director of the Human Rights Division visiting a country which the United Nations had condemned for violating the most basic principles of the Universal Declaration of Human Rights. It may have been a mistake for me to go there; but as far as I know my visit went unnoticed, notwithstanding the fact that my identity clearly appeared on my passport. If the police followed my movements they must have had a dull time. As always in a strange city, I walked a good deal and even made one uninteresting excursion into the suburbs. I did see some of the signs of racial segregation: separate buses for blacks and whites, and in the parks separate benches, of which there didn't seem to be too many. But I had already seen that kind of thing in the United States. The thing that impressed me most was the expressions on the faces of the people, white and black. It may have been a coincidence, but I didn't see anyone smile all the time I was in Johannesburg.

I flew up the west coast to Accra. The plane came down for an hour at Leopoldville, which was the nearest I ever got to the United Nations operation in the Congo. In Accra, I visited my friends Wilfred and Tressa Benson. Wilfred was now the resident representative of the U.N. technical assistance board in Ghana. He drove me on New Year's Day to the home of the controversial Englishman, Geoffrey Bing, who was Nkrumah's attorney general, with whom he left me alone for two hours. Bing must have felt himself under some kind of impulsion to defend the record of the Nkruman government and his part in it. He paced the room, waving a glass of champagne, while he expounded on the necessities for and the virtues of the preventive detention laws under which many of Nkrumah's political enemies were then languishing in prison. I don't remember that I had an opportunity to say very much myself. That night the Bensons gave a big party. I had planned to fly to Lagos the next morning, but it happened that two English professors who were at the party were driving to Lagos also to attend the conference and they invited me to come with them. We left early in the morning because we wanted to be in Lagos before dark. When we reached the Togolese border I discovered that neither of my companions had a passport, something that would have been serious enough at any time; but the fact that, because of some dispute between the two countries, the border between Ghana and Togo was closed made it much worse. A large number of people were waiting patiently at the barrier, most of whom belonged to the same tribe as the people in the country they were trying to enter. They politely made way for us, but, although I myself had both a Canadian diplomatic passport and a U.N. laisser-passer, we were of course challenged by the immigration officers. To my great surprise we were then sent to the French embassy in Lomé, where our difficulties were quickly ironed out. The incident was not without significance. Officially Togo was an independent country, but it was the French ambassador who made the decision. We had no difficulty at the Dahomey border; and, by the time we reached Nigeria it was so late that the border post was closed and we crossed over without challenge. Apart from some stretches of the road through Dahomey, where I especially remember one beautiful lake in the still waters of which a man was fishing from a dug-out not far from some huts nestled on stilts, the drive along the flat coast was not as interesting as I had expected. I had seen places in the West Indies more like what I had imagined Africa would be like.

There were lawyers at the conference from all over the world, many of whom I met, including Gerald Gardiner (later Lord Gardiner)—the British barrister who had just successfully defended the right of Penguin Books to publish *Lady Chatterley's Lover*. After my retirement from the United Nations, I became a member of the International Commission of Jurists myself and am now one of its vice-presidents; but at the Lagos conference I was only an observer. The commission has consultative status with the United Nations and is one of the most influential international nongovernmental organizations dedicated to the promotion of human rights and respect for the rule of law. One of the questions canvassed at Lagos was whether the African countries should be encouraged to create a regional human rights commission like the European Commission. I favored this, but I did not subscribe to the view so often expressed that a regional approach to the international protection of human rights is more likely to succeed than the universal approach in the United Nations. If the experiment has worked so well in Western Europe it is chiefly because this is a relatively cohesive community with shared traditions in the process of economic and political integration.

Lagos was lively and colorful and, in 1960, full of hope for the future but (outside the air-conditioned hotel) hot and humid, the hottest place, I think, I have ever been in. I had, moreover, had quite enough adventure for one month and after less than a week in Nigeria was glad to board a plane for London and on to New York.

Australia, New Zealand, Romania and Mexico (1961)

I was back in New York in time for the thirteenth session of the Sub-Commission on the Prevention of Discrimination and the Protection of Minorities. It had been doing useful if unexciting work ever since it began its series of studies on various aspects of discrimination, one of which, Charles Ammoun's study of discrimination in education, had just borne fruit in the form of a UNESCO convention. The main item on the 1961 agenda was Santa Cruz's draft report on discrimination in the enjoyment of political rights. The bulky document analyzed information contained in fifty-four country monographs and then went on to draw conclusions and make tentative proposals. It was discussed in detail, chapter by chapter; and the rapporteur was asked to complete his report in time for the next session. The next study in the series would be on the right of everyone to leave any country, including his own, and to return to his country. Judge Ingles, the rapporteur (who was also the chairman of this session of the sub-commission) made a progress report. According to the rhythm that had now become routine, a draft report would be ready for 1962.

The sub-commission was now concentrating on the first part of its mandate, which was the prevention of discrimination, having decided (in the light of the negative attitude of governments as revealed by decisions of the Human Rights Commission) to take no further steps in the protection of minorities, the second part of the mandate, until so directed by the commission. In 1959, however, the Secretariat had circulated a note on the activities of the United Nations relating to minorities, and this was still on the agenda. It was in this connection that the Austrian ambassador, Franz Matsch (who had been elected to the sub-commission in 1960) moved that the Secretariat be instructed to prepare for consideration at the next session a compilation and analysis of the texts of all contemporary international treaties which provide special protective measures for ethnic, religious or linguistic groups. Although not expressed in debate, the motivating factor here was Austrian interest in the fate of the German-speaking minority in the Italian Tyrol. The motion was adopted by a vote of seven in favor and five abstentions. Austria was also a member of the Human Rights Commission, at the next session of which its representative tried to have the sub-commission asked to evaluate the principles contained in the treaties; but the commission, always suspicious when the question of minorities was raised and particularly so when a specific issue was involved, took no action. A year later, an Italian, Professor Francesco Capotorti, was elected to the sub-commission so that both countries in cause now had their man on the spot. Ambassador Matsch would return to the matter, but all he was ever able to achieve was an instruction to the Secretariat to publish the 1959 note. The incident illustrates both how difficult it sometimes is to bring a specific case before the United Nations and also how undeclared political motives may influence a procedural debate.

I had to leave headquarters before the end of the session on another long mission. This time it was to New Zealand and Australia, and I took my wife with me. The government of New Zealand was hosting a seminar in Wellington on the protection of human rights in the administration of criminal justice. I also wanted to talk to people in Canberra about a seminar on the role of the police. After a day in Vancouver and one in Honolulu, we flew on to Australia. In Sydney we looked up my old colleague Mary Tenison-Woods (at one time the chief of the section on the status of women) and Harold Snelling, the solicitor-general of New South Wales, who had been at the Tokyo seminar. It was very hot. The day Jeanne and I visited the famous zoo, I thought she would have a heat stroke. She decided not to undertake the trip to Canberra.

For a Canadian there is nothing exotic about Canberra, and it lacked the life of Sydney; built up out of nothing it might just as well have been a town in the Canadian West; even the trees had been imported. On my next visit I would get out into the bush country, admire some of the famous gum trees and even do some bird-watching; but this was a quick visit and I didn't get outside the city. I spent most of my time with Sir Kenneth Bailey, the solicitor-general of the commonwealth, and Ralph Harry who had represented Australia on the Human Rights Commission. When I left the capital I was reasonably sure that there would be a seminar on the role of the police in the promotion of human rights and that it would be in Canberra. My hosts wanted me to see Chief Justice Sir Owen Dixon, in Melbourne, where I therefore went next. I was happy to meet this distinguished Australian, but he wasn't particularly interested in the proposed seminar and we talked about the United Nations and his experience as U.N. mediator in Kashmir.

It was frustrating to have to leave Australia after such a short visit, but I consoled myself with the thought that I would probably be returning for the seminar. We flew on to Auckland, where we very nearly missed our plane for Wellington, the departure of which was announced while we were going through customs. I protested loudly; if we didn't make the plane some very highly placed officials would be disappointed. This worked, the plane was stopped on the runway and we were able to take our seats. Dick Wild, the solicitor-general, his wife and some other people were waiting for us at the Wellington airport. We were also welcomed by a high wind that nearly blew the plane off the tarmac. Later in Wild's house, where we were taken for a late supper, Wild confided that he had been worried whether we would be able to land, and he went on the describe the gales for which Cook Strait is famous. Because we were so obviously very tired our hosts allowed us to retire early to the Waterloo Hotel, where we put up for the next fortnight and where most of the participants at the conference were also staying. The hotel was on a busy street overlooking the harbor. Its chief drawback was that, like everything else in New Zealand, it seemed to be completely under the control of the trade unions, and it was quite impossible to get anything to eat there after seven o'clock in the evening, a real problem because our meetings often adjourned late and there was usually work to be done after that. It was solved by our being allowed to eat in a clubroom by I know not what violation of trade-union rights.

The seminar was held in the legislative council chamber and opened by the prime minister. Wild was the chairman, one of the best I have ever worked with. The prime minister invited me to go with him to the Bay of Islands on the north coast for a ceremony commemorating the signing of the Treaty of Waitangi, under which the British crown assumed sovereignty over the country in 1841. I was sorely tempted to accept, but it would have meant an absence of three days from Wellington and I didn't think that this would be appropriate. The New Zealand government took the conference very seriously, partly I suppose because it had brought so many distinguished Asians to the country, which was also probably the reason for the elaborate hospitality. On the first weekend we were taken on a trip to Hamilton and to see the thermal phenomena in the Rotorua district, which is also a Maori center. Our hosts were anxious to show us something of Maori life; but, back in Wellington, a government official told me that integration wasn't working too well under the stresses of urban conditions.

The conference ended on 20 February. In his closing speech the minister of justice had high praise for the seminars which, he said, were not occasions for the exchange of easy platitudes; the New Zealand experience was that they had real, practical benefits for the participating countries. His government was introducing legislation to create an office of ombudsman (the first such office in an English-speaking country), which was an institution that had been discussed by the United Nations seminar in Ceylon, and there could be little doubt, he said, that the legislation setting it up in New Zealand was a result of what participants had learned at Kandy. The minister then went on to say that his government had undertaken a review of the work of administrative tribunals, which was another subject that had been discussed in Kandy, and was giving further consideration to capital punishment, which had been discussed in Tokyo. I wished that some of my critics back at United Nations Headquarters could have heard the minister's speech.

On our way back over the Pacific, we spent three days in Fiji.

The seventeenth session of the Human Rights Commission had already begun by the time we reached New York. There was some discussion of the report of its committee on the right of everyone to be free from arbitrary arrest, detention and exile, which was instructed to finish its study in time for the next session and also to undertake, as suggested by the Vienna seminar, a separate study on the right of arrested persons to communicate with anyone they needed to consult in order to ensure their defense and protect their essential interests. Some fifty-nine governments having reported under the resolution by which ECOSOC had asked states to report on developments and progress achieved in the matter of human rights, the commission decided to appoint a committee of six of its members to examine the summaries of these reports that had been prepared by the Secretariat—an examination that was unlikely to have significant results, however, because the members of the committee would not be independent experts but representatives of governments. Other matters discussed were the advisory services program, the prevention of discrimination and freedom of information. The session ended on 17 March. In the meantime, on 13 March, the fifteenth session of the Commission on the Status of Women had begun in Geneva. I did not attend, but I did go to the seminar on the status of women in family law which met in Bucharest from 19 June to 3 July.

The Romanian seminar was the first to be held in a communist country, and I was especially pleased that the government had agreed to sponsor it. The Americans did not want us to have any seminars in these countries, and even Sir Humphrey Trevelyan had agreed with them. But to turn down the invitation would have been discriminatory. It seemed to make good sense, moreover, to have as many of the seminars as possible in communist countries. In my philosophy one of the chief purposes of the program was to carry the human rights flag into as many places as possible, especially countries with authoritarian regimes where the United Nations presence was weak. Romania had only recently become a member of the organization and the seminar on the status of women was the first conference to be held there under its auspices. It attracted participants from twenty-three countries and observers from sixteen nongovernmental organizations. The discussions, which were good, ranged over a wide field including marriage and its dissolution, the rights and duties of parents, the status of unmarried women and the law of inheritance. There was only one sour note. The foreign office official who saw me off at the airport complained about one of my officers: "Never bring her on a mission to a socialist country again," he said.

Walking one evening with my sister, who had interrupted a European holiday to be with me in Bucharest, I slipped at a curb (we were talking about some paintings the late Emily Carr had given her and I wasn't looking where I was going) and turned my left foot. I limped back to our hotel and, the pain being so bad, called the diplomatic clinic which sent around a couple of nurses. "Only a sprain," they said, and bound up my foot. The next morning a doctor diagnosed a compound fracture. This confined me to my room for several days, during which the minister for foreign affairs came to see me. As he was leaving he said that he didn't think that I had been given a good enough room; and, over my objection—my room was a very good one with large windows overlooking a square —he insisted on having me moved into a suite which, among other things, contained a very fine radio set. He also left a large case containing a bottle of, I think, every kind of wine and brandy produced in Romania. The wine and brandy are gone, but I still have a very fine icon that I had been admiring in a second hand shop the day before my fall and which Mircea Malitza gave me. I had struck up a friendship with Malitza when he first came to the United Nations representing Romania in a relatively junior capacity. He was now high up in the establishment and would soon be a minister. A mathematician by training, he was a man of considerable intellectual attainment and wide culture. He once told me that if he had his way he would be a teacher.

At the diplomatic clinic my doctor did a fine job of setting the broken bones; I have never had any trouble with the foot, although I had it in a cast for the rest of the summer. In my closing speech to the seminar, I said that if anyone were silly enough to break a foot, the place to do it was Romania. The accident prevented me from going on a weekend excursion to the Carpathians; but my sister and I joined the excursion to the Black Sea resort of Mamaia the next Saturday, amusing ourselves on our way bird-watching from the train window. Perched on the telegraph wires were such exotic specimens as rollers, kingfishers and, I am fairly sure, bee-eaters. The delta of the Danube, is, of course, one of the finest places in the world for birds. We toured Constanta before driving on to Mamaia, where we were put up in a comfortable hotel full of Scandinavian tourists. Returning to Bucharest the next day, I was amused to see a first-class waiting room at the station. Romania may be an egalitarian country, but the principle did not extend to foreign tourists. Nor did it apply to all Romanians. I had lunch one day with a deputy minister whose son was finishing his studies. He had had an education that was well beyond the reach of most of his compatriots and several government agencies were already bidding for his services.

The summer session of the Economic and Social Council opened in Geneva the day after the adjournment of the seminar. Freedom of information was again on the agenda. In 1959, the Council had asked for a report on developments since 1954; and I had asked my old colleague, Hilding Eek, who was now a professor of international law in the University of Stockholm, to prepare the report which was now before the Council. One of Eek's conclusions questioned the feasibility of proceeding further with the proposed convention on freedom of information (the original draft of which had been adopted by the information conference over thirteen years earlier); and because of this, three countries, including the Soviet Union and Poland, abstained when it was moved that the report be sent to governments. There could have been no better proof of the bankruptcy of freedom of information in the United Nations than the fact that it was the countries that were not practicing it that were now the principal advocates of the convention. It was at this session that the Council recommended that the General Assembly adopt a convention on consent to marriage, minimum age of marriage and registration of marriages, a draft text of which had been approved by the Commission on the Status of Women at its last session. The Council also increased the membership of the Human Rights Commission from eighteen to twenty-one. In 1966 the membership was again increased to thirty-two. The "equitable" distribution of seats then established, which guarantees that the developing countries will have a comfortable majority (twenty out of the thirty-two seats), is not the least of the reasons for the radical changes that have taken place in the performance of the commission since 1966. The membership has again increased to 42, with, however, the same imbalance in the distribution of seats.

My duties at the Council over, I returned to headquarters but was away again in less than a fortnight for Mexico and the seminar on *amparo* and *habeas corpus*. My colleague, John Male, who would be the secretary of the seminar, was at the airport to meet me on my arrival in Mexico City. He had done his usual efficient job with the arrangement but, from what he told me, I gathered that the Mexican government was not being overcooperative. The seminar lasted from 15 to 28 August. It wasn't as good as I had hoped, which was annoying because the American participant was the U.S. Deputy Attorney General, Nicholas Katzenbach, whom I wanted to return to Washington with a good impression. The agenda was pertinent enough to the protection of human rights. The English remedy of *habeas corpus*, by which the legality of detention can be tested, has spread all over the world. *Amparo* is a Spanish institution that also protects physical freedom, but it can also be used to protect other human rights and, in some countries, even to challenge the constitutional validity of the law. It was useful to compare the two institutions and appropriate, as I pointed out in my opening remarks, that this should be done in Mexico, where *amparo* has had an especially interesting development.

The seminar was held in the Hotel del Prado, where most of the participants and secretariat also lived. After a few days most of them were ill with the endemic Mexican intestinal complaint. I went to the regional office of the World Health Organization and returned to the hotel with a flight bag filled with antibiotics, which I distributed at the next meeting. The remedy seemed to work.

We always had to count on the possibility that a United Nations seminar on human rights could become an occasion for manifestations aimed at the host government, and this is what happened in Mexico when leftist militants protested in the streets against the incarceration of the painter, David Alfaro Siqueros. This agitation, or the fear of it, may have been the reason the government tended to play down the seminar and there was so little official entertainment, a relief which made it possible for me to visit again many of the show places my wife and I had seen when we were in Mexico for several weeks back in 1940, including the pyramids at San Juan Teotihuacan. On one Sunday, however, we were all taken to the ranch of one of the Mexican participants to eat turtle and drink tequila. The turtle was unappetizing, but thanks perhaps to the tequila, we ate it with no bad results.

Back in New York the first thing I did was to get a doctor to take the cast off my foot, but I continued for several weeks to use the cane that my Romanian doctor had given me. It had been such a busy summer that the nearest thing I had to a holiday was one long weekend at Hampton Beach on Long Island. On our return to Manhattan we learned that Hammarskjold had been killed in an airplane crash on his way from Leopoldville to Northern Rhodesia. The last time I had talked to him had been when he was passing through Geneva in July. U Thant was appointed Acting Secretary-General on 3 November. One result of the tragic accident was that Narasimhan replaced Cordier as the Secretary-General's executive assistant and next to the Secretary-General became the most powerful man in the establishment. He also became Under Secretary for General Assembly Affairs.

The sixteenth session of the General Assembly began on 19 September with the Covenant on Civil and Political Rights still the most important item on the agenda of its Third Committee. Eight more articles were now adopted, one of which recognized the right of everyone to hold opinions without interference and to "seek, receive and impart" information. In 1959, much to my disgust, the Third Committee had substituted the weaker word "gather" for "seek" in a similar provision of the draft Convention on Freedom of Information. Seven African and Asian states now moved that the covenant be amended in the same way, but this was defeated. The draft article recognized that the enjoyment of these rights could be subjected to certain restrictions, including those necessary to ensure the rights or reputations of others and "for the protection of national security or of public order or of public health or morals." The Irish moved that the words "public order" be qualified by the addition in the English version of the French civil law expression *ordre public*, a qualification which, as already explained, greatly widened the scope of permissible restrictions on the enjoyment of the rights. This was adopted by a vote of 71 to 7 with 12 abstentions. The same addition had already been made to two other articles, on freedom of movement and fair trial (and would later be made to the rights of assembly and association) but that didn't make the Irish initiative any less mischievous.

The Somalian delegation introduced but later withdrew (because it would have hampered the activities of trade unions) an amendment that would have had the covenant recognize, as the Universal Declaration does, the right not to belong to an association. Other articles adopted in 1961 included one prohibiting war propaganda and any advocacy of national, racial or religious hatred which is an incitement to discrimination, hostility or violence; an article on marriage and the family; an article on the right of every citizen to take part in the conduct of public affairs and to vote and be elected at genuine periodic elections which are to be by universal and equal suffrage and by secret ballot; an article on equality before the law; and an article on minorities. The last of these (Article 27 of the covenant) says that members of ethnic, religious or linguistic minorities shall not be denied the right, in community with the other members of their group, to enjoy their own culture, to profess and practice their own religion, or to use their own language. I once thought that, while this article might be specific enough to prohibit any positive interference by a contracting state in the exercise of any of the rights listed—and in certain circumstances that could be very important—it really had very little meaning. Quite recently, however, a Canadian Indian woman complained, under the optional protocol, to the Human Rights Committee (the implementation body set up under the Covenant on Civil and Political Rights) that she was being discriminated against because, under the Canadian Indian Act, she lost her rights as an Indian and in her Indian band when she married a non-Indian; whereas an Indian man who married a non-Indian woman brought his wife into the band. Curiously enough the Human Rights Committee did not find that there was discrimination as prohibited by the covenant. But it did find that Canada was in default under Article 27 of that instrument. There can be no doubt however that the article, which is drafted in negative terms, does not require the state to take any steps to help a minority retain its identity, for example, by providing special schools or protecting the use of minority languages in the courts and legislative bodies. The committee also adopted two more articles for the Convention on Freedom of Information, and the preamble and two articles for the Convention on Consent to Marriage, Minimum Age of Marriage and Registration of Marriages; but it did nothing on the proposed declarations on freedom of information and the right of asylum.

On 10 December there was a concert in the Assembly Hall commemorating the adoption of the Universal Declaration of Human Rights. The tradition went back to 1949, but after the celebration of the tenth anniversary in 1958 Hammarskjold had discontinued the concerts because, he said, one United Nations concert a year was enough and it should be held on 24 October, the anniversary of the coming into force of the Charter. Some weeks after Hammarskjold's death, I suggested to Narasimhan that the human rights concerts be resumed, and this was done. The arrangements (which were complicated because an orchestra and a conductor as well as individual artists had to be found) were made by the Office of Public Information, but I had to make most of the decisions. I remember a detail which throws some light on the extent to which the work of the Secretariat was centralized under Hammarskjold. An officer in the O.P.I. called me one day about some change that would be necessary in the program. I listened to his explanations and told him to go ahead with what he had proposed. "But aren't you going to consult U Thant?" he asked. I explained that I couldn't bother the Secretary-General about such a detail. "Hammarskjold decided all these things," he said. I last attended one of these human rights concerts in 1973, when I went to New York to address the General Assembly on the occasion of the twenty-fifth anniversary of the adoption of the Universal Declaration. I was shocked to discover that the concerts were now little more than good variety shows and that the audience was made up almost exclusively of members of the Secretariat. I remembered a conversation I had had with Narasimhan when he objected that the symphony concerts were too Western oriented. What he would like, he said, would be more participation by the African and Asian countries. This has been largely achieved, but the programs of folk music and dancing do not lend themselves to the original idea, which was to have a concert at headquarters that could be broadcast to all corners of the world.

It was again being suggested that the Human Rights Division be moved to Geneva. The building on Turtle Bay which lodged the Secretariat was only a little over ten years old, but it was already too small and the office of general services was looking for some unit that could be moved out. David Vaughan, the director of the office, telephoned me one day to tell me that my division had been chosen and that we would be moved to the European headquarters. Personally I liked Geneva and would have been happy to live there, but I realized right away that to move the Division away from the political center at headquarters would not be a good thing for the human rights program. It happened that Vaughan made his decision during the absence of Narasimhan. When the latter returned to headquarters, I pointed out that he had not been consulted, and he immediately called Vaughan to say that he could not agree to the proposal. The result was that the Human Rights Division remained at headquarters as long as I was its director. I can throw no light on the later controversial decision (which was interpreted in certain quarters as an attempt to downgrade human rights in the United Nations) to move the Division to Geneva.

India, Afghanistan, Saltsjobaden and Dublin (1962)

Refreshed after a Christmas holiday in Jamaica, I was back at headquarters in time for the January session of the Sub-Commission on the Prevention of Discrimination, the chief business of which was Santa Cruz's final report on political rights, a draft report on the right of everyone to leave any country, including his own, and to return to his country, and a new study of discrimination against persons born out of wedlock, for which Judge Saario of Finland was to be the rapporteur. The sub-commission adjourned on 2 February, by which time however I was on my way to India and a seminar on freedom of information. The route I followed could hardly have been less direct. First I went to Dakar, where I spent most of three days in government departments, in each of which I was cordially received by the minister with whom my talks always began; but there was always a Frenchman present, the *conseiller technique,* to whom the minister invariably turned when the time came to make a decision. I couldn't imagine this happening in one of the former British colonies. The result of these talks was that the government decided to sponsor a seminar on human rights in developing countries. It was held in February 1966, and was the last seminar I attended before retiring from the Secretariat. On this, my first visit to Dakar, I saw very little of the city and nothing of the surrounding countryside. What I did see seemed very French, and had it not been for the black faces and colorful costumes—the women were especially handsome and chic—I might just as well have been somewhere in the south of France.

From Dakar I flew on to Accra where, there being then no air service between Ghana and Togo, I hired a car to drive me to Lomé, where I wanted to organize a seminar on the status of women. I remember that the owner of the garage cheated me very badly. I spent the night in Accra and the next morning, a Sunday, had the time before leaving for Lomé to visit the waterfront. The new deep water harbor had not yet been built, and several ships were being unloaded by lighters in the roadstead. I watched the oarsmen, their wet black bodies glistening in the sun, as they brought the colorful boats over the heavy surf to the beach.

The Togolese government very quickly agreed to sponsor the seminar. I had the time before returning to Accra to drive a short distance up the coast, ostensibly to see the headman of one of the villages, who was the uncle of a woman who had represented Togo at the General Assembly. I never did meet her uncle, but as we were walking through the village I noticed a group of women dressed in light blue performing some ritualistic dance. It was such an unusual sight for me that I wanted to come nearer so that I could take a picture; but my companion discouraged me, so I did not insist. I put her reluctance down to modesty because the breasts of the dancers were bare; but later someone told me that what I had seen was a religious ceremony and that if we had gone nearer my companion might have had her clothes stripped from her: it would be an insult to the god for a woman to approach him with her breasts covered.

Back in Accra I had the time to have tea with a retired U.N. colleague and to attend a reception at the home of the Canadian high commissioner before boarding a plane at midnight for Rome to take another for Beirut where I had decided to break my trip for a night before going on to New Delhi. I was pretty tired by the time I got to Rome on Friday morning, but I had a whole weekend to rest, mostly walking on the Capitoline and in the Forum. I also visited the foreign office, which agreed to sponsor a seminar on freedom of information.

There was a particularly fine view of the coast as my plane circled over the sea approaching Beirut. After dinner at the St. Georges Hotel I started out for a walk. The presence of soldiers on guard outside the hotel should have warned me that there was some kind of alert. Returning to the hotel I learned there would be an excursion to Baalbek and Byblos the next day. The autocar, the advertisement said, would be back in Beirut at six o'clock in the evening. My plane for New Delhi was to leave at seven thirty. I decided to risk it and was glad that I did, for the drive was spectacular, including a splendid view of the Mediterranean from the hills above Beirut and of the Bekaa. The mountains were covered with snow and it was quite cool; only three weeks earlier the roads through the passes had been blocked and I could not have made the trip. Our car was stopped several times at military checkpoints and carefully searched. They were looking, it seemed, for some infiltrators who were trying to cross the border into Syria. After all I had just seen in Rome, Baalbek, although spectacular, was disappointing. The ruins of the temples were impressive notwithstanding the depredations of crusaders, Arabs and Turks and the earthquake of 1759; but the temples had not been built in the period of best taste. I have better memories of Byblos, of the coast coming south back to Beirut and of a monastery whose name I have forgotten.

I had no difficulty catching my plane and was in New Delhi the next morning. The seminar, which was held in the Vigyan Bhavan, was attended by participants from all over Asia and from Australia and New Zealand, and there were observers from the United Kingdom and the United States and from two specialized agencies and many nongovernmental organizations. It was opened on 20 February by Vice President of India Dr. Radakrishnan. This was the first seminar on freedom of information and, therefore, I thought, particularly useful because (after the liquidation of the Sub-Commission on Freedom of Information and of the Press in 1952) there was no longer any expert organ in the United Nations specifically concerned with this fundamental right. The agenda covered most of the thorny questions, including the role of government, of publishers and proprietors and professional journalists, press laws and standards in the profession. Notwithstanding the competition of an election campaign, the seminar made a strong local impact. Prime Minister Nehru came to and addressed the closing meeting. It was a proud moment for me when I accompanied this great leader into the conference chamber.

Apart from one or two official receptions there was very little entertaining, and most evenings we were left to the questionable amenities of the Janpath Hotel, where the participants and the Secretariat put up. Thinking it would be a good idea if as many as possible of the participants were to eat together, I arranged to have a special common table prepared. This so disturbed the habits of the waiters—who may have been afraid they would not be getting the usual tips—that a violent quarrel developed and one day at lunch one of them chased another through the dining room with a large carving knife, whereupon I decided not to pursue my attempt to encourage fraternization. I was invited one evening with some others to dine at the home of a government official, a rare experience in India, where foreigners are not easily admitted to the privacy of the family circle. The dinner party was obviously a major ordeal for the official's wife, who never once sat down at table. I would have liked to help her with the service but did not dare to interfere.

Like the New Zealanders a year earlier, our Indian hosts organized an elaborate tour taking us, one weekend, first to Agra to see the Taj Mahal and to Fatepur Sikkri and then, by special train, north into the mountains to inspect a fertilizer plant and a hydroelectric development. Due to no fault of our hosts the visit was a fiasco; for when, after a night on the train, we arrived at our destination, it was raining so hard that we were able to make only a perfunctory tour of the industrial development that they were so anxious for us to see. The thing I remember best about the trip was the sight from the train window early in the morning as we returned to New Delhi. The fields were full of people kneeling before little bowls and performing the rites of the morning toilet—hardly the impression of industrial development that our hosts had intended us to take back to our respective countries.

On my last weekend in India my two colleagues, Kamalshwar Das and John Male, and I hired a car and drove into Rajasthan as far as Jaiput, where we spent a night. Back in New Delhi I packed my bags and took off for Tokyo, where I spent two days discussing with the Japanese government the final arrangements for the seminar on the status of women that was to meet in May. I stopped in Honolulu for a weekend on my way back to New York, where I arrived on 3 March.

There were no important developments at the sixteenth session of the Commission on the Status of Women or the eighteenth session of the Human Rights Commission, both of which opened the same day a fortnight after my return to headquarters—apart from the fact that the membership of both bodies had now been increased to comprise twenty-one states. I did not have long in my office after they adjourned. The Tokyo seminar on the status of women was to begin on 8 May, but instead of flying straight to Japan I again went around the world.

Abdul Pazhwak, who represented Afghanistan on the Human Rights Commission and was one of the most outspoken representatives of the Third World in the General Assembly, was very anxious that I visit his country and, hoping that the Afghans would sponsor a seminar, I accepted an invitation to spend a week in Kabul on my way to Tokyo. But first I went to Moscow, where I used four days of my annual leave sightseeing. It was my first visit to the Soviet Union and I made the best of it. I went to the Bolshoi Theater, saw a puppet show, roamed around Red Square and the Kremlin, rode on the famous subway, visited museums and art galleries and even a run-down mansion in the country that had once been owned by some aristocrat. On some of these excursions I was accompanied by an Intourist guide who tried to convert me to communism. She was shocked and very obviously did not believe me when, replying to something she had said, I remarked that one of the most conservative influences in the United States was organized labor. But mostly I was alone.

The director of the United Nations information center with whom I dined the night I left Moscow had agreed to drive me to the airport; but he was enjoying himself so much that we were late leaving my hotel and reached the airport only a few minutes before my plane was to take off. The woman at the wicket told me (she spoke excellent English) that I would have to pay an airport tax, but—because it was against the law to take them out of the country—I had used up all my rubles. Looking through my papers I discovered that I had an American Express voucher that had been given to me to meet just such an eventuality; but the functionary refused even to look at it, whereupon I asked to see the manager, but this was also refused. My Russian colleague then took over with an equally negative result. In the meantime my plane had been called. He then did the only decent thing in the circumstances and paid the tax, which must have been about ten dollars. "But how can I ever repay you?" I asked. "It is nothing," he said. "There are some books that I would like to have from New York. You can send them to me." I left him promising that I would send the books, but before I could do so I learned that he had died of a heart attack.

I climbed into the big jet just before takeoff and after some hours was in Tashkent, where I changed to a much smaller plane for Kabul. Although Ambassador Pazhwak had arranged for me to spend a full week in Afghanistan, it took me less than an hour to complete my business with the government. I was surprised when I learned that I would be seeing the king, Mohammed Zahu Shah, himself. If he agreed, I was told, that was all that would be needed and there would be a seminar; but my hosts were skeptical because Afghanistan had never before hosted an international conference, and there was some hesitation about undertaking what they thought might be a difficult experiment. I was taken to the palace and received by the king alone in a small office. I told him, in French, that if the government would provide a meeting place, a few offices and some secretarial help, the United Nations would accept full responsibility for running the conference and that I would personally guarantee its success. He was apparently convinced because I had his consent by the time I left his office, much to the surprise of the officials who were waiting for me outside. My business in Kabul was now over, but the government had me on their hands for the rest of the week and I had to be kept busy. They provided me with a car and driver and, after making the round of government offices I was taken to visit hospitals, factories and the fine historical museum. The driver, who was a good Moslem, always stopped at prayer time and, laying a small carpet by the side of the road and falling on his knees, would bend his body several times towards Mecca touching the ground with his forehead. This same driver, accompanied by an official from the foreign office, also drove me (this time by jeep) to Bamyan, an excursion that took the best of three days. The road followed the spectacular Hindu Kush, which at places towered above us at a height of twenty thousand feet. Occasionally the jeep would leave the road and climb to a point from which we had an even finer view. From a distance I also saw several encampments of nomads living in black felt tents, which I would have liked to visit, but we kept our distance because of the vicious dogs which kept strangers at bay.

At Bamyan I was taken to a hotel which had been closed for the winter but had been opened for my benefit. My room was bitterly cold and although there was a stove (which looked like a Quebec heater) in it, the wood was so dry that it burned up like paper and I might just as well have been outside. To add to my discomfort the doorway leading to the bathroom was only about five feet high and every time I went through it I managed to bump my head. All this was forgotten the next morning when I looked through my window; for at a distance of about half a mile, behind the mud-brick houses in the village, I could see two great Buddhas carved in a precipice and behind them the Hindu Kush. I spent most of that day inspecting these wonders. The monuments are in remarkably good condition notwithstanding the attempts that vandals have made to destroy them. One story is that Genghis Khan's archers could not reach the heads with their arrows; but the feet of both Buddhas have been destroyed, the work of the Mogul Emperor Aurangzeb in the seventeenth century, who had them bombarded with field artillery. One can only be thankful that his soldiers were not better shots. I also visited the ancient city of Shar-i-Gholhola which, however, is not much more now than a pile of rubble.

That night I had dinner with the governor of the province. Since he spoke neither English nor French, the conversation dragged, notwithstanding the efforts of my foreign office friend to interpret. Making conversation I said something about trout fishing; wouldn't some of the streams I had seen be likely places for the sport? The governor was interested. Would I like to go fishing, he asked? I said that there was nothing that I would like better. So early next morning after breakfast three jeeps were waiting at the hotel door. I noticed that there was no fishing tackle but imagined that this would be picked up later; but I soon discovered that it wasn't to be that kind of a fishing trip, for when we reached the river, I was horrified to have to watch it being dynamited. But the governor had made his point; there had been fish in the river and dozens of them were soon floating dead with their bellies turned up. I didn't even taste the fish because once the performance was over I immediately started on my trip back to Kabul. This wasn't as pleasant as it had been coming up, for the sky was filled with heavy clouds and it was cold in the open jeep. I was thankful for the *chapan* (a kind of homespun greatcoat) that the governor had given me as a parting gift. Soon we were caught in a cloudburst, which turned the never-too-good road into a river of mud. We sought refuge in a peasant's adobe cabin, but I wasn't invited inside and had to make do with the little protection provided by a small balcony. I guessed that the reason for this inhospitality must have been that there were women inside. In the Afghan countryside, traditions apparently die hard and infidels are not allowed to see women unveiled. We were in Uzbek country, and I had noticed that the gaily dressed women working in the fields always drew their veils over their faces as our jeep approached. What a contrast to their cousins, the smart-looking Uzbek girls whom I had seen at the Tashkent airport. In Kabul, however, while many women still wore the *chador*, it was stylish for women to go unveiled, the royal family having given the example. The government was, it seemed, genuinely reformist, but the mullahs were still strong, particularly in the country, and progress could be made only slowly and with extreme caution. Not so very long ago, King Amanullah had returned from Europe full of reformist zeal only to be deposed when he tried to put some of his new ideas into practice.

I was ready to leave Kabul, but there was still some uncertainty as to the exact time of my departure; for the little airplane in which I was to fly over the mountains to Amritsar left only in good weather. At Amritsar I changed to an Indian plane and flew on to Delhi, where it was hot and humid, but I had less than a day there, hardly time to visit an emporium to buy some things that I had been coveting ever since my last visit.

The Tokyo seminar on the status of women in family law lasted from 8 to 21 May and was held in the same Shinagawa Prince Hotel where the seminar on the protection of human rights by criminal law had met in 1960. The participants came from all over Asia, Australia and New Zealand. The presence of all these women at an official United Nations conference apparently posed a problem for our hosts. The Japanese are very hospitable to foreigners, but one seldom sees the wives of officials at their elaborate dinner parties and receptions. At this conference they brought their wives to the parties, a practice which, one of them told me, was quite new in Japanese etiquette. That, I thought, was an achievement in itself. Returning to the hotel one night after a big reception at the foreign office, I was the only man in a bus full of women. As we were driving through the center of the city it occurred to me that most of these women had probably never seen the Ginza. So I passed the word around that I was planning to walk from one end of it to the other and that anyone who would like to come with me would be welcome. Some twenty of them, most of them dressed in colorful national costumes, accepted my invitation; we were an exotic sight as we proceeded down the Ginza.

C.V. Narasimhan turned up while the conference was in session and attended one of the meetings. The Japanese wanted to do something to entertain him and, because he was a vegetarian, all the United Nations people in Tokyo (about a dozen of us) were invited to a dinner party in a Buddhist temple. I counted over a score of delicately served dishes, none of which I could identify with certainty. After dinner we were entertained by a Geisha who taught us how to play some frivolous little games like scissors and paper.

The seminar went so smoothly that I have very little memory of it, or indeed of this visit to Tokyo. I remember that I went several times to the big department stores, not so much because I wanted to buy as because in Tokyo they are as much social centers as anything else. Most evenings there was a reception of some kind, and since the Shinagawa Prince Hotel was a good distance from the center of the city, I usually settled for a walk afterwards in the hotel grounds.

The Tokyo seminar over, I returned to New York only to leave on 6 June for Sweden, where there was a seminar on judicial and other remedies against the abuse of administrative authority, and on to Geneva for the summer session of the Economic and Social Council. The seminar was held in the Grand Hotel in Saltsjobaden, a summer resort within easy reach of Stockholm. It was an ideal place for a conference, and the arrangements were perfect. So was the weather. Its being June and in the north, the nights were so short that one had to make a special effort to go to bed.

It was natural that a human rights conference in Sweden should be especially concerned with the typically Scandinavian institution of the ombudsman. Stephen Hurwitz, the *Folkstingets Ombudsman* of Denmark, and his colleague, Pol Hansen, were amongst the participants and, although not a participant, the Swedish ombudsman, Alfred Bexelius (whom I was to know better later) addressed the seminar. Because the office of procurator in the Soviet Union and other Eastern European countries resembles the Scandinavian institution in some respects, the presence at the seminar of Vladimir Terebilov, a member of the Collegium of the Procurator's Office of the U.S.S.R. and of Aleksey Bondar, the Procurator of Byelorussia, gave special interest to the discussions. The Russians played an active part and I remember that, just as at meetings at headquarters, we had some trouble with them about the report. I have no doubt that the discussions at this, the Kandy, and other human rights seminars helped stimulate world-wide interest in the institution of the ombudsman which, in one form or another, has now been copied in many countries.

Stockholm's being so easy to reach by electric train, I spent many evenings there. I particularly remember a dinner party at the Irish embassy where Andreas O'Keeffe, the Irish attorney general, and I were guests. O'Keeffe wanted to have a seminar in Ireland and invited me to visit Dublin after the summer session of the Economic and Social Council.

One Saturday afternoon, our Swedish hosts took the participants sailing on the archipelago. When we stopped at one of the islands for tea, I walked to the inn, which was some distance from the dock, with one of our hosts, who was a very high official in the Swedish civil service. He immediately began to talk about Hammarskjold whom, I gathered, he had known very well. He said that Hammarskjold had had very few if any close friends in the civil service, and that his practice was to work alone. On the following Saturday the seminar was taken to Uppsala to visit the late Secretary-General's grave on which, as the representative of his successor, I placed a wreath of flowers.

The seminar ended on 25 June and three days later I was in Geneva for the summer session of the Economic and Social Council. Very little was done at this session to advance the cause of human rights. Given the political climate in the early sixties, the opposition of governments to the creation of any effective international system for the implementation of human rights, and the conventional wisdom conveniently shared by most of them that there would be no significant developments until after the General Assembly had approved the two covenants, we were in a kind of doldrums. In these circumstances the seminars were still the most vital part of the program. I was therefore pleased when, on 24 July, the Council unanimously recommended that the General Assembly expand the advisory services program, a recommendation which the Assembly approved on 7 December.

After the adjournment of the Council, I went to Dublin hoping that, as Andreas O'Keeffe had suggested, the Irish government would sponsor one of the seminars. I slept at the Shelbourne Hotel, but my real hosts were the O'Keeffes, who did everything they could to make my visit pleasant. O'Keeffe took me one afternoon to Government House to see President De Valera. After a few minutes, O'Keeffe quietly slipped out of the room leaving me alone with the president for about an hour. He seemed relaxed and apparently glad to have someone to talk to, for he was practically blind. I don't remember that I reminded the president of our conversation thirteen years earlier in Strasbourg when we had argued about the meaning of the word "dissolution" in an article of the Universal Declaration on equality in marriage. I also attended a session of the Dail Eireann, after which I had lunch with several of the members, including the foreign minister, Frank Aiken, whom I had already met in New York, and F.H. Bolton, who was president of the General Assembly in 1960. It was Bolton who one afternoon when he was presiding over the Assembly broke his mallet when calling the representative of Romania to order. It happened that Edvard Mezcincescu, the man in question, dined at my apartment that same evening. Describing the incident, which had caused a sensation, he told me that he had just mentioned the word, Ireland, when the president brought down his mallet. Bolton was apparently expecting some derogatory reference to his country, but Mezcincescu told me that he had no such intention.

O'Keeffe had me meet the people whose decisions counted, but, for reasons that were never explained to me, the Irish government never did sponsor a seminar. I do not think that their decision could have been influenced by the *Lawless* case, although emergency legislation made necessary by the activities of the I.R.A. may have had something to do with it. O'Keeffe, who argued the *Lawless* case on behalf of Ireland before the European Court of Human Rights, told me that he suspected that, in their eagerness to have a case come before the Court (which had never had one on its docket), the Secretariat of the Council of Europe had maneuvered to have the European Commission refer the case to the Court. I didn't say that I would probably have done the same thing had I been in their place. Lawless, who was suspected of belonging to the I.R.A., was being detained without trial under the provisions of the Offenses against the State Act. The Court, which decided the case in 1961, held that this was in violation of Article 5 of the European Convention for the Protection of Human Rights and Fundamental Freedoms, under which an arrested person must be brought promptly before a judge and is entitled to a trial within a reasonable time or to release pending trial. However, the Irish government had exercised its right, under Article 15 of the convention, under which "in time of war or other public emergency threatening the life of the nation" a contracting party may take measures derogating from its obligations under the convention "to the extent strictly required by the exigencies of the situation . . .;" and the Court held that the derogation was justified. But it went on to say—and this is one of the reasons why the decision was so important—that it was for itself and not the government to decide whether the conditions laid down in the article for the exercise of the exceptional right of derogation had been fulfilled. I never quite understood why O'Keeffe was upset about the case going to the Court because the judgment should have pleased the Irish government.

Back in New York, the seventeenth session of the General Assembly began on 18 September and the most important human rights item on the agenda of its Third Committee was still the covenants. The committee discussed but did not adopt at this session the texts of two new articles for the Covenant on Civil and Political Rights, one of them on the rights of children (which was referred to the Human Rights Commission for study) and the other on the right to asylum, further consideration of which was postponed to the next session of the Assembly, which did not adopt it. Six articles were adopted, two for the Covenant on Civil and Political Rights and four for the other convention, but none of these defined particular rights. Article 2 of the Covenant on Economic, Social and Cultural Rights obliges the state parties to take steps to achieve "progressively" by all appropriate means the full realization of the rights recognized in the instrument. The rights are to be enjoyed without discrimination of any kind; but "developing countries, with due regard to human rights and their national economy, may determine to what extent they would [sic] guarantee the economic rights recognized in the present covenant to non-nationals." The exact meaning of this provision, which was suggested by Poland and adopted by a small majority, is obscure, but it would seem to be doubly discriminatory in that only "developing countries" are permitted to discriminate against nonnationals.

The General Assembly also approved and opened for signature the Convention on Consent to Marriage, Minimum Age for Marriage and Registration of Marriages, which is now in force. A disappointing feature is its failure to fix any minimum age for marriage; the convention says that no one below a minimum age shall marry, but it is left to the contracting states to decide what this age shall be. In 1965, however, the General Assembly recommended that the minimum age be fifteen, unless a dispensation is granted by a competent authority in the interests of the persons to be married.

The Assembly also called for the preparation of draft declarations and conventions on the elimination of all forms of racial discrimination and of religious intolerance. The Declaration on the Elimination of All Forms of Racial Discrimination was unanimously adopted a year later, in 1963; and in 1965 a convention on the same subject was opened for signature and is now in force; but the United Nations has not yet been able to adopt either a declaration or a convention on the elimination of religious intolerance.

On 7 November, I was grieved to hear that Mrs. Roosevelt had died. She had been ill for some time and it had been some months since I had seen her. On behalf of her family Adlai Stevenson invited my wife and me to attend the funeral. We drove to Hyde Park on a cold, wet day. The rose garden, where she was buried beside her illustrious husband, was filled with distinguished personalities, including the president of the United States and two past presidents. It was a great tribute to a great person.

The Canberra Seminar on the Role of the Police (1963)

All my years at the United Nations were eventful, but the one that now began was especially so. Various missions continued to take me abroad. I went to Australia, Poland and South Vietnam, and there were sessions in Geneva of both the Human Rights Commission and ECOSOC. The Canberra seminar on the role of the police was the best in the series; and apart from being a unique personal experience the General Assembly fact-finding mission to South Vietnam, of which I was the principal secretary, established important new precedents in United Nations practice. The year 1963 also saw the birth of an imaginative proposal for creating an office of United Nations High Commissioner for Human Rights.

My wife and I saw the New Year in on the pleasant island of St. Maarten, after which we visited Guadaloupe, Martinique, Antigua and Jamaica before returning refreshed to New York in time for the opening of the fifteenth session of the Sub-Commission on the Prevention of Discrimination. Well over half of the session was devoted to the final report on the study of the right of everyone to leave any country including his own and to return to his country, which together with draft principles were sent to the Human Rights Commission. The sub-commission also discussed a preliminary report on the study of discrimination against persons born out of wedlock, appointed Chief Justice Abu Rannat as its rapporteur to undertake a study on equality in the administration of justice and drew up a first draft of the instrument (already mentioned) that became the United Nations Declaration on the Elimination of All Forms of Racial Discrimination.

The session ended on 1 February, a month after which I was in Warsaw making arrangements for a seminar on the rights of children, to be held in August. It was a bad time of year to be in Poland, for it was miserably cold. Apart from a few churches, which seemed to be well attended, what I saw of the city had little interest. I put this down to the too-quick work of reconstruction after the war, and wished that I had the time to visit Cracow. I consoled myself with the thought that I could probably do this in August, but, as things turned out, I did not attend the seminar. There was one building that dominated everything else, the Palace of Culture and Science, built in the Moscow style, a gift of the Soviet Union. I heard more than one joke about this and also assurances that never again would such a building go up in Warsaw. The Poles are famous for their jokes, many of which are politically loaded. As a commentary on the seriousness of the Cuban crisis, Wojciech Ketrzynski, the brilliant Polish member of the Sub-Commission on the Prevention of Discrimination who was my effective host, told me that Poles weren't even making jokes about it. Ketrzynski gave a party for me one evening to which he invited people I had met at various United Nations meetings. I noted a large crucifix over the door as I came into his apartment. That an important government official should parade his religious convictions so openly seemed to show that, as I had seen in Romania, freedom of religion could still have some meaning in a communist country.

In Geneva, although spring hadn't quite come the weather was more pleasant. There was also a comfortable hotel, good food, walks in the country on weekends and, more important, the good free air of Switzerland. The nineteenth session of the Human Rights Commission opened on 11 March and lasted until 5 April. Overlapping at headquarters was the seventeenth session of the Commission on the Status of Women.

The first item on the agenda and the one to which the Human Rights Commission devoted most attention at this session (seventeen out of thirty-five meetings) was on the draft declaration on the elimination of all forms of racial discrimination. Although the General Assembly had asked for texts of both a declaration and a convention, the commission, like its sub-commission, decided to give priority to the declaration, a draft of which had been prepared by the sub-commission. The commission's draft, which was unanimously adopted, was sent to ECOSOC for transmission to the General Assembly where, after further amendment, it was adopted 20 November.

The Assembly had also asked for drafts of a declaration and convention on the elimination of all forms of religious intolerance. Neither the commission nor the sub-commission made any attempt to prepare them in 1963; but the sub-commission did draw the attention of the commission to the draft principles forwarded to it in 1960 in connection with its study on freedom and nondiscrimination in the matter of religious rights and practices which, it pointed out, contained the basic principles which should be included in these instruments. But just as it had done in the three previous years, the commission also postponed consideration of these principles. Nor did it take any action on the draft principles on discrimination in the enjoyment of political rights, which had been prepared by its sub-commission or on its own studies on arbitrary arrest and detention and the right to counsel.

For the first time, Canada had become a member of the commission. Its representative was Margaret Aitken, who had been a Conservative member of Parliament but had been defeated in the elections of 1962, a classic qualification in Canada for representing the country at the United Nations. As it turned out, the party of which she was a member was defeated in the elections that took place shortly after the adjournment of the commission, when the government headed by John Diefenbaker was replaced by the Liberals. Miss Aitken continued to represent Canada for the next two years; and I have heard it said that the circumstance that she was now a member of the party in opposition explains the mediocre Canadian performance on the commission. However that may be—and the explanation is not convincing because Canada and not Miss Aitken was the member—there was nothing in the situation as it existed at the nineteenth session to prevent Canada from playing an active role. The delegation apparently wanted to take some initiative with which the name of Canada could be associated and which had some chance of being adopted at that session, because Jean Boucher, the alternate representative, came to see me looking for suggestions. It happened that I had no significant proposal for which I was looking for a sponsor, and I am not expert in pulling rabbits out of hats; but I had been thinking that it might be useful if governments were asked to sponsor regional training courses on human rights as part of the advisory services program. The participants at the seminars were for the most part very senior people, much too senior to be expected to follow any organized course of teaching. It would be useful, therefore, if some kind of more or less formal instruction were provided for junior and even intermediate officials. Although the idea wasn't exciting I passed it on to Boucher, and the Canadians decided to sponsor a resolution recommending that ECOSOC request the Secretary-General to organize regional training courses on an experimental basis in 1964 and 1965, and this was adopted. A similar resolution was adopted in the Economic and Social Council, but nothing came of it until after I left the Secretariat, partly because the Human Rights Division never had the necessary funds. Had the Canadians been serious about the matter they would have offered to act as the first hosts of a course and seen to it that we were provided with a budget large enough to make the program viable. I remember that Marietta Tree, the American representative on the commission, was upset by the Canadian plan which, she apparently thought, might become a rival of the seminars and other aspects of the advisory services program to which her delegation attached more importance. Whether the Americans put any pressure on the Canadians to drop the courses I don't know. In the three years Canada was on the commission its delegation took no other initiative.

The commission devoted some eight meetings, which were largely a waste of time, to an Assembly resolution by which it was instructed "to study and to encourage the adoption of measures designed to accelerate the promotion of respect for human rights and fundamental freedoms and to devote special attention to this matter during the United Nations Development Decade." This was a real opportunity to push forward the program, but the commission's "first report and recommendations" was little more than a review of the work program.

The commission adjourned on 5 April and I returned to New York, but I was soon off on another mission—to Australia for a seminar on the role of the police in the promotion of human rights, which met in Canberra. The Canberra seminar was one of the best in the series. The subject, which I had myself suggested, was a good one: the police are sometimes guilty of violating the most fundamental rights, but they also protect human rights. The excellent discussions were well covered by the press and we made a real impact on the public. Even the taxi drivers knew all about it. The participants came from all over Asia; but it was the Australian delegation, which was made up largely of judges and police commissioners (who could be expected to have radically different points of view) that kept the debate going. The report of the seminar still makes useful reading. One of its conclusions was that a well-trained, efficient police force is more likely to promote human rights and not violate them than one that is poorly trained; police training colleges are therefore a good investment.

I liked Canberra better this time than I had on my short visit in 1962, and I managed to see something of the Australian countryside. One weekend the participants and secretariat were taken on a long expedition into the Snowy Mountains. Thick groves of eucalyptus trees with their blue-green leaves and whitish trunks reminded me of old tapestries as we sped by them in our buses. Twice I went bird-watching with Ray Whitrod, the federal police commissioner, once to a lake not far from Canberra, where we saw black swans, ibises, spoonbills and other exciting specimens. In the bushes near the shore were many colorful small birds, but I never heard a song. The last man he had taken there, Whitrod said, was the Duke of Edinburgh. When I asked him whether the duke had been able to identify all the birds, he said that he was pretty good but that, when faced with a difficulty, he put down simply "little brown bird."

On my way back to New York I stopped for two or three days in Tahiti. There was much noise and hula dancing at the airport when my plane arrived there five hours late in the middle of the night, a demonstration which I found highly artificial, but that was perhaps because I was so tired. I can think of half a dozen islands in the West Indies, none of which I would trade for Tahiti. I almost regretted visiting the island, for seeing it destroyed illusions nursed by Gaugin, Captain Cook and Robert Louis Stevenson. The Tahitians were, it seemed to me, being pushed off the island by French and Chinese just as East Indians were taking over Fiji.

In New York office work had been piling up, but nothing worth reporting happened in the six weeks I spent there before going on to Geneva and the summer session of the Economic and Social Council. I had wanted to visit Copenhagen on my way to Geneva, but the bureau of the budget objected at the last moment and I did not go. The result was that we never had a seminar in Denmark. And I was in Geneva for only a fortnight, which was a much shorter time than I usually spent at the summer session of the Council; but as it happened the human rights items were disposed of very quickly. When the Council asked the Secretary-General to appoint a special rapporteur to bring up to date the 1955 report on slavery, I arranged to have Mohammed Awad of the United Arab Republic appointed to the post. Slavery still existed in Saudi Arabia, and the slave trade in northern Africa. The special rapporteur could, I hoped, become a pivot around which quiet negotiations could be conducted to bring this to an end; and it would be easier for a Moslem to play the role. I immediately thought of Awad, whom I also knew as one of the most capable members of the Sub-Commission on the Prevention of Discrimination and the Protection of Minorities. If he was unable to play the diplomatic role that I had envisaged, it was at least partly the fault of the bureau of the budget, which refused to provide the necessary resources. The Council also adopted a calendar of conferences for 1964, which made no provision for meetings of functional commissions other than the Commission on Narcotic Drugs. Apparently it wasn't only members of the Human Rights Division whose travel was to be restricted. But, at its next session, the General Assembly requested the Council to reconsider its decision and to make arrangements for the Commission on Human Rights to continue to meet annually.

I was also prevented from attending the seminar in Poland that summer on the rights of the child, the arrangements for which I had made in April. Instead, my wife and I had a very pleasant holiday on Martha's Vineyard. Nor did I attend the seminar on the status of women in Bogotá in December. The reasons were the same as those which had prevented my going to Copenhagen.

A United Nations High Commissioner for Human Rights (1963)

The 1963 session of the General Assembly began on 17 September. Three days later I found myself sitting next to Harlan Cleveland, the American under secretary of state, at a luncheon given by the Secretary-General for President Kennedy and Prime Minister Pearson. Making conversation, he asked me whether I had heard the president's speech in the General Assembly that morning. When I replied that I had not, he said that it was too bad because the president had said that the time had come to take a long step forward in the human rights program, and he went on to say something about prolonging the mandate of the chairman of the Human Rights Commission so that he could act between sessions. I didn't think that this would be a very long step forward and said so. I pointed out that the chairman was only a presiding officer who had no mandate to extend, and that, if it were proposed to give him one, it should be remembered that his was a purely political appointment. "What would you suggest?" Cleveland asked somewhat nettled. "I would like to give that question some thought," I replied. "All right," he said, "I will have someone call on you next week and you can let us have your ideas." I then asked him why the United States had supported the move in ECOSOC to cancel next year's session of the Human Rights Commission. That, I suggested, wasn't a step forward. His reply was that it wasn't a particularly useful commission.

On the Friday following, Ambassador Bingham, the United States representative on the Economic and Social Council, Marietta Tree, U.S. representative on the Human Rights Commission and Richard Gardner of the state department called at my office. We talked for nearly an hour and a half. Their suggestion, as I noted it down in my diary, was that there should be a full-time, paid chairman of the commission who would report to it annually on the observance of human rights in the world. I had a quite different idea: the General Assembly should appoint an independent officer who could help the Human Rights Commission deal with the periodic reports and other matters. I was concerned by the fact that, although governments were reporting, the commission had not set up any procedures for a critical examination of the reports. A United Nations High Commissioner for Human Rights could, I added, have other duties. He could, for example, also be available to assist governments, at their request, in various ways, including the investigation of situations and the mediation of disputes. Gardner told me later that the state department had been working that summer on a proposal coming from Marietta Tree that there should be a kind of United Nations ombudsman. I am pretty sure that they did not mention this at our meeting, although the idea of a full-time, paid chairman of the commission may have been inspired by it. In any event, the United Nations High Commissioner for Human Rights, as I envisaged the office, would not have been an ombudsman. He would not have dealt with complaints nor reported on the observance of human rights. I never thought for a moment that governments would agree to give such wide powers to a single individual whatever his office. Nor was my suggestion the same as one (with which it is often confused) that had been made over ten years earlier by the observer at the United Nations of one of the nongovernmental organizations, Moses Moskowitz, and taken up by the Uruguayan delegation that there should be a United Nations Attorney General or High Commissioner. Moskowitz's suggestion was a response to the argument so often heard that if individuals were given the right to petition the United Nations, the organization would be swamped with complaints. For the principal function of the proposed United Nations Attorney General would have been to sift the complaints and decide which of them should be pursued. This was a brilliant idea, but it had very little in common with the suggestion I was now making to the Americans. The upshot of the meeting was that the Americans left my office full of enthusiasm for my suggestion, and I was pretty sure that the high commissioner would be President Kennedy's long step forward.

About a month after this meeting I went to South Vietnam as the principal secretary of a United Nations mission which President Diem had reluctantly invited to investigate allegations that the Buddhist community in that country was being persecuted by a Roman Catholic government. I will have something to say about that mission later. The point that I want to make now is that this experience convinced me that a United Nations High Commissioner for Human Rights could perform some very useful functions indeed. It would have been far better from the point of view of both the United Nations and the Vietnamese government had that investigation been conducted by an independent officer of the General Assembly rather than by a politically oriented mission of ambassadors, some of whom were representing countries which in the General Assembly had already accused the Diem government of violating the rights of the Buddhists. As a result of this experience and even while I was in Vietnam, I began to refine the ideas that I had hastily outlined to the Americans. What was needed, I thought, was an independent officer of great authority who would be available to act in a situation like the one in Vietnam if asked to do so by a government or by some United Nations body. But he would not be a United Nations ombudsman or have the kind of powers proposed for the United Nations Attorney General. If the idea were to be accepted by a majority of states one would have to be careful not to propose for the high commissioner any powers that would make the office politically unacceptable. I figured that if the office could be created, it would take on importance and increased powers by the operation of time chiefly through the instrumentality of an annual report on his activities which the high commissioner would make to the General Assembly and the debates to which it would give rise.

President Kennedy was assassinated on 22 November, not long after my return from Vietnam, and the interest of the Americans in a United Nations High Commissioner for Human Rights seemed to disappear with him. But by this time I was convinced that the idea had merit, and I was determined not to let it die. If necessary I would find another sponsor. Some months later I went to Rome for a seminar on freedom of information and stopped off in London to address a meeting of officers of nongovernmental organizations in the offices of Amnesty International. I referred in my talk to the high commissioner and, after the meeting, a small group of us decided we would take steps to bring about his appointment. And in July, when I was in Geneva for the summer session of ECOSOC, we drew up in Sean MacBride's office at the International Commission of Jurists a draft resolution for adoption by the General Assembly. On my suggestion this was given to Ambassador Fernando Volio Jimenez of Costa Rica, partly because he represented a small country—small countries were usually more amenable to suggestions coming from the Secretariat or from nongovernmental organizations than the big powers—but chiefly because Volio had been on the mission to Vietnam, and I wanted him to be able to say that the institution would have been useful in that situation. Back in New York I had another opportunity to put in a word for the high commissioner. Jacob Blaustein, an American businessman who had been one of the consultants representing voluntary organizations whom the United States delegation had invited to advise it at the San Francisco Conference, asked me to write a speech which he was to deliver in the Dag Hammarskjold series at Columbia University. Because I knew that Blaustein had influence at the state department, I put the high commissioner into the speech and the proposal became known in the United States as the Blaustein plan. A few days after he had made the speech he came to my office with a letter from Adlai Stevenson asking some questions about the plan. I helped him draft an appropriate reply.

The proposal to create an office of United Nations High Commissioner for Human Rights was to have a long history, most of it extending beyond my retirement from the Secretariat. I will discuss it here. When the draft resolution was given to Ambassador Volio in the summer of 1964, it was too late for him to raise the question before the Human Rights Commission that year. He did this in 1965, but the commission did not discuss it, ostensibly because there was no time. He therefore brought it up in the General Assembly, which referred the matter to the commission. When the latter dealt with it at its twenty-second session in March, 1966 (the last which I attended as the director of the Division) the proposal was bitterly attacked by the Soviet Union. "It was," said Nasinovsky, "utopian to suppose that a single individual could act as an arbitrator, adviser or even judge in resolving the questions relating to human rights which would arise under various legal, philosophical or religious systems." And, he went on to say, as did Nedbailo of the Ukrainian S.S.R., that the office if created would impair the sovereignty of states. "The High Commissioner," said Nedbailo, "would be a kind of investigator enjoying extraterritorial status: that was contrary to the principles of the sovereignty of states and of nonintervention in their internal affairs, which were the very foundation on which the United Nations rested." There was nothing in the Costa Rican proposal as it was originally presented which could possibly justify this kind of language, for its authors had carefully avoided putting anything into it that could reasonably frighten governments and prevent its adoption. The underlying philosophy was that the high commissioner would have only such powers as governments or United Nations bodies might see fit to give him in a particular case.

I had already known that the Soviet Union was opposed to the plan because their objections had affected me personally. Throughout my twenty years as director of the Human Rights Division my relations with the communist countries had been good, if not cordial. Although I could not approve of their attitude towards human rights, I was conscious of the international character of my post and I leaned over backwards to be fair—to the point that there were times when I was suspected of favoring the communists—and I think my objectivity was appreciated by both sides in the Cold War. I know, for example, that when, in 1964, the date of my normal retirement from the Secretariat was approaching, both Ambassador Stevenson, on behalf of the United States, and Ambassador Morozov, on behalf of the Soviet Union, suggested to the Secretary-General that my tenure of office be extended beyond the normal retirement age of sixty. Morozov even invited me to an excellent lunch for the express purpose of asking my permission before making the *démarche*, because, as he put it, such an intervention by the Soviet Union might do me no good. But all this had now changed. The Russians had discovered that the proposed high commissioner was my invention and they didn't forgive me for passing the idea on to the Americans. As a consequence, my relations with them were now very bad, and this was compounded by difficulties I was having with a Russian chief of section in my division. In a conversation with Morozov during the 1966 session of the Human Rights Commission, only a few weeks before my retirement, I tried to explain my attitude towards the high commissioner and the philosophy I had of the office. His only reply was a frosty, "I am glad that your real position is now clear," as if to say, "I am glad you are now removing your mask." The Russians were unalterably opposed to the creation of any kind of international machinery for the implementation of human rights and, although the proposal for setting up an office of United Nations High Commissioner for Human Rights did not (as I had originally conceived it and in the form in which it was then being discussed) give any power to the commissioner to interfere in the internal affairs of governments, they saw in it a sinister plan to undermine the sovereignty of states.

They took their revenge at the same session of the commission. In the light of my imminent retirement from the Secretariat, the Canadian government had nominated me to become a member, in my personal capacity, of the Sub-Commission on the Prevention of Discrimination and Protection of Minorities, the membership of which was being increased by three seats. The Russians pointedly said that all three of the new places should go to African countries and that they would vote against candidates from any other, but I was elected notwithstanding their opposition.

The Human Rights Commission did not vote on the Costa Rican proposal at its 1966 session, but by majority vote it did appoint a working group of nine of its members to study "all relevant questions" relating to it and to report to the 1967 session of the commission. On the basis of a document prepared by the Secretariat after my retirement, which would never have been circulated had I still been the director of the Division, this working group quite abandoned the caution that had presided over the original plan and suggested a number of changes in the Costa Rican proposal, all of which were designed to strengthen the powers of the high commissioner. He was now to have, amongst other powers, the right to look at all communications received by the United Nations alleging violations of human rights and, when he deemed it appropriate, to bring them to the attention of the governments concerned. And, in his annual report to the General Assembly, he was to comment on

developments in the field of human rights, including his observations on the implementation of the relevant declarations and instruments adopted by the United Nations and the specialized agencies and his evaluation of significant progress and problems.

Such new functions could take the high commissioner very far indeed. Over the opposition of the Soviet bloc and the doubts of some of the Afro-Asian countries, the commission now adopted the Costa Rican proposal as amended, and in June of the same year it was adopted, much to my surprise, by the Economic and Social Council. The long history of the proposal in the General Assembly and of the controversies and frustrations to which it gave rise do not belong to the period covered by this book. The item was postponed from year to year and, in 1971, for two years; in 1973 it was not only postponed but the very wording of the item was changed so that there is no longer any specific mention in it of the high commissioner. The proposal which was greeted with so much enthusiasm in 1963 by nongovernmental organizations and some governments now seems to be dead, at least in the form in which it was adopted by the Human Rights Commission in 1967. The malady of which the patient died may have been brought about by the excessive zeal of some of its well-wishers.

The story of the high commissioner has taken me well beyond 1963 and the eighteenth session of the General Assembly. At this session, the Third Committee adopted Articles 2, 4 and 24 of the Covenant on Civil and Political Rights. By Article 2, one of the most important in the instrument, a contracting state undertakes

> to respect and to ensure to all individuals within its territory and subject to its jurisdiction the rights recognized in this Covenant, without distinction of any kind, such as race, colour, sex, language, religion, political or other opinion, national or social origin, property, birth or other status.

To this end the contracting states agree "to adopt such legislative or other measures as may be necessary to give effect to the rights recognized in the Covenant." They also agree to ensure that any person whose rights are violated shall have an effective remedy which shall be determined by competent judicial, administrative, legislative or other authorities, and that such remedies when granted shall be enforced by the competent authorities. There were several abstentions when the article was voted paragraph by paragraph. The United Kingdom, quite rightly I thought, proposed the deletion of the provision that calls for the adoption of legislative or other measures necessary to give effect to the covenant, on the ground that civil and political rights should, generally speaking, be immediately implemented and that consequently an undertaking to take steps toward their realization, without setting any time limit, weakened the article. But the British withdrew the motion when it became clear that the paragraph as drafted represented the maximum the majority was willing to accept.

Article 4 is another of the most important in the covenant. It provides that

> in time of public emergency which threatens the life of the nation and the existence of which is officially proclaimed, the states parties hereto may take measures derogating from their obligations under this Covenant to the extent strictly required by the exigencies of the situation provided that such measures are not inconsistent with

their other obligations under international law and do not involve discrimination solely on the ground of race, colour, sex, language, religion or social origin.

The article recognizes, however, that certain basic rights cannot be subject to derogation even in time of public emergency. To avail themselves of the right of derogation states parties must immediately inform the other parties through the Secretary-General of the provisions from which they have derogated and the reasons by which they were actuated.

Article 24 is the article on the rights of children, concerning which the Assembly had at its last session sought the advice of the Human Rights Commission. The commission had not been able to agree on how to advise the Assembly and had therefore merely forwarded to it the record of its deliberations. In the Third Committee there was the same disagreement, certain delegations arguing that the article was unnecessary because the covenant applied to everyone irrespective of age or status. But a majority favored the inclusion of the article, and it was adopted by a vote of 38 to 1 with 38 abstentions. The committee then adopted a provision on the right to be free from hunger, which was added to Article 11 (on the right to an adequate standard of living) of the Covenant on Economic, Social and Cultural Rights. This provision was suggested by the Food and Agriculture Organization after a conversation in my office. The F.A.O. was so pleased by the result that it was easy for me to get them to agree to provide the facilities for the seminar on freedom of information which took place in Rome, where they had their headquarters, the next spring.

The General Assembly also adopted the Declaration on the Elimination of All Forms of Racial Discrimination, a draft of which had been prepared by the Human Rights Commission, but consideration of the declaration on the right of asylum, which had been on its agenda since 1960, was again postponed. Also postponed was further work on the convention and declaration on freedom of information. Two resolutions on the status of women were adopted: one on the participation of women in national, social and economic development, and the other on a proposed declaration on the elimination of discrimination against women, which was adopted in 1967.

The fifteenth anniversary of the adoption of the Universal Declaration of Human Rights was celebrated on 9 December by a special plenary session of the General Assembly and, on the tenth, by the traditional concert. The anniversary was also widely celebrated throughout the world. On 12 December, the General Assembly unanimously decided to designate 1968, the year of the twentieth anniversary, as International Year for Human Rights.

Mission to South Vietnam (1963)

I have already mentioned the mission of inquiry that went to South Vietnam in the fall of 1963 to investigate charges that the Buddhist majority in that country was being persecuted by the Roman Catholic government of Ngo Dinh. The charges were serious. The government, it was said, had interfered with the right of the Buddhists to freedom of thought, conscience and religion, including their right to manifest their religion. Some nine people had been killed when government troops had prevented the people of Hue from celebrating the birthday of the Buddha, and feeling in the country was so high that five monks and a nun had immolated themselves. Armed police had entered the Xa Lai pagoda in Saigon and carried off hundreds of nuns to prison, and the operation had been repeated in pagodas throughout the country. Some one thousand monks were said to be in prison and hundreds of students arrested. The death toll was unknown.

The debate on the item had hardly begun in the General Assembly when its president read out a letter from the observer of South Vietnam (that country not being a member state) inviting "representatives of several member states to visit Vietnam . . . in order that they may find out for themselves the true situation regarding the relations between the government and the Vietnamese Buddhist community." Whether this was an invitation to the United Nations to send a mission of inquiry to South Vietnam is open to doubt; but on 11 October the president appointed such a mission consisting of representatives of Afghanistan, Brazil, Ceylon, Costa Rica, Dahomey, Morocco and Nepal. Whatever its real intention, the Diem government was in real trouble and in no position to insist on niceties. As Diem's brother Ngo Dinh Nhu, later told the mission: "I will be frank. The government was forced to invite you to come and see anything you wanted." We now know from *The Pentagon Papers* that the United States was on the point of withdrawing its support from a government it had helped create and always supported.

The chairman of the mission was Ambassador Abdul Rahman Pazhwak from Afghanistan, the chairman that year of the Human Rights Commission, and it was, I have no doubt, on his insistence that I became the principal secretary of the mission. We left New York on the night of Tuesday, 21 October, and flew straight to Saigon with only one night for sleep in San Francisco. The planning by the U.N. field services could hardly have been worse, for we arrived at our destination at 12:30 in the morning of the 24th (having lost a day crossing the International Date Line) dead tired. As a result we got away to a bad start. When it became necessary to have a meeting of the mission on our arrival at the Majestic

Hotel—where our headquarters were to be—at two o'clock in the morning, one cranky ambassador even refused to attend.

We were greeted at the Saigon airport by a press corps—national and international but chiefly American—which put on one of the worst performances I have ever witnessed. The reporters recognized Pazhwak, whose picture they had seen in the newspapers, but the rest of us were rudely pushed aside as if we had been interlopers. "What are you doing here?" a reporter asked me. "Are you a reporter?" "No," I answered, "I am the principal secretary of the mission." He could not have been less impressed. The government had provided cars to take the ambassadors to the Majestic Hotel, each one flying the flag of the diplomat's country, a courtesy about which we made our first protest the next morning because, as we insisted, we were in Vietnam as a United Nations body. No provision was made for the transportation of the Secretariat, but I was at the hotel in time to make arrangements for the night meeting I have already mentioned.

We had urgent business to transact. At the airport the secretary general of the foreign office had handed the chairman a tentative program of the mission's activities which were to begin that same day. The proposal was that we should spend three days in Saigon, then go on to Vung-Tau (Cap St. Jacques) to see a pagoda, and then to Dalat, where there would be more visits to pagodas, and to educational establishments and tourist centers. There were also to be visits to Hue, Phan-Rang, Phan-Thiet, Ba-Xuyen and Vinh-Binh. This would have been an attractive program for tourists, and I for one would certainly have liked to see, in other circumstances, the Imperial City and other exotic places like the River of Perfumes; but, as the chairman had said at the airport, we had come to Vietnam "determined to report the facts." We did accept the program planned for the first day, which included courtesy calls on the secretaries of state for foreign affairs and of the interior, talks at the ministry of the interior, an audience with President Ngo Dinh Diem and a dinner party hosted by the secretary of the interior. We had a second, longer meeting later in the morning after we had all had some much-needed sleep, when we also decided to accept most of the government's suggestions for our second day in Saigon. There would be an audience with Vice-President of the Republic Ngo Dinh Nhu, and visits to three pagodas for talks with Buddhist leaders, but we suggested that a reception to be given that evening by the secretary of state for foreign affairs be postponed until the mission had completed its work. It never did take place. As for the future, the mission would make its own plans and the government was so informed.

President Diem was a thickset, nervous little man who courteously received us neatly dressed in white. He was obviously under great strain—much greater than we could then imagine—and, like his brother whom we met the next day, a chain smoker. Speaking in French, he described the events which had led up to the incident in Hue when nine demonstrators were alleged to have been shot by government troops. The government had, he said, come to an agreement with the Buddhists, but the monks became impatient and said the agreement was not being respected. Their demands were supported, the president said, by certain political forces which provoked a series of public demonstrations, the main theater of which had been the pagodas, where the monks installed loudspeakers through which they harangued the public. On the advice of the Army (the next day Diem's brother Nhu told us that Diem's hand had been forced) he had declared martial law. The pagodas were then searched, but no one had been killed. He also mentioned interference by foreign

governments, and it was perfectly clear to me that he was not talking about either the Soviet Union or China. I came away from this meeting favorably impressed by the man. Obviously an aristocrat and probably an autocrat, he was also a loyal Vietnamese who was
passionately concerned about the future of his country. A week later he and his brother
Nhu were dead, murdered by soldiers in a coup d'état for which the green light had been
given by the foreign government that had brought him to power.

We had an audience the next day with Ngo Dinh Nhu. His large office in the palace
was furnished in exquisite taste with great Chinese vases, red lacquered chests and, on the
walls, French postimpressionist paintings, all of which would soon be in a shambles. Nhu
spoke for about an hour. Of slighter build and smarter in appearance than his brother, he
was also neatly dressed in white. He too was in a highly nervous state and smoked cigarette
after cigarette. There was something in his face that marked him as a man of superior intelligence. I was attracted to him immediately, notwithstanding the bad image the world
press had given him. When I remarked to a colleague that I was surprised that such a man
would permit his wife to create such an unfavorable image abroad, he replied that Nhu
probably couldn't do anything about it.

Nhu's opening remarks are worth repeating:

> The principal problem facing us is a problem of underdevelopment. . . . . . The
> Buddhist question is only one aspect of that problem. Political, social and religious
> movements have grown considerably since the country became independent. But
> there is a lack of cadres both in these movements and in the government. The latter
> has been obliged to seek the assistance of foreign technicians in all fields (adminis-
> tration, education and so on) but these aliens have their own ideology, and their pres-
> ence in Vietnamese organs has its drawbacks as well as its advantages and is a source
> of friction. The same situation obtains in the Buddhist movement; it has expanded
> enormously, but its cadres are inadequate, a fact that has inevitably led to aberra-
> tions. I consider that the line taken by the Vietnamese government has also suffered
> certain inevitable aberrations. The problem of freedom is not the only one the Viet-
> namese people has to solve; the main problem is a problem of justice. The masses
> have to be mobilized for industrialization; but so long as political, economic and so-
> cial privileges have not been abolished that will not be possible. The military and
> economic problems cannot be divorced from the social problem. All the less devel-
> oped countries have their problems, both with their friends and with their enemies.

In the light of the events that were to follow and the revelations of *The Pentagon Papers*,
Nhu's reference to friends and enemies had a meaning which escaped us at the time. He
spoke for nearly an hour and then offered to answer questions. It was a remarkable performance. His remarks were penetrating and to the point; and as they appear in the report of
the mission one might think that they had been carefully drafted (the quotations reproduced
here suffer by the fact that they are in translation), but he was speaking *ex tempore* without
notes.

Nothing came out of the interview that could possibly substantiate a charge that the
Buddhists were being persecuted. Ambassador Gunewardene's questions were all directed
to getting some admission on that score, but the impression with which we were left was

quite the opposite. Nhu said many things that would be worth quoting, but this is not possible here. However, one other reference to the United States does need to be quoted:

> The United States advocates liberty as the solution to underdevelopment. But liberty is not liberation. The liberation advocated by communism is not freedom. A liberator is not automatically a liberal, a liberal is not necessary a liberator . . . United States assistance, which is very valuable to us, contains the seeds of decay: How can one mobilize the masses with a freedom which does not entail the suppression of privileges? On the contrary, we are being asked to retain them, while at the same time making progress; this is a myth.

He also spoke of foreign agitators, "especially the American press." The published record does not contain one thing that I distinctly remember Nhu saying, for I attached great significance to it at the time. He spoke, possibly privately to a smaller group—I do not remember—of the complementary natures of the economies of North and South Vietnam. After the coup d'état in which he was murdered I wondered whether the reason the Americans abandoned the two brothers wasn't possibly that they feared they had entered or were about to enter into some kind of discussion with the northern leaders.

The same day we visited two pagodas, where we interviewed monks, nuns and Buddhist leaders. It was in these pagodas that I began to have real trouble with the press. The monks and nuns were afraid that anything they might say would come to the attention of the government. We had therefore to gain their confidence and the worst possible thing that we could have done would be to allow the press to be present. The reporters dogged our every step and set up television cameras within view of the places where we were conducting the interviews. My press officer, Valieri Stavridi, had his hands full keeping them at a distance. These people also created the impression abroad that the government was pulling the wool over our eyes whereas, as a matter of fact, Ngo Dinh Nhu had agreed to every request we had made, and we were now working on our own timetable. It was a very simple thing for me to follow what was being reported in the press, particularly in the United States, because I received full accounts every day from New York. We had our own interpreters and no Vietnamese official ever accompanied us to the pagodas or to the prisons and concentration camps that we later visited. It is possible, of course, that some of these places may have been "bugged," although I always did examine them very carefully.

On 26 October we issued a statement, which was published in the local press and carried over the radio, that the mission would hear witnesses at its headquarters in the Majestic Hotel. For a United Nations body to conduct such an inquiry in a sovereign independent country was a precedent of some importance. We then gave the government a list of witnesses we wanted to question, a number of whom were among those who appeared before the mission at its headquarters; others were interviewed in the pagodas, prisons and concentration camps.

Among those who testified at our headquarters was a young monk who had been picked up by the police to prevent him from immolating himself as others had done, some while the mission was in Saigon. His story was pathetic. He had intended to commit suicide at the National Day celebrations. He had, he said, been approached by a student who asked him to join the movement, given him two suits (because, the student said, it was dangerous to appear in the streets dressed as a monk) and later introduced him to two other men:

"The first man's name was Thanh and the other man was a monk disguised as a civilian wearing a nylon hat. They told me they were happy to see me. They also told me that the United Nations mission would soon come to Vietnam to inquire into the relations between the government and the Buddhist community. Then they told me that they needed ten volunteers, and they wanted to know if I would accept to be one of the ten. I accepted because I felt so upset about what I had heard earlier about the government's treatment of monks. I thought that I would end up the same way sooner or later myself. So that is why I accepted. I was also told that a monk named Phanh My would commit suicide by burning in front of the Redemptionist Church and another nun in front of Tan Dinh Church on Hai Batrung Road. They said I should do so at the National Day celebration because many people would be there, including members of the United Nations mission. I asked him how I would get into the area because it had been cordoned off. I was told not to worry, that the suicide promotion group would make all the arrangements for me. I asked what kind of arrangements, and they answered that on 26 October I would be given a white suit and a yellow robe soaked in gasoline. They would provide me with a car bearing a sticker enabling the car to go into the area. When the car got there I was to get out in a normal manner. The car would then be driven away. I was then to sit down, put the yellow robe on and strike a match and set myself on fire. Also, before this, they would give me some pills so that I would not feel the pain. Then they told me that I could go. They gave me a hundred piastres for carfare.

Two days later the student had him sign three letters, one addressed to the president of the republic, the second to the chief monk at the An Quang pagoda and the third to the United Nations mission. He was picked up by the police the day before the national celebrations. The young monk's story could have been manufactured for our benefit; but I do not think so, for there was a note of veracity in it that convinced me in any event, and he stuck to it during cross-examination.

We visited the LeVan Duyet Youth Camp in which students who had taken part in manifestations were being kept for periods averaging two weeks, after which they were returned to their parents. We talked to some of them. They were a healthy-looking, neatly dressed lot, and I couldn't help thinking that some of them were rather enjoying the experience. We wanted very much to interview the monk, Thich Tri Quang, who according to the foreign minister, "was the real leader of all Buddhist political insurrectionist movements," but he had sought asylum in the United States embassy, with which the mission wanted to have no contact.

One day Pazhwak asked me to charter an airplane to take the mission to Hue. I thought about this for a few minutes and then suggested that it was not a very good idea. By that time it was perfectly obvious that we had outworn our welcome, which had never been very enthusiastic. We had gone beyond anything the government could ever have contemplated when it agreed to the mission's coming to Vietnam, and they must have been wondering what would happen when our report came before the General Assembly. An easy solution—although the thought was admittedly far-fetched and in retrospect I do not think that they would have had recourse to such a measure—would have been to have something happen to the mission. If our plane were to be brought down in flight, it could be blamed on the Vietcong, who were operating so close to Saigon that gunfire could be heard from our hotel. I therefore suggested that only half the mission go to Hue. There would then be no incentive for skullduggery. Pazhwak agreed that the risk wasn't worth taking and we proceeded as I had suggested. I wanted to go to Hue myself, but the chairman had business with the foreign office and insisted on my remaining with him in Saigon.

By the time our colleagues had returned from Hue we were beginning to hear rumors about an impending coup d'état. My administrative officer, Alain Dangeard, who was a Frenchman, had mingled with the crowd watching the great military parade on National Day (an invitation to which the mission had rejected) and had also been in touch with the French embassy. There would be trouble, he warned, but we discounted his warnings. The government seemed to be firmly enough in control—something which the great military parade seemed to confirm—and it had, we thought, the support of the United States. So we laughed when he came to the table where Pazhwak and I were having lunch on the first of November, to report that he had a message from the French embassy that it would be better if the mission were to remain in the hotel that afternoon. But before we could finish our lunch the sound of gunfire in the streets made it only too obvious that Dangeard had not been crying wolf.

I went with Pazhwak and some others to our offices on the mezzanine, the large windows of which overlooked the Saigon river where some ships of the Vietnamese fleet were moored. We hadn't been there long when we noticed warplanes coming in towards the ships; and before we could realize what was happening there was a deafening outburst of anti-aircraft fire. All of us except Pazhwak, who continued to look out of the window, dropped to the floor. I wormed my way into the corridor for greater protection, with on one side of me Ambassador Gunewardene and on the other an American soldier on leave from his barracks in the outskirts of the city. "I wish I were in the barracks," he said. We were afraid the planes would bomb the ships, some of which were only a few hundred yards from the hotel. The admiral had remained loyal to Diem and the Air Force had come in as a warning, but he was shot by one of his officers, which soon brought the fleet over to the side of the insurgents. The street fighting continued through the afternoon and into the night, but nobody interfered with us at the hotel.

The next morning I was awakened by my room boy who, crossing his hand over his throat, murmured excitedly "Diem," and at breakfast I learned that both the president and his brother had been killed. Later in the morning I went out into the streets which were full of tanks and soldiers. The palace, with all of Nhu's fine pictures and furniture, was in a shambles. Crossing at a street corner I ran into Gordon Cox, the Canadian member of the International Supervisory Commission, at whose house in the diplomatic compound I had had dinner a few nights earlier. It had been a kind of cloak-and-dagger affair; the Canadians apparently didn't want it to be known that they were entertaining the principal secretary of the United Nations mission and they had arranged for their car to pick me up not at the Majestic Hotel but several blocks away.

That afternoon, sitting in the mission's office on the mezzanine floor of the hotel, I noticed a great crowd of people busy demolishing a monument on the quay some distance up the Saigon River. It had been recently erected in memory of the two sisters who, a thousand years ago, had ridden out of Saigon on elephants to repulse a Chinese army, and had been modeled by Madame Nhu and her daughter. The crowd, taking its revenge by tearing the monument to pieces, then began to move along the quay towards the hotel. We soon learned why they had been distracted from their vandalism. Buu Hoi, (the observer of South Vietnam at the United Nations, who had come with us from New York to be the government's liaison officer with the mission) was now on his way in an open car with a message from the Military Revolutionary Council that the mission would be welcome to stay in Vietnam as long as it liked. The son of a nun who had threatened to immolate herself in protest against the Diem government and a marked man because he had supported that government, the crowd had recognized him and were following him to the hotel. He came up to the mezzanine where I and several others were waiting. Some of the more militant people in the crowd had followed him into the hotel, but none of them climbed the stairs to the mezzanine. There was a great deal of noise and much shouting. Some hotheads wanted to lynch Buu Hoi and even to attack the United Nations people who had been invited to Vietnam by the Diem government. Since the beginning of the fighting the mission had had no police protection whatsoever, Nhu's elite guard—which had been an embarrassment because it intimidated witnesses coming to the hotel—having long since disappeared. There wasn't even a traffic policeman. I turned to the army major who had accompanied Buu Hoi. "Good God," I said, "do something." He got on the telephone but it wasn't working. After five or ten minutes of this and after Buu Hoi had disappeared to some other part of the hotel, I figured that it was time to think about my own safety and that of my colleague, Ilhan Lütem, with whom I retired down the corridor to my room. After about twenty minutes, we returned to the mission's office; everything was now quiet, the crowd had gone and the hotel was surrounded by troops.

The mission had already decided that there was nothing more it could do in Vietnam. We had been asked to investigate certain charges against the Diem government and that government no longer existed. We, therefore, informed the military council of our intention to leave Saigon on 3 November, a departure time which turned out not to be easy, since all the airports were closed, but with the permission of the new government we were able to arrange with Cathay Pacific Airlines to pick us up. We were driven to the airport in a cavalcade escorted by police, and all along the long ride the streets were lined with soldiers. I had inquired about Buu Hoi but nobody knew where he was. When we got to the airport, I was relieved to discover that he had been with us in the convoy and boarded the plane with us. That plane took us to Hong Kong, which had never looked so good, and where Lütem and I and some of the others spent a couple of days before continuing our journey. Back in New York I supervised the preparation of the mission's report to the General Assembly which, on 13 December, decided that in the light of events it need not pursue the matter further.

A few days after this my wife and I were in Jamaica. It was a combination of business and pleasure. I wanted the government to sponsor one of our human rights seminars and had an appointment with Hugh Shearer, who was a member of the Jamaican cabinet. We quickly reached an agreement, and shortly after my retirement from the Secretariat I attended the seminar there on local remedies for the protection of human rights, as one of two participants from Canada. On Shearer's recommendation we spent our holiday in the Shaw Park Hotel at Ocho Rios, which was near the hospital in which our friend, Dr. Leonard Jacobs, was the chief surgeon. Jacobs suggested to me that there might be a place in the University of the West Indies for me after my retirement from the Secretariat, and he arranged for me to meet Dr. Sherlock, the principal of the university. But although my wife and I both liked Jamaica and I probably would have accepted an appointment had one been offered me nothing came out of the interview.

Mongolia, Kabul and Other Adventures (1964)

At its sixteenth session, which opened on 13 January, the Sub-Commission on the Prevention of Discrimination prepared the first drafts of the important Convention on the Elimination of All Forms of Racial Discrimination and of the Declaration on the Elimination of All Forms of Religious Intolerance. Other business included reports on its studies of discrimination against persons born out of wedlock and on equality in the administration of justice. The rapporteur for the latter study was represented by his alternate, M.Y. Mudawi, a judge of the Supreme Court of the Sudan, a man who so impressed me that I later recommended that, if the choice did not fall on Edward Lawson (who was unlikely to be appointed because there were so many American directors in the Secretariat), he become my successor as the director of the Human Rights Division. I saw more of Mudawi at Dakar in 1965; and, after a coup d'état in the Sudan when he resigned from the bench, I helped him find an academic post in an African university.

The twentieth session of the Human Rights Commission also met at headquarters. Its one concrete achievement was its approval, after amendment, of the draft convention on racial discrimination that had been prepared by the sub-commission; but it did not find the time to approve the draft declaration on religious intolerance. It did set up a thirty-four member committee, of which Sir Egerton Richardson (Jamaica) was the chairman, to recommend a program for the International Year for Human Rights in 1968. This committee met many times throughout the year.

Apart from the Racial Convention, the most important item on the commission's agenda related to the periodic or as they were now called, the triennial, reports covering the years 1960-62. By the end of 1964, sixty-five governments had reported in the third round. I thought and still do that, as in the International Labor Organization, an effective implementation system could have been built up around these reports. The Secretariat had prepared summaries to make the commission's work easier, and I hoped it would examine them critically. It did appoint a committee of eight member states to examine the summaries. This committee was also to prepare a survey of developments as well as its conclusions and recommendations "of an objective and general character" and to recommend a procedure to be followed by the Secretariat in the controversial matter of what to do with the comments and observations received from nongovernmental organizations. The committee held sixteen meetings during the year and made several recommendations, but none of them touched on the crucial matter of the creation of machinery for the critical examination of the reports by independent experts.

In April I went to Rome for the seminar on freedom of information, which was held at the headquarters of the Food and Agriculture Organization, an arrangement made possible partly because of the help I had given this specialized agency at the last session of the General Assembly, when a reference to the right to freedom from hunger was included in the Covenant on Economic, Social and Cultural Rights. The seminar, which brought together participants from twenty-five European countries, discussed the roles of government, press laws, the publisher and proprietor and the professional journalist, as well as standards of journalism and the role of the reader. Ordinarily I did not encourage the seminars to adopt resolutions, but this time I used all the influence I had to get the seminar to adopt the resolutions on a code of ethics and international machinery for the promotion of freedom of information already mentioned. A highlight of the seminar was an audience with Pope Paul, which all the participants attended, including the Russians and their friends from Eastern Europe who donned their best clothes for the occasion. The Pope made a very good speech, which was later reproduced in *L' Osservatore Romano*. He then descended from his throne to chat with the participants, passing around medallions from a generous supply in a pocket under his white soutane. When he came to me, he paused and said: "I don't suppose you want one." Someone must have told him that the representative of the Secretary-General was a heretic.

From Rome I went to Mongolia to organize a seminar on the status of women. In this case I had made my first contact through a young officer in my own division. I talked to Orso, he talked to the Mongolian delegation and it invited me to come to Ulan Bator which wasn't as far out of my way as it might seem, because I was going to Central Asia in any event for a seminar in Afghanistan. But first I went to Moscow, where I spent a weekend mostly admiring the icons in the churches of the Kremlin.

At Ulan Bator airport I was received by a foreign office delegation, a big Zim car—longer than a Cadillac—a chauffeur and an interpreter. The Mongolians hadn't had much experience with United Nations officials—they had been in the organization for less than three years—and I must have been one of the very first to visit the country. Instead of taking me to the perfectly good hotel in the city, where I stayed a year later, I was driven to a V.I.P. establishment some six miles outside the city limits. When the big Zim car approached this place we were stopped at a barrier by a heavily armed guard. It was a moonlit night and I could see that the hotel was in a narrow valley. I later learned that it had been given to the Mongolian people by the People's Republic of China. Although already in need of repair—the plumbing in my room didn't work properly—it was as luxurious as any hotel I have ever been in. That first night I dined there with officials from several government departments. After they had left and I had retired to my room, I noticed that the place was peculiarly quiet; and, to my consternation, I soon realized that I was absolutely alone in the building, or so in any event it seemed. All the servants had gone, and as far as I could gather there wasn't even a night watchman; but I remembered the soldiers at the gate. I turned out my lights and looked out of the windows. Silhouetted against the sky on the hill near the hotel were several sentinels. I felt like the prisoner of Zenda. The next morning when I awoke the place was humming again and there were even two or three government people waiting to have breakfast with me. For breakfast I was offered caviar and vodka. Other mornings they gave me a kind of porridge made of millet. Government officials came to dine with me nearly every evening. They were a jolly lot, and I enjoyed their company. But after they had left it was always the same and as far as I knew I was the only person left in the hotel. I might have questioned my hosts about this, but I didn't want them to think I was afraid. I finally concluded that the hotel was part of a compound where members of the Politburo came for recreation and other purposes; that would explain why it was so heavily guarded.

I visited a number of government departments, where I met many personalities, and soon finished the business I had come to transact. The Mongolians were proud of the equality enjoyed by their women, and it didn't take much urging to convince them that they should sponsor the seminar. From the viewpoint of the United Nations it would be an opportunity to fly the flag in a country where there had never been an international conference attended by participants from beyond the Soviet bloc. Mongolia was obviously very much under Soviet influence. All the young men with whom I dealt were graduates of Russian universities and, of course, spoke Russian as a second language; some of them also spoke very good English or French. There were no noncommunist embassies in Ulan Bator and, in the growing ideological conflict between China and the Soviet Union, sympathies were firmly on the side of the Russians.

It was fascinating to see what was happening to Ulan Bator, a city which not so long ago wasn't much more than an agglomeration of felt yurts. In an almost straight line bulldozers were destroying the yurts, and construction gangs—some of them Chinese—were building a new city. The best view of all this was from a hill just outside the city, to which I drove several times. The city now had a university, hospitals and even a theater. It was probably as good an example of rapid industrialization as could be seen anywhere. And most if not all of this was being done with the help of Russian experts. The Russians were obviously very popular, and I saw no sign of the kind of nationalistic resentment which in other countries, for example the Philippines, I had detected against countries providing technical assistance.

I asked my hosts whether the Buddhists were free to practice their religion. This resulted in arrangements being immediately made for me to visit the Gandantehehingling Pagoda which, it seems, was one of the rare pagodas still operating in the country; some of the others had been turned into museums. After visiting the pagoda and listening to the most cacophonous service that could be imagined, I was invited to the abbot's yurt, a very large felt tent decorated with many carpets, where I was seated on a kind of throne near the abbot, who made a speech welcoming me to Mongolia. Although not prepared for it, I felt that I was expected to respond and made a short speech in which I compared Buddhist philosophy with the aims and principles of the United Nations. I don't know how this went down with my hosts. There was then a feast consisting of brandy, fermented mare's milk, Russian chocolates and chunks of mutton. I was surprised to find meat in an abbot's yurt. The explanation was that the Mongolians were traditionally nomads who lived chiefly on mutton and mare's milk and that the Buddhist taboo on meat was therefore not observed.

Before leaving the yurt, I was able to talk to some of the monks, most of whom were old men. I told them about my experiences in Vietnam, the alleged persecution of the monks there and the immolations. They had heard nothing about these things and were shocked by what I told them. The quick gesture they made could have been mistaken for the sign of the cross. When I later remarked to a foreign office official that the pagoda I had visited was apparently the only one still operating in Ulan Bator, he said that the government had not had to take any special measures against the monks; it had simply made conditions outside the monasteries so attractive that the pagodas could no longer recruit acolytes.

On the weekend I was driven in my Zim car to a trade-union rest house about fifty miles from Ulan Bator. There were conventional roads for only a few miles outside the city, after which we drove over the plains on tracks which, at some points, went off in all directions. At one place we forded a river. We passed several great herds of horses and stopped at one place to examine a dead colt that must have been born only the night before and was already being attacked by birds of prey.

The Terelj rest house wasn't particularly comfortable, and I was left to my own devices all the time I was there. I spent my time walking, mostly on a hill back of the hostel where the only attraction was some yaks—another animal that must have been put together by a committee. There was a brook not far from the rest house in which I imagined there must be trout, but I had no tackle. There were hardly any birds and I could not identify those I did see. I was glad when the time came to climb into my Zim car and drive back to my V.I.P hotel, particularly because I couldn't get used to the smell of mutton, which permeated every corner of the hostel.

My mission in Ulan Bator completed I had over a week to put in before the Kabul seminar and was planning to visit Tashkent and perhaps Samarkand and Bukhara. When I went to the Aeroflot offices to make reservations, however, they told me that I would have to return to Moscow and fly to Tashkent from there. This seemed so ridiculous that I protested, but the agency was adamant and I resigned myself to a long and tiring trip. The first leg took me back to Irkutsk in Siberia, where I had stopped to change planes on my way to Ulan Bator. I remember the fine view of Lake Baikal as the low-flying plane came in over it. Going through immigration in Irkutsk, I said I was on my way to Tashkent. "Sorry," came the reply in perfect English, "the plane for Novosibirsk has just left. You will have to spend the night here." This suited me, so I accepted an offer of dinner, and after a walk retired for the night in a kind of dormitory where I was the only guest. Next morning after a breakfast consisting mainly of red caviar and tea, I inquired about the possibility of seeing something of the city, for there were still a few hours left before my plane would leave. But I was told this was impossible and I very soon gave up the idea.

I changed planes at Novosibirsk but again saw nothing of the city except from the air. From there I flew to Alma Ata in Kazakhstan. On the seat next to me was a young soldier with Asiatic features. Once he pointed excitedly to the ground, from which I gathered that this was where he lived. The plane remained in Alma Ata—Father of the Apple—for over an hour, long enough to admire the great orchards of blooming apple trees which seemed to stretch to the Tien Shan mountains far in the distance.

A protocol officer from the Uzbek Foreign Office was waiting for me when I arrived at Tashkent. The authorities had apparently caught up with my movements although they said nothing about my failure to follow instructions. The protocol officer was a Ukrainian who spoke such good English that one might have thought he had just come down from Oxford or Cambridge, but he told me that he had never been outside the Soviet Union.

I had no official business in Tashkent and had now decided to spend only a short time there and then go on to Bukhara and Samarkand. But the Uzbek Foreign Office had a plan for my entertainment that would keep me fully occupied until the time came to leave for Kabul, and I thought that it would be more courteous to accommodate myself to it. The program included a visit to a very large factory, where I was escorted by the chief engineer—a smartly dressed young woman—calls on various personalities, including the head of the Uzbek Republic, who was also a woman, visits to hospitals, and so on. One afternoon I went to a boarding school in the country where all the students—they ranged in age from about seven to twenty—were specializing in music while also following a regular school curriculum. I heard a symphony orchestra and another in which all the instruments were Uzbek and also watched a ballet. My visit to the school was to have lasted for only about an hour, but I was obviously enjoying myself so much that my enthusiastic hosts kept me there for most of the afternoon. Before leaving I planted a vine in the school garden, a ceremony in which I was helped by a little girl of about seven, whose special duty it would be to look after the vine. On the way back to Tashkent we stopped at a hospital for sick children. The children could not leave their beds, but they did a dance with their hands; it was one of the most charming performances I have ever witnessed, and the obvious devotion of the doctors and nurses to their charges warmed my heart.

At my hotel I was left to my own resources, which was embarrassing because none of the waiters understood English or French and I was in danger of starving. However, there were three or four men at a table near mine who were obviously Americans, sociologists as it turned out who were in Tashkent on some exchange program. They invited me to their table and my eating problem was solved. I went with them several times to the theater just across a square from the hotel, where we saw some very good ballet and Uzbek dancing. The audience roared its approval of the Uzbek dances. One evening, after the theater, one of the American professors asked me if I would accompany him to an Easter service. We took a ramshackle tramway to the outskirts of the city, where there was a small Baptist church in a courtyard surrounded by high walls, the entrance to which, I was surprised to see, was guarded by husky-looking women armed with large staffs. We went into the yard, but the church was so full of people that it was impossible to get inside. There was a commotion outside the walls which, we soon discovered, was the work of young toughs playing banjos and hurling insults at the faithful. Since there was no room for us in the church, we soon left the place. Waiting for the tramway I noticed a black maria which had just arrived. Ah, I thought, the police are going to protect the right of the faithful to manifest their religion. Not so, they had come to arrest beggars who, in the Soviet Union, are still attracted by any large gathering of people.

The Kabul seminar on human rights in developing countries began on 12 May and attracted participants from sixteen countries and many observers. Opening the conference I referred to the opinion so often expressed at the United Nations that economically developing countries face special difficulties in promoting respect for human rights. Was that true? The answers of the participants were, as I had expected, in the affirmative.

This second visit to Afghanistan, although longer, was not nearly so interesting as my first, when I had been taken to Bamiyan; but there were compensations, including a day-long drive north on the new road that had been built by the Russians and a drive down the Khyber Pass. The Americans were building roads in the south, and between them and the Russians the Afghans were doing very well. Nearly every morning, before driving to the fine new university on the outskirts of Kabul where the seminar was held, I managed a stroll in the old part of the city or along the river. With its narrow streets and high adobe houses the old city was like a page out of the Arabian nights, and life went on, I imagined, as it must have done for a thousand years. Here most of the men were armed and the woman wore the traditional *chador*. What a contrast at the university. Arriving there one morning, I watched a young woman take off her veil as she walked through the gates—a gesture as indicative of what I thought was happening in Afghanistan as anything I could have seen.

Moscow, Irkutsk, Ulan Bator, Alma Ata, Tashkent and Kabul—it had been an exotic experience, but there was more to come. The Iranian government had invited me to stop off in Tehran on my way back to New York to discuss a seminar on the status of women which they wanted to sponsor. The Ganji family, which had entertained me so lavishly on my first visit, were at the airport to meet me; they refused to allow me to go to a hotel and took me to their home, where I stayed all the time I was in Tehran. I was also summoned to have dinner with Princess Ashraf Pahlavi, the twin sister of the shah. My instructions were to arrive half an hour before the other guests for a private talk. When she said that the seminar was to be part of an effort to improve the condition of Iranian women and I realized that she wanted to do something that would have real impact, I suggested that instead of sponsoring a seminar, the government should invite the Commission on the Status of Women to hold one of its regular sessions in Iran. She quickly agreed. I pointed out that it would cost a large sum of money, but this wasn't an obstacle; she invited the foreign minister and the minister of finance into the room and informed them that the commission would meet in Iran.

Before leaving Iran I also visited the ancient city of Isfahan. In the meantime a cablegram arrived from New York asking me to go to Colombo, where the United Nations Association of Ceylon was holding a conference at which they were anxious to have a representative of the Secretary-General. This was an unusual request and it was even more unusual that the Secretariat should have agreed to send anyone such a long distance for such a purpose. There must be, I guessed, something special about the meeting and Ambassador Gunewardene must have put great pressure on the Secretary-General, but I couldn't anticipate what I was in for. When I got to Colombo, I discovered that most of the people at the conference were Tamils and that one of the chief topics to be discussed was the treatment of the Tamil minority by the Singhalese majority. I had learned something about this when I was in Ceylon in 1959 for the Kandy seminar, and it was because I had not wanted to become involved that I had cut short my visit. Now I was in the thick of it. To make things worse, I was seated on the podium next to the chairman and everytime he or someone else made a point he would turn to me and say, "And isn't that right, Dr. Humphrey?" I was somewhat relieved when Mrs. Bandaranaike, now prime minister, invited me to her house for tea, which I took to mean I had not compromised the United Nations.

On the weekend before leaving Ceylon, I managed to drive to Kandy, which I was glad to see again, and on my way back to New York stopped off for three days in Madras. After about a month at headquarters, I moved on to Geneva for the summer session of the Economic and Social Council. This was when, with several others in Sean MacBride's office at the International Commission of Jurists, I drafted the resolution on the United Nations High Commissioner for Human Rights which we gave to the Costa Rican ambassador.

There was an item on the Council's agenda concerning measures that might be taken to implement the recently adopted Declaration on the Elimination of All Forms of Racial Discrimination; but although the Secretariat had prepared a report on the question, all the Council managed to do in response to a request from the General Assembly was to recommend that the Assembly adopt a resolution calling on states "in which racial discrimination was practiced" to implement the Declaration and to prosecute or outlaw organizations promoting such discrimination, which could have been done without consulting the Council. It was like a kind of merry-go-round except that it wasn't merry. The Council also forwarded to the Assembly the articles that had been prepared by the Human Rights Commission and its sub-commission for an international convention on the same subject. Exceptionally there was no report from the Commission on the Status of Women before this session of the Council, because, pursuant to the decision taken in 1963, that commission did not meet in 1964. Realizing its mistake, the Council now decided that henceforth this commission would meet annually.

In October I went to Edmonton, Alberta, to represent the Secretary-General at celebrations commemorating the coming into force of the United Nations Charter. Shortly after returning to New York I attended a cocktail party at which U Thant made a speech in which he said that the work of the three councils of the United Nations corresponded to its three principal purposes and went on to mention the maintenance of international cooperation for the solution of economic and social problems. But he said nothing about human rights, even though the principal purposes of the United Nations also include, in the words of the first article of the Charter, "promoting and encouraging respect for human rights." His failure to mention human rights specifically in an apparently unprepared statement was significant. He was enthusiastic about the role of the Trusteeship Council in preparing colonial peoples for independence, thereby betraying a bias very near to his heart, but even though in speeches prepared for him by his staff he would come out strongly on the side of human rights, he gave no priority to the work of the United Nations for their promotion.

At meetings in November of the committee on periodic reports from governments on their performance in the matter of human rights, the Americans made some interesting suggestions, which were energetically opposed by the Russians and Poles, one of them that the reports, which up until that time had been summarized by the Secretariat, should be published in full. The second—my own idea—was that the report should be sent to the Sub-Commission on the Prevention of Discrimination for preliminary examination. Because the members of this body were elected in their personal capacity, I thought they would be less inhibited in criticizing the reports than the representatives of governments on the Human Rights Commission. I didn't like the third American suggestion, which was that in the future governments should report annually in three-year cycles: in the first year on civil and political rights, in the second on economic, social and cultural rights and in the third on freedom of information. This formula, which was later adopted and entailed a cycle extending over six years, meant that a very long time could elapse between the events being reported on and their consideration (if any) by the United Nations. The Americans were therefore guilty of emasculating their own original reporting scheme. The fact is, however, that governments never had any intention of making the system work, and, as already indicated, it was abandoned in 1981.

One of the most frustrating experiences an international official can have is to have to sit silently while a committee member sabotages a good idea, particularly if it is his own, which is what happened to me when the delegate from the Philippines tried for reasons that I could not fathom to emasculate the proposal to send the reports to the sub-commission. But notwithstanding his efforts and the opposition of the Soviet Union and Poland, the committee did recommend that the reports be sent to the sub-commission. I was so confident that the sub-commission would respond positively to the challenge that I thought these committee meetings had been the most useful that had been held on a human rights question for a long time. But when the time came the performance of the sub-commission was no better than that of the commission.

The nineteenth session of the General Assembly did not begin until the first of December. This was the session at which—because it was feared that the sanction provided by Article 19 of the Charter would be invoked against the Soviet Union and in all probability provoke the withdrawal of that country from the United Nations—there was until the very end no voting. Article 19 says that a member state which is in arrears in the payment of its financial contribution to the organization shall have no vote in the General Assembly if the amount of its arrears equals or exceeds the amount of the contributions due from it for the preceding two years. Dues owing by the Soviet Union were now in arrears in this amount, the government of that country having refused to recognize the legality of sums expended by the United Nations in the Congo. The danger of a confrontation which could destroy the United Nations was therefore very great; and this was why the opening of the session had been postponed for so long beyond its normal opening date. The Secretary-General now suggested that only the most urgent business should be transacted, and that by consensus or acclamation. A *modus vivendi* was worked out along these lines. This crisis brought to the surface some of the inherent weaknesses of the United Nations; but the fact that all member states were willing until the very end of the session, to have recourse to patently irregular devices in order to avoid a confrontation which threatened the life of the organization was eloquent proof of the great importance they attached to it. I happened to be in the Assembly Hall the day the delegate from Albania, then generally considered to be the voice of the People's Republic of China, not then a member state, nearly upset the applecart by moving a procedural motion which required a decision. I watched the president while he consulted his advisers and wondered what would happen. The crisis was met by Adlai Stevenson who said that a vote on that procedural motion would not be considered a vote within the meaning of Article 19, a statement which although an act of statesmanship was by any interpretation an American capitulation. The drama of the incident was heightened when Jamil Baroody, the representative of Saudi Arabia, walked to the podium and attempted to conduct the Albanian back to his seat. One result of this crisis was that although there were a number of human rights items on the agenda, including the draft Convention on the Elimination of All Forms of Racial Discrimination, no decisions were taken on any of them at this session.

The Foreign Minister of Dahomey gave an elaborate and, for such a small country, very expensive dinner dance at the Plaza Hotel. Ambassador Morozov, who was there, told me that he had talked to the Secretary-General about extending my contract beyond the normal retirement age, which was now only a little over a year away. "It may do you no good," he said. When the director of personnel offered to extend my tenure by a year he did not mention this *démarche* or a similar one that Adlai Stevenson had made. I was fairly sure, however, that had it not been for them my contract would not have been extended; for not long afterwards Narasimhan told me that my career in the Secretariat would end on 30 April 1966. I was more popular with the staff than with certain parts of the establishment. The day after the Dahomey party, the chairman of the staff council asked me if he could put my name forward as the staff nominee for the appointments and promotion board, but I didn't want to repeat my earlier experience with this board and declined the honor. The day after the Human Rights Concert on 10 December, Edward Lawson showed me copies of the *New York Journal American* and *New York News*, both of which had front page stories about the concert and the Universal Declaration of Human Rights. The reason why the popular press had suddenly become interested in the Declaration was that "Jackie" Kennedy had been at the concert; it was, according to the stories, her first "official" appearance since the death of her husband. There was a rumor that the Americans were backing her for a directorship in the Secretariat. Later that morning, I received a delegation of South Koreans who had with them a petition in over a hundred large volumes and signed, they said, by over a million people, alleging that many thousands of South Koreans who had been captured by the communists during the war had never been heard of since. Only a few minutes before receiving this delegation I had been disturbed by a loud explosion. Looking out my window I could see a disturbance in the water about halfway across the East River and later learned that the explosion was part of an anti-Castro demonstration that was taking place on the other side of the building. Not long before this I had received a delegation of war resisters headed by Norman Thomas.

Tehran, Ljubljana and Mongolia Again
(1965)

My wife and I spent the Christmas holidays on the delightful West Indian Island of St. Vincent, where we went chiefly because one of my colleagues, governor of the island [later Sir] Rupert John, had invited us to his daughter's marriage. I was back at headquarters in time to go to Geneva for the annual meetings of the Sub-Commission on the Prevention of Discrimination, but the Under Secretary told me that my place was in my office and I did not attend the session. The sub-commission prepared a first draft of the yet-to-be-adopted Convention on the Elimination of All Forms of Religious Intolerance. Other matters on the agenda were the studies on discrimination against persons born out of wedlock, on equality in the administration of justice and in the political, economic and cultural spheres. I followed these activities as best I could from New York, where I was much less usefully employed than I would have been in the driver's seat in Geneva.

At headquarters much time was being devoted to the Committee on the International Year for Human Rights (1968), which held thirty-six plenary meetings at various times and produced a report of over a hundred pages. If there ever was proliferation in the human rights program this was it. One suggestion was that there should be a special international conference on human rights in 1968, the chief purpose of which would be to review the program as it had developed over two decades and to make recommendations for the future. But the committee was now saying that this conference should also review the progress that had been made in the actual enjoyment of human rights, which was something quite different. An exercise like that could be very useful, but if it were undertaken at a conference of representatives of governments it could and probably would be an occasion for political recrimination, a possibility which frightened the American and some other delegations, who were suggesting that the progress review should be made at regional seminars. I was as skeptical about the American as I was about the committee's plan. If the conference became a forum for political recrimination it was unlikely that it would do any useful work leading to the strengthening of the program, but I was just as much opposed to politicizing the seminars. Nor did I think the American plan could keep the conference on a technical level, because the seminars were to report to it. The Americans showed me a memorandum suggesting something even worse; the conference should be convened as a committee of the twenty-third session of the General Assembly. That, I thought, would be simply another version of the Third Committee. The question continued to be discussed throughout the year by the committee, by the Human Rights Commission, by ECOSOC and by the General Assembly. When, on 20 December, the Assembly recommended elaborate measures for the celebration of the anniversary, these included the holding of a conference which was to review the progress that had been made since the adoption of the Universal Declaration of Human Rights, evaluate the methods used, especially for the elimination of racial discrimination and apartheid, and prepare a program for the future. The conference was held in Tehran. Because I had by that time retired from the Secretariat, the Canadian government invited me to be a member of its delegation, but my wife was so ill that spring that Dean Ronald Macdonald of the University of Toronto took my place.

There was much talk in the corridors at Turtle Bay about the proposed United Nations High Commissioner for Human Rights, and I was encouraged when in a speech to the General Assembly—the nineteenth session of which had resumed after the Christmas holiday—Lord Caradon gave his support to the new office. The chief difficulty now, a member of the American delegation said to me, was to get the right man appointed to the post. What if the Assembly appointed some demagogue? I had to admit that this was a danger. What we needed was a new Nansen.

Andrew Brewin, a New Democrat member of the Canadian parliament, called to tell me that I would soon be receiving an invitation from the chairman of the Standing Committee on External Affairs of the House of Commons to appear before it in connection with certain bills dealing with genocide and group libel. A formal invitation to appear before the committee soon followed, but when I spoke to Narasimhan about it, he said that I could not accept it, and he stuck to his decision even though I pointed out that in 1947 I had testified before a joint committee of the senate and commons when they were discussing a Canadian Bill of Rights and that, in 1950, two of my colleagues had stood in for me at meetings of a committee of the Canadian Senate. I therefore had to refuse the invitation but did arrange to have some United Nations documents sent to the committee. Early in February I did go to Montreal to address a dinner meeting in connection with a model United Nations, which was being sponsored jointly by McGill University and the Université de Montréal. Sitting next to me at the dinner was Professor Pierre Elliot Trudeau of the Université de Montréal, who introduced me with a witty speech in which he referred to me as a New Brunswicker who had met a French-Canadian girl on board ship, married her in Paris and become an assimilated Quebecer. The next time I met him, at a dinner meeting in Ottawa celebrating the twentieth anniversary of the adoption of the Universal Declaration of Human Rights, he was the prime minister of Canada. I was thanked by Jacques Yvan Morin, another professor at the Université de Montréal, who is now a minister in the separatist *Patri Quebecois* government of Quebec.

My talk with the Princess Ashraf had borne fruit, for the Iranian government invited the Commission on the Status of Women to meet in Tehran. On my way to this meeting—my third visit to Iran—I spent three nights in Athens, long enough to visit Delphi, the Archeological Museum and, of course, the Acropolis. I also went with a Greek friend to Pireus for lunch, before which we ate cuttlefish and drank *ouzo*. He then drove to Marathon, but we had eaten so well that he very nearly went to sleep at the wheel and we had to stop at the side of the road for a siesta. My next visit to Athens was in 1973, after my retirement from the Secretariat, when I was one of three observers sent by the International Commission of Jurists and the International League for the Rights of Man to inquire into violations of human rights by the government of the colonels. We were treated as unwelcome intruders, but I like to think that our report helped educate world public opinion and bring about the fall of a despotic government.

I arrived in Tehran on a Saturday evening and hadn't been there a day when I was already suffering from symptoms of Iranian tummy. The meetings were held in the Royal Hilton Hotel, which is on the outskirts of the city on the very edge of the desert. In the evenings I sometimes walked in the vicinity, but I had been warned not to go too far because there were packs of wild dogs in the neighborhood. Being isolated in that hotel was like being on a ship without a promenade deck. On Sunday afternoon, I went with members of the commission to lay a wreath on the tomb of the shah's father, Reza Shah. Outside the mausoleum a group of women stood watching, most of them wearing the traditional *chador*. It was primarily to improve the condition of women like this that the Commission on the Status of Women existed.

The Americans were agitated lest some delegation might challenge the presence on the commission of the representative of Taiwan. If they didn't provoke the very thing they wanted to prevent I would be very much surprised. But that was their business. It wasn't their business to interfere with the work of the Secretariat, and I was annoyed when a state department official came to say that Mrs. Tillet, the American representative, was concerned about who would be sitting on the podium when the empress opened the session. She was afraid that the women members of the Secretariat would not be sufficiently in evidence.

Like the Iranian tummy, the China question proved to be a false alarm. There wasn't even a whimper from the Russians. It was my job to conduct the empress to and from the podium at the opening meeting, but there was such a press of people around her that both times I found myself at the end of the line; I could hardly push myself in front of the cabinet ministers and courtiers who surrounded her. The security arrangements were elaborate; on Sunday evening the police had combed the public rooms of the hotel and I had even seen one of them poking in a pot containing a palm. But in the excitement of the event, all these precautions, some of which had been carefully explained to me, evaporated. I therefore had no opportunity on this occasion to talk to the empress, but I could see that she was a very beautiful woman who conducted herself with real majesty.

That night Prime Minister Hoveida gave a dinner party at the ministry of foreign affairs. There were over a thousand guests, and it was quite impossible to approach the elaborate buffet. I gave a cocktail party myself on Tuesday evening but hardly enjoyed myself. When the guests began to arrive, the prime minister's brother stormed down the stairs to the hotel lobby in a great fury and announced that he would not attend the reception. He would also, he loudly proclaimed, ask the princess to boycott it. He had been having a row, it seemed, with one of my people from headquarters, an Iranian, about who should be invited to the party. I left the receiving line and pleaded with Hoveida, who finally relented.

By Thursday I really had Iranian tummy, but I went to the Shah Reza mausoleum again that afternoon, this time with the Ganji family (in whose house I had stayed on my visit to Iran a year earlier) for ceremonies to mark the fortieth day after the assasination of the late prime minister, Hassan Ali Masur, who had been Mrs. Ganji's cousin. It was an impressive ceremony, but it must have been a harrowing experience for the friends and relatives of the murdered man; it lasted over two hours. There were readings from the Koran and Mansur's voice was reproduced over loudspeakers. I admired the courage of the new prime minister who stood at attention during most of the ceremony. There was a great crowd of people present, and it would not have been too hard for a fanatic to pick him off.

Because we were in Moslem country the commission did not sit on Fridays. Walking near the hotel on the first of these holy days, I met Djalal Abdoh, who had been the administrator of the United Nations Temporary Executive Authority in West Iran and whom I had known at headquarters. After we had walked for a while he asked me if I liked to bowl. I hadn't bowled since Baguio, when the sport had been the principal pastime at the first human rights seminar, but I said I would like to try again. He took me to a fine alley owned by his brother, where on the following Monday I had lunch with him and the Canadian ambassador on some of the finest caviar I have ever eaten.

One weekend most of the members of the commission and of the Secretariat went to Isfahan, Shiraz and Persepolis. It was a very tiring trip, but I was glad to see Isfahan again and even more to see Persepolis. We paid our own expenses, and it would have been better had the government left us to our own resources; but they gave the trip an official character and we had to cope with unwanted entertainment and women's committees. I saw very little in Isfahan that I had not already seen in 1964, but the architecture is so rich that it can be seen many times. Our visit to Shiraz was much too short, and we had only a little more than an hour in Persepolis. Flying back to Tehran on Saturday afternoon, we ran into a dust storm that nearly prevented us from landing. Later, from my hotel window, through which I had a magnificent view of the Alborz mountains, I could see that the snow-covered summits were tinted with red dust.

The shah came to the hotel on Tuesday for some function connected with the state visit of President Bourgiba of Tunisia. The lobby was full of soldiers armed with submachine guns and there were plain clothes police everywhere. That night I did not go for a walk. Wild dogs were bad enough but, with the shah in the hotel, anyone lurking in the grounds would surely be shot. On Wednesday the Princess Ashraf gave a reception which the empress attended. This time I did not have to fight for my food. The princess invited all the V.I.P.'s—and I was included—to a private room where we were served by waiters. Everyone else had to fend for themselves. A few days after this Princess Ashraf (who was the chairman of the commission) gave a luncheon in the palace. There was some kind of entertainment nearly every day, but we were fortunately coming to the end of the session.

From Tehran I flew to Geneva for the twenty-first session of the Human Rights Commission, which opened on 22 March. Salvador Lopez of the Philippines, whom I knew well, was elected chairman. He had been coming to the United Nations ever since 1946, when he was one of General Romulo's assistants.

Ambassador Volio had no trouble having his item on the high commissioner included in the agenda, but I wasn't too happy about the way the business was managed: he had even mentioned Jacob Blaustein's speech—the one that I had written—in the supporting memorandum, an act that could have alienated the Arabs. But I was able to talk him into leaving the draft resolution (which some overzealous people wanted him to strengthen) in the form in which it had been given to him by the group that had drafted it. I said that if he made the changes that were being suggested, the people with whom the idea had originated would hold him responsible if anything went wrong; there was, I added, some very strong backing for the text as it stood. The nongovernmental organizations were overplaying their role, and I wondered whether I had not made a mistake in passing the idea on to them and putting it into Blaustein's speech; but I consoled myself with the thought that if I had not done these things the proposal might have never got off the ground.

The most time-consuming item on the commission's agenda was the proposed Convention on the Elimination of All Forms of Religious Intolerance. The debate got off to a good start and I began to think that my early skepticism, when the commission had been discussing the draft principles emanating from Krishnaswami's study on religious rights and practices, that the United Nations would never agree on standards in a matter like religion had been unwarranted. But the momentum with which the debate began soon slowed down and, after nearly three weeks, the commission had been able to agree on only a preamble and four articles. The convention has still to be adopted. Other matters discussed at this session included plans for International Year for Human Rights and periodic reports.

As usual there were many receptions, dinner parties and luncheons. Nasinovsky of the Soviet delegation took me to dinner. My relations with the Russians were still good and there was nothing extraordinary about his inviting me to dinner; but this kind of *tête-à-tête* was rare with the Russians unless there was a reason for it. The reason this time was that he wanted me to meet a countryman who was a candidate for a post in my division that was being vacated by another Russian. The Russians never allowed their people to remain very long in the Secretariat. We had vodka, caviar and all the rest. I also had lunch with Prince Zadruddin Khan who was then a director in the office of the high commissioner for refugees and not yet the high commissioner. He entertained me with *aperçus* of Iranian history. His family had, he said, come from Iran before going to Pakistan and had always considered themselves as Persians. The Canadians gave a party at the home of the ambassador. Miss Aitken's alternate this year was Charles Lussier, whose brother was the rector of the Université de Montréal. When he asked me what I would be doing when I retired from the United Nations, I said that I would probably return to academic life if I could find a post. Would I be interested in the Université de Montréal, and could he write to his brother? I told him to go ahead.

The commission adjourned on Thursday, 15 April, without reaching the item on the high commissioner for human rights. Volio decided to bring it up at the next session of the General Assembly. After a weekend in Rome I returned to New York. On 30 April I reached my sixtieth birthday which, in the United Nations Secretariat, is the normal age of retirement. My tenure had been extended, but Narasimhan had told me that I would be leaving the Secretariat in exactly a year. As I had no intention of retiring from an active life, I began to look around for other employment. There were several possibilities, including teaching appointments at the Université de Montréal and Carlton University. I finally accepted a professorship at my old university, McGill, where I would straddle law and political science. They told me that I could take up the post either that fall or in January or May 1966. I chose to return to my old university on the later date and am still teaching there.

Soon after this, I left New York on another long trip, which would keep me away from headquarters for three months. My first stop was London, where I spent three days. The Minority Rights Group had asked me whether I would be interested in the directorship of the group, and, although I was now committed to McGill, I had already accepted to have lunch with several members of the group at the offices of the *Jewish Chronicle* : I suggested the names of several people who might take on the job. One result of this visit was that the *Observer* sent a special correspondent to Ljubljana to cover the seminar on the multinational society. I also went to the home office for talks about a seminar in Britain on the role of the police.

On Saturday I was in Budapest for talks about a seminar on participation in local government as a means of promoting human rights which the government had agreed to host. Officials from the foreign office met me at the airport and took me to the Gellert Hotel, where I was left to my own devices for the rest of that day; but they called for me early Sunday morning and drove me around Lake Balaton, famous for its wine. There was a long meeting on Monday morning at the Academy of Sciences to discuss an agenda for the seminar, and that afternoon I inspected various places where it might be held. Dr. Imxe Szabo, the director of the Institute of Law and Science, speaking of the draft Covenants on Human Rights, said the communist countries would have to review their attitude towards their implementation. This was encouraging. There was another meeting on Tuesday morning, after which a foreign office car drove me to the end of Margaret Island, from where I returned by foot—a long walk—to my hotel. That evening Szabo took me to a restaurant so big that there was a band at each end. I remember that it was full of people drinking wine and singing. I visited his institute the next morning after which, my business finished, I was taken to see parts of the city where I had not yet been, including the Fisherman's Bastion and the Coronation Church, and then by car into the hills of Buda.

I was up early the next morning to catch a plane for Belgrade. Officials from the foreign office met me at the airport and took me to a lounge where, notwithstanding the early hour, I was given a glass of slivovic, perhaps to test my manhood. I then called on the assistant secretary of state for foreign affairs, who questioned me about the financial crisis at the United Nations; but I had to tell him that all I knew about it I had read in the newspapers. There was a meeting the next day with Anton Vratusa, who was to be the chairman of the seminar; and that evening I dined with a foreign office official and his fiancee. I remember her radical views: unlike the communist stereotype she wanted to be a simple housewife which was, I thought, a very difficult ambition to achieve in a communist country.

The seminar on the multinational society was to be in Ljubljana which was at the other end of Yugoslavia. Since I wanted to see something of the country, the foreign office provided me with a Mercedes and driver for the long trip. The countryside between Belgrade and Zagreb, where we had lunch, was flat but rich; but from Zagreb on, as we drove through Slovenia, there was a dramatic change in scenery, with many wooded farms and villages that reminded me of Austria or Switzerland. There were also many small churches, each of which had a fine steeple different from the others. My heart missed a beat when speeding around a curve the car swerved to the left as we narrowly missed a stork which had been resting on the road. I was glad to add him to my list but would have preferred to see him under other circumstances.

At Ljubljana I put up at the Lev Hotel which was modern and first-class in every way. On Sunday and Monday I was busy making arrangements for the seminar; but late Sunday afternoon I took our government-provided car and drove with Secretariat colleagues to Trieste for dinner. We had no difficulty crossing the border even though the immigration officers on both sides had never seen a U.N. *laissez passer* before; our driver had no identification papers of any kind. The iron curtain wasn't very tight here!

The meetings began on Tuesday morning in the Festival Hall. Unlike the other seminars, which were regional, the participants at this one came from more than one continent. There were also many alternates, assistants and observers from nongovernmental organizations. More important, it was the first time the United Nations had made a visible effort to cope with the pressing problem of the protection of minorities. Yugoslavia made an ideal host country for such a conference because it really is a multinational society. That first morning the vice-president of the Council of Government of the Republic of Slovenia, the mayor of Ljubljana and I all made speeches. Vratusa was elected chairman and Chief Justice Wold of Norway one of the vice-presidents. I was flattered when the American participant quoted from my opening speech. Daniel Moynihan was the American assistant secretary of labor and, rumor had it, would be the Democratic candidate for the mayoralty of New York. He was a good speaker who had the knack of saying the right thing at the right time. I thought (as I wrote in my diary) that he was one of the most effective speakers the Americans had ever sent, in my experience at least, to a United Nations meeting. I could not guess that he would play the role in the United Nations which he did ten years later.

After the meeting on Thursday morning, Ivan Macek, the President of the Slovenian Assembly, gave a reception. I sat with him eating sausages. He was an old-time communist who had once been a carpenter and joined the partisans during the war. Later I walked back to the hotel with Vratusa, who told me that he had joined the Community Party as a result of his experiences with the partisans when he was a liaison officer with the Italian resistance; he was now a member of the Central Committee of the Slovenian Communist Party. He had great personal charm and was certainly one of the most capable people at the seminar. Later he became the head of the Yugoslav mission to the United Nations.

On Saturday the participants were taken on an excursion down the Adriatic coast: the Yugoslavs wanted us to see what they were doing for the Italian-speaking minority in Istria. Professors Sperduti and Capotorti, accompanied by an official from the Italian foreign office, had come to me on Friday complaining about this trip to a territory the sovereignty over which had not yet, they said, been finally settled. I referred them to the host government. I do not remember whether they came on the excursion. The Austrians came and made favorable comments about the present state of Slovenia compared to what it had been when it was an Austrian province.

Vratusa gave a party at which I incited Lord Stoneham to sing the Red Flag, which he did very well. The seminar was now going well. There was some animated discussion about the right of members of minority groups to associate across national borders. A foreign office man from Moscow, a cocky little fellow who was inclined to throw his weight around, insisted that there could be no such right. I gathered that other members of the Soviet delegation were much more important; one of them was the first secretary of the Central Committee of the Communist Party of Tajikistan. The Russians came to me at the end of the seminar with a statement, most of it quite irrelevant, which purported to sum up the discussions. When I said that there would have to be unanimous agreement before we could put it in the report, Vratusa backed me up and we finally agreed that the Soviet and American participants would annex separate statements. It took the whole of that day to adopt the report so that by the evening much of the spirit of international cooperation that everyone had been praising had evaporated. This was partly the fault of an Austrian foreign office official, who was particularly difficult, and this notwithstanding the fact that she had arrived in Ljubljana only a day before the adjournment of the conference and had not heard the discussions.

The conference over, I drove to Zagreb and the next morning boarded a plane for Zurich where I took the TransEurope Express to Strasbourg for talks with the Human Rights Directorate of the Council of Europe. A.H. Robertson, the head of the Directorate, met me at the station and drove me to the *Maison d'Europe* where we spent the rest of the day discussing various aspects of the United Nations program in which he was interested. That evening there was a dinner party at his house, where there was much talk about the Belgian language cases which were coming up before the European Court of Human Rights. I had a long talk the next morning with P. Modinos, the deputy secretary-general of the Council of Europe, after which I had lunch at the residence—a magnificent place—of the Secretary-General, Peter Smithers. On Saturday I had lunch with A.B. MacNulty, the secretary of the European Human Rights Commission and in the afternoon Robertson drove me to Riquewihr, where they make some of the best Alsatian wine, after which we had dinner in the home of Dr. Golsong, who was the registrar of the European Court of Human Rights.

On Monday I went to Geneva for the summer session of the Economic and Social Council. Although it wasn't on the agenda, there was a good deal of talk in the corridors about the proposed United Nations High Commissioner for Human Rights and the name of Lord Caradon was being mentioned as a possible incumbent. The Russians and their allies were dead against. So was Schneider, the high commissioner for refugees, who I heard campaigning against it at U Thant's luncheon. After this luncheon I listened to the Secretary-General's speech to the Council. Again he didn't say a word about human rights, which seemed to be one of his blind spots. I wrote to Narasimhan drawing his attention to the omission. Word soon got around that I didn't like the speech, whereupon Martin Hill told me that it had been written by de Seynes' ghost writer and that Narasimhan, who had seen it twice, had raised no objections. Martin said that he was writing another speech which the Secretary-General would make the next day. Would I put something into it about human rights? He sent me the draft that afternoon while I was busy in the Social Committee. I puzzled over it as best I could in the circumstances but could find nowhere in the draft where something could be added that would not sound artificial; and I finally decided that any reference to human rights in this speech would only compound the felony.

I was expecting Mohammed Awad in Geneva to present his report on slavery. But he had a heart attack on his way from Cairo. When I went to the hospital to see him, I found him in good spirits and obviously glad to see me; but his doctor told me that he would have to remain in the hospital for several weeks and perhaps months. It would therefore be impossible for him to present his report personally. The introduction, which he had written himself and which I very much liked, put things in proper perspective, naming countries when they needed to be named. I hoped that, notwithstanding his illness, Awad's mandate would be extended for at least another year. This was done, but the Council took no substantive decisions, ostensibly because the report hadn't yet been circulated in all the working languages. The French, Gabonese and Argentinians even refused to take part in the debate. There was, it seemed to me, something wrong with their priorities. But the report was nevertheless sent to the Human Rights Commission, which sent it on to the sub-commission which, in 1967, called for international police action to intercept the transportation of persons in danger of enslavement and to bring the traders to justice. The sub-commission also recommended that a study be made of measures that could be taken against states that were violating their international obligations. None of these recommendations have been implemented.

In the Social Committee the Russians attacked the Americans for what they were doing in Vietnam. The sad thing was that nearly everything they said was true. The committee approved the recommendations which the Human Rights Commission had made for reforming the periodic reporting system. I didn't like them all but was happy about the decision to send the reports to the sub-commission for preliminary examination. Since the members of this body were supposed to act in their personal capacities I thought they would be less inhibited than the representatives of governments in the Human Rights Commission. But it didn't work out that way in practice; for they didn't relish the responsibility and their mandate was revoked before they could recover from their first mismanagement of the business.

Laugier was holidaying at Gex, where at dinner with him one night, he nagged me about the book he wanted me to write about human rights and the United Nations to which, he said, I should devote my full time after retiring; it was mercenary of me, he said, to want to return to McGill. I had such a deep feeling of friendship for him that I could easily accept this kind of bullying, but other people didn't take it so kindly.

The Council adjourned on 31 July, but by that time I was in Moscow, where I spent three days before going on to Mongolia and the seminar on the participation of women in public life. There had been some question almost at the last moment whether we would go ahead with this seminar; for shortly before I left New York the Mongolian ambassador called on me to announce that, because of the worsening situation in Southeast Asia, his government would not issue visas to participants from Taiwan, South Korea or South Vietnam. Pointing out that it was unlikely that requests for visas would come from any of these countries and even less likely that anyone from them would want to come to the seminar, I had to tell him that if the visas were refused we would have to cancel the seminar; and I pressed him for an early answer, to which he replied that he would consult his government. Several days later he told me that they would go ahead with the seminar; and when I asked him if I could assume that the visas would be issued if requested, he said that this was correct. Later, when I was in Geneva, the South Vietnamese suddenly announced that they would be sending participants and asked the Secretariat to guarantee their safety en route to and in Mongolia. This was a patent attempt to sabotage the seminar, and I suspected the fine hands of the Americans; but I wasn't really worried because the request was unreasonable and South Vietnam wasn't a member of the United Nations. As it turned out no participants came from South Vietnam or from Taiwan or South Korea.

Flying from Moscow to Ulan Bator I had a long wait at Irkutsk changing planes, but, as on my two previous stops there, saw nothing of that city. The best part of the trip was again the view flying over Lake Baikal, but what I saw this time could not be compared with the view when the mountains surrounding the lake were covered with snow. It was late in the afternoon when I arrived in Ulan Bator. The Mongolians had apparently learned something about how unimportant international officials really are and this time there was no fuss at the airport and I was taken not to the V.I.P. hotel, where I had stayed on my previous visit, but to an ordinary one in the city.

The seminar opened the next morning, 3 August, in the government building. I made a speech, laid a wreath at the national shrine and gave a reception. The chairman of the seminar, whom I had already met on my first visit to Ulan Bator, was Mrs. Sonomyn Udval, who was a member of the Presidium of the Great People's Hural and the chairman of the Committee of Mongolian Women. She was obviously a very important person (the authorities chose the occasion of the seminar to give her the Order of Lenin), but I did not find it easy to work with her. There were five discussion leaders, one of whom, Mrs. Lakshmi Menon from India, had once been the chief of the section on the status of women in my division. The long agenda covered every aspect of the participation of women in public life.

Later in the week, the chairman took the participants and secretariat on a picnic in a wooded valley about ten miles from Ulan Bator, where we were received in a large yurt with tea, oranges—a great delicacy in Mongolia—Russian chocolates and, for the more adventurous, fermented mare's milk. I had again been warned about this drink, which the World Health Organization man in Ulan Bator told me was a breeding place for all kinds of germs. After these preliminaries we were taken to a big open tent where there was a great feast which lasted for over two hours. This was folllowed by singing, some of it very good, and, after a walk in the valley (where there were camels and yaks as well as the more familiar cattle and horses) more tea in the yurt. Boarding the bus for the drive back to Ulan Bator I noticed that one of my colleagues was missing. I finally found him asleep under a tree. The next day I had diarrhea, but because I had already had nausea in the morning before going to the picnic I did not hold it responsible, nor indeed even the fermented mare's milk.

One afternoon, Mrs. Gladys Tillett (who was the American representative on the Commission on the Status of Women and an observer at the seminar) and two officers from the U.S. state department came to complain that Mrs. Blume Grégoire, who was a member of the World Peace Council (which did not have consultative status with the United Nations) wanted to speak on the next item on the agenda. They were afraid she would raise some irrelevant political question, possibly connected with the American presence in Vietnam. I explained that although the World Peace Council did not have consultative status, Mrs. Blume Grégoire was, with the agreement of the Secretary-General, at the seminar as the guest of the Mongolian government. There had been, I added, a precedent for this at the Romanian seminar and the reason was that the government felt that representation from the nongovernmental sector would be slanted in favor of the West, which indeed it was. Mrs. Blume Grégoire made her speech the next morning and, as the Americans had feared, attacked their intervention in Vietnam, making a number of allegations which, although they were undoubtedly true, were quite out of place at a seminar on the status of women. The chairman did not interfere, nor did she when this speech was followed by one in which a Mongolian participant also attacked the United States. Mrs. Udval then somewhat tardily appealed to the participants to stick to the agenda, but the damage had been done. Mrs. Tillett's reply was restrained. When the session was resumed in the afternoon, the Mongolians returned to the attack. I had no doubt that the incident had been carefully planned. It was a very foolish thing for the host country to do. For they marred an otherwise almost perfect performance and gave reason to the critics who had said that if we had a seminar in Mongolia something like that was almost bound to happen.

One evening at a reception at the Hungarian embassy I was standing near the door when the ambassador of the People's Republic of China came into the room. He stopped to salute me, but when I said that I was the representative at the conference of the Secretary-General of the United Nations, he turned on his heels and walked away. I mentioned the incident to a Mongolian acquaintance. ''There must have been some mistake,'' he said. ''He must have thought that you said the United States. I will take you over and introduce you properly,'' which he did, but the ambassador repeated the performance. He had been standing with the ambassadors of North Korea and North Vietnam, with whom I had a pleasant conversation.

There was some kind of entertainment nearly every evening, including visits to the circus and the ballet. Both were very good, but I couldn't say the same of an exhibition of paintings, which were worse than Russian realism. On our last weekend we were taken to the same rest house at Terelj where I had been on my first visit to Mongolia. We stopped for lunch at a big collective farm, where it fell on me to cut first into a barbecued sheep. Afterwards there was a fine demonstration of horsemanship. The riders lassoed wild horses with a contraption consisting of a kind of loop on a long pole, and there was racing with small boys as the jockeys. The horses are now kept chiefly for their milk, and we visited a place where they were being milked mechanically. I have never mixed champagne and buttermilk but I imagine that it would taste very much like the fermented milk which is the national drink. I figured that I could drink it safely on a collective farm. A few days before this a man from the Czech embassy had again warned me not to drink it and to underline his point had sent a case of Pilsener beer to my hotel.

There were no meetings on the last Monday because the Secretariat was preparing the report. I went for a walk with two men from the U.S. state department who were unhappy because a communication from the Democratic Republic of Germany, which the chairman had had circulated outside the seminar, had been reproduced on a United Nations mimeographing machine. I explained the circumstances. Mrs. Udval had, in her capacity as chairman, wanted to circulate the communication as part of the documentation of the seminar. We had talked her out of this and I didn't think the fact that the document had been reproduced on our machine had any importance whatsoever. They were also upset because, they said, the seminar had no publicity in the Mongolian press. It was obvious that they had come to Ulan Bator to find fault. I sympathized with them because, apart from the incident about Vietnam, they would have very little to put in their report to the state department.

On Tuesday morning, the Mongolians had some politically inspired amendments to the report and more than once Mrs. Udval departed from her role as chairman to support the Mongolian position. She did not come to a reception that evening in the big V.I.P. hotel outside the city, where I had stayed on my first visit to the country; nor was any explanation given for her absence.

I would have liked to return to New York by the railroad across the Gobi desert to Peking and on across the Pacific; but I didn't have the right papers, and I doubt very much whether at that time it would have been possible for a United Nations official to get them. By way of compensation I decided to visit Leningrad.

Leningrad was more attractive than Moscow but terribly run-down, even shabby. After touring the city by car with a guide, I walked from the Astoria Hotel to the Peter and Paul Fortress and back through the Summer Garden. Compared to the beautiful churches in the Kremlin, the interior of the Peter and Paul Cathedral was disappointing. I looked for one beautiful thing and did not find it. After dinner I went to the ballet with Mrs. Ambhorn Meesook who had been at the seminar representing Thailand. While we were standing in the hotel lobby waiting for a taxi, a couple came up, introduced themselves as Vietnamese and asked Mrs. Meesook if she were Japanese. Their friendly attitude did not change when they learned that she was Thai and I a Canadian and a United Nations official. The place of honor at the theater was occupied by a North Vietnamese general and his suite, who were given an enthusiastic ovation.

Next day it rained and Leningrad looked even more run-down. I spent the morning in the Hermitage, which was packed like an underground station with large organized groups pacing through the salons stopping only when their guides pointed out some purple patch. After lunch I went to the Cathedral of St. Isaacs. Decorated in the worst nineteenth century style, it deserved its fate, for it had become a museum. I then walked along the Neva admiring the old buildings.

I was up at five the next morning to board my plane for Helsinki, where I had to wait for three hours before going on to London, time enough for a long walk on a road leading from the airport. Had it not been for some heather on the roadside, I might have been somewhere in the Maritime Provinces of Canada. I had the weekend in London and on Monday had lunch with Kenneth Pridham of the foreign office, to discuss plans for the seminar the British government was to host after my retirement from the Secretariat.

I was back in New York the next day. One of my first visitors was Peter Smithers, the Secretary-General of the Council of Europe, who wanted to know how the Council could enter into a closer relationship with the United Nations. I suggested a first step would be to get ECOSOC to invite them to send an observer to the Human Rights Commission. He then invited me to attend the opening of the *Maison des Droits de l'homme* in Strasbourg at the end of September, but when I talked to Narasimhan about this he said that I could not accept the invitation.

Last Months at the United Nations
(1965–1966)

It had been such a busy summer that my wife and I missed our now usual holiday on Prince Edward Island, but we did have a week on Martha's Vineyard, the American resort we liked best. We were back in New York in time for the opening of the twentieth session of the General Assembly. The Costa Ricans had had no trouble getting the item on the high commissioner for human rights on to the agenda; but the Americans, who came to see me about it, told me that no special leadership was being given to the business; they favored it themselves but apparently did not want to give it too much visible support at this stage, thinking perhaps that this could be the kiss of death. The item was referred to the Third Committee which sent it on to the Human Rights Commission. It might have been better had the Assembly discussed it in plenary session. All that remained to be done, I had said somewhat overoptimistically to the Americans, was to find the right man for the post and get him elected; but I had to admit that this would not be easy. A few days later Jamil Baroody told me that he wouldn't trust his father with the job and had some other unkind things to say about the proposal. I didn't tell him that it was my own brain child. The representative of India called it "a hive of wasps." But I was pleased by the support coming from the Western democracies.

The crisis resulting from the failure of the Soviet Union to pay its financial contribution had prevented any voting at the nineteenth session of the Assembly and consequently our making any progress on the covenants in 1964. Nor did we in 1965. But the Assembly did adopt the Convention on the Elimination of All Forms of Racial Discrimination. The fact that priority was given to this convention over instruments on which the United Nations had been working for nearly two decades, and even more that the provisions for its implementation are appreciably stronger than those adopted a year later for the Covenant on Civil and Political Rights throws a good deal of light on the human rights priorities of governments. There are good reasons perhaps why there is more international support for the elimination of racial and some other forms of discrimination than for the protection of the traditional civil and political rights, including the reaction to colonialism and the new importance given to ethnicity in contemporary society. But it is also a fact that a government can take a strong stand against discrimination without surrendering any of its powers over the lives and rights of the people under its jurisdiction. It is only too easy to imagine a situation where there is no or very little discrimination and yet no enjoyment of fundamental civil and political rights.

The covenants were in real danger at the twentieth session because some delegations wanted to adopt them without further delay and without any provisions in them for their international implementation except possibly reporting. The talk in the corridors was that a system for reporting was as far as the Afro-Asian and communist delegations would go. Even Francisco Cuevas Cancino, who had been in the Human Rights Division and was now the chairman of the Third Committee, was pushing for the adoption of the covenants at this session even though this could mean that there would be no provisions in them for their international implementation. When I spoke to him about this at one of the weekly luncheons the president of the Assembly gave for the chairmen of committees, he said that the prestige of the Third Committee didn't come that high on my scale of values; I would rather have no covenants than instruments that made no provision for their implementation; that kind of covenant could only weaken the authority of the Universal Declaration.

In the Human Rights Commission the Americans had proposed that the racial convention include a provision condemning anti-Semitism and calling on states to take appropriate action for its speedy eradication. When the Soviet Union moved that the provision be broadened to include "Nazism, including all its manifestations, (neo-nazism), genocide, anti-Semitism as well as other forms of racial discrimination," the question became so controversial that further discussion was left over until the draft convention would come before the General Assembly. The Americans now re-introduced their proposal. But the Afro-Asian bloc reacted so sharply to it that the committee adjourned to give the Americans a chance to reconsider their position, which they nevertheless decided to maintain. The Russians thereupon moved a much more controversial amendment than the one they had sponsored in the Human Rights Commission, which would have treated anti-Semitism, Zionism and colonialism as equivalent. They were obviously exploiting the anti-Israeli sentiment which continuing hostilities in the Near East had generated in so many countries. A week later the Americans were roundly defeated when (by a roll call vote of 82 to 12 with 10 abstentions) the Third Committee decided that there would be no mention in the convention of any specific form of racial discrimination. The American initiative was probably badly conceived in that, as the representative of Ghana pointed out, the original text was adequate for the purpose sought by them. But this hardly excuses the racist reaction of the Soviet Union and Afro-Asian bloc, which was itself a manifestation of anti-Semitism.

As prepared by the Human Rights Commission, the convention's fourth article would have had the states parties "condemn all propaganda and organizations which are based on ideas or theories of the superiority of one race or group of persons of one color or ethnic origin," adopt measures designed to eradicate all incitement to racial discrimination, and declare "an offense punishable by law all incitement to racial discrimination resulting in acts of violence." It will be noted that according to the commission's text, there would be no punishable offense unless the incitement resulted in an act of violence. The Assembly changed this by dropping the qualifying reference to "acts of violence" so that states parties were required:

to declare an offense punishable by law all dissemination of ideas based on racial superiority or hatred, incitement to racial discrimination, as well as all acts of violence or incitement to such acts against any race or group of persons. . . .

Any dissemination of ideas based on racial superiority was therefore to be an offense whether or not it resulted in violence, a challenge to freedom of expression so great that the committee then felt it necessary to add a reference in the article to the "principles embodied in the Universal Declaration of Human Rights." Whether the qualification is strong enough to protect freedom of expression is a moot question. The article is a good example of United Nations overkill.

The Human Rights Commission had not included in its draft any provisions for the international implementation of the convention and many delegations felt that there should be none. The delegation of Ghana first raised the question in the General Assembly. When they continued to push their suggestions notwithstanding the objections of some of the other African countries, the speculation in the corridors was that they did so because they were annoyed by the Russians who had, it seems, reproached them for playing into the hands of the United States—an accusation that so infuriated them that they pushed proposals which had been originally launched more or less as a kite. Whatever their motives, the fact is that the Assembly finally adopted measures for the international implementation of the convention which, although weak, are nevertheless stronger than those adopted only a year later for the Covenant on Civil and Political Rights.

The Racial Convention created a committee on the elimination of racial discrimination consisting of eighteen experts acting in their personal capacity to which the states parties undertake to report "(a) within one year after the entry into force of the Convention; and (b) thereafter every two years and whenever the Committee so requests" on the legislative, judicial, administrative or other measures they have adopted to give effect to the convention. If, moreover, a state party considers that another party to the convention is not giving effect to its provisions, it may address a complaint to the committee which then appoints an ad hoc conciliation commission which can make recommendations for the amicable settlement of the dispute. More important, because experience shows that states only rarely use such procedures, a state party may at any time recognize the competence of the committee to receive and consider complaints from individuals and groups under its jurisdiction. Jamil Baroody, who did not like the idea of an individual right of petition to an international body, came to see me one day when these matters were being discussed with an alternative plan under which the states parties could establish or designate some national body to which communications from their nationals could be addressed. His plan had very little merit and was obviously meant to circumvent the possibility that the Assembly might give an international right of petition to individuals. I therefore suggested and was surprised when he accepted the further idea that if a petitioner did not obtain satisfaction at the national level he could then petition the racial discrimination committee; and I helped him draft an appropriate text which was adopted as part of the convention.

I have said that the provisions adopted in December 1966, for the international implementation of the Covenant on Civil and Political Rights are weaker than those contained in the racial convention and that this is evidence of the higher priority given in the United Nations to matters like racial discrimination over the traditional civil and political rights. Like the racial convention, the covenant creates a committee of experts for its implementation, the Human Rights Committee, to which the state parties undertake to report on measures they have adopted to give it effect and the progress made in the enjoyment of the rights recognized by it. The reports are to be made within a year after the covenant enters into force for the state concerned and thereafter "whenever the Committee so requests." There is no automatic continuing obligation to report every two years as under the convention. The Human Rights Committee may also receive and consider complaints from the state parties; but, under the covenant, acceptance of these arrangements is optional: a state can therefore ratify that instrument without running the risk that its conduct will be called into account by another contracting state. More important, the covenant gives no individual right of petition, not even on an optional basis. It is true that under a separate optional protocol which was adopted by a much smaller majority at the same time as the covenant, a state may recognize the competence of the Human Rights Committee to receive and consider communications from individuals subject to its jurisdiction; but all the committee can do after examining a communication (which it must do in closed session) is to "forward its views to the state party concerned and the individual." It must however include a summary of its activities under the protocol in its annual report to the General Assembly. The Human Rights Committee has interpreted these provisions liberally, and has indeed not hesitated to find states in default for not respecting their obligations under the covenant, so that there is in fact little difference between the expressions of its "views" and a judicial determination. I could not anticipate this development when the covenant was adopted in 1966.

The twentieth session of the General Assembly was my last and it ended on 29 December; but some ten days before this my wife and I were already in Grenada on a winter holiday. There was nothing to keep us in New York after the adjournment of the Third Committee and my attending to one other bit of business, a visit to Montreal to speak at a meeting organized by the Canadian Citizenship Council, the Canadian Council for International Cooperation Year and the United Nations Association. Part of my speech was in French and I had something to say about the "Quiet Revolution" in Quebec which, from my perspective in New York, seemed like a constructive development and a good thing for Canada. My remarks about biculturalism—in my opinion a great national asset—were widely reported, but there was one man in the audience who did not like what I said. Joseph Thorsen, who presided over the meeting—the man who later unsuccessfully challenged the Canadian Official Languages Act in the Court—was visibly upset and in his short speech of thanks took exception to a reference I had made to the "two founding races." But Jean Lesage, the premier of Quebec, wrote me a letter thanking me for saying that what the francophobes of Canada were asking for "were not concessions but the essential conditions of Canadian unity."

The little paradise of Grenada would soon be disturbed by the ambition and greed of one man. The labor leader and soon-to-be premier, Eric Gairy, was pointed out to me as he climbed into his big white car at a supermarket in St. George's. Someone must have told him who I was because he turned up at my hotel the next evening and we spent two hours talking in the garden. Nothing he said could have made me guess that he would become a petty dictator.

I was back in New York in time for the opening of the eighteenth session of the Sub-Commission on the Prevention of Discrimination, most of which, like others in recent years, was devoted to its program of studies. This was good, solid work, but from the point of view of establishing effective procedures for the international protection of human rights not nearly as important as another item on its agenda, and here the sub-commission lost an opportunity. ECOSOC had asked it, it will be remembered, to study the periodic reports being received from governments with a view to sending its comments and recommendations to the Human Rights Commission. Because its members were elected to act in their personal capacity, I had hoped they would make the critical examination of the reports that the representatives of governments in the commission obviously had no intention of making. But this body of ostensibly independent experts had no stomach for the job and did nothing at this session under its new mandate. One member said that they had reached a "frontier," but it was a frontier they did not dare to cross. Instead of performing the very clear mandate of the commission, the sub-commission adopted a resolution (based on a Soviet draft) which asked the commission "to indicate more precisely how the sub-commission could more usefully discharge its functions in relation to periodic reports." Another test came a year later after the commission had clarified the mandate (although this was really not necessary) and by which time I had myself become a member of the sub-commission. The disgraceful performance showed quite clearly that the majority of the members were acting not as independent experts but as the representatives of their governments. On the initiative of the Americans the rapporteur of the sub-commission, Judge Zeev Zeltner of Israel, was appointed a special rapporteur to examine the periodic reports, prepare with the help of the Secretariat a short study covering salient developments revealed by them, and bring his comments and recommendations to the attention of the sub-commission. When the time came to discuss it, both Zeltner and his report were bitterly attacked, most of the criticism being directed to one of four annexes to the report which summarized information emanating from nongovernmental organizations and the comments of the governments concerned, and which, because the role of the n.g.o.'s in the reporting system was so controversial, the Secretariat had circulated as a restricted document. The information emanating from the nongovernmental organizations was, some of the experts said, slanderous, the annex should never have been circulated as a U.N. document and the rapporteur had exceeded his mandate. Nasinovsky, the Soviet member, then moved the annex be destroyed, whereupon by a vote of eight to six against (including my own) and four abstentions the sub-commission decided to withdraw the document. The acrimonious debate was further embittered by the fact that the rapporteur was an Israeli and some of the n.g.o. observations related to Arab countries, with the result that many Arab delegations sent observers to the meetings who took part in the debate, giving it a political flavor quite inappropriate for the deliberations of a body of experts. The upshot of all this was that the sub-commission again drew the attention of the Human Rights Commission to "the doubts and difficulties" involved in its examination of the reports and asked it to give further consideration to the matter. In the circumstances, the commission, which in the meantime had appointed an ad hoc committee of its own members (who were, of course, representatives of states) to look at the reports, could hardly be blamed when on its recommendation ECOSOC revoked the sub-commission's mandate to examine the reports. It was therefore the fault of the sub-commission itself that a procedure whereby independent experts would examine the reports was abandoned, but I have no doubt whatsoever that governments were relieved when the experiment failed. It was another case of an opportunity lost. Had the mandate of the sub-commission not been revoked, it would in time, I have no doubt, have developed procedures for an objective and perhaps critical examination of the reports.

I return to 1966. Working as always on a tight schedule, I was on my way less than a week after the sub-commission adjourned to Dakar and the seminar on human rights in developing countries. Stopping for the weekend in Paris, I arrived in Dakar on Monday, 7 February, where Ibrahim Boye, the *procureur général* of Senegal who would be the chairman of the seminar, met me at the airport and took me to the uncomfortable Hotel Croix du Sud.

The participants came from all over Africa, with the noticeable exception of the Republic of South Africa, and there were observers from a number of other countries, including France, the Soviet Union and the United States, and of many nongovernmental organizations. The agenda, which covered a wide range of topics, had been drawn up in the light of conditions in Africa; and the spirited discussions reflected the widely different political orientations represented in the chamber, one persistent theme being the conflict between individual rights and the ''necessities'' of development in industrially backward countries. One participant argued that the one-party system was a new and better kind of democracy. I could not hide my annoyance when the representative of UNESCO said that the Universal Declaration of Human Rights did not reflect the aspirations of African people because they had had no part in drafting it; and although I felt very strongly that international officials should not intervene, as she had just done, when matters of substance were being debated, I thought it was necessary to reply. Was there anything in the Declaration, I asked, with which Africans could not agree, and what special African aspirations had not been expressed in it? And then I asked her if she were speaking for UNESCO or for herself.

Dakar itself is very French and were it not for the black faces and colorful dress one could think one was somewhere in southern France. The government had put a car at my disposal. I used it one Saturday to drive to Kayar and on the Sunday went to M'Boro. I also visited the island of Goree. Once outside of Dakar one moves back a thousand years as it were in time. The country was flat and, at that time of the year in any event, arid. There were many signs of poverty, but the people were good-looking and colorfully dressed, and some of the women were very beautiful.

On Saturday, 19 February, I flew to Geneva by way of Lisbon. Walking by the lake on Sunday morning I noticed that the primroses and daisies were beginning to bloom. I had come to Geneva to attend part of the session of the Commission on the Status of Women, the session at which it finished preparing its draft of the Declaration on the Elimination of Discrimination against Women which the General Assembly unanimously adopted in November 1967. At one of the meetings Mrs. Helvi Sipila, who was in the chair, said a few pleasant things about my imminent retirement. In Paris, where I went on Friday, I attended meetings of the European nongovernmental organizations interested in human rights which, at a dinner given by the World Veterans Federation, presented me with a fine clock marked simply ''in appreciation.''

Back at headquarters, the twenty-second session of the Human Rights Commission opened on 8 March. The Poles nominated Peter F. Nedbailo of the Ukraine as chairman—a far cry from Eleanor Roosevelt—and this was seconded by India and the U.S.S.R., but Nedbailo withdrew from the race on the understanding that he would have the post in 1967. Nedbailo was awarded one of the United Nations human rights prizes in 1973.

The first of the over twenty items on the agenda related to the proposed declaration and convention on the elimination of all forms of religious intolerance, to which well over a third of the session was devoted; but the commission adopted only five more articles. One matter on the agenda could have created an important precedent had it been better handled. The International Labor Organization had asked the commission to consider certain alleged violations of human rights in Burundi, including the execution without trial of trade unionists. I was present at a meeting in the Secretary-General's office with the Burundian ambassador who argued that the commission was not competent to entertain the complaint. U Thant was exceedingly prudent and I thought too accommodating, but the ambassador promised that ''there would be no more executions.'' I passed this on to P.L. Blamont, the representative of the I.L.O., who said that if the ambassador would make a similar commitment to the commission, the I.L.O. would not press the matter and asked me to give the message to the Burundians. When I talked to them, the ambassador asked for time to consider but later the same day said that they would make the statement—that there would be no more executions without fair trial. He never made this statement but did say that his government would send a mission to Geneva to discuss the matter with the I.L.O., whereupon Blamont said that he would not press the matter. The Office of Public Information published a press release saying that the commission had refused to put the item on its agenda, but this was quite wrong.

It will be remembered that the General Assembly had forwarded the Costa Rican proposal on the high commissioner to the Human Rights Commission which now, as already indicated in an earlier chapter, decided over the protests of the Soviet Union to appoint a committee to study the matter and report back to the commission's twenty-third session in 1967. Ambassador Morozov damned the proposal in a vehement speech full of abuse; it was, he said, ''an obscene machination'' invented by the United States to undermine the covenants to which that country would not become a party. The Americans were, he said, trying to divert the commission from its proper functions. The only element of truth in this diatribe was the fact that the Americans had long since said that they would not ratify the covenants. In the logic of the Cold War, once the Americans had abandoned their role of leadership, the Russians should pose as the advocates of the two treaties. But the truth was that they were opposing and would continue to oppose any international machinery for their implementation, and the real reason for their bitter hostility to an office of high commissioner was their adamant opposition to any kind of international implementation of human rights. Although he did not mention me in his speech I was also a target. Maurice Perlzweig (the observer for the World Jewish Congress) told me later that Nasinovsky had said to him that the high commissioner was President Kennedy's idea and that he got it from Humphrey. I have never been more flattered.

The session was drawing to a close and my days at the United Nations were numbered. But there was one way in which I might retain a tenuous link with the organization. The membership of the Sub-Commission on the Prevention of Discrimination and the Protection of Minorities was being increased, and the Canadian government had nominated me for election to one of the four new seats. The sub-commission was becoming an important cog in the United Nations apparatus for the protection of human rights, and I always had a high opinion of its members. I was therefore looking forward to becoming one of them and, as a retiring United Nations official, would have liked to be unanimously elected. I knew however that this could not be, for my relations with the Russians—which had been reasonably good for the greater part of my twenty years in the Secretariat—had soured. But I never imagined that they would oppose my candidacy as openly as they did when, in a speech immediately before the elections, Nasinovsky pointedly said that the Soviet Union would vote only for candidates from Africa and Asia. They would not forgive me for inventing the idea of a high commissioner, although there may have also been another reason for their hostility: the bad blood between me and a Russian chief of section in my division who had been challenging my objectivity and who was now accusing me of deliberately hampering the preparation of documentation for the summer session of the Economic and Social Council. This man once took issue with me because I was having published in the Human Rights Yearbook the texts of certain laws that the General Assembly had called on South Africa to repeal. I patiently explained that one reason for publishing the texts was to bring pressure on South Africa and that, when Trygve Lie was Secretary-General, we had a first-class row with the South Africans because we had insisted on publishing certain texts. But he was sure that in some way we were favoring South Africa. The Russians later tried to have this man appointed deputy director of the Human Rights Division.

In the result, I was elected by only fourteen out of twenty-one votes notwithstanding the fact that most of the seven who did not vote for me had promised their support either to the Canadian delegation or to me personally. Even the Poles—I do not know how they voted—had sought me out to promise their support. My ruffled feelings were slightly improved when Judge Haim Cohn told me afterwards that many delegations thought the four new seats were indeed meant for the Afro-Asian countries and that my election to one of them was therefore a personal victory.

The same afternoon I found myself in another embarrassing position and at the center of another controversy when, without consulting me or anyone else, Judge Cohn circulated a draft resolution by which the commission would have thanked me for the services I had rendered it over a period of twenty years. The Iraqi delegation said that they would not vote for the resolution because the Israelis had moved it, and the Russians and Ukrainians then said that they too would not support it. After the meeting I went to Judge Cohn and asked him to withdraw the motion, and although he said that he would not, nothing more was heard of it, so that I left the Secretariat without the formal thanks of the commission. There was a little round of complimentary speeches when the commission adjourned on 5 April, but the Russians were noticeably silent. Other people were more friendly, including the deputy head of the Hungarian mission, who had me to lunch and later sent me a flattering letter, a bottle of wine and a vase. Apparently I still had some friends in Eastern Europe.

My last days in the Secretariat were not happy ones. I caught a miserable cold which my doctor thought might be pleurisy; I was still having trouble with my Russian chief of section who, right up until the eve of my departure, kept insisting that I was being unfair to socialist—by which he meant communist—countries; and I was kept busy until the last moment. There were also the usual extra-curricular activities. Jamil Baroody gave a big luncheon for me and Sir Mohamed Zafrullah Khan, who had been elected to the World Court; the World Jewish Congress gave me a luncheon and a citation; I spoke at a meeting in Freedom House to launch Amnesty International in the United States; the New York branch of the Canadian Institute of International Affairs gave a dinner at the Canadian

Club, after which I presided for the last time over a meeting of the branch; and there was a Secretariat reception for me in the Press Bar. It was all very friendly and flattering, but in my mood at the time—I did not want to retire—I enjoyed very little of it and was glad when all the formalities were over. On 30 April I reached my sixty-first birthday and the end of my career as an international official. The ''great adventure'' Henri Laugier had promised and that I had been living for twenty years was over.

Index